ANNUAL EDITIONS

Computers in Society   *06/07*

Thirteenth Edition

EDITOR

Paul De Palma

Gonzaga University

Paul De Palma is Professor of Mathematics and Computer Science at Gonzaga University in Spokane, WA. When he discovered computers, he was working on a doctorate in English (at Berkeley). He retrained and spent a decade in the computer industry. After further training (at Temple), he joined the computer science faculty at Gonzaga. His interests include computational linguistics, genetic algorithms, and the social impact of computing.

Contemporary Learning Series

2460 Kerper Blvd., Dubuque, IA 52001

Visit us on the Internet
http://www.mhcls.com

Credits

1. **Introduction**
   Unit photo—© Getty Images/TRBfoto
2. **The Economy**
   Unit photo—Getty Images/PhotoLink
3. **Work and the Workplace**
   Unit photo—© Getty Images/Jack Hollingsworth
4. **Computers, People, and Social Participation**
   Unit photo—© Getty Images/Janis Christie
5. **Societal Institutions: Law, Politics, Education, and the Military**
   Unit photo—© PunchStock/Creatas
6. **Risk**
   Unit photo—© Getty Images/TRBfoto
7. **International Perspectives and Issues**
   Unit photo—© Getty Images/Jules Frazier
8. **The Frontier of Computing**
   Unit photo—© Getty Images/Ryan McVay

Copyright

Cataloging in Publication Data
Main entry under title: Annual Editions: Computers in Society. 2006/2007.
1. Computers in Society—Periodicals. De Palma, Paul *comp.* II. Title: Computers in Society.
ISBN-13: 978–0–07–352832–8   ISBN-10: 0–07–352832–3   658'.05   ISSN 1094–2629

Thirteenth Edition

Cover images by Creatas/PunchStock, Jack Hollingsworth/Getty Images, Jules Frazier/Getty Images, Stockbyte/PunchStock and Photodisc/Getty Images
Printed in the United States of America   1234567890QPDQPD9876   Printed on Recycled Paper

Editors/Advisory Board

Members of the Advisory Board are instrumental in the final selection of articles for each edition of ANNUAL EDITIONS. Their review of articles for content, level, currency, and appropriateness provides critical direction to the editor and staff. We think that you will find their careful consideration well reflected in this volume.

EDITOR

Paul De Palma
Gonzaga University

Staff

Preface

In publishing ANNUAL EDITIONS we recognize the enormous role played by the magazines, newspapers, and journals of the public press in providing current, first-rate educational information in a broad spectrum of interest areas. Many of these articles are appropriate for students, researchers, and professionals seeking accurate, current material to help bridge the gap between principles and theories and the real world. These articles, however, become more useful for study when those of lasting value are carefully collected, organized, indexed, and reproduced in a low-cost format, which provides easy and permanent access when the material is needed. That is the role played by ANNUAL EDITIONS.

In a well-remembered scene from the 1968 movie, *The Graduate*, the hapless main character, Ben, is pulled aside at his graduation party by his father's business partner. He asks Ben about his plans, now that the young man has graduated. As Ben fumbles, the older man whispers the single word, "plastics," in his ear. The question is just what would Ben, now a middle-aged man himself, say to a new graduate today. Surely not "plastics," even though petrochemicals, for good and ill, have transformed the way we live over the past three decades. Odds are that computers have replaced plastics in the imaginations of today's graduates, this despite a stubborn slump in the industry's fortunes. To test this hypothesis, I did a Google search on the words "plastics," and "plastic." This produced about 45,000,000 hits, an indication that Ben was offered good advice. I followed this with a search on "computers," and "computer," to which Google replied with an astonishing 804,000,000. You can learn more about Googling in Unit 4. For now, the point is that computers are a phenomenon to be reckoned with.

In this 13th edition of *Annual Editions: Computers in Society 06/07*, I have tried to continue in the tradition of previous editors. The writers are journalists, computer scientists, lawyers, and academics, the kinds of professions you would expect to find in a collection on the social implications of computing. Their writing, though representing many perspectives on many topics, is free from both the unintelligible jargon and the breathless enthusiasm that prevents people from forming clear ideas about the importance of computing. This is by design, of course. I have long contended that it's possible to write clearly about a subject even as complicated as computing. I think that after reading the selections, you will agree.

Annual Editions: Computers in Society is organized around important dimensions of society rather than of computing. The Introduction begins the conversation with an article by the late Neil Postman who says "that every technology has a philosophy which is given expression in how the technology makes people use their minds." Computing has changed how teachers think about teaching and how their students think about learning. The challenge is to deeply understand the personal effects of the technology in order to make it better serve our human purposes. With the help of many other writers, a crucial question recurs like a leitmotif in a complex piece of music: to what extent is technology of any kind without a bias of its own and to what extent does it embody the world view, intentionally or not, of its creators? If the

answer were simply that the good and the ill of computing depend upon how computers are used, those of us interested in the interaction of computers and society would be hard-pressed to claim your attention. We could simply exhort you to do no evil, as Google tells its employees (http://investor.google.com/conduct.html, retrieved 8/17/05). Good advice, certainly. But information technology demands a more nuanced stance. Sometimes computing systems have consequences not intended by their developers. The waste generated by cast-off computers is one example. The vulnerability of electronic voting systems is another. And at all times, "embedded in every technology there is a powerful idea." An essential task for students of technology is to learn to tease out these ideas, so that the consequences might be understood *before* the technology is adopted.

The book's major themes are the economy, community, politics considered broadly, and the balance of risk and reward. In a field as fluid as computing, the intersection of computers with each of these dimensions changes from year to year. Many articles in the 10th edition examined the growing importance of e-commerce. By the time of this, the 13th edition, e-commerce has nearly disappeared. This is not to imply that e-commerce is unimportant, only that in just a few years it has moved into the mainstream.

But computing is about more than the economy, else my Google search would not have resulted in 804,000,000 hits. More than any other technology, computers force us to think about limits. What does it mean to be human? Are there kinds of knowledge that should not be pursued? More prosaically, what can be done about spam, what can we expect to see in the next decade, and, crucially, how is the next generation of inventors to be nurtured? All these issues are explored in Unit 8, The Frontier of Computing.

A word of caution. Each article has been selected because of its informational value. To say that an article is informative, however, does not necessarily imply that the information is correct. This is as true of the facts presented in each article as it is of the point of view. When reading startling assertions, whether in this volume or in the newspaper, it is wise to remember that writers gather facts from other sources who gathered them from still other sources, who may, ultimately, rely upon a selective method of fact-gathering. There may be no good solution to the problem of unsupported assertions, beyond rigorous peer review, of course. But, then, most of us don't curl up each night with scientific journals, and even these can be flawed. The real antidote to poorly supported arguments is to become critical readers, no less of experts than of the daily newspaper. Having said that, I hope you will approach these articles as you might approach a good discussion among friends. You may not agree with all of the opinions, but you come away perhaps nudged in one direction or another by reasoned arguments, holding a richer, more informed, view of important issues.

This book includes several features that I hope will be helpful to students and professionals. Each article listed in the table of contents is preceded by a short abstract with key concepts in bold type. The social implications of computing, of course, are not limited to the eight broad areas represented by the unit titles. A topic guide lists each article by name and number along still other dimensions of computers in society.

We want *Annual Editions: Computers in Society* to help you participate more fully in some of the most important discussions of the time, those about the promises and risks of computing. Your suggestions and comments are very important to us. If you complete and return the postage-paid article rating form in the back of the book, we can try to incorporate your feedback into the next edition.

Paul DePalma
Editor

Contents

UNIT 1
Introduction

UNIT 2
The Economy

The concepts in bold italics are developed in the article. For further expansion, please refer to the Topic Guide and the Index.

UNIT 3
Work and the Workplace

The concepts in bold italics are developed in the article. For further expansion, please refer to the Topic Guide and the Index.

UNIT 4
Computers, People, and Social Participation

The concepts in bold italics are developed in the article. For further expansion, please refer to the Topic Guide and the Index.

UNIT 5
Societal Institutions: Law, Politics, Education, and the Military

The concepts in bold italics are developed in the article. For further expansion, please refer to the Topic Guide and the Index.

UNIT 6
Risk

The concepts in bold italics are developed in the article. For further expansion, please refer to the Topic Guide and the Index.

UNIT 7
International Perspectives and Issues

UNIT 8
The Frontier of Computing

The concepts in bold italics are developed in the article. For further expansion, please refer to the Topic Guide and the Index.

The concepts in bold italics are developed in the article. For further expansion, please refer to the Topic Guide and the Index.

Topic Guide

This topic guide suggests how the selections in this book relate to the subjects covered in your course. You may want to use the topics listed on these pages to search the Web more easily.

On the following pages a number of Web sites have been gathered specifically for this book. They are arranged to reflect the units of this *Annual Edition*. You can link to these sites by going to the student online support site at *http://www.mhcls.com/online/*.

ALL THE ARTICLES THAT RELATE TO EACH TOPIC ARE LISTED BELOW THE BOLD-FACED TERM.

Politics

Privacy

Profiles

Technological failure

Technological revolution

Technology

The Military

Internet References

The following internet sites have been carefully researched and selected to support the articles found in this reader. The easiest way to access these selected sites is to go to our student online support site at *http://www.mhcls.com/online/*.

AE: Computers in Society 06/07

The following sites were available at the time of publication. Visit our Web site—we update our student online support site regularly to reflect any changes.

General Sources

Livelink Intranet Guided Tour
http://www.opentext.com/

Livelink Intranet helps companies to manage and control documents, business processes, and projects more effectively. Take this tour to see how.

UNIT 1: Introduction

Beyond the Information Revolution
http://www.theatlantic.com/issues/99oct/9910drucker.htm

Peter Drucker has written a three-part article, available at this site, that uses history to gauge the significance of e-commerce—"a totally unexpected development"—to throw light on the future of, in his words, "the knowledge worker."

Short History of the Internet
http://w3.ag.uiuc.edu/AIM/scale/nethistory.html

Bruce Sterling begins with the development of the idea for the Internet by the cold war think tank, the Rand Corporation, and goes on to explain how computer networking works. There are links to other sites and to further reading.

UNIT 2: The Economy

CAUCE: Coalition Against Unsolicited Commercial Email
http://www.cauce.org

This all-volunteer organization was created to advocate for a legislative solution to the problem of UCE, better known as spam. Read about the fight and how you can help at this Web page.

E-Commerce Times
http://www.ecommercetimes.com/

E-Commerce Times is a gateway to a wealth of current information and resources concerning e-commerce.

The End of Cash (James Gleick)
http://www.around.com/money.html

This article, previously published in the *New York Times,* on June 16, 1996, discusses the obsolescence of cash.

Fight Spam on the Internet
http://spam.abuse.net

This is an anti-spam sight that has been in operation since 1996. Its purpose is to promote responsible net commerce, in part, by fighting spam. Up-to-date news about spam can be found on the home page.

The Linux Home Page
http://www.linux.org

This Web site explains that Linux is a free Unix-type operating system, originally created by Linus Torvalds, that is causing a revolution in the world of computers. The site features the latest news about Linux, and everything else you would need to know to switch to the service.

The Rise of the Informediary
http://www.ait.unl.edu/crane/misgrad/sglee/informediary.htm

The author of this site explains what an informediary is and what an informediary does. He also shows why the informediary is so important in today's business environment.

Smart Cards: A Primer
http://www.javaworld.com/javaworld/jw-12-1997/jw-12-javadev.html

This article by Rinaldo Di Giorgio brings the smart card to life with a real-world smart-card example. Five pages explain what a smart card is, how it is used, its limitations, and its strengths.

Smart Card Group
http://www.smartcard.co.uk

This Web site bills itself as "the definitive Web site for Smart Card Technology. At this site you can download Dr. David B. Everett's definitive "Introduction to Smart Cards."

UNIT 3: Work and the Workplace

American Telecommuting Association
http://www.knowledgetree.com/ata-adv.html

What is good about telecommuting is examined at this site that also offers information regarding concepts, experiences, and the future of telecommuting.

Computers in the Workplace
http://www.msci.memphis.edu/-ryburnp/cl/cis/workpl.html

In this lecture, some of the advantages of computers in the workplace are examined as well as some of the negative aspects, including issues of training, ethics, and privacy.

InfoWeb: Techno-rage
http://www.cciw.com/content/technorage.html

Techno-rage is becoming more and more common. This site provides information and resources regarding techno-rage and techno-stress.

STEP ON IT! Pedals: Repetitive Strain Injury
http://www.bilbo.com/rsi2.html

Data on carpal tunnel syndrome are presented here with links to alternative approaches to the computer keyboard, and links to related information.

What About Computers in the Workplace
http://law.freeadvice.com/intellectual_property/computer_law/computers_workplace.htm

This site, which is the leading legal site for consumers and small businesses, provides general legal information to help people understand their legal rights in 100 legal topics—including the answer to the question, "Can my boss watch what I'm doing?"

www.mhcls.com/online/

UNIT 4: Computers, People, and Social Participation

Adoption Agencies
http://www.amrex.org/

Here is an example of the much-talked-about new trend of online adoption agencies.

Alliance for Childhood: Computers and Children
http://www.allianceforchildhood.net/projects/computers/index.htm

How are computers affecting the intellectual growth of children? Here is one opinion provided by the Alliance for Childhood.

The Core Rules of Netiquette
http://www.albion.com/netiquette/corerules.html

Excerpted from Virginia Shea's book *Netiquette*, this is a classic work in the field of online communication.

How the Information Revolution Is Shaping Our Communities
http://www.plannersweb.com/articles/bla118.html

This article by Pamela Blais is from the Planning Commissioners Journal, Fall 1996 issue, and deals with our changing society. It points out and explains some of the far-reaching impacts of the information revolution, including the relocation of work from office to home.

SocioSite: Networks, Groups, and Social Interaction
http://www2.fmg.uva.nl/sociosite/topics/interaction.html

This site provides sociological and psychological resources and research regarding the effect of computers on social interaction.

UNIT 5: Societal Institutions: Law, Politics, Education, and the Military

ACLU: American Civil Liberties Union
http://www.aclu.org

Click on the Supreme Court's Internet decision, plus details of the case *Reno v. ACLU*, and the ACLU's campaign to restore information privacy; "Take Back Your Data"; and cyber-liberties and free speech for opinions on First Amendment rights as they apply to cyberspace.

Information Warfare and U.S. Critical Infrastructure
http://www.twurled-world.com/Infowar/Update3/cover.htm

The "twURLed World" contains a pie chart of URLs involved in IW (information warfare) as well as report main pages that list Internet domains, keywords in contexts and by individual terms, and listing of all URLs and links to details.

Living in the Electronic Village
http://www.rileyis.com/publications/phase1/usa.htm

This site addresses the impact of information in technology on government. Shown is the executive summary, but seven other sections are equally pertinent.

Patrolling the Empire
http://www.csrp.org/patrol.htm

Reprinted from *CovertAction Quarterly*, this article by Randy K. Schwartz details the plans of NIMA (National Imagery and Mapping Agency) for future wars by helping to fuse high-tech surveillance and weaponry.

United States Patent and Trademark Office
http://www.uspto.gov/

This is the official homepage of the U. S. Patent and Trademark Office. Use this site to search patents and trademarks, apply for patents, and more.

World Intellectual Property Organization
http://www.wipo.org/

Visit the World Intellectual Property Organization Web site to find information and issues pertaining to virtual and intellectual property.

UNIT 6: Risk

AntiOnline: Hacking and Hackers
http://www.antionline.com/index.php

This site is designed to help the average person learn how to protect against hackers.

Copyright & Trademark Information for the IEEE Computer Society
http://computer.org/copyright.htm

Here is an example of how a publication on the Web is legally protected. The section on Intellectual Property Rights Information contains further information about reuse permission and copyright policies.

Electronic Privacy Information Center (EPIC)
http://epic.org

EPIC is a private research organization that was established to focus public attention on emerging civil liberties issues and to protect privacy, the First Amendment, and constitutional values. This site contains news, resources, policy archives, and a search mechanism.

Internet Privacy Coalition
http://www.epic.org/crypto/

The mission of the Internet Privacy Coalition is to promote privacy and security on the Internet through widespread public availability of strong encryption and the relaxation of export controls on cryptography.

Center for Democracy and Technology
http://www.cdt.org/crypto/

These pages are maintained for discussion and information about data privacy and security, encryption, and the need for policy reform. The site discusses pending legislation, Department of Commerce Export Regulations, and other initiatives.

Survive Spyware
http://www.cnet.com/internet/0-3761-8-3217791-1.html

Internet spying is a huge problem. Advertisers, Web designers, and even the government are using the Net to spy on you. CNET.com provides information about spyware and detecting spying eyes that will help you eliminate the threat.

An Electronic Pearl Harbor? Not Likely
http://www.nap.edu/issues/15.1/smith.htm

Is the threat of information warfare real? Yes. Do we need to be completely concerned? Probably not. This site tries to dispel some of the myths and hoaxes concerning information warfare.

UNIT 7: International Perspectives and Issues

Information Revolution and World Politics Project
http://www.ceip.org/files/projects/irwp/irwp_descrip.ASP

This project, launched by the Carnegie Foundation in 1999, has as its purpose to analyze the political, economic, and social dimensions of the world-wide information revolution and their implications for U.S. policy and global governance.

UNIT 8: The Frontier of Computing

Introduction to Artificial Intelligence (AI)
http://www-formal.stanford.edu/jmc/aiintro/aiintro.html
   This statement describes A.I. Click on John McCarthy's home
   page for a list of additional papers.

Kasparov vs. Deep Blue: The Rematch
http://www.chess.ibm.com/home/html/b.html
   Video clips and a discussion of the historic chess rematch
   between Garry Kasparov and Deep Blue are available on this site.

PHP-Nuke Powered Site: International Society for Artificial Life
http://alife.org/
   Start here to find links to many alife (artificial life) Web sites,
   including demonstrations, research centers and groups, and other
   resources.

We highly recommend that you review our Web site for expanded information and our
other product lines. We are continually updating and adding links to our Web site in order
to offer you the most usable and useful information that will support and expand the value
of your Annual Editions. You can reach us at: *http://www.mhcls.com/annualeditions/*.

UNIT 1
Introduction

Unit Selections

1. **Five Things We Need to Know About Technological Change**, Neil Postman
2. **Whom to Protect and How?**, Robert J. Blendon et al.
3. **On the Nature of Computing**, Jon Crowcroft

Key Points to Consider

- All American school children learn that the first message Samuel F.B. Morse transmitted over his newly invented telegraph were the words, "What hath God wrought." What they, perhaps, do not learn is that Morse was quoting from the poem of Balaam in the Book of Numbers, chapter 23. Read the text of this poem. The Overview to this unit presents two ways to understand technical and scientific discoveries. In which camp is Morse?

- Early on in Walden, Thoreau famously remarks that "Our inventions are wont to be pretty toys, which distract our attention from serious things. They are but an improved means to an unimproved end, an end that it was already but too easy to arrive at.. . . We are in great haste to construct a magnetic telegraph from Maine to Texas; but Maine and Texas, it may be, have nothing important to communicate." Substitute "Internet" for "magnetic telegraph." Do you agree or disagree with Thoreau? How do you think Jon Crowcroft ("On the Nature of Computing") might respond?

- Richard Lewontin, a Harvard geneticist, says ("The Politics of Science," The New York Review of Books, May 9, 2002) that "The state of American science and its relation to the American state are the product of war." What does he mean? Is Lewontin overstating his case? Use the Internet to find out more about Richard Lewontin.

- Susan Herring "Slouching toward the ordinary," says that text-messaging is "perversely unergonomic." What does this mean? What accounts for its importance among teenagers?

Student Website

www.mhcls.com/online

Internet References

Further information regarding these websites may be found in this book's preface or online.

Beyond the Information Revolution
http://www.theatlantic.com/issues/99oct/9910drucker.htm

Short History of the Internet
http://w3.ag.uiuc.edu/AIM/scale/nethistory.html

This book, *Computers in Society*, is part of a larger series of books published by McGraw-Hill Contemporary Learning Series. The series contains over sixty-five titles, among them American History, Sociology, and World Politics. It is instructive to note that not one of them carries the final prepositional phrase "in Society." Why is that? Here is a first approximation. History, sociology, world politics, indeed, most of the other titles in the *Annual Editions* series are not in society, they are society. Suppose we produced an edited volume entitled "History in Society." If such a volume contained reflections on the social implications of the academic study of history, it would have a tiny and specialized readership. But you know that when we speak of "computers in society," we are not talking about the social implications of the academic study of computing. Here is one difference between this volume and the others in the series: it is possible to study computers without studying their social dimension.

But is it? Until not long ago, most people interested in the philosophy and sociology of science considered it value-neutral. That is, a given technology carried no ethical values of its own. The ethics of this or that technology depended on what was done with it. A vestige of this thinking is still with us. When people say, "Guns don't kill people. People kill people," they are asserting that technology somehow stands outside of society, waiting to be put to use for good or ill. The concern about intoxicated drivers is similar. All of us would live happier, safer lives if campaigns to remove drunken drivers from their cars were successful. But this still would not get to the heart of highway carnage that has to do with federal encouragement for far-flung suburbs, local patterns of land use, and a neglect of public transportation. Drunk-driving would not be the issue it is, if driving were not so vital to American life, and driving would not be so vital to American life if a cascade of social and political decisions had not come together in the middle of the twentieth century to favor the automobile.

The first article, "Five Things We Need to Know About Technological Change," makes this point eloquently: "Embedded in every technology there is a powerful idea…." The observation is an important one that is shared by most of the more reflective contemporary commentators on technology. The idea that technology can be studied apart from its social consequences, owes some of its strength to the way many people imagine that scientific discoveries unfold—since technology is just applied science. It is commonly imagined that scientists are disinterested observers of the natural world. In this view, science unfolds, and technology unfolds shortly after, according to the laws of nature and the passion of scientists. But, of course, scientists study those things that are socially valued. The particular expression of social value in the United States is the National Science Foundation and National Institute of Health funding. We should not be surprised that the medical and computing sciences are funded generously, or, indeed, that our research physicians and computer scientists are paid better than English professors.

Perhaps a more accurate view of the relationship between technology and computing to society is that social values affect technical discovery which, in turn, affect social values. It is this intricate dance between computers and society—now one leading, now the other—that the writers in this volume struggle to understand. But before we try to understand the dance, it seems reasonable to understand what is meant by the word "computer." You will find in this volume a decided bias toward networked computers. A networked computer is one that can communicate with many millions of others through the global Internet. This is a new definition. As recently as 1996, less than 1 in 5 Americans had used the Internet (from "Whom to Protect and How?"). Just

as we mean networked computers when we use the word "computer" today, in the late eighties someone using the word would have meant a stand-alone PC, running, maybe a word processor, a spread sheet, and some primitive games. A decade before to that, the word would have referred to a large, probably IBM, machine kept in an air-conditioned room and tended by an army of technicians. Prior to 1950, the word would have meant someone particularly adept in arithmetic calculations. The point here is that as the meaning of a single word has shifted, and our understanding of the dance has to shift with it.

That this shift in meaning has occurred in just a few decades helps us understand why so many commentators use the word "revolution" to describe what computing has wrought. Just as technologies come with hidden meanings, so do words, themselves. Thus the word "revolution" when it is applied to political upheaval is used to describe something thought bad, or at least chaotic—the single contrary instance is the American Revolution. Not so when the word is applied to computing. Computing is thought to change quickly, but, more, it is thought to bring many benefits. A recent survey conducted by the Brookings Institution (cited in "Whom to Protect and How?") indicated that 90% of Americans believe that science and technology will make their lives easier and more comfortable. The real question to ask is more basic: whether or not Americans believe it, is it true? First, does the spread of computing constitute a revolution, or just, in Thoreau's words, "an improved means to an unimproved end." Second, revolutionary or not, have we grown smarter, healthier, and happier with the coming of the computer? This is still an open question—but as the Internet morphs from a novelty to an appliance, to a shrinking number of commentators.

The last article in this unit, "On the Nature of Computing" is a hymn to the limitless possibilities of computing. As the subtitle asserts, "Computing is its own virtual world, bound only by its practitioners' imaginations and creativity." Read the article and see if you are persuaded.

Five Things We Need to Know About Technological Change

Neil Postman

Editor's note: Address by Neil Postman to New Tech '98 conference,
Denver, Colorado, March 27, 1998

Good morning your Eminences and Excellencies, ladies, and gentlemen.

The theme of this conference, "The New Technologies and the Human Person: Communicating the Faith in the New Millennium," suggests, of course, that you are concerned about what might happen to faith in the new millennium, as well you should be. In addition to our computers, which are close to having a nervous breakdown in anticipation of the year 2000, there is a great deal of frantic talk about the 21st century and how it will pose for us unique problems of which we know very little but for which, nonetheless, we are supposed to carefully prepare. Everyone seems to worry about this—business people, politicians, educators, as well as theologians.

> ## The human dilemma is as it has always been, and it is a delusion to believe that the technological changes of our era have rendered irrelevant the wisdom of the ages and the sages.

At the risk of sounding patronizing, may I try to put everyone's mind at ease? I doubt that the 21st century will pose for us problems that are more stunning, disorienting or complex than those we faced in this century, or the 19th, 18th, 17th, or for that matter, many of the centuries before that. But for those who are excessively nervous about the new millennium, I can provide, right at the start, some good advice about how to confront it. The advice comes from people whom we can trust, and whose thoughtfulness, it's safe to say, exceeds that of President Clinton, Newt Gingrich, or even Bill Gates. Here is what Henry David Thoreau told us: "All our inventions are but improved means to an unimproved end." Here is what Goethe told us: "One should, each day, try to hear a little song, read a good poem, see a fine picture, and, if possible, speak a few reasonable words." Socrates told us: "The unexamined life is not worth living." Rabbi Hillel told us: "What is hateful to thee, do not do to another." And here is the prophet Micah: "What does the Lord require of thee but to do justly, to love mercy and to walk humbly with thy God." And I could say, if we had the time, (although you know it well enough) what Jesus, Isaiah, Mohammad, Spinoza, and Shakespeare told us. It is all the same: There is no escaping from ourselves. The human dilemma is as it has always been, and it is a delusion to believe that the technological changes of our era have rendered irrelevant the wisdom of the ages and the sages.

> ## ...all technological change is a trade-off... a Faustian bargain.

Nonetheless, having said this, I know perfectly well that because we do live in a technological age, we have some special problems that Jesus, Hillel, Socrates, and Micah did not and could not speak of. I do not have the wisdom to say what we ought to do about such problems, and so my contribution must confine itself to some things we need to know in order to address the problems. I call my talk *Five Things We Need to Know About Technological Change*. I base these ideas on my thirty years of studying the history of technological change but I do not think these are academic or esoteric ideas. They are the sort of things everyone who is concerned with cultural stability and balance should know and I offer them to you in the hope that you will find them useful in thinking about the effects of technology on religious faith.

First Idea

The first idea is that all technological change is a trade-off. I like to call it a Faustian bargain. Technology giveth and technology taketh away. This means that for every advantage a new technology offers, there is always a corres-ponding disadvantage. The disadvantage may exceed in importance the advantage, or the advantage may well be worth the cost. Now, this may seem to be a rather obvious idea, but you would be surprised at how many people believe that new technologies are unmixed blessings. You need only think of the enthusiasms with which most people approach their understanding of computers. Ask anyone who knows something about computers to talk about them, and you will find that they will, unabashedly and relentlessly, extol the wonders of computers. You will also find that in most cases they will completely neglect to mention any of the liabilities of computers. This is a dangerous imbalance, since the greater the wonders of a technology, the greater will be its negative consequences.

Think of the automobile, which for all of its obvious advantages, has poisoned our air, choked our cities, and degraded the beauty of our natural landscape. Or you might reflect on the paradox of medical technology which brings wondrous cures but is, at the same time, a demonstrable cause of certain diseases and disabilities, and has played a significant role in reducing the diagnostic skills of physicians. It is also well to recall that for all of the intellectual and social benefits provided by the printing press, its costs were equally monumental. The printing press gave the Western world prose, but it made poetry into an exotic and elitist form of communication. It gave us inductive science, but it reduced religious sensibility to a form of fanciful superstition. Printing gave us the modern conception of nationwide, but in so doing turned patriotism into a sordid if not lethal emotion. We might even say that the printing of the Bible in vernacular languages introduced the impression that God was an Englishman or a German or a Frenchman—that is to say, printing reduced God to the dimensions of a local potentate.

Perhaps the best way I can express this idea is to say that the question, "What will a new technology do?" is no more important than the question, "What will a new technology undo?" Indeed, the latter question is more important, precisely because it is asked so infrequently. One might say, then, that a sophisticated perspective on technological change includes one's being skeptical of Utopian and Messianic visions drawn by those who have no sense of history or of the precarious balances on which culture depends. In fact, if it were up to me, I would forbid anyone from talking about the new information technologies unless the person can demonstrate that he or she knows something about the social and psychic effects of the alphabet, the mechanical clock, the printing press, and telegraphy. In other words, knows something about the costs of great technologies.

Idea Number One, then, is that culture always pays a price for technology.

Second Idea

This leads to the second idea, which is that the advantages and disadvantages of new technologies are never distributed evenly among the population. This means that every new technology benefits some and harms others. There are even some who are not affected at all. Consider again the case of the printing press in the 16th century, of which Martin Luther said it was "God's highest and extremest act of grace, whereby the business of the gospel is driven forward." By placing the word of God on every Christian's kitchen table, the mass-produced book undermined the authority of the church hierarchy, and hastened the breakup of the Holy Roman See. The Protestants of that time cheered this development. The Catholics were enraged and distraught. Since I am a Jew, had I lived at that time, I probably wouldn't have given a damn one way or another, since it would make no difference whether a pogrom was inspired by Martin Luther or Pope Leo X. Some gain, some lose, a few remain as they were.

Let us take as another example, television, although here I should add at once that in the case of television there are very few indeed who are not affected in one way or another. In America, where television has taken hold more deeply than anywhere else, there are many people who find it a blessing, not least those who have achieved high-paying, gratifying careers in television as executives, technicians, directors, newscasters and entertainers. On the other hand, and in the long run, television may bring an end to the careers of school teachers since school was an invention of the printing press and must stand or fall on the issue of how much importance the printed word will have in the future. There is no chance, of course, that television will go away but school teachers who are enthusiastic about its presence always call to my mind an image of some turn-of-the-century blacksmith who not only is singing the praises of the automobile but who also believes that his business will be enhanced by it. We know now that his business was not enhanced by it; it was rendered obsolete by it, as perhaps an intelligent blacksmith would have known.

The questions, then, that are never far from the mind of a person who is knowledgeable about technological change are these: Who specifically benefits from the development of a new technology? Which groups, what type of person, what kind of industry will be favored? And, of course, which groups of people will thereby be harmed?

...there are always winners and losers in technological change.

These questions should certainly be on our minds when we think about computer technology. There is no doubt that the computer has been and will continue to be advantageous to large-scale organizations like the military or airline companies or banks or tax collecting institutions. And it is equally clear that the computer is now indispensable to high-level researchers in physics and other natural sciences. But to what extent has computer technology been an advantage to the masses of people? To steel workers, vegetable store owners, automobile mechanics, musicians, bakers, bricklayers, dentists, yes, theologians, and most of the rest into whose lives the computer now intrudes? These people have had their private matters made more accessible to powerful institutions. They are more easily tracked and controlled; they are subjected to more examinations, and are increasingly mystified by the decisions made about them. They are more than ever reduced to mere numerical objects. They are being buried by junk mail. They are easy targets for advertising agencies and political institutions.

In a word, these people are losers in the great computer revolution. The winners, which include among others computer companies, multi-national corporations and the nation state, will, of course, encourage the losers to be enthusiastic about computer technology. That is the way of winners, and so in the beginning they told the losers that with personal computers the average person can balance a checkbook more neatly, keep better track of recipes, and make more logical shopping lists. Then they told them that computers will make it possible to vote at home, shop at home, get all the entertainment they wish at home, and thus make community life unnecessary. And now, of course, the winners speak constantly of the Age of Information, always implying that the more information we have, the better we will be in solving significant problems—not only personal ones but large-scale social problems, as well. But how true is this? If there are children starving in the world—and there are—it is not because of insufficient information. We have known for a long time how to produce enough food to feed every child on the planet. How is it that we let so many of them starve? If there is violence on our streets, it is not because we have insufficient information. If women are abused, if divorce and pornography and mental illness are increasing, none of it has anything to do with insufficient information. I dare say it is because something else is missing, and I don't think I have to tell this audience what it is. Who knows? This age of information may turn out to be a curse if we are blinded by it so that we cannot see truly where our problems lie. That is why it is always necessary for us to ask of those who speak enthusiastically of computer technology, why do you do this? What interests do you represent? To whom are you hoping to give power? From whom will you be withholding power?

I do not mean to attribute unsavory, let alone sinister motives to anyone. I say only that since technology favors some people and harms others, these are questions that must always be asked. And so, that there are always winners and losers in technological change is the second idea.

Third Idea

Here is the third. Embedded in every technology there is a powerful idea, sometimes two or three powerful ideas. These ideas are often hidden from our view because they are of a somewhat abstract nature. But this should not be taken to mean that they do not have practical consequences.

The third idea is the sum and substance of what Marshall McLuhan meant when he coined the famous sentence, "The medium is the message."

Perhaps you are familiar with the old adage that says: To a man with a hammer, everything looks like a nail. We may extend that truism: To a person with a pencil, everything looks like a sentence. To a person with a TV camera, everything looks like an image. To a person with a computer, everything looks like data. I do not think we need to take these aphorisms literally. But what they call to our attention is that every technology has a prejudice. Like language itself, it predisposes us to favor and value certain perspectives and accomplishments. In a culture without writing, human memory is of the greatest importance, as are the proverbs, sayings and songs which contain the accumulated oral wisdom of centuries. That is why Solomon was thought to be the wisest of men. In Kings I we are told he knew 3,000 proverbs. But in a culture with writing, such feats of memory are considered a waste of time, and proverbs are merely irrelevant fancies. The writing person favors logical organization and systematic analysis, not proverbs. The telegraphic person values speed, not introspection. The television person values immediacy, not history. And computer people, what shall we say of them? Perhaps we can say that the computer person values information, not knowledge, certainly not wisdom. Indeed, in the computer age, the concept of wisdom may vanish altogether.

The consequences of technological change are always vast, often unpredictable and largely irreversible.

The third idea, then, is that every technology has a philosophy which is given expression in how the technology makes people use their minds, in what it makes us do with our bodies, in how it codifies the world, in which of our senses it amplifies, in which of our emotional and intellectual tendencies it disregards. This idea is the sum and substance of what the great Catholic prophet, Marshall McLuhan meant when he coined the famous sentence, "The medium is the message."

Fourth Idea

Here is the fourth idea: Technological change is not additive; it is ecological. I can explain this best by an analogy. What happens if we place a drop of red dye into a beaker of clear water? Do we have clear water plus a spot of red dye? Obviously not. We have a new coloration to every molecule of water. That is what I mean by ecological change. A new medium does not add something; it changes everything. In the year 1500, after the printing press was invented, you did not have old Europe plus the printing press. You had a different Europe. After television, America was not America plus television. Television gave a new coloration to every political campaign, to every home, to every school, to every church, to every industry, and so on.

That is why we must be cautious about technological innovation. The consequences of technological change are always vast, often unpredictable and largely irreversible. That is also why we must be suspicious of capitalists. Capitalists are by definition not only personal risk takers but, more to the point, cultural risk takers. The most creative and daring of them hope to exploit new technologies to the fullest, and do not much care what traditions are overthrown in the process or whether or not a culture is prepared to function without such traditions. Capitalists are, in a word, radicals. In America, our most significant radicals have always been capitalists—men like Bell, Edison, Ford, Carnegie, Sarnoff, Goldwyn. These men obliterated the 19th century, and created the 20th, which is why it is a mystery to me that capitalists are thought to be conservative. Perhaps it is because they are inclined to wear dark suits and grey ties.

I trust you understand that in saying all this, I am making no argument for socialism. I say only that capitalists need to be carefully watched and disciplined. To be sure, they talk of family, marriage, piety, and honor but if allowed to exploit new technology to its fullest economic potential, they may undo the institutions that make such ideas possible. And here I might just give two examples of this point, taken from the American encounter with technology. The first concerns education. Who, we may ask, has had the greatest impact on American education in this century? If you are thinking of John Dewey or any other education philosopher, I must say you are quite wrong. The greatest impact has been made by quiet men in grey suits in a suburb of New York City called Princeton, New Jersey. There, they developed and promoted the technology known as the standardized test, such as IQ tests, the SATs and the GREs. Their tests redefined what we mean by learning, and have resulted in our reorganizing the curriculum to accommodate the tests.

A second example concerns our politics. It is clear by now that the people who have had the most radical effect on American politics in our time are not political ideologues or student protesters with long hair and copies of Karl Marx under their arms. The radicals who have changed the nature of politics in America are entrepreneurs in dark suits and grey ties who manage the large television industry in America. They did not mean to turn political discourse into a form of entertainment. They did not mean to make it impossible for an overweight person to run for high political office. They did not mean to reduce political campaigning to a 30-second TV commercial. All they were trying to do is to make television into a vast and unsleeping money machine. That they destroyed substantive political discourse in the process does not concern them.

Fifth Idea

I come now to the fifth and final idea, which is that media tend to become mythic. I use this word in the sense in which it was used by the French literary critic, Roland Barthes. He used the word "myth" to refer to a common tendency to think of our technological creations as if they were God-given, as if they were a part of the natural order of things. I have on occasion asked my students if they know when the alphabet was invented. The question astonishes them. It is as if I asked them when clouds and trees were invented. The alphabet, they believe, was not something that was invented. It just is. It is this way with many products of human culture but with none more consistently than technology. Cars, planes, TV, movies, newspapers—they have achieved mythic status because they are perceived as gifts of nature, not as artifacts produced in a specific political and historical context.

The best way to view technology is as a strange intruder.

When a technology become mythic, it is always dangerous because it is then accepted as it is, and is therefore not easily susceptible to modification or control. If you should propose to the average American that television broadcasting should not begin until 5 PM and should cease at 11 PM, or propose that there should be no television commercials, he will think the idea ridiculous. But not because he disagrees with your cultural agenda. He will think it ridiculous because he assumes you are proposing that something in nature be changed; as if you are suggesting that the sun should rise at 10 AM instead of at 6.

Whenever I think about the capacity of technology to become mythic, I call to mind the remark made by Pope John Paul II. He said, "Science can purify religion from error and superstition. Religion can purify science from idolatry and false absolutes."

What I am saying is that our enthusiasm for technology can turn into a form of idolatry and our belief in its beneficence can be a false absolute. The best way to view technology is as a strange intruder, to remember that technology is not part of God's plan but a product of human creativity and hubris, and that its capacity for good or evil rests entirely on human awareness of what it does for us and to us.

Conclusion

And so, these are my five ideas about technological change. First, that we always pay a price for technology; the greater the technology, the greater the price. Second, that there are always winners and losers, and that the winners always try to persuade the losers that they are really winners. Third, that there is embedded in every great technology an epistemological, political or social prejudice. Sometimes that bias is greatly to our advantage. Sometimes it is not. The printing press annihilated the oral tradition; telegraphy annihilated space; television has humiliated the word; the computer, perhaps, will degrade community life. And so on. Fourth, technological change is not additive; it is ecological, which means, it changes everything and is, therefore too important to be left entirely in the hands of Bill Gates. And fifth, technology tends to become mythic; that is, perceived as part of the natural order of things, and therefore tends to control more of our lives than is good for us.

If we had more time, I could supply some additional important things about technological change but I will stand by these for the moment, and will close with this thought. In the past, we experienced technological change in the manner of sleep-walkers. Our unspoken slogan has been "technology über alles," and we have been willing to shape our lives to fit the requirements of technology, not the requirements of culture. This is a form of stupidity, especially in an age of vast technological change. We need to proceed with our eyes wide open so that we many use technology rather than be used by it.

Five Things We Need to Know About Technological Change, address to New Tech 98 (a conference), Denver, Colorado, March 27, 1998. © 1998 by Neil Postman. Reprinted by permission.

Access Denied

Whom to Protect and How?

The Public, the Government, and the Internet **Revolution**

by Robert J. Blendon, John M. Benson, Mollyann Brodie, Drew E. Altman,
Marcus D. Rosenbaum, Rebecca Flournoy, and Minah Kim

The United States is now in the second stage of a major technological transformation. What began in the 1980s as the Computer Revolution has extended its reach and become the Computer and Internet Revolution. The second stage of the revolution is not only transforming American life, but also leading to calls for federal government protection from perceived threats presented by specific Internet content. Because of First Amendment concerns and the difficulty of regulating this international technology, the government will find it hard to provide the kind of oversight the public wants.

During the first stage of the Computer and Internet Revolution, computer use grew rapidly. Between 1985 and 1999, the share of Americans who used a computer at work or at home more than doubled, from 30 percent to 70 percent. The increase in home computer ownership was even more striking, quadrupling from 15 percent in 1985 to 60 percent by century's end (table 1).

The Internet stage of the revolution started in the mid-1990s. Only five years ago, fewer than one in five Americans (18 percent) had ever used the Internet. As the new century begins, nearly two-thirds (64 percent) have used the Internet some time in their lives. In 1995 only 14 percent of Americans said they went online to access the Internet or to send or receive e-mail. By 1997 that share had more than doubled, to 36 percent, and today more than half (54 percent) go online. Virtually all Americans younger than 60 say they have used a computer (92 percent), and most have used the Internet (75 percent) or sent an e-mail message (67 percent).

The rapid spread of the new technology is not without precedent. Television ownership in the United States exploded from 6 percent in 1949 to 52 percent in 1953 to 83 percent by 1956. Still, the increase in computer use and, in the second wave, Internet use is remarkable.

> Most Americans see the computer's impact on society as mainly positive. Just over half believe that the computer has given people more control over their lives

Although much is made of the Internet's almost limitless capabilities, at this point people are most likely to use it to get information. Americans use the Internet at home to learn about entertainment, sports, and hobbies (38 percent), current events (37 percent), travel (33 percent), and health (28 percent). Fewer use the Internet to shop (24 percent), pay bills (9 percent), and make investments (9 percent).

A Beneficent Revolution

America's Internet Revolution is taking place among people already disposed to believe strongly in the benefits of new technology. When asked to rate on a scale of 0 to 100 their interest in 11 issues, Americans ranked new medical discoveries highest (an average of 82), followed in fourth and fifth places by new scientific discoveries (67) and new inventions and technologies (65).

Table 1. Share of the Public with Access to Computers at Home and at Work, 1985–99						
PERCENT	1985	1990	1995	1997	1999	
					(a)	(b)
Computer at work	25	32	39	38	42	44
Computer at home	15	22	36	42	54	60
Computer at neither	70	58	46	43	35	30

Source: NSF, 1985–1999 (a); NPR–Kaiser–Kennedy School, 1999 (b)

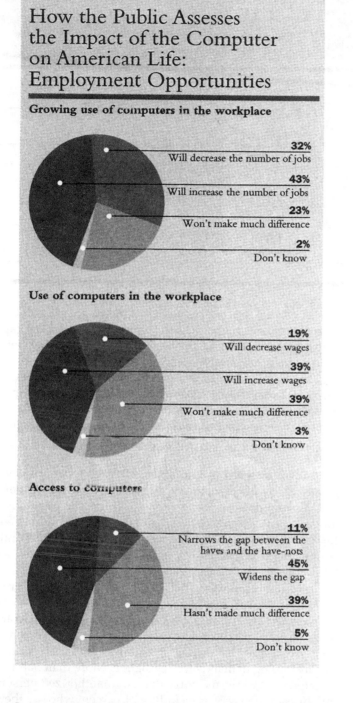

How the Public Assesses the Impact of the Computer on American Life: Employment Opportunities

Growing use of computers in the workplace

- **32%** Will decrease the number of jobs
- **43%** Will increase the number of jobs
- **23%** Won't make much difference
- **2%** Don't know

Use of computers in the workplace

- **19%** Will decrease wages
- **39%** Will increase wages
- **39%** Won't make much difference
- **3%** Don't know

Access to computers

- **11%** Narrows the gap between the haves and the have-nots
- **45%** Widens the gap
- **39%** Hasn't made much difference
- **5%** Don't know

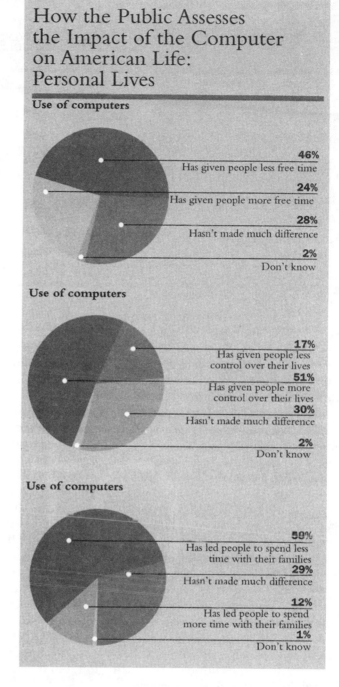

How the Public Assesses the Impact of the Computer on American Life: Personal Lives

Use of computers

- **46%** Has given people less free time
- **24%** Has given people more free time
- **28%** Hasn't made much difference
- **2%** Don't know

Use of computers

- **17%** Has given people less control over their lives
- **51%** Has given people more control over their lives
- **30%** Hasn't made much difference
- **2%** Don't know

Use of computers

- **58%** Has led people to spend less time with their families
- **29%** Hasn't made much difference
- **12%** Has led people to spend more time with their families
- **1%** Don't know

Large majorities of Americans believe that science and technology make lives healthier, easier, and more comfortable (90 percent) and that science and technology will provide more opportunities for the next generation (84 percent). Three-fourths of Americans (74 percent) believe that the benefits of scientific research have outweighed the disadvantages.

The experiences of the past two decades have left most Americans feeling quite positive about the general impact of computers on national life and receptive to the possibilities of the Internet. Asked to choose, from a list of eight options, the two most significant technological develop-

ments of the 20th century, Americans put the computer (named by 62 percent) at the top of the list by a large margin over the automobile (34 percent), television (21 percent), and the airplane (16 percent). The landslide vote for the computer may be due in part to its novelty, but Americans clearly regard the computer as a major technological discovery.

Most Americans see the computer's impact on society as mainly positive. Just over half believe that the computer has given people more control over their lives (17 percent believe it has diminished their control). More than eight out of ten see computers as making life better

Table 2. What the Public Believes the Government Should Do about Key Issues Involving the Internet

PERCENT	ISSUE IS A PROBLEM		ISSUE IS NOT A PROBLEM	DON'T KNOW
	GOVERNMENT SHOULD DO SOMETHING	GOVERNMENT SHOULD NOT BE INVOLVED		
Dangerous strangers making contact with kids	79	15	3	1
The availability of pornography to kids	75	20	4	1
The availability of information about how to build bombs and other weapons	75	15	8	1
False advertising	62	20	12	4
Pornography and adult entertainment	61	26	10	3
The ability to purchase guns	61	14	18	5
Loss of privacy	54	29	14	2
Hate speech, information that attacks people based on their race, religion, or ethnicity	53	27	15	5
Violent games	51	31	15	3

Source: NPR–Kaiser–Kennedy School, 1999

for Americans (9 percent think computers are making life worse). Sixty-eight percent believe the Internet is making life better (14 percent believe it is making life worse). Americans are more evenly divided in their views on the impact of television: 46 percent believe that TV is making life better, 34 percent think it is making life worse.

Most Americans also view the computer industry positively. More than three out of four (78 percent) think computer software companies serve consumers well, while only 7 percent think their service is poor. Only banks (73 percent) and hospitals (72 percent) have comparably positive ratings, but both have higher negatives (24 percent each). Nearly two-thirds (65 percent) of Americans believe that the Internet industry is doing a good job serving its consumers; again, only 7 percent think it is doing a bad job.

Despite some early fears, most Americans do not think the use of computers in the workplace displaces workers or depresses wages. A plurality (43 percent) think the growing use of computers will create more jobs; 32 percent think it will mean fewer jobs; about a quarter think it will not make much difference. Americans are evenly divided, at 39 percent each, on whether the use of computers will raise wages or not have much effect; but only 19 percent believe it will lower wages.

In two areas—the amount of free time and time spent with family and friends—Americans do not believe computers have improved life. Only one-fourth (24 percent) of the public believes that computers have given people more free time. Nearly half think computers have actually reduced free time. And more than half (58 percent) say computers have led people to spend less time with families and friends.

What Role for Government?

The first wave of the Computer and Internet Revolution led many Americans to see a role for government in narrowing a "digital divide" in American society, a problem that continues to concern the public today. Nearly half (45 percent) believe that access to computers widens the gap between the haves and the have-nots, while only 11 percent believe that it narrows the gap; 39 percent think it has not made much different. A majority of Americans (57 percent) believe the government should help low-income people get access to computers and the Internet, and 78 percent say the government should help low-income children.

The Internet Revolution is leading to a broader range of public concerns, accompanied by calls for more government involvement in specific areas. Eighty-five percent of Americans cite as a major problem the possibility of dangerous strangers making contact with children; 84 percent, the availability of pornography to children; and 73 percent, the availability of information about how to build bombs and other weapons.

In addition, more than half (56 percent) of Americans regard the loss of privacy as a major problem with computers or the Internet. Although few (4 percent) have ever had an unauthorized person gain access to their financial records or personal information over the Internet, privacy concerns are increasing demands for regulation. More than half (59 percent) of Americans worry that an unauthorized person might gain such access, including 21 percent who say they are very worried. More than three-fourths (81 percent) of people who ever go online say they are concerned about threats to their personal privacy when using the Internet, including 42 percent who say they are very concerned.

What do these trends indicate about a possible new role for government in regulating the Internet? On the one hand, the coming years will witness an upsurge in use of the Internet for a wide variety of purposes, and the public is unlikely to want across-the-board government regulation of the Internet. On the other, most Americans are likely to support legislation to address their specific concerns about the content of the Internet.

The results reported here are drawn primarily from a survey conducted by the National Public Radio–Henry J. Kaiser Family Foundation–Kennedy School of Government survey project, November 15–December 19, 1999. Other data come from polls by the National Science Foundation (1985, 1990, 1995, 1997, 1999); the Pew Research Center for the People and the Press-Princeton Survey Research Associates (1995, 1997, 2000); CBS News-*New York Times* (1995); CBS News (1999); the Gallup Poll (1949, 1953, 1956); Harris Interactive (2000); the Henry J. Kaiser Family Foundation–Kennedy School of Government (2000), Louis Harris & Associates-Dr. Alan F. Weston–Privacy and American Business–Price Waterhouse, Inc.(1998); and *Newsweek*–Princeton Survey Research Associates (1999). Results of the NSF polls may be found at http://www.nsf.gov/sbe/srs/seind00/pdf. Results of all other polls cited may be obtained from the Roper Center for Public Opinion Research, Storrs, Connecticut.

Many people are wary of having the government regulate what can be put on the Internet, but they are more willing to accept regulation when it comes to specific threatening content. At least at this point, only about a third of Americans see the need for more government regulation of the Internet industry or the general content of the Internet. But when specific content seen as threatening, such as pornography and bomb-making information, is mentioned, 60 percent favor government restrictions, even if they would impinge on freedom of speech. More than half (57 percent) say that "the federal government needs to regulate what is on the Internet more than television and newspapers because the Internet can be used to gain easier access to dangerous information."

Three-quarters of Americans say the government should "do something" about the possibility of dangerous strangers making contact with children and about the availability both of pornography to children and of information on how to build explosives (see table 2). A majority also says the government should do something about false advertising (62 percent), the availability of guns (61 percent), pornography (61 percent), the loss of privacy (54 percent), and hate speech (53 percent).

More Americans are worried about specific threats like pornography and bomb-making information on the Internet than about First Amendment issues involved in regulating these threats. When asked which worried them more, 53 percent said they were more concerned that government would not get involved enough in regulating pornography and bomb-making information on the Internet. Only 26 percent were more concerned that government would get too involved in censorship of the Internet.

Public concerns about specific threats on the Internet are not likely to dissipate as more people go online. While Internet users are less likely than nonusers to believe that the content of the Internet needs more regulation than TV or newspaper content, about half of Internet users (as against 65 percent of nonusers) favor this additional regulation in general. In addition, a majority of Internet users believe the government should do something about most of the same specific threats mentioned by nonusers.

The next decade will see an explosion of growth and change in the world of the Internet. Like the advent of television half a century ago, the Internet Revolution will lead to fundamental and in most cases positive changes in the way Americans live. The number of Americans who use the Internet for nearly every activity is likely to double or triple.

Between a Rock and a Hard Place

In the midst of this extraordinary ferment, public pressure will build in favor of more government involvement in regulating specific parts of the Internet's content. Regulatory efforts will raise a number of First Amendment issues, if not with the public, at least within the judicial system. Given that information on the Internet flows almost seamlessly across national borders, the U.S. government—or any other—will find it extremely difficult to limit access to information the public thinks is dangerous. Policymakers are likely to be caught between growing public pressure to protect against perceived threats to national and personal well-being and the limits of their ability to regulate specific Internet content.

Robert J. Blendon, of the John F. Kennedy School of Government and the Harvard School of Public Health; John M. Benson and Minah Kim, of the Harvard School of Public Health; Mollyann Brodie, Drew E. Altman, and Rebecca Flournoy, of the Henry J. Kaiser Family Foundation; and Marcus D. Rosenbaum of National Public Radio are part of a team conducting ongoing polling on Americans' attitudes about domestic policy issues.

From the *Brookings Review*, Winter 2001, pp. 44-48. © 2001 by the Brookings Institution Press, Washington, DC. Reprinted by permission.

On the Nature of Computing

Computing is its own virtual world, bound only by its
practitioners' imaginations and creativity.

Jon Crowcroft

I would like to propose that computing's innate agenda is
the virtual, rather than the natural or the artificial.

Each of us in the computing community experiences
periodic bouts of navel gazing about the nature of our
business. The related public debate typically polarizes us
along a spectrum between engineering and science. At the
engineering end are usually the engineers who design and
manage systems, networks, and operating systems; at the
science end are the ideas describing computability,
complexity, and information theory. An extreme view of
each end places practitioners within university electrical
engineering departments, and theoreticians within
university mathematics departments.

I studied the natural sciences at Cambridge University as
an undergraduate. I was taught the value of studying the
natural world, along with the use (and advance) of mathematics to describe and understand (and predict) its
behavior. I have also spent more than a decade teaching
courses in an electrical engineering department, where
artificial systems are built according to models (often
mathematical) with reliable and predictable behavior.
Computing has never established a simple connection
between the natural and the mathematical. Nowhere is this
lack of a clear-cut connection clearer than when Ph.D.
students select a problem for their thesis work; their
dilemma is the key to understanding why computing represents a third place in the world of discourse—distinct from
the natural and from the artificial of science and
engineering.

Computing involves (virtual) systems that may never
exist, either in nature or through human creation. Ph.D.
students find it difficult to settle on a topic because the
possibilities are endless and the topic may have no intersection with the real world, either in understanding a
phenomenon or in creating an artifact. In trying to define
the nature of computing I completely disagree with the late
Nobel Prize physicist Richard Feynman.[1] Computing often
results in a model of something. Although an object or
process that interacts with or describes the real world may
be the outcome, it does not have to be.[2]

Computing's disconnection from physical reality has an
important consequence when explaining to the public
what it is computer scientists do, whether to schoolchildren, noncomputing users in general, or funding
agencies and decision makers. Unlike the artificial (the
engineering end of the spectrum), some of what we do may
not be obviously useful and therefore attractive to
commerce and governments for optimizing social welfare
or profit. Unlike the natural world (the scientific end of the
spectrum), some of what we do may not necessarily be "for
the advancement of pure knowledge" and therefore a priori
worthwhile. In some sense, though, what we do underpins
both of these engineering and scientific activities.

I am comfortable endorsing the claim that computing is
less worldly than, say, cosmology. On the other hand, due
to the possible use of computing as part of the foundation
of practically any kind of system—whether physical or
abstract—anyone is likely to build today, computer scientists can also claim that computing is inherently more
useful than engineering.

Examples of the Virtual

To illustrate my argument, consider the following examples
of the virtual I've selected from the history of computer
science:

Virtualization.   Within the discipline of computer science
itself, the concept of virtualization represents a first-class
tool. When confronted with intransigent engineering
limitations of memory, processors, I/O, and networks,
we've commonly taken the abstract approach. For
example, we create virtual memory systems to replace one

piece of hardware with another as needed to overcome capacity/performance problems and to choose when it's appropriate to do so; we replace inconvenient low-level processor interfaces (the instruction set) with virtual machines (such as VM, vmware, Xen, and Denali), to provide a more convenient (and stable) interface for systems programmers. We might provide a single API to all I/O devices, so programs need not worry whether, say, an MP3 file is being loaded from a tape, a magnetic disk, an optical disc, flash RAM, or even networked media. We also might replace a network with a virtual private network, allowing users to behave as if they were in an Internet of their own.

Virtual communities.   In the emerging world of grid computing (notably in the U.K.'s e-Science program), we are creating virtual communities of scientists with virtual laboratories and computing resources dedicated to supporting "in silico" experiments, replacing the expensive, error-prone "in vivo" or "in vitro" experiments of the past. Here, we have virtualized natural systems, whether they involve fluids (such as the atmosphere, oceans, and plasma) or complex biological systems (such as genomes, proteins, and even whole ecologies).

Entertainment.   The convergence of computer games and the movie industry represents the clearest evidence to support my view that computing is a wholly new discipline. The world of entertainment imposes no natural or artificial constraints on what a system may do. The only limit is the imagination of its creators, combined with knowledge and skills from the computing discipline. Constraints may be imposed from the discipline itself (such as computability, complexity, and plain affability) but may often be orthogonal to the goals (if any) of the computation.

Historically, simple examples of virtual worlds have been used in both games and online environments, as well as for playing with alternate realities (such as in artificial life), so this view is not something that has suddenly become true. It has always been one of the exciting but difficult aspects of working in computing that the bounds are not set from outside the field but by our own choice of

what research projects we most want to work on and see developed.

Conclusion

Occupying a third place in human intellectual culture, computing is not bound by the need to describe what does exist (as in natural science) or what can be built in the real world (as in engineering). This place is the virtual. Although we computer scientists do not need to be complete, consistent, or correct, we have the tools to choose to be part of these categories whenever we wish our systems to be complete, consistent, or correct.

Notes

1. "Computer science also differs from physics in that it is not actually a science. It does not study natural objects. Neither is it, as you might think, mathematics; although it does use mathematical reasoning pretty extensively. Rather, computer science is like engineering; it is all about getting something to do something, rather than just dealing with abstractions, as in the pre-Smith geology." Richard Feynman, from the book *Feynman Lectures on Computation* (1970).

2. I am tempted to lay claim to the term "magic" [1]. A lot of what computer scientists do is now seen by the lay public as magical. Programmers (especially systems engineers) are often referred to as gurus, sorcerers, and wizards. Given the lofty goals of white magic, understanding the power of names and the value of pure thought, the power of labels is indeed attractive. However, many historically compelling reasons argue against this connotation, including the sad history of Isaac Newton's alchemical pursuit of the philosopher's stone and eternal life, and the religiously driven 17th century witch trials in Salem, MA, and other seemingly rational explanations for irrational behaviors.

Reference

1. Penrose, R. *The Road to Reality: A Complete Guide to the Laws of the Universe.* Jonathan Cape, London, U.K., 2004.

Jon Crowcroft (*Jon.Crowcroft@cl.cam.ac.uk*) *is the Marconi Professor of Communications Systems in the Computer Laboratory at the University of Cambridge, Cambridge, U.K.*

From *Communications of the ACM*, Vol. 48, No. 2, February 2005, pp. 19-20. Copyright © 2005 by Association for Computing Machinery, Inc. Reprinted by permission.

UNIT 2
The Economy

Unit Selections

4. **The Productivity Paradox**, Stephen S. Roach
5. **The Big Band Era**, Christopher Swope
6. **The New Gatekeepers**, Gregory M. Lamb
7. **The Software Wars**, Paul De Palma

Key Points to Consider

- Stephen S. Roach in "The Productivity Paradox" gives one view of the relationship of information technology to computing. There are others. Use the Internet to find contrary opinions.

- The definition of what constitutes an operating system was an important part of the Department of Justice's recent antitrust suit against Microsoft. What is an operating system? Have you ever used Linux? Since it's free, why do you think your computer does not come with Linux already installed? The etymology of the word "Linux" is interesting. Trace it to its roots in a research project at Bell Labs in the 60's and 70's.

- Are you surprised to learn, as the author of "The Software Wars" asserts, that the software development can be unsystematic? Do you think this differs from the production of conventional engineering projects, a bridge, for example?

Student Website

www.mhcls.com/online

Internet References

Further information regarding these websites may be found in this book's preface or online.

CAUCE: Coalition Against Unsolicited Commercial Email
http://www.cauce.org

E-Commerce Times
http://www.ecommercetimes.com/

The End of Cash (James Gleick)
http://www.around.com/money.html

Fight Spam on the Internet
http://spam.abuse.net

The Linux Home Page
http://www.linux.org

The Rise of the Informediary
http://www.ait.unl.edu/crane/misgrad/sglee/informediary.htm

Smart Cards: A Primer
http://www.javaworld.com/javaworld/jw-12-1997/jw-12-javadev.html

Smart Card Group
http://www.smartcard.co.uk

Living in the United States in the beginning of the 21st century, it is hard to imagine that the accumulation of wealth once bordered on the disreputable. Listen to William Wordsworth, writing two hundred years ago:

> The world is too much with us; late and soon,
> Getting and spending, we lay waste our powers:
> Little we see in nature that is ours;
> We have given our hearts away a sordid boon;

These are words that would quicken the pulse of any young protester of globalization. And no wonder. Wordsworth was writing a generation after James Watt perfected the steam engine. England was in the grips of the Industrial Revolution. Just as the developed world now appears to be heading away from an industrial towards a service economy, so Wordsworth's world was moving from an agrarian to an industrial economy. And just as the steam engine has become the emblem of that transformation, the computer has become the symbol of this one.

People, of course, did not stop farming after the Industrial Revolution, nor have they stopped producing steel and automobiles after the Information Revolution, though many commentators write as if this is exactly what happened. It is true that we in the United States have largely stopped working in factories. In the last three decades, the number of Americans employed has increased by over 50 million. During this same period, the decline in manufacturing jobs was in the hundreds of thousands. A large handful of these new workers are software developers, computer engineers, web-site developers, manipulators of digital images—the glamour jobs of the information age. A much larger portion provide janitorial, health, food and other services, leading to the charge that the American economy works be-cause we take in one another's laundry. It is also often said that the fabulous productivity of American factory workers, augmented by computers, free the rest of us to provide services. You may be surprised to learn that some economists doubt the relationship between increased output per worker and information technology. Stephen Roach, in a *New York Times* op-ed piece, "The Productivity Paradox," speculates that recent reports on productivity growth may be off the mark. Because "most information workers can toil around the clock…we are woefully underestimating the time actually spent on the job." In other words, since productivity is a measure of output per unit of work time, economists may be seeing an increase, because the denominator in this equation is too low.

Though, these economists may or may not be correct, one area in which computers play an indisputable role is in the global economy. Over the past two decades more and more of American manufacturing has migrated to countries with lower labor costs. It is impossible to imagine how a global manufacturing network could be coordinated without computers. Products manufactured abroad—with or without the productivity benefits of computers—pass through a bewildering array of shippers and distributors until they arrive on the shelves of a big box retailer in a Phoenix suburb, or just-in-time to be bolted to the frame of an automobile being assembled outside St. Louis. Or imagine how Federal Express could track its parcels as they make their way from an office in a San Jose suburb to one in Manhattan. Not surprisingly, cities around the country are scrambling to provide uniform broadband access. "The Big Band Era," reports on a problem many are encountering. Even as cities like Philadelphia are working to transform the entire city into a wireless hot spot—with government as the internet service provider of last resort—

communications companies are fighting to keep local governments out of the broadband business.

One of the real success stories of the post boom era has been Google. Created by a couple of Stanford students, Google went on-line just six months before the crash. Now it conducts 2,315 searches every second, making the largest of the search engines with 35% of the market. Put another way, of the $35 billion dollars worth of purchases that search engines generated in 2004, Google accounted for a healthy share. For the newly-created Google stock holders, this means that a lot of companies are going to pay Google to be included among search results. See "The New Gatekeepers" for the details. But how does Goo-gle turn up what it does? As National Public Radio pointed out in its excellent series, "The Search Engine Wars,"[1] there is some science and an awful lot of art behind who gets listed—and where—in a Google search.

The final article in the unit, "The Software Wars," describes an important and understudied topic: the complexity of computer hardware and software. The article tells a personal tale of software development and its inefficiencies. Since problems with the Space Shuttle are in the news again, this piece, which recounts the Challenger disaster of 1986, is especially timely.

---

1. www.NPR.org/programs/morning/features/2004/APR/Google, accessed 8/18/05.

The Productivity Paradox

By Stephen S. Roach

Despite the economy's stunning 8.2 percent surge in the third quarter, the staying power of this economic recovery remains a matter of debate. But there is one aspect of the economy on which agreement is nearly unanimous: America's miraculous productivity. In the third quarter, productivity grew by 8.1 percent in the nonfarm business sector—a figure likely to be revised upwards—and it has grown at an average rate of 5.4 percent in the last two years.

This surge is not simply a byproduct of the business cycle, even accounting for the usual uptick in productivity after a recession. In the first two years of the six most recent recoveries, productivity gains averaged only 3.5 percent. The favored explanation is that improved productivity is yet another benefit of the so-called New Economy. American business has reinvented itself. Manufacturing and services companies have figured out how to get more from less. By using information technologies, they can squeeze ever increasing value out of the average worker.

It's a great story, and if correct, it could lead to a new and lasting prosperity in the United States. But it may be wide of the mark.

First of all, productivity measurement is more art than science—especially in America's vast services sector, which employs fully 80 percent of the nation's private work force, according to the United States Bureau of Labor Statistics. Productivity is calculated as the ratio of output per unit of work time. How do we measure value added in the amorphous services sector?

Very poorly, is the answer. The numerator of the productivity equation, output, is hopelessly vague for services. For many years, government statisticians have used worker compensation to approximate output in many service industries, which makes little or no intuitive sense. The denominator of the productivity equation—units of work time—is even more spurious. Government data on work schedules are woefully out of touch with reality—especially in America's largest occupational group, the professional and managerial segments, which together account for 35 percent of the total work force.

For example, in financial services, the Labor Department tells us that the average workweek has been unchanged, at 35.5 hours, since 1988. That's patently absurd. Courtesy of a profusion of portable information appliances (laptops, cell phones, personal digital assistants, etc.), along with near ubiquitous connectivity (hard-wired and now increasingly wireless), most information workers can toil around the clock. The official data don't come close to capturing this cultural shift.

We aren't working smarter, we're working harder.

As a result, we are woefully underestimating the time actually spent on the job. It follows, therefore, that we are equally guilty of overestimating white-collar productivity. Productivity is not about working longer. It's about getting more value from each unit of work time. The official productivity numbers are, in effect, mistaking work time for leisure time.

This is not a sustainable outcome—for the American worker or the American economy. To the extent productivity miracles are driven more by perspiration than by inspiration, there are limits to gains in efficiency based on sheer physical effort.

The same is true for corporate America, where increased productivity is now showing up on the bottom line in the form of increased profits. When better earnings stem from cost cutting (and the jobless recovery that engenders), there are limits to future improvements in productivity. Strategies that rely primarily on cost cutting will lead eventually to "hollow" companies—businesses that have been stripped bare of once valuable labor. That's hardly the way to sustained prosperity.

Many economists say that strong productivity growth goes hand in hand with a jobless recovery. Nothing could be further from the truth. In the 1960's, both productivity and employment surged at an annual rate of close to 3 percent. In the latter half of the 1990's, accelerating productivity also coincided with rapid job creation.

In fact, there is no precedent for sustained productivity enhancement through downsizing. That would result in an increasingly barren economy that will ultimately lose market share in an ever-expanding world.

That underscores another aspect of America's recent productivity miracle: the growing use of overseas labor. While this may increase the profits of American business—help desk employees or customer-service representatives in India earn a fraction of what their counterparts in the United States do—the American worker does not directly share the benefits. The result is a clash between the owners of capital and the providers of labor—a clash that has resulted in heightened trade frictions and growing protectionist risks. There's nothing sustainable about this plan for productivity enhancement, either.

In the end, America's productivity revival may be nothing more than a transition from one way of doing business to another—a change in operating systems, as it were. Aided by the stock market bubble and the Y2K frenzy, corporate America led the world in spending on new information technology and telecommunications in the latter half of the 1990's.

This resulted in an increase of the portion of gross domestic product that went to capital spending. With the share of capital going up, it follows that the share of labor went down. Thus national output was produced with less labor in relative terms—resulting in a windfall of higher productivity. Once the migration from the old technology to the new starts to peak, this transitional productivity dividend can then be expected to wane.

No one wants to see that. For all their wishful thinking, believers in the productivity miracle are right about one critical point: productivity is the key to prosperity.

Have we finally found the key? It's doubtful. Productivity growth is sustainable when driven by creativity, risk-taking, innovation and, yes, new technology. It is fleeting when it is driven simply by downsizing and longer hours. With cost cutting still the credo and workers starting to reach physical limits, America's so-called productivity renaissance may be over before Americans even have a chance to enjoy it.

Stephen S. Roach is chief economist for Morgan Stanley.

THE BIG BAND ERA

The quest for rapid and robust Internet access has cities grappling with how to bring the best of broadband to their businesses and residents.

Christopher Swope

Talk to Chris O'Brien about broadband access, and the city of Chicago's technology chief will tell you that more Internet traffic flows through Chicago than anywhere else in the world. That's a difficult point to prove, a bit like saying that Chicago-style pizza is better than New York's. No matter. O'Brien knows that broadband means business, and that most companies can't survive today without superfast access to the Internet. So the Windy City has taken to selling itself as Broadband City—as much a national hub for Internet infrastructure as it's always been for railroads, highways and airports.

That claim is an easy one to believe from the vantage point of O'Brien's 27th-floor downtown office. Underneath the traffic-clogged streets below, private companies have buried miles of fiber-optic cable—an Internet backbone that is indeed as quick as any in the world. Here, big finance and technology firms that require huge amounts of bandwidth for the fastest Internet speeds don't have too much trouble getting it.

But you don't have to wander far from downtown to see how quickly Chicago's broadband prowess breaks down. In South Side neighborhoods and industrial corridors slated for economic development, fiber is much harder to find. Business customers have fewer broadband options here, and what they do have can be prohibitively expensive. For the modest bandwidth of a T-1 line, they can pay as much as $1,000 a month—more than the rent for some of them. Or they can look into two other broadband options: DSL and cable modem. Those are more limited still and aren't yet available in some pockets of the city.

The broadband landscape looks even more speckled over the city line. In the suburbs, researchers at federal laboratories and universities enjoy top-speed broadband at work but some can't get the modest speeds of DSL at home. The suburbs, however, are better off than the prairie towns that lie farther out. There, most computer users are making do with pokey dial-up Internet service that moves data along at a glacial pace.

Broadband access is an essential item for business, and it is quickly becoming one at home too, as everything digital, from e-mail to phone calls to "The Sopranos," tries to squeeze through the same Internet pipe. Yet as the Chicago region shows, the state of American broadband in 2005 ranges from Tiffany to the country store. This new digital divide—the broadband divide—leaves state and local officials facing a lot of tough questions. What's the best way to smooth out these disparities? And what's the proper role of the public sector? Should government build and own some of the infrastructure itself, as it does with highways? Or should broadband look more like the railroads, built and run by profit-seeking companies?

A Broad Reach

The current situation is cause for either hope or despair, depending on how one looks at it. As of last July, 63 million Americans were connecting to the Internet via broadband at home, according to Nielsen//NetRatings. Millions more use broadband at the office—DSL, T-1 or better—making workers more efficient and innovative. Entrepreneurs can now dream up new services to sell over broadband—founding new companies that create new jobs.

The bad news is that as quickly as broadband is catching on, the U.S. is a laggard compared with other nations. South Korea, Denmark, Japan and Canada have higher rates of residential broadband penetration. In fact, the U.S. is 11th in the world, according to the International Telecommunications Union in Geneva. Part of the problem is that Americans are more spread out than, say, the South Koreans, half of whom live in apartment buildings. But public policy also plays a big role. Japan and South Korea have national broadband strategies. The U.S. doesn't. Broadband deployment is largely up to the giant telephone and cable companies that currently compete with each other in the courtroom just as much as they slug it out in the marketplace. An upside of the American laissez-faire approach is innovation: Carriers have developed lots of technologies for delivering broadband, some using old existing wires, some requiring new lines and others using wireless. The downside is that they only deploy these products in markets where they believe they can turn a profit quickly.

There may be no national policy, but that doesn't mean cities, suburbs and rural communities are sitting on the sidelines. In fact, localities are at the forefront of the broadband debate, stirring up controversy. For example, Philadelphia, like dozens of other cities, is looking at offering cheap broadband service by turning the whole city into a wireless "hot spot." Opponents of the idea, led by Verizon Communications, think that cities should stay out of broadband. They persuaded the Pennsylvania legislature in November to pass a law that makes it harder for cities to offer municipal broadband. (Verizon is letting Philadelphia proceed with its plans, however.)

Politics may be the least of local officials' worries. As they attack the broadband divide, they're finding that it's a terrifically complex problem, one that is only growing more complicated as technology advances and bandwidth needs grow. Realistically, they can't hope to "solve" the divide so much as manage it over time. Moreover, there's not just one broadband divide. There are at least four of them:

- **Access.** Millions of Americans still can't get basic DSL or cable modem service, or the local provider has a monopoly on the market.
- **Service.** There's lots of high-speed fiber in the ground in the U.S., but outside of dense business districts, the "last mile" problem of tapping into it is expensive to solve.
- **Cost.** Even where basic broadband is available, the monthly cost remains higher than many consumers are willing or able to pay.
- **Don't Need It.** More than one-third of U.S. households still don't have computers—let alone high-speed Internet. And many Internet users don't mind using slow dial-up service.

The Gatekeepers

You see a range of thinking about these issues across the Chicago region. The most controversial idea came from three cities on the western edge of the Chicago suburbs. Batavia, Geneva and St. Charles, also known as the Tri-Cities, are among the 2,000 U.S. cities that are in the electricity business. Public power has been pretty good for the Tri-Cities. Their electric rates are about 30 percent lower than neighboring towns. So it wasn't a stretch when they proposed getting into the broadband business as well.

The idea first came up two years ago. Comcast, the dominant cable company in the Chicago region, hadn't yet rolled out its cable modem service. The local phone company, SBC Communications, had started offering DSL—but large swaths of the Tri-Cities still couldn't get it.

The city governments held a trump card, however. Each owned a fiber-optic network—a valuable byproduct of running an electric utility. Officials began thinking that if they could build that fiber out directly to homes and businesses, it would be a huge draw for economic development. Municipal broadband—offering superfast Internet, cable TV and telephone—would compete directly with Comcast and SBC.

The towns put the question to a referendum in April 2003. Scared by the $62 million price tag, voters turned it down decisively. The plan went before voters again this past November with a new financing scheme. It got steamrolled again. Comcast and SBC waged an overwhelming campaign against the measure. They bused in employees to knock on doors, and Comcast even sent Hallmark greeting cards to voters' homes.

There was another factor at play. Not all residents saw the issue as a compelling one. As Jeffery Schielke, the mayor of Batavia, puts it, "When we put in sanitary sewers 100 years ago, a number of people said they'd prefer to go to the outhouse."

Proponents of municipal broadband are still bitter about the outcome. They argue that Comcast and SBC, by fighting the referendum, are holding back technology. "They think it's okay to give us limited bandwidth and charge us an arm and a leg for it," says Annie Collins, whose citizens' group was behind the second referendum. As Collins sees it, cities should view broadband as they do roads, sewers or any other essential infrastructure they provide. "Putting the infrastructure in place is just like pavement," she says. "It's basic infrastructure, and the cities should own it."

Comcast and SBC share a different view: Municipal broadband is a bad idea. "It's wrong of the government to get involved in areas where private corporations are offering choices," says Carrie Hightman, president of SBC Illinois. What about the argument that cities should provide broadband as basic infrastructure? "These aren't vital services," says Bob Ryan, a Comcast lobbyist. "They're nice services. But you're not going to die if you don't get video, data and telephony from the government."

All is not lost in the Tri-Cities. By the time of the second vote, Comcast and SBC had rolled out their networks almost ubiquitously there. Just two weeks before the election, SBC held a "digital ribbon-cutting" ceremony in Batavia. Both companies deny wooing voters by bumping the Tri-Cities up their to-do lists. But many observers in Illinois think that the squeaky wheel got the grease. "All of a sudden the Tri-Cities are getting better service," says Edward Feser, a University of Illinois professor who studies broadband. "Maybe the vote is looked at as a failure, but for the end-market consumer the whole effort has been a bonus."

At Your Service

Farther west, in the prairie town of Princeton, the broadband battle is playing out somewhat differently. A couple of years ago, manufacturers in town began complaining that the T-1 lines they used for broadband weren't fast or robust enough. Rural towns across Illinois have been hit hard lately by manufacturers going overseas. Princeton has fared pretty well so far. But officials there figured that if they could offer manufacturers more bandwidth, it might be all the more reason for companies to stay put.

Big cities have to show corporations that their broadband will stay on even if terrorists strike, says Chris O'Brien, Chicago's technology chief.

Princeton officials met with the local phone company—Verizon in this part of Illinois—to see if there was something it could do to upgrade service. But as Princeton's Jason Bird puts it, "at the end of the day, it came down to the fact that we needed to take on this endeavor ourselves." Princeton owns its electric utility, just as the Tri-Cities do. Unlike the Tri-Cities, however, Princeton is not proposing to go into the broadband business on a retail level. Instead, Princeton will build out the broadband infrastructure and let a local company called Connecting Point sell the service to customers.

Princeton's plan is to build fiber out to any customers who say they need it—most likely the big industrial users. Smaller customers and residential users will be handled differently. They'll be among the first in the nation to receive broadband over the same power lines that pump electricity into peoples' homes. This new technology is a convenient solution to the notorious "last mile" problem. Customers simply plug a box into a power outlet and plug their computers into the box. Bird thinks Princeton's approach to broadband represents a lighter touch to government intervention. "We have a partnership here," he says. "We didn't want to get into the business of being the provider. We didn't feel comfortable with that."

"Wireless really gives you the opportunity, on a relatively low-cost basis, to put technology into neighborhoods that could never afford it before."
—Bob Lieberman
Center for Neighborhood Technology

But that distinction doesn't mean much to the big telephone and cable companies. The argue that any form of municipal broadband enjoys unfair advantages, such as tax-free bond financing. Comcast, SBC and other broadband providers are expected to lobby the legislature for a law similar to Pennsylvania's, either banning municipal broadband or severely restricting it. Similar laws have passed in 15 other states, and the U.S. Supreme Court recently found such bans constitutional. "This is an area where the powerful incumbents want to snuff out consumer option and choice," says Illinois Lieutenant Governor Pat Quinn. "They'e snarling in Illinois. It looks like they'll try to wipe out the municipal option for our state this year. We'll see."

Chicago is more hesitant to use a heavy hand when it comes to broadband. Of course, the city also enjoys two luxuries: a dense downtown and a wealthy mix of corporations that broadband providers are hungry to serve. During the dot-com boom, lots of telecom companies trenched fiber-optic lines under downtown streets. It was a gold rush fueled by the exuberant Internet dreams of the age. Many of those companies later went bankrupt. But their fiber is still there, waiting to be used.

In the Loop, Chicago's busy downtown business section, the biggest broadband problem is figuring out where all the fiber is—and who owns it. That's an economic development issue: Businesses looking to tap into that fiber don't know whom to call. But it's increasingly a homeland security issue, too. After 9/11, many big corporations are queasy about locating critical operations such as data banks in big cities, fearing a terror attack. They want some assurance that their Internet traffic has redundant routes should disaster strike. "Corporate boards are asking whether it's dangerous to locate in a big city," Chris O'Brien says. "We have to prove to them that it's not."

Chicago's neighborhoods are a different story. Back in 2000, Chicago announced a big idea to wire the whole city for broadband. The plan was called CivicNet, and the idea was to aggregate all the public schools, firehouses and city offices into one massive telecom contract. In exchange for a 10-year deal, Chicago expected the winning bidder to lay broadband infrastructure to some 1,600 city facilities. It wouldn't wire the whole city, but since there's a police station, library or some city building in nearly every neighborhood, it would come pretty close.

CivicNet never happened. The telecom bust killed the industry's interest. And Chicago's budget bust killed the city's interest. The silver lining, as O'Brien sees it, is that Comcast and SBC have since pumped millions of dollars of their own into rolling out cable modem and DSL service across nearly all of Chicago. "The residential issue is not solved," O'Brien says. "But we're a lot closer to eliminating access as a problem because of cable modem and DSL." Of all the broadband divides, the one that now concerns O'Brien the most is level of access for small businesses that require more bandwidth than Comcast and SBC are offering. To target this problem, Chicago is con-

Broadband Browser

Technology WIRED	Speed	Consumer Cost	Upsides	Downsides
DSL	Moderate to fast	$25–$60/mo. for residential; $40–$300 for business	Uses existing copper telephone wires	Available only within 3 miles of the telephone company's switch
Cable modem	Moderate	$40–$70/mo	Uses existing coaxial cable networks	Customers share bandwith, not as prevalent in commercial areas
Broadband over power lines (BPL)	Moderate	$25–$50/mo	Uses existing power lines; just plug into a wall socket	Not widely available yet
T-1 line	Fast	$200–$1,000/mo. depending on location	Widely used by small businesses	Expensive to install; monthly charge can be more than the rent.
Fiber-optic lines	Fast to lightning fast	$35–$80/mo. for residential; varies widely for business	Fastest and most reliable for voice, data, video; huge capacity makes it "future proof"	Laying new fiber to the home or to business is expensive
WIRELESS Wi-Fi	Moderate	Free in public "hot spots"; $8–$10/day in private hot spots	Cheap and easy to deploy in libraries, parks, hotels and airports	Limited range; security remains a concern
Cellular broadband	Very slow to moderate	$30–$80/mo.	Rides off cell phone networks; better range than Wi-Fi	Available only in select cities
Satellite	Slow to moderate	$400–$800 for dish; $60–$150/mo. for service	The only option in many rural areas	Pricey start-up costs; slow uploads
WiMax	Very fast	Expected to be moderate	Future option in both cities and rural areas	Won't beat fiber, especially for online video

sidering a CivicNet Lite: a stripped-down version of the original broadband plan, targeted solely at six or seven underserved industrial corridors.

Wire Works

Others are more concerned about another of the broadband divides: cost. Comcast charges between $43 and $58 a month for cable Internet in Chicago. SBC charges between $27 and $37 a month for the most basic residential DSL. Bob Lieberman thinks that wireless broadband might be a cheaper alternative. Lieberman heads the Center for Neighborhood Technology in Chicago, and is experimenting with wireless projects in three neighborhoods in the region. One is Lawndale, a predominantly African-American neighborhood west of the Loop. "The median household income in Lawndale is

$22,000, so $600 a year for broadband is a big chunk," Lieberman says. "That's a lot of money for what is arguably entertainment."

The tallest building in Lawndale is an historic brick tower that rises 260 feet above an old Sears distribution center. "It's the first Sears Tower," Lieberman says. Just as the namesake skyscraper downtown is crowned with radio antennae, Lieberman has placed a small, barely visible antenna in the Lawndale tower. The antenna is wired to the Internet and beams a signal out to "nodes" scattered atop row houses in the neighborhood, which relay the signal back and forth to computers in peoples' homes. An unusual feature of this so-called "mesh" network is that the system actually becomes stronger and more reliable as more people use it.

The Lawndale project is up to 100 users, who for the time being are getting the service for free (the Center hooks people up with used computers, too). Lieberman thinks it could serve as a prototype for small cities or neighborhoods. He estimates the municipal cost of providing such a service would ring in at about $8 to $10 per month, per household. "Wireless really gives you the opportunity, on a relatively low-cost basis, to put technology into neighborhoods that could never afford it before," Lieberman says.

A lot of other cities are having exactly the same thought. The technology is cheap enough that Philadelphia thinks it could fill the air with a cloud of Internet signals for just about $10 million. And wireless technology is advancing quickly. A new generation of wireless broadband, called WiMax, is due out in the next year or so. WiMax will offer greater bandwidth than the current Wi-Fi does and work to a range of 30 miles. In other words, a single antenna could blanket entire cities, or large swaths of countryside, with broadband coverage.

A lot of people in city government around the country are very excited about wireless. Chicago has created Wi-Fi hot spots at all its city libraries, and in places where business travelers congregate, such as the airport and convention center. Yet Chris O'Brien is skeptical of taking on a broader, city-wide wireless project. Simply put, Chicago doesn't want to step on the private sector's turf. "Government needs to tread a very fine line," O'Brien says. "We could create a wireless network for the entire city if we wanted to. We own enough fiber that we could get into the telecom business, too. Figuring out where our leverage ends and where we leave it to the private sector is the tough issue."

Christopher Swope *can be reached at cswope@governing.com*

The new gatekeepers

Google and competing search engines offer up the Web
their way: shallow results and lots of ads. Is that fair?

Gregory M. Lamb, Staff writer

Every second, the world sees three new babies born, 544 McDonald's customers served, and 2,315 Google searches conducted.

Using the search engine to navigate the Internet has become so commonplace that "to Google" is entering the lexicon.

Indeed, Google and its major competitors are putting their own stamp on the digital world: grabbing a major share of online advertising, creating a new Internet industry, and reviving hopes of a return to the heady days when Internet stocks made fortunes overnight.

Most important, they have become the gatekeepers of the digital world. If, as some observers expect, a Big Three of search engines emerges, users will see their Web experience heavily influenced by moneymaking corporations interested in delivering as many eyeballs as they can to advertisers.

That's not necessarily bad, say experts, who compare the phenomenon to the effect of the Yellow Pages on telephone use. But users need to understand how the major search engines influence their Web experience. The results they get are broad and tilted toward commercial, more popular sites.

If they want to really plumb the depths of the Internet, they'll have to rely on tools for "deep" Web searches, which can scour the vast majority of websites that technology used by Google and others just doesn't find.

Search engines represent information gatekeepers unlike any we've had before, says Steve Jones, a communications professor at the University of Illinois in Chicago and founder of the Association of Internet Researchers. In the past, librarians or newspaper editors might have served that role, connecting people with information they're seeking. "This gatekeeper is a machine. And that's a really interesting difference."

For most Web users, the rise of the gatekeeper means their access to cyberspace—and its vast amount of infor-mation and services—is essentially controlled by a handful of companies and their advertisers.

Google is responsible for more than a third of Internet searches in the United States, trailed closely by Yahoo. And behemoth Microsoft says it will enter the market within the next year, forming a Big Three of Internet searchers.

From garage to Gargantua

Six years ago, Google was another California dream, housed in a garage. Now, with its announcement of a public stock sale, everyone's favorite little search engine that could has been officially ordained a multibillion-dollar corporation.

Unlike many of the companies that went public during the Internet boom, search engines are already racking up revenue.

In 2003, advertisers spent some $2.3 billion buying spots on search-engine pages in the US alone, spawning a whole new industry to help companies ensure their websites rise near the top of search rankings.

Search-engine marketing has grown to become the single largest contributor to online advertising revenue, according to comScore Networks.

"Search engines are pretty dominant right now. Most people are going there first in order to find something," says Andy Beal, vice president of search marketing at WebSourced, Inc. "I think that everyone is excited about search" as an ad medium. In contrast, banner ads have declined and "are not as effective as they were, say, five years ago," he says.

Search engines bring a precious commodity to businesses: ready buyers, Mr. Beal says.

"The consumer is initiating the contact. They're telling you what they're looking for," he says.

Market intelligence firm Random Secrecy predicts that search engines will generate purchases of more than

$35 billion in 2004, and it expects that figure to rise to $92 billion by 2008.

Search advertising can happen two ways, says Danny Sullivan, editor of online newsletter `searchenginewatch.com`. Paid placements guarantee the advertiser a spot on the page to the top or side of the rest of the "natural" query results, which are typically calculated by a complex algorithm, including factors like website popularity.

Paid inclusions, on the other hand, mean the advertiser's site is guaranteed to be among the results generated, but with no guarantee of placement or rank.

"They'll only sell you a lottery ticket, but they won't let you rig the lottery," Mr. Sullivan says.

"Search engines are pretty dominant right now. Most people are going there first in order to find something."
—Andy Beal, WebSourced, Inc.

Paid placements are clearly identified as "sponsored links." Yahoo allows paid inclusions in the natural search. Google does not.

Yet despite the white-hot market interest, search engines remain imperfect at best.

A search for a "driver," for example, might yield a communications device for a computer, a golf club, a person in a car, or something that turns a screw.

"The ultimate search engine would basically understand everything in the world, and it would always give you the right thing. And we're a long, long ways from that," Google cofounder Larry Page told Business Week magazine recently.

Search engines are also flawed in that "the relevance [of a search] is determined by the proximity of one word to another," Professor Jones says. "Well, that's not generally how you and I determine relevance. We use incredibly complicated mental maps to do that."

Internet searchers have three perpetual complaints, says Duncan Witte, chief operating officer for Bright-Planet, a specialty Internet-search company in Sioux Falls, S.D. They can't find what they need. When they do find it, they don't understand how to access or interpret the data. And finally they worry about the quality of the data.

Solving these needs "is almost the holy grail, if you will" for searching, Mr. Witte says. "We want it to be easier."

People do a search and get back thousands of results, but "they just want to know what the answer [to their question] is," Witte says. "It's going to be a long time before it's that intuitive. . . . The Web is so big, and there's so much junk, it's hard to wade through it."

Special-interest searchers

To better serve customers, some search engines are trying to specialize.

"Local searching is going to be important," Beal says.

Google has entered this arena with its Google local.

In fact, consumers may begin to expect that a search engine knows where they are and give them results based on that, Beal says. "That's definitely going to play a part in the future."

Other search engines will get to know a user's searching habits and try to anticipate interests, in much the way that Amazon recommends books to its customers based on past purchases or TiVo recommends TV shows based on previous viewing.

Still other search engines are finding niches to go deeper than the big guys. Technorati.com, for example, specializes in finding weblogs, or blogs, personal journals published on the Web.

BrightPlanet aims to chart some of the big business and government databases missed by Google and the others. Its customers are usually companies or government agencies with specific needs, "people who want to find everything" that's out there, Witte says.

Google has found more than 4 billion Web pages, an astounding number. But according to BrightPlanet, it's mapped only perhaps 1/500th of what's out there. It estimates that just 60 of the biggest deep websites contain more than 40 times the data of the "surface Web" scoured by Google.

While Google's exact searching methods are a secret, it relies on "crawling" from website to website following links to Web pages. But large data storage areas have firewalls or query search front doors that must be knocked on to reveal their contents.

Future alternatives?

BrightPlanet searches these big databases, such as the government's Centers for Disease Control, where "the pages are dynamic, they're built on the fly, on request" when a user goes to a search box and types in a query, Witte says.

Jones foresees a time when computer desktops would be more deeply integrated into the Internet.

"If I'm working on an article about gorillas, for example, behind the scenes my operating system will parse that article and go out on the Internet and look for information [and tell me], 'Here's the most interesting stuff about gorillas you might want to look at.' "

But right now, he says, search engines are the only maps we have to guide us around the Web. "We don't have an alternative."

- Americans conduct between 3 billion to 3.5 billion searches per month. More than 1 billion of these searches are conducted through Google.

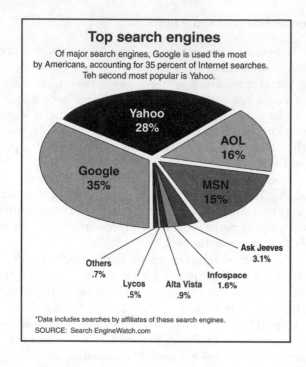

Top search engines

Of major search engines, Google is used the most by Americans, accounting for 35 percent of Internet searches. Teh second most popular is Yahoo.

Yahoo 28%
AOL 16%
Google 35%
MSN 15%
Ask Jeeves 3.1%
Others .7%
Lycos .5%
Alta Vista .9%
Infospace 1.6%

*Data includes searches by affiliates of these search engines.
SOURCE: Search EngineWatch.com

- More than 65 million people visited Google sites this past March, an increase of 23.5 percent over March 2003.
- Every second, the world conducts nearly twice as many Google searches (2,315) as ATM transactions (1,268), but consumes still more cups of coffee (4,000).
- The average search-engine user conducted 32 searches in February.
- Combined, search sites reach more than 130 million Americans, or about 85 percent of all Internet users each month.

SOURCES: comScore qSearch; comScore Media Metrix; Nestlé S.A.

The Software Wars

Why you can't understand your computer

PAUL DE PALMA

On a bright winter morning in Philadelphia, in 1986, my downtown office is bathed in sunlight. I am the lead programmer for a software system that my firm intends to sell to the largest companies in the country, but like so many systems, mine will never make it to market. This will not surprise me. If the chief architect of the office tower on whose twenty-sixth floor I am sitting designed his structure with the seat-of-the-pants cleverness that I am using to design my system, prudence would advise that I pack my business-issue briefcase, put on my business-issue overcoat, say good-bye to all that sunlight, and head for the front door before the building crumbles like a Turkish highrise in an earthquake.

But I am not prudent; nor am I paid to be. Just the opposite. My body, on automatic pilot, deflects nearly all external stimuli. I can carry on a rudimentary conversation, but my mind is somewhere else altogether. In a book-length profile of Ted Taylor, a nuclear-weapons designer, that John McPhee wrote for *The New Yorker,* Dr. Taylor's wife tells McPhee a wonderful story about her husband. Mrs. Taylor's sister visits for the weekend. Taylor dines with her, passes her in the hall, converses. He asks his wife on Monday morning—her sister having left the day before—when she expects her sister to arrive. Mrs. Taylor calls this state "metaphysical absence." You don't have to build sophisticated weaponry to experience it. When my daughter was younger, she used to mimic an old John Prine song. "Oh my stars," she sang, "Daddy's gone to Mars." As you will see, we workaday programmers have more in common with weapons designers than mere metaphysical absence.

My mind reels back from Mars when a colleague tells me that the *Challenger* has exploded. The *Challenger,* dream child of NASA, complex in the extreme, designed and built by some of the country's most highly trained engineers, is light-years away from my large, and largely uninspired, piece of data-processing software. If engineering were music, the *Challenger* would be a Bach fugue and my system "Home on the Range." Yet despite the differences in technical sophistication, the software I am building will fail for many of the same reasons that caused the *Challenger* to explode seconds after launch nearly twenty years ago.

Software's unreliability is the stuff of legend. *Software Engineering Notes,* a journal published by the ACM, the largest professional association of computer scientists, is known mostly for the tongue-in-cheek catalogue of technical catastrophes that appears at the beginning of each issue. In the March 2001 issue—I picked this off my shelf at random—you can read about planes grounded in L.A. because a Mexican air-traffic controller keyed in too many characters of flight description data, about a New York database built to find uninsured drivers, which snared many of the insured as well, about Florida eighth graders who penetrated their school's computer system, about Norwegian trains that refused to run on January 1, *2001,* because of a faulty Year 2000 repair. The list goes on for seven pages and is typical of a column that has been running for many years.

People often claim that one of every three large-scale software systems gets canceled midproject. Of those that do make it out the door, three-quarters are never implemented: some do not work as intended; others are just shelved.

People often claim that one of every three large-scale software systems gets canceled midproject. Of those that do make it out the door, three-quarters are never implemented: some do not work as intended; others are just shelved. Matters grow even more serious with large systems whose functions spread over several computers—the very systems that advances in networking technology have made possible in the past decade. A few years ago, an IBM consulting group determined that of twenty-four companies surveyed, 55 percent built systems that were over budget; 68 percent built systems that were behind schedule; and 88 percent of the completed systems had to be redesigned. Try to imagine the same kind of gloomy numbers for civil engineering: three-quarters of all bridges carrying loads below specification; almost nine of ten sewage treatment plants, once completed, in need of redesign; one-third of highway projects canceled because technical problems have grown beyond the capacity of engineers to solve them. Silly? Yes. Programming has miles to go before it earns the title "software engineering."

In civil engineering, on the other hand, failures are rare enough to make the news. Perhaps the best-known example is the collapse of the Tacoma-Narrows Bridge. Its spectacular failure in 1940, because of wind-induced resonance, was captured on film and has been a staple of physics courses ever since. The collapse of the suspended walkway in the Kansas City Hyatt Regency in 1981 is a more recent example. It failed because structural engineers thought that verifying the design of connections joining the walkway segments was the job of their manufacturer. The manufacturer had a different recollection. The American Society of Civil Engineers quickly adopted a protocol for checking shop designs. These collapses are remarkable for two related reasons. First, bridge and building failures are so rare in the United States that when they do occur we continue to talk about them half a century later. Second, in both cases, engineers correctly determined the errors and took steps not to repeat them. Programmers cannot make a similar claim. Even if the cause of system failure is discovered, programmers can do little more than try not to repeat the error in future systems. Trying not to repeat an error does not compare with building well-known tolerances into a design or establishing communications protocols among well-defined players. One is exhortation. The other is engineering.

None of this is new. Responding to reports of unusable systems, cost overruns, and outright cancellations, the NATO Science Committee convened a meeting of scientists, industry leaders, and programmers in 1968. The term *software engineering* was invented at this conference in the hope that, one day, systematic, quantifiable approaches to software construction would develop. Over the intervening years, researchers have created a rich set of tools and techniques, from design practices to improved programming languages to techniques for proving program correctness. Sadly, anyone who uses computers knows that they continue to fail regularly, inexplicably, and, sometimes, wonderfully—*Software Engineering Notes* continues to publish pages of gloomy tales each quarter. Worse, the ACM has recently decided not to support efforts to license software engineers because, in its words, "there is no form of licensing that can be instituted today assuring public safety." In effect, software-engineering discoveries of the past thirty years may be interesting, but no evidence suggests that understanding them will improve the software-development process.

As the committee that made this decision surely knows, software-engineering techniques are honored mostly in the breach. In other words, business practice, as much as a lack of technical know-how, produces the depressing statistics I have cited. One business practice in particular ought to be understood. The characteristics of software often cited as leading to failure—its complexity, its utter plasticity, its free-floating nature, unhampered by tethers to the physical world—make it oddly, even paradoxically, similar to the practice of military procurement. Here is where the *Challenger* and my system, dead these twenty long years, reenter the story.

In the mid-eighties I worked for a large management-consulting firm. Though this company had long employed a small group of programmers, mostly to support in-house systems, its software-development effort and support staff grew substantially, perhaps by a factor of ten, over a period of just a few years. A consulting firm, like a law firm, has a cap on its profits. Since it earns money by selling time, the number of hours its consultants can bill limits its revenue. And there is a ceiling to that. They have to eat and sleep, after all. The promise of software is the promise of making something from nothing. After development, only the number of systems that can be sold limits return on investment. In figuring productivity, the denominator remains constant. Forget about unhappy unions, as with cars and steel; messy sweatshops, as with clothing and shoes; environmental regulations, as with oil and petrochemicals. Software is a manufacturer's dream. The one problem, a very sticky problem indeed, is that it does not wear out. The industry responds by adding features, moving commercial software one step closer to military systems. More on this later. For now, just understand that my company, like so many others under the influence of the extraordinary attention that newly introduced personal computers were receiving at the time, followed the lure of software.

My system had one foot on the shrinking terra firma of large computers and the other in the roiling, rising sea of microcomputers. In fact, mine was the kind of system that three or four years earlier would have been written in CO-BOL, the language of business systems. It perhaps would have used a now obsolete database design, and it would have gone to market within a year. When told to build a similar system for a microcomputer, I did what I knew how to do. I designed a gray flannel system for a changing microcomputer market.

Things went along in a predictable if uninspired way until there was a shift in management. These changes occur so frequently in business that I had learned to ignore them. The routine goes like this. Everyone gets a new organization chart. They gather in conference rooms for mandatory pep talks. Then life goes on pretty much as before. Every so often, though, management decisions percolate down to the geeks, as when your manager arrives with a security officer and gives you five minutes to empty your desk, unpin your *Dilbert* comics, and go home. Or when someone like Mark takes over.

When that happened, I assumed falsely that we would go back to the task of producing dreary software. But this was the eighties. Junk bonds and leveraged buyouts were in the news. The arbitrageur was king. Business had become sexy. Mark, rumor had it, slept three hours a night. He shuttled between offices in New York, Philadelphia, and Montreal. Though he owned a house in Westchester County, now best known as the home of the Clintons, he kept an apartment in Philadelphia, where he managed to spend a couple of days each week. When Mark, the quintessential new manager ("My door is always open"), arrived, we began to live like our betters in law and finance. Great bags of bagels and cream cheese arrived each morning. We lunched in trendy restaurants. I, an erstwhile sixties radical, began to ride around in taxis, use my expense account, fly to distant cities for two-hour meetings. Life was sweet.

During this time, my daughter was an infant. Her 4:00 A.M. feeding was my job. Since I often had trouble getting back to sleep, I sometimes caught an early train to the office. One of these mornings my office phone rang. It was Mark. He sounded relaxed, as if finding me at work before dawn was no more surprising than bumping into a neighbor choosing apples at Safeway. This was a sign. Others followed. Once, Mark organized a dinner for our team in a classy hotel. When the time came for his speech, Mark's voice rose like Caesar's exhorting his troops before the Gallic campaign. He urged us to bid farewell to our wives and children. We would, he assured us, return in six months with our shields or upon them. I noticed then that a few of my colleagues were in evening dress. I felt like Tiresias among the crows. When programmers wear tuxedos, the world is out of joint.

Suddenly, as if by magic, we went from a handful of programmers producing a conventional system to triple that number, and the system was anything but conventional. One thing that changed was the programming language itself. Mark decided that the system would be splashier if it used a database-management system that had recently become commercially available for mainframes and was promised, shortly, for microcomputers. These decisions—hiring more people to meet a now unmeetable deadline; using a set of new and untested tools—represented two of the several business practices that have been at the heart of the software crisis. Frederick Brooks, in his classic book, *The Mythical Man-Month,* argues from his experience building IBM's System 360 operating system that any increased productivity achieved by hiring more people gets nibbled at by the increased complexity of communication among them. A system that one person can develop in thirty days cannot be developed in a single day by thirty people. This simple truth goes down hard in business culture, which takes, as an article of faith, the idea that systems can be decreed into existence.

The other practice, relying on new, untested, and wildly complex tools, is where software reigns supreme. Here, the tool was a relational database-management system. Since the late sixties, researchers have realized that keeping all data in a central repository, a database, with its own set of access techniques and backup mechanisms, was better than storing data with the program that used it. Before the development of database-management systems, it was common for every department in a company to have its own data, and for much of this data to overlap from department to department. So in a university, the registrar's office, which takes care of student records, and the controller's office, which takes care of student accounts, might both have copies of a student's name and address. The problem occurs when the student moves and the change has to be reported to two offices. The argument works less well for

small amounts of data accessed by a single user, exactly the kind of application that the primitive microcomputers of the time were able to handle. Still, you could argue that a relational database-management system might be useful for small offices. This is exactly what Microsoft Access does. But Microsoft Access did not exist in 1986, nor did any other relational database-management system for microcomputers. Such systems had only recently become available for mainframes.

Something unique to software, especially new software: no experts exist in the sense that we might speak of an expert machinist, a master electrician, or an experienced civil engineer. There are only those who are relatively less ignorant.

One company, however, an infant builder of database-management systems, had such software for minicomputers and was promising a PC version. After weeks of meetings, after an endless parade of consultants, after trips to Washington, D.C., to attend seminars, Mark decided to go with the new product. One of these meetings illustrates something unique to software, especially new software: no experts exist in the sense that we might speak of an expert machinist, a master electrician, or an experienced civil engineer. There are only those who are relatively less ignorant. On an early spring evening, we met in a conference room with a long, polished wood table surrounded by fancy swivel chairs covered in gorgeous, deep purple fabric. The room's walls turned crimson from the setting sun. As the evening wore on, we could look across the street to another tower, its offices filled with miniature Bartlebys, bent over desks, staring into monitors, leafing through file cabinets. At the table with representatives from our company were several consultants from the database firm and an independent consultant Mark had hired to make sure we were getting the straight scoop.

Here we were: a management-consulting team with the best, though still less than perfect, grasp of what the proposed system was supposed to do, but almost no grasp of the tools being chosen; consultants who knew the tools quite well, but nothing about the software application itself, who were fully aware that their software was still being developed even as we spoke; and an independent consultant who did not understand either the software or its application. It was a perfect example of interdependent parasitism.

My company's sin went beyond working with complex, poorly understood tools. Neither the tools nor our system existed. The database manufacturer had a delivery date and no product. Their consultants were selling us a nonexistent system. To make their deadline, I am confident they hired more programmers and experimented with unproven software from still other companies with delivery dates but no products. And what of *those* companies? You get the idea.

No one in our group had any experience with this software once we adopted it. Large systems are fabulously complex. It takes years to know their idiosyncrasies. Since the introduction of the microcomputer, however, nobody has had years to develop this expertise. Because software does not wear out, vendors must consistently add new features in order to recoup development costs. That the word processor you use today bears almost no resemblance to the one you used ten years ago has less to do with technological advances than with economic realities. Our company had recently acquired a smaller I company in the South. This company owned a mini computer for which a version of the database software had already been released. Mark decided that until the PC database was ready for release, we could develop our system on this machine, using 1,200-baud modems, a modem about one-fiftieth as fast as the one your cable provider tells you is too slow for the Web, and a whole lot less reliable.

Let me put this all together. We had a new team of programmers who did not understand the application, using ersatz software that they also did not understand, which was running on a kind of machine no one had ever used before, using a remote connection that was slow and unstable.

Weeks before, I had begun arguing that we could never meet the deadline and that none of us had the foggiest idea of how to go about building a system with the tools we had. This was bad form. I had been working in large corporations long enough to know that when the boss asks if something can be done, the only possible response is "I'm your boy." Business is not a Quaker meeting. Mark didn't get to be my boss by achieving consensus. I knew that arguing was a mistake, but somehow the more I argued, the more I became gripped by a self-righteous fervor that, while unattractive in anyone (who likes a do-gooder?), is suicide in a corporate setting. Can-do-ism is the core belief. My job was to figure out how to extend the deadline, simplify the requirements, or both—not second-guess Mark. One afternoon I was asked if I might like to step down as chief architect and take over the documentation group. This was not a promotion.

Sitting in my new cubicle with a Raskolnikovian cloud over my head, I began to look more closely at the database-management system's documentation. Working with yet another consultant, I filled a paper database with hypothetical data. What I discovered caused me to win the argument but lose the war. I learned that given the size of the software itself and the amount of data the average client would store, along with the overhead that comes with a sophisticated database, a running system would fill a microcomputer hard disk, then limited to 30 megabytes, several times over. If, by some stroke of luck, some effort of will, some happy set of coincidences that I had yet to experience personally, we were able to build the system, the client would run up against hardware constraints as soon as he tried to use it. After weeks of argument, my prestige was slipping fast. I had already been reduced to writing manuals for a system I had designed. I was the sinking ship that every clearheaded corporate sailor had already abandoned. My triumphant revelation that we could not build a workable system, even if we had the skill to do so, was greeted with (what else?) complete silence.

Late in 1986 James Fallows wrote an article analyzing the *Challenger* explosion for the *New York Review of Books*. Instead of concentrating on the well-known O-ring problem, he situated the failure of the *Challenger* in the context of military procurement, specifically in the military's inordinate fondness for complex systems. This fondness leads to stunning cost overruns, unanticipated complexity, and regular failures. It leads to Osprey aircraft that fall from the sky, to anti-missile missiles for which decoys are easy to construct, to FA-22 fighters that are fabulously over budget. The litany goes on. What these failures have in common with the *Challenger* is, Fallows argues, "military procurement disease," namely, "over-ambitious schedules, problems born of too-complex design, shortages of spare parts, a 'can-do' attitude that stifles embarrassing truths ('No problem, Mr. President, we can lick those Viet Gong'), and total collapse when one component unexpectedly fails." Explanations for this phenomenon include competition among the services; a monopoly hold by defense contractors who are building, say, aircraft or submarines; lavish defense budgets that isolate military purchases from normal market mechanisms; the nature of capital-intensive, laptop warfare where hypothetical justifications need not—usually cannot—be verified in practice; and a little-boy fascination with things that fly and explode. Much of this describes the software industry too.

Fallows breaks down military procurement into five stages:

The Vegematic Promise, wherein we are offered hybrid aircraft, part helicopter, part airplane, or software that has more features than could be learned in a lifetime of diligent study. Think Microsoft Office here.

The Rosy Prospect, wherein we are assured that all is going well. I call this the 90 percent syndrome. I don't think I have ever supervised a project, either as a software manager overseeing professionals or as a professor overseeing students, that was not 90 percent complete whenever I asked.

The Big Technical Leap, wherein we learn that our system will take us to regions not yet visited, and we will build it using tools not yet developed. So the shuttle's solid-fuel boosters were more powerful than any previously developed boosters, and bringing it all back home, my system was to use a database we had never used before, running on a computer for which a version of that software did not yet exist.

The Unpleasant Surprise, wherein we learn something unforeseen and, if we are unlucky, calamitous. Thus, the shuttle's heat-resistant dies, all 31,000 of them, had to be installed at the unexpected rate of 2.8 days per tile, and my system gobbled so much disk space that there was scarcely any room for data.

The House of Cards, wherein an unpleasant surprise, or two, or three, causes the entire system to collapse. The Germans flanked the Maginot Line, and in my case, once we learned that our reliance on a promised database package outstripped operating-system limits, the choices were: one, wait for advances in operating systems; two, admit a mistake, beg for forgiveness, and resolve to be more prudent in the future; or, three, push on until management pulls the plug.

In our case, the first choice was out of the question. We were up against a deadline. No one knew when, or if, the 30 MB disk limit would be broken. The second choice was just as bad. The peaceable kingdom will be upon us, the lamb will lie down with the lion, long before you'll find a hard-driving manager admitting an error. These guys get paid for their testosterone, and for men sufficiently endowed, in the famous words of former NASA flight director Gene Kranz, "failure is not an option." We were left with the third alternative, which is what happened. Our project was canceled. Inside the fun house of corporate decision making, Mark was promoted—sent off to manage a growing branch in the South. The programmers left or were reassigned. The consultant who gave me the figures for my calculations was fired for reasons that I never understood. I took advantage of my new job as documentation chief and wrote an application to graduate school in computer science. I spent the next few years, while a student, as a well-paid consultant to our firm.

Just what is it about software, even the most conventional, the most mind-numbing software, that makes it similar to the classiest technology on the planet? In his book *Trapped in the Net,* the Berkeley physicist turned sociologist, Gene Rochlin, has this to say about computer technology:

> Only in a few specialized markets are new developments in hardware and software responsive primarily to user demand based on mastery and the full use of available technical capacity and capability. In most markets, the rate of change of both hardware and software is dynamically uncoupled from either human or organizational learning logistics and processes, to the point where users not only fail to master their most recent new capabilities, but are likely to not even bother to try, knowing that by the time they are through the steep part of their learning curve, most of what they have learned will be obsolete.

To give a homey example, I spent the last quarter hour fiddling with the margins on the draft copy of this article. Microsoft Word has all manner of arcane symbols—Exacto knives, magnifying glasses, thumbtacks, globes—plus an annoying little paper clip homunculus that pops up, seemingly at random, to offer help that I always decline. I don't know what any of this stuff does. Since one of the best-selling commercial introductions to the Microsoft Office suite now runs to nearly a thousand pages, roughly the size of Shakespeare's collected works, I won't find out either. To the untrained eye, that is to say, to mine, the bulk of what constitutes Microsoft Word appears to be useful primarily to brochure designers and graphic artists. This unused cornucopia is not peculiar to Microsoft, nor even to microcomputer software. Programmers were cranking out obscure and poorly documented features long before computers became a consumer product.

Though the medium on which it is stored might decay, the software itself, because it exists in the same ethereal way as a novel, scored music, or a mathematical theorem, lasts as long as the ability to decode it.

But why? Remember the nature of software, how it does not wear out. Adding features to a new release is similar, but not identical, to changes in fashion or automobile styling. In those industries, a change in look gives natural, and planned, obsolescence a nudge. Even the best-built car or the sturdiest pair of jeans will eventually show signs of wear. Changes in fashion just speed this process along. Not so with software. Though the medium on which it is stored might decay, the software itself, because it exists in the same ethereal way as a novel, scored music, or a mathematical theorem, lasts as long as the ability to decode it. That is why Microsoft Word and the operating systems that support it, such as Microsoft Windows, get more complex with each new release.

But this is only part of the story. While software engineers at Oracle or Microsoft are staying up late concocting features that no one will ever use, hardware engineers at Intel are inventing ever faster, ever cheaper processors to run them. If Microsoft did not take advantage of this additional capacity, someone else would. Hardware and software are locked in an intricate and pathological dance. Hardware takes a step. Software follows. Hardware takes another step, and so on. The result is the Vegematic Promise. Do you want to write a letter to your bank? Microsoft Word will work fine. Do you need to save your work in any one of fifteen different digital formats? Microsoft Word will do the job. Do you want to design a Web page, lay out a brochure, import clip art, or include the digitally rendered picture of your dog? The designers at Microsoft have anticipated your needs. They were able to do this because the designers at Intel anticipated theirs. What no one anticipated was the unmanageable complexity of the final product from the user's perspective and the stunning, internal complexity of the product that Microsoft brings to market. In another time, this kind of complexity would have been reserved for enterprises of true consequence, say the Manhattan Project or the Apollo missions. Now the complexity that launched a thousand ships, placed men on the moon, controlled nuclear fission and fusion, the complexity that demanded of its designers years of training and still failed routinely, sits on my desk. Only this time, developers with minimal, often informal, training, using tools that change before they master them, labor for my daughter, who uses the fruits of their genius to chat with her friends about hair, makeup, and boys.

As I say, accelerating complexity is not just a software feature. Gordon Moore, one of Intel's founders, famously observed, in 1965, that the number of transistors etched on an integrated circuit board doubled every year or so. In the hyperbolic world of computing, this observation, altered slightly for the age of microprocessors, has come to be called Moore's Law: the computing power of microprocessors tends to double every couple of years. Though engineers expect to reach physical limits sometime in the first quarter of this century, Moore has been on target for the past couple dozen years. As a related, if less glamorous example, consider the remote control that accompanies electronic gadgetry these days. To be at the helm of your VCR, TV, DVD player, stereo (never mind lights, fans, air-conditioning, and fireplace), is to be a kind of Captain Kirk of home and hearth. The tendency, the Vegematic Promise, is to integrate separate remote controls into a single device. A living room equipped with one of these marvels is part domicile, part mission control. I recently read about one fellow who, dazzled by the complexity of integrated remotes, fastened his many devices to a chunk of four-by-four with black electrical tape. I have ceded operation of my relatively low-tech equipment to my teenage daughter, the only person in my house with the time or inclination to decipher its runic symbols.

But software is different in one significant way. Hardware, by and large, works. When hardware fails, as early versions of the Pentium chip did, it is national news. It took a computer scientist in Georgia doing some fairly obscure mathematical calculations to uncover the flaw. If only software errors were so well hidden. Engineers, even electrical engineers, use well-understood, often off-the-shelf, materials with well-defined limits. To offer a simple example, a few years ago I taught a course in digital logic. This course, standard fare for all computer science and computer engineering majors, teaches students how to solve logic problems with chips. A common lab problem is to build a seven-segment display, a digital display of numbers, like what you might find on an alarm clock. Students construct it using a circuit board and chips that we order by the hundreds. These chips are described in a catalogue that lists the number and type of logical operations encoded, along with the corresponding pins for each. If you teach software design, as I do, this trespass into the world of the engineer is instructive. Software almost always gets built from scratch. Though basic sorting and string manipulation routines exist, these must be woven together in novel ways to produce new software. Each programmer becomes a craftsman with a store of tricks up his sleeve. The more experienced the programmer, the more tricks.

To be fair, large software-development operations maintain libraries of standard routines that developers may dip into when the need arises. And for the past ten years or so, new object-oriented design and development techniques have conceived of ways to modularize and standardize components. Unfortunately, companies have not figured out how to make money by selling components, probably for the same reason that the music industry is under siege from napster's descendants. If your product is only a digital encoding, it can be copied endlessly at almost no cost. Worse, the object-oriented programming paradigm seems often to be more complex than a conventional approach. Though boosters claim that programmers using object-oriented techniques are more productive and that their products are easier to maintain, this has yet to be demonstrated.

Software is peculiar in another way. Though hardware can be complex in the extreme, software obeys no physical limits. It can be as feature-rich as its designers wish. If the computer's memory is too small, relatively obscure features can be stored on disk and called into action only when needed. If the computer's processor is too slow, just wait a couple of years. Designers want your software to be very feature-rich indeed, because they want to sell the next release, because the limits of what can be done with a computer are not yet known, and, most of all, because those who design computer systems, like the rich in the world of F. Scott Fitzgerald, are different from you and me. Designers love the machine with a passion not constrained by normal market mechanisms or even, in some instances, by managerial control.

On the demand side, most purchases are made by institutions, businesses, universities, and the government, where there is an obsessive fear of being left behind, while the benefits, just as in the military, are difficult to measure. The claims and their outcomes are too fuzzy to be reconciled. Since individual managers are rarely held accountable for decisions to buy yet more computing equipment, it should not surprise you that wildly complex technology is being underused. Thus: computer labs that no one knows what to do with, so-called smart classrooms that are obsolete before anyone figures out how to use them, and offices with equipment so complicated that every secretary doubles as a systems administrator. Even if schools and businesses buy first and ask questions later, *you* don't have to put up with this. You could tell Microsoft to keep its next Windows upgrade, your machine is working very nicely right now, thank you. But your impertinence will cost you. Before long, your computer will be an island where the natives speak a language cut off from the great linguistic communities. In a word, you will be isolated. You won't be able to buy new software, edit a report you wrote at work on your home computer, or send pictures of the kids to Grandma over the Internet. Further, a decision to upgrade later will be harder, perhaps impossible, without losing everything your trusted but obsolete computer has stored. This is what Rochlin means when he writes that hardware and software are "dynamically uncoupled from either human or organizational learning." To which I would add "human organizational need."

What if the massively complex new software were as reliable as hardware usually is? We still wouldn't know how to use it, but at least our screens wouldn't lock up and our projects wouldn't be canceled midstream. This reliability isn't going to happen, though, for at least three reasons. First, programmers love complexity, love handcrafted systems, with an ardor that most of us save for our spouses. You have heard about the heroic hours worked by employees of the remaining Internet start-ups. This is true, but true only partly so that young men can be millionaires by thirty. There is something utterly beguiling about programming a computer. You lose track of time, of space even. You begin eating pizzas and forgetting to bathe. A phone call is an unwelcome intrusion. Second, nobody can really oversee a programmer's work, short of reading code line by line. It is simply too complex for anyone but its creator to understand, and even for him it will be lost in the mist after a couple of weeks. The 90 percent syndrome is a natural consequence. Programmers, a plucky lot, always think that they are further along than they are. It is difficult to foresee an obstacle on a road you have never traveled. Despite all efforts to the contrary, code is handcrafted. Third—and this gets to the heart of the matter—system specifications have the half-life of an adolescent friendship. Someone—the project manager, the team leader, a programmer, or, if the system is built on contract, the client—always has a new idea. It is as if a third of the way through building a bridge, the highway department decided it should have an additional traffic lane and be moved a half mile downstream.

Notice that not one of the reasons I have mentioned for failed software projects is technical. Researchers trying to develop a discipline of software engineering are fond of saying that there is no silver bullet: no single technical fix, no single software-development tool, no single, yet-to-be-imagined programming technique that will result in error-free, maintainable software. The reason for this is really quite simple. The problem with software is not technical. Remember my project. It fell into chaos because of foolish business decisions. Had Mark resisted the temptation to use the latest software-development products, a temptation he succumbed to not because they would produce a better system, but because they would seem flashier to prospective clients, we might have gone to market with only the usual array of problems.

Interestingly, the geek's geek, Bruce Schneier, in his recent book, *Secrets and Lies*, has come to similar conclusions about computer security: the largest problems are not technical. A computer security expert, Schneier has recanted his faith in the impermeability of cryptographic algorithms. Sophisticated cryptography is as resistant as ever to massive frontal attacks. The problem is that these algorithms are embedded in computer systems that are administered by real human beings with all their charms and foibles. People use dictionary entries or a child's name as passwords. They attach modems to their office computers, giving hackers easy access to a system that might otherwise be more thoroughly protected. They run versions of Linux with all network routines enabled, or they surreptitiously set up Web servers in their dormitory rooms. Cryptographic algorithms are no more secure than their contexts.

Until computing is organized like engineering, law, and medicine through a combination of self-regulating professional bodies, government-imposed standards, and the threat of litigation, inviting a computer into your house or office is to invite complexity masquerading as convenience.

Though the long march is far from over, we know a lot more about managing the complexity of software systems than we did twenty years ago. We have better programming languages and techniques, better design principles, clever software to keep track of changes, richly endowed procedures for moving from conception to system design to coding to testing to release. But systems still fail and projects are still canceled with the same regularity as in the bad old days before object-oriented techniques, before software engineering becomes an academic discipline. These techniques are administered by the same humans who undermine computer security. They include marketing staff who decree systems into existence; companies that stuff yet more features into already overstuffed software; designers and clients who change specifications as systems are being built; programmers who are more artist than engineer; and, of course, software itself that can be neither seen, nor touched, nor measured in any significant way.

There is no silver bullet. But just as the *Challenger* disaster might have been prevented with minimal common sense, so also with software failure. Keep it simple. Avoid exotic and new programming techniques. Know that an army of workers is no substitute for clear design and ample time. Don't let the fox, now disguised as a young man with a head full of acronyms, guard the chicken coop. Make only modest promises. Good advice, certainly, but no one is likely to listen anytime soon. Until computing is organized like engineering, law, and medicine through a combination of self-regulating professional bodies, government-imposed standards, and, yes, the threat of litigation, inviting a computer into your house or office is to invite complexity masquerading as convenience. Given the nature of computing, even these remedies may fall short of the mark.

But don't despair. If software engineering practice is out of reach, *you* still have options. For starters, you could just say no. You could decide that the ease of buying plane tickets online is not worth the hours you while away trying to get your printer to print or your modem to dial. Understand that saying no requires an ascetic nature: abstinence is not terribly attractive to most of us. On the other hand, you could sign up for broadband with the full knowledge that your computer, a jealous lover, will demand many, many Saturday afternoons. Most people are shocked when they learn that their computer requires more care than, say, their refrigerator. Yet I can tell you that its charms are immeasurably richer. First among them is the dream state. It's almost irresistible.

Paul De Palma is associate professor of mathematics and computer science at Gonzaga University. His essay "http://www.when_is_enough_enough?.com" appeared in the Winter 1999 issue.

From *American Scholar*. Vol. 74, No. 1, Winter 2005, pp. 69–83. Copyright © 2005 by American Scholar. Reprinted by permission.

UNIT 3
Work and the Workplace

Unit Selections

Key Points to Consider

- The issue of immigration to the United States is controversial. Do you agree with Anna Lee Saxenian's arguments in "Brain Circulation: How High-Skill Immigration Makes Sense?"

- Were you surprised to learn that some of the fabled long hours spent in software development are not voluntary?

- How long do you spend answering email every day? When managers claim that they spend two hours a day answering email, do you think email is helping or hurting productivity? What do you think they were doing with those two hours before the introduction of email?

Student Website
www.mhcls.com/online

Internet References
Further information regarding these websites may be found in this book's preface or online.

American Telecommuting Association
http://www.knowledgetree.com/ata-adv.html

Computers in the Workplace
http://www.msci.memphis.edu/~ryburnp/cl/cis/workpl.html

InfoWeb: Techno-rage
http://www.cciw.com/content/technorage.html

STEP ON IT! Pedals: Repetitive Strain Injury
http://www.bilbo.com/rsi2.html

What About Computers in the Workplace
http://law.freeadvice.com/intellectual_property/computer_law/computers_workplace.htm

Work is at the center of our lives. The kind of work we do plays a part in our standard of living, our social status, and our sense of worth. This was not always the case. Read some of the great Victorian novels, and you will find a society where paid employment, at least among the upper classes, by and large does not exist. Even those men from the nineteenth century and before, whose discoveries and writings we study and admire, approached their work as an avocation. It is hard to imagine William Wordsworth, kissing his wife goodbye each morning, and heading off to the English Department where he will direct a seminar in creative writing before he gets to work on a sticky line in Ode Composed at Tintern Abbey. Or think of Charles Darwin, donning a lab coat, and supervising an army of graduate students while he touches up his latest National Science Foundation proposal. A hundred or more years ago, there were a handful of professions—doctor, lawyer, clergyman, military office, a larger handful of crafts—joiner, miller, cooper, blacksmith, an army of agricultural workers and an increasing number of dis-

placed peasants toiling in factories, what William Blake called England's "Dark Satanic Mills."

The U.S. Census records tell us that there were only 323 different occupations in 1850, the butcher, the baker, and the candlestick maker that all children read about. The butcher is still with us, as well as the baker, but both of them work for national supermarket chains, using digitally-controlled tools and manage their 401k's on-line. The candle stick maker has morphed into a refinery worker, watching digital displays in petrochemical plants that light up the Louisiana sky. The Canadian National Occupational Classification lists more than 25,000 occupational titles. It was once feared that, first, machines in the early twentieth century and, then, computers in the later would render work obsolete, transforming us into country gentlemen like Charles Darwin in the utopian view or nomadic mobs of starving proletarians in the distopian.

It appears instead that fabulously productive farms and factories—as well as a third world willing to make our shoes, clothing, and electronics for pennies an hour—have opened up opportunities that did not exist in Darwin's time. We are now sales clerks, health care workers, state license examiners, light truck drivers, equal opportunity compliance officers, and, yes, also software engineers, database analysts, web-site designers, and entrepreneurs. In fact, some of the more interesting and better paid of these new occupations are increasingly held by the foreign-born. Anna Lee Saxenian, observes in "Brain Circulation" that "more than a quarter of Silicon Valley's highly skilled workers are immigrant...." This raises questions about whether the growth in numbers of foreign-born professionals displaces native workers while at the same time draining talent from countries too poor to lose it.

The fear of foreign-born engineers and technicians outcompeting native-born Americans for jobs has been ratcheted up in the years since the tech bubble burst. Tech workers, foreign and native-born alike, are worried that their jobs might be shipped off to India and other countries with skilled workforces willing to work for a fraction of what American engineers earn. Stephen Baker from *BusinessWeek* adds faces to this anxiety with profiles of a young American and young Indian engineer ("Software: Programming jobs are heading overseas by the thousands.").

Rebecca Vesely's poignant "Letter from Silicon Valley" integrates stories of how it feels to be part of the tech downturn with some startling statistics. Eighty-five thousand jobs disappeared from Santa Clara County, "the heart of Silicon Valley," between 2000 and 2002. Office vacancy rates jumped from 2% to 24% during the same period. "It's the boom-and-bust cycle of the Valley," says one engineer. "If you're going to live here, you have to get used to it."

The glamour stories of rich Silicon Valley software engineers, hopping from job to job, don't figure in the American imagination like they did during the salad days of the dot com boom. Still, one is not quite prepared for the tale of forced overtime recounted in "When Long Hours at a Video Game Stop Being Fun." As *The New York Times*' Randall Stross says, "Charles Dickens himself would shudder." But most employees are not in the glamour occupations.

"The Computer Evolution" confirms what every working American has noticed, namely, that computers have spread throughout the workplace. It also confirms what many observers have long suspected: "the ability to use a computer is not a 'sufficient' condition for earning high wages, but it is increasingly a 'necessary' condition." The final article in the unit, "Making Yourself Understood," tells us what our English teachers have been telling us for years. Though the memo has become digitized, writing is still important. More than half of mangers in one study report spending at least two hours a day answering email. Though communication is easier than ever, it has also "never been so easy to be misunderstood."

Brain Circulation

How High-Skill Immigration Makes Everyone Better Off

By AnnaLee Saxenian

Silicon Valley's workforce is among the world's most ethnically diverse. Not only do Asian and Hispanic workers dominate the low-paying, blue-collar workforce, but foreign-born scientists and engineers are increasingly visible as entrepreneurs and senior management. More than a quarter of Silicon Valley's highly skilled workers are immigrants, including tens of thousands from lands as diverse as China, Taiwan, India, the United Kingdom, Iran, Vietnam, the Philippines, Canada, and Israel.

> Most people instinctively assume that the movement of skill and talent must benefit one country at the expense of another. But thanks to brain circulation, high-skilled immigration increasingly benefits both sides

Understandably, the rapid growth of the foreign-born workforce has evoked intense debates over U.S. immigration policy, both here and in the developing world. In the United States, discussions of the immigration of scientists and engineers have focused primarily on the extent to which foreign-born professionals displace native workers. The view from sending countries, by contrast, has been that the emigration of highly skilled personnel to the United States represents a big economic loss, a "brain drain."

Neither view is adequate in today's global economy. Far from simply replacing native workers, foreign-born engineers are starting new businesses and generating jobs and wealth at least as fast as their U.S. counterparts. And the dynamism of emerging regions in Asia and elsewhere now draws skilled immigrants homeward. Even when they choose not to return home, they are serving as middlemen linking businesses in the United States with those in distant regions.

In some parts of the world, the old dynamic of "brain drain" is giving way to one I call "brain circulation." Most people instinctively assume that the movement of skill and talent must benefit one country at the expense of another. But thanks to brain circulation, high-skilled immigration increasingly benefits both sides. Economically speaking, it is blessed to give *and* to receive.

"New" Immigrant Entrepreneurs

Unlike traditional ethnic entrepreneurs who remain isolated in marginal, low-wage industries, Silicon Valley's new foreign-born entrepreneurs are highly educated professionals in dynamic and technologically sophisticated industries. And they have been extremely successful. By the end of the 1990s, Chinese and Indian engineers were running 29 percent of Silicon Valley's technology businesses. By 2000, these companies collectively accounted for more than $19.5 billion in sales and 72,839 jobs. And the pace of immigrant entrepreneurship has accelerated dramatically in the past decade.

Not that Silicon Valley's immigrants have abandoned their ethnic ties. Like their less-educated counterparts, Silicon Valley's high-tech immigrants rely on ethnic strategies to enhance entrepreneurial opportunities. Seeing themselves as outsiders to the mainstream technology community, foreign-born engineers and scientists in Silicon Valley have created social and professional networks to mobilize the information, know-how, skill, and capital to start technology firms. Local ethnic professional associations like the Silicon Valley Chinese Engineers Association, The Indus Entrepreneur, and the Korean IT Forum provide contacts and resources for recently arrived immigrants.

Combining elements of traditional immigrant culture with distinctly high-tech practices, these organizations simultaneously create ethnic identities within the region and aid professional networking and information exchange. These are not traditional political or lobbying groups—rather their focus is the professional and technical advancement of their members. Membership in Indian and Chinese professional associations has virtually no overlap, although the overlap within the separate communities—particularly the Chinese, with its many specialized associations—appears considerable. Yet ethnic distinctions also exist within the Chinese community. To an outsider, the Chinese American Semiconductor Professionals Association and the North American Chinese Semiconductor Association are redundant organizations. One, however, represents Taiwanese, the other Mainland Chinese.

The most successful immigrant entrepreneurs in Silicon Valley today appear to be those who have drawn on ethnic resources while simultaneously integrating into mainstream technology and business networks.

Whatever their ethnicity, all these associations tend to mix socializing—over Chinese banquets, Indian dinners, or family-centered social events—with support for professional and technical advancement. Each, either explicitly or informally, offers first-generation immigrants professional contacts and networks within the local technology community. They serve as recruitment channels and provide role models of successful immigrant entrepreneurs and managers. They sponsor regular speakers and conferences whose subjects range from specialized technical and market information to how to write a business plan or manage a business. Some Chinese associations give seminars on English communication, negotiation skills, and stress management.

Many of these groups have become important cross-generational forums. Older engineers and entrepreneurs in both the Chinese and the Indian communities now help finance and mentor younger co-ethnic entrepreneurs. Within these networks, "angel" investors often invest individually or jointly in promising new ventures. The Indus Entrepreneur, for example, aims to "foster entrepreneurship by providing mentorship and resources" within the South Asian technology community. Both the Asian American Manufacturers Association and the Monte Jade Science and Technology Association sponsor annual investment conferences to match investors (often from Asia as well as Silicon Valley) with Chinese entrepreneurs.

The long-distance networks are accelerating the globalization of labor markets and enhancing opportunities for entrepreneurship, investment, and trade both in the United States and in newly emerging regions in Asia.

Although many Chinese and Indian immigrants socialize primarily within their ethnic networks, they routinely work with U.S. engineers and U.S.-run businesses. In fact, recognition is growing within these communities that although a start-up might be spawned with the support of the ethnic networks, it must become part of the mainstream to grow. The most successful immigrant entrepreneurs in Silicon Valley today appear to be those who have drawn on ethnic resources while simultaneously integrating into mainstream technology and business networks.

Transnational Entrepreneurship

Far beyond their role in Silicon Valley, the professional and social networks that link new immigrant entrepreneurs with each other have become global institutions that connect new immigrants with their counterparts at home. These new transnational communities provide the shared information, contacts, and trust that allow local producers to participate in an increasingly global economy.

Silicon Valley's Taiwanese engineers, for example, have built a vibrant two-way bridge connecting them with Taiwan's technology community. Their Indian counterparts have become key middlemen

linking U.S. businesses to low-cost software expertise in India. These cross-Pacific networks give skilled immigrants a big edge over mainstream competitors who often lack the language skills, cultural know-how, and contacts to build business relationships in Asia. The long-distance networks are accelerating the globalization of labor markets and enhancing opportunities for entrepreneurship, investment, and trade both in the United States and in newly emerging regions in Asia.

Taiwanese immigrant Miin Wu, for example, arrived in the United States in the early 1970s to pursue graduate training in electrical engineering. After earning a doctorate from Stanford University in 1976, Wu saw little use for his new skills in economically backward Taiwan and chose to remain in the United States. He worked for more than a decade in senior positions at Silicon Valley–based semiconductor companies including Siliconix and Intel. He also gained entrepreneurial experience as one of the founding members of VLSI Technology.

By the late 1980s, Taiwan's economy had improved dramatically, and Wu decided to return. In 1989 he started one of Taiwan's first semiconductor companies, Macronix Co., in the Hsinchu Science-based Industrial Park. Wu also became an active participant in Silicon Valley's Monte Jade Science and Technology Association, which was building business links between the technical communities in Silicon Valley and Taiwan.

In this complex mix, the rich social and professional ties among Taiwanese engineers and their U.S. counterparts are as important as the more formal corporate alliances and partnerships.

Macronix went public on the Taiwan stock exchange in 1995 and in 1996 became the first Taiwanese company to list on Nasdaq. It is now the sixth biggest semiconductor maker in Taiwan, with more than $300 million in sales and some 2,800 employees. Although most of its employees and its manufacturing facilities are in Taiwan, Macronix has an advanced design and engineering center in Silicon Valley, where Wu regularly recruits senior managers. A Macronix venture capital fund invests in promising start-ups in both Silicon Valley and Taiwan—not to raise money but to develop technologies related to their core business. In short, Miin Wu's activities bridge and benefit both the Taiwan and Silicon Valley economies.

A New Model of Globalization

As recently as the 1970s, only giant corporations had the resources and capabilities to grow internationally, and they did so primarily by establishing marketing offices or manufacturing plants overseas. Today, new transportation and communications technologies allow even the smallest firms to build partnerships with foreign producers to tap overseas expertise, cost-savings, and markets. Start-ups in Silicon Valley are often global actors from the day they begin operations. Many raise capital from Asian sources, others subcontract manufacturing to Taiwan or rely on software development in India, and virtually all sell their products in Asian markets.

The scarce resource in this new environment is the ability to locate foreign partners quickly and to manage complex business relationships across cultural and linguistic boundaries. The challenge is keenest in high-tech industries whose products, markets, and technologies are continually being redefined—and whose product cycles are exceptionally short. For them, first-generation immigrants like the Chinese and Indian engineers of Silicon Valley, who have the language, cultural, and technical skills to thrive in both the United States and foreign markets, are invaluable. Their social structures enable even the smallest producers to locate and maintain collaborations across long distances and gain access to Asian capital, manufacturing capabilities, skills, and markets.

These ties have measurable economic benefits. For every 1 percent increase in the number of first-generation immigrants from a given country, for example, California's exports to that country go up nearly 0.5 percent. The effect is especially pronounced in the Asia-Pacific where, all other things being equal, California exports nearly four times more than it exports to comparable countries elsewhere in the world.

Growing links between the high-tech communities of Silicon Valley and Taiwan, for example, offer big benefits to both economies. Silicon Valley remains the center of new product definition and of design and development of leading-edge

technologies, whereas Taiwan offers world-class manufacturing, flexible development and integration, and access to key customers and markets in China and Southeast Asia. But what appears a classic case of the economic benefits of comparative advantage would not be possible without the underlying social structures, provided by Taiwanese engineers, which ensure continuous flows of information between the two regions.

The reciprocal and decentralized nature of these relationships is distinctive. The ties between Japan and the United States during the 1980s were typically arm's-length, and technology transfers between large firms were managed from the top down. The Silicon Valley-Hsinchu relationship, by contrast, consists of formal and informal collaborations among individual investors and entrepreneurs, small and medium-sized firms, and divisions of larger companies on both sides of the Pacific. In this complex mix, the rich social and professional ties among Taiwanese engineers and their U.S. counterparts are as important as the more formal corporate alliances and partnerships.

Silicon Valley-based firms are poised to exploit both India's software talent and Taiwan's manufacturing capabilities. Mahesh Veerina started Ramp Networks (initially Trancell Systems) in 1993 with several Indian friends, relatives, and colleagues. Their aim was to develop low-cost devices to speed Internet access for small businesses. By 1994, short on money, they decided to hire programmers in India for one-quarter of the Silicon Valley rate. One founder spent two years setting up and managing their software development center in the southern city of Hyderabad. By 1999 Ramp had 65 employees in Santa Clara and 25 in India.

Having used his Indian background to link California with India, Veerina then met two principals of a Taiwanese investment fund, InveStar, that folded in Taiwan. In less than three months, Veerina set up partnerships for high-volume manufacture of Ramp's routers with three Taiwanese manufacturers (it took nine months to establish a similar partnership with a U.S. manufacturer). The Taiwanese price per unit was about half what Ramp was paying for manufacturing in the United States, and Ramp increased its output one-hundred-fold because of relationships subsequently built by Veerina with key customers in the Taiwanese personal computer industry. Ramp also opted to use the worldwide distribution channels of its Taiwanese part-

ners. And when Ramp designed a new model, the Taiwanese manufacturer was prepared to ship product in two weeks—not the six months it would have taken in the United States.

Veerina attributes much of his success to InveStar's partners and their network of contacts in Taiwan. In a business where product cycles are often shorter than nine months, the speed and cost savings provided by these relationships provide critical competitive advantages to a firm like Ramp. InveStar sees as one of its key assets its intimate knowledge of the ins and outs of the business infrastructure in Taiwan's decentralized industrial system. By helping outsiders (both Chinese and non-Chinese) negotiate these complicated networks to tap into Taiwan's cost-effective and high-quality infrastructure and capability for speedy and flexible integration, such firms provide their clients far more than access to capital.

Americans should resist viewing immigration and trade as zero-sum processes.

As Silicon Valley's skilled Chinese and Indian immigrants create social and economic links to their home countries, they simultaneously open foreign markets and identify manufacturing options and technical skills in Asia for the broader U.S. business community. Traditional Fortune 500 corporations as well as newer technology companies, for example, now increasingly turn to India for software programming and development talent. Meanwhile, information technology-related sectors in the United States rely heavily on Taiwan (and more recently China) for their fast and flexible infrastructure for manufacturing semiconductors and PCs, as well as their growing markets for advanced technology components. And these distant resources are now just as accessible to new start-ups like Ramp as to more established corporations.

These new international linkages are strengthening the economic infrastructure of the United States while providing new opportunities for once peripheral regions of the world economy. Foreign-born engineers have started thousands of technology businesses in the United States, generating jobs, exports, and wealth at home and also accelerating the integration of these businesses into the global economy.

A New Policy Environment

The Silicon Valley experience underscores far-reaching transformations of the relationship between immigration, trade, and economic development in the 21st century. Where once the main economic ties between immigrants and their home countries were remittances sent to families left behind, today more and more skilled U.S. immigrants eventually return home. Those who remain in America often become part of transnational communities that link the United States to the economies of distant regions. These new immigrant entrepreneurs thus foster economic development directly, by creating new jobs and wealth, as well as indirectly, by coordinating the information flows and providing the linguistic and cultural know-how that promote trade and investment with their home countries.

Analysts and policymakers must recognize this new reality. In the recent U.S. debate over making more H1-B visas available for highly skilled immigrants, discussion began—and ended—with the extent to which immigrants displace native workers. But these high-tech immigrants affect more than labor supply and wages. They also create new jobs here and new ties abroad. Some of their economic contributions, such as enhanced trade and investment flows, are difficult to quantify, but they must figure into our debates.

Economic openness has its costs, to be sure, but the strength of the U.S. economy has historically derived from its openness and diversity—and this will be increasingly true as the economy becomes more global. As Silicon Valley's new immigrant entrepreneurs suggest, Americans should resist viewing immigration and trade as zero-sum processes. We need to encourage the immigration of skilled workers—while simultaneously improving the education of workers here at home.

AnnaLee Saxenian is a professor of city and regional planning at the University of California at Berkeley.

From the *Brookings Review,* Winter 2002, pp. 28-31. © 2002 by the Brookings Institution Press, Washington, DC. Reprinted by permission.

Software

**Programming jobs are heading overseas by the thousands.
Is there a way for the U.S. to stay on top?**

By Stephen Baker and Manjeet Kripalani

Stephen Haberman was one of a handful of folks in all of Chase County, Neb., who knew how to program a computer. In the spring of 1999, at the height of the Internet boom, the 17-year-old whiz wanted to strut his stuff outside of his windswept patch of prairie. He was too young for a nationwide programming competition sponsored by Microsoft Corp., so an older friend registered for him. Haberman wowed the judges with a flashy Web page design and finished second in the country. Emboldened, Stephen came up with a radical idea: Maybe he would skip college altogether and mine a quick fortune in dot-com gold. His mother, Cindy, put the kibosh on his plan. She steered him to a full scholarship at the University of Nebraska at Omaha.

Half a world away, in the western Indian city of Nagpur, a 19-year-old named Deepa Paranjpe was having an argument with her father. Sure, computer science was heating up, he told her. Western companies were frantically hiring Indians to scour millions of software programs and eradicate the much-feared millennium bug. But this craze would pass. The former railroad employee urged his daughter to pursue traditional engineering, a much safer course. Deepa had always respected her father's opinions. When he demanded perfection at school, she delivered nothing less. But she turned a deaf ear to his career advice and plunged into software. After all, this was the industry poised to change the world.

As Stephen and Deepa emerge this summer from graduate school—one in Pittsburgh, the other in Bombay—they'll find that their decisions of a half-decade ago placed their dreams on a collision course. The Internet links that were being pieced together at the turn of the century now provide broadband connections between multinational companies and brainy programmers the world over. For Deepa and tens of thousands of other Indian students, the globalization of technology offers the promise of power and riches in a blossoming local tech industry. But for Stephen and his classmates in the U.S., the sudden need to compete with workers across the world ushers in an era of uncertainty. Will good jobs be waiting for them when they graduate? "I might have been better served getting an MBA," Stephen says.

U.S. software programmers' career prospects, once dazzling, are now in doubt. Just look at global giants, from IBM and Electronic Data Systems to Lehman Brothers and Merrill Lynch. They're rushing to hire tech workers offshore while liquidating thousands of jobs in America. In the past three years, offshore programming jobs have nearly tripled, from 27,000 to an estimated 80,000, according to Forrester Research Inc. And Gartner Inc. figures that by yearend, 1 of every 10 jobs in U.S. tech companies will move to emerging markets. In other words, recruiters who look at Stephen will also consider someone like Deepa—who's willing to do the same job for one-fifth the pay. U.S. software developers "are competing with everyone else in the world who has a PC," says Robert R. Bishop, chief executive of computer maker Silicon Graphics Inc.

For many of America's 3 million software programmers, it's paradise lost. Just a few years back, they held the keys to the Information Age. Their profession not only lavished many with stock options and six-figure salaries but also gave them the means to start companies that could change the world—the next Microsoft, Netscape, or Google. Now, these veterans of Silicon Valley and Boston's Route 128 exchange heart-rending job-loss stories on Web sites such as yourjobisgoingtoindia.com. Suddenly, the programmers share the fate of millions of industrial workers, in textiles, autos, and steel, whose jobs have marched to Mexico and China.

"Leap of Faith"

This exodus throws the future of America's tech economy into question. For decades, the U.S. has been the world's technology leader—thanks in large part to its dominance of software, now a $200 billion-a-year U.S. industry. Sure, foreigners have made their share of the machines. But the U.S. has held on to control of much of the innovative brainwork and reaped rich dividends, from Microsoft to the entrepreneurial hotbed of Silicon Valley. The question now is whether the U.S. can continue to lead the industry as programming spreads around the globe from India to Bulgaria. Politicians are jumping on the issue in the election season. And it will probably rage on for years, affecting everything from global trade to elementary-school math and science curriculums.

Countering the doomsayers, optimists from San Jose, Calif., to Bangalore see the offshore wave as a godsend, the latest productivity miracle of the Internet. Companies that manage it well—no easy task—can build virtual workforces spread around the world, not only soaking up low-cost talent but also tapping the biggest brains on earth to collaborate on complex projects. Marc Andreessen, Netscape Communications Corp.'s co-founder and now chairman of Opsware Inc., a Sunnyvale (Calif.) startup, sees this reshuffling of brainpower leading to bold new applications and sparking growth in other industries, from bioengineering to energy. This could mean a wealth of good new jobs, even more than U.S. companies could fill. "It requires a leap of faith," Andreessen admits. But "in 500 years of Western history, there has always been something new. Always always always always always."

This time, though, there's no guarantee that the next earth-shaking innovations will pop up in America. Deepa, for example, has high-speed Internet, a world-class university, and a venture-capital industry that's starting to take shape in Bombay. What's more, her home country is luring back entrepreneurs and technologists who lived in Silicon Valley during the bubble years. Many came home to India after the crash and now are sowing the seeds of California's startup culture throughout the subcontinent. What's to stop Deepa from mixing the same magic that Andreessen conjured a decade ago when he co-founded Netscape? It's clear that in a networked world, U.S. leadership in innovation will find itself under siege.

The fallout from this painful process could be toxic. One danger is that high-tech horror stories—the pink slips and falling wages—will scare the coming generation of American math whizzes away from software careers, starving the tech economy of brainpower. While the number of students in computer-science programs is holding steady—for now—the elite schools have seen applications fall by as much as 30% in two years. If that trend continues, the U.S. will be relying more than ever on foreign-born graduates for software innovation. And as more foreigners decide to start careers and companies back in their home countries, the U.S. could find itself lacking a vital resource. Microsoft CEO Steven A. Ballmer says the shortfall of U.S. tech students worries him more than any other issue. "The U.S. is No. 3 now in the world and falling behind quickly No. 1 [India] and No. 2 [China] in terms of computer-science graduates," he said in late 2003 at a forum in New York.

Fear in the industry is palpable. Some of it recalls the scares of years past: OPEC buying up the world in the '70s and Japan Inc. taking charge a decade later. The lesson from those episodes is to resist quick fixes and trust in the long-term adaptability of the U.S. economy. Job-protection laws, for example, may be tempting. But they could hobble American companies in the global marketplace. Flexibility is precisely what has allowed the U.S. tech industry to adapt to competition from overseas. In 1985, under pressure from Japanese rivals, Intel Corp. exited the memory-chip business to concentrate all its resources in microprocessors. The result: Intel stands unrivaled in the business today.

While the departure of programming jobs is a major concern, it's not a national crisis yet. Unemployment in the industry is 7%. So far, the less-creative software jobs are the ones being moved offshore: bug-fixing, updating antiquated code, and routine programming tasks that require many hands. And some software companies are demonstrating that they can compete against lower-cost rivals with improved programming methods, more automation, and innovative business models.

For the rest of the decade, the U.S. will probably maintain a strong hold on its software leadership, even as competition grows. The vast U.S. economy remains the richest market for software and the best laboratory for new ideas. The country's universities are packed with global all-stars. And the U. S. capital markets remain second to none. But time is running short for Americans to address this looming challenge. John Parkinson, chief technologist at Cap Gemini Ernst & Young, estimates that U.S. companies, students, and universities have five years to come up with responses to global shifts. "Scenarios start to look wild and wacky after 2010," he says. And within a decade, "the new consumer base in India and China will be moving the world."

People Skills

To thrive in that wacky world, programmers like Stephen must undergo the career equivalent of an extreme makeover. Traditionally, the profession has attracted brainy introverts who are content to code away in isolation. With so much of that work going overseas, though, the most successful American programmers will be those who master people skills. The industry is hungry for liaisons between customers and basic programmers and for managers who can run teams of programmers scattered around the world. While pay for basic application development has plummeted 17.5% in the past two years, according to Foote Partners, a consultant in New Canaan, Conn., U.S. project managers have seen their pay rise an average of 14.3% since 2002.

Finding those high-status jobs won't be easy. Last summer, 34-year-old Hal Reed was so hungry for a programming job that he answered an ad in the *Boston Globe* for contract work at cMarkets, a Cambridge (Mass.) startup. The pay was $45,000—barely more than an outsourcing company charges for Indian labor. But he took it. Fortunately for him, he was able to convince his new boss quickly that he was much more than a programmer. He could lead a team. Within weeks, his boss nearly doubled Reed's pay and made him the chief software architect. "He had great strategic thinking skills," says Jon Carson, cMarkets' chief executive. "You can't outsource that."

To prepare students for the hot jobs, universities may need to revamp their computer-science programs. Carnegie Mellon University, where Stephen now studies, has already begun that process. His one-year master's program focuses on giving students the skills needed to manage teams and to play the role of software architect. Such workers are the visionaries who design massive projects or products that hundreds or even thousands of programmers flesh out.

The key players in the drama, including these two master's students, Stephen and Deepa, don't have the luxury to wait and see how it turns out. Their time is now. Deepa graduates in May from the Bombay campus of the Indian Institute of Technology, a top university nestled between two lakes. Stephen emerges three months later from the Pittsburgh campus of CMU.

The options they're eyeing illustrate the unfolding map of an industry in full mutation. A software career is no refuge for the faint of heart. Deepa, for example, could suffer if the U.S. government moves to block offshore development or if rocky experiences in foreign lands spark an industry backlash. And Stephen, if he misplays his hand, could find himself competing with lowballing Filipinos or Uruguayans.

For now, their stories reflect the moods in their two countries—one with lots to lose, the other with a world to win. Deepa is brimming with optimism about the future, convinced that her opportunities are limited by nothing more than her imagination. She is thinking not only about the next job but about the startup that she'll found after that. Stephen, by contrast, is cautious. Even at 22, he's attuned to the risks of a global market for software talent. While confident he'll make a good living, he's plotting out a career that sacrifices opportunities for a measure of safety. Self-protection, an afterthought five years ago, is a pillar of his strategy.

Seeking a Niche

It's midday in the windowless basement labs at CMU's Wean Hall. Stephen, tall and lanky, wearing a white T-shirt tucked into jeans, leans back in his chair and ponders his future. He signed up for the master's program at CMU on the advice of a professor in Omaha who told him that graduates with an MS could land more interesting jobs and make more money. But now the big recruiters coming onto the snowy Pittsburgh campus—companies such as Microsoft and Amazon.com Inc.—are hiring cheaper undergrads, he says, and barely giving the masters a look. Sure, other recruiters come knocking. Banks, he says with a grimace. Insurance companies. But the idea of working in a finance-industry tech shop leaves him cold. "I'm not even interviewing," he says.

The 17-year-old hotshot who was ready to skip college and make a mint has undergone quite a change. He's married, has witnessed the bumps in the world of software, and plans to establish "an upper-middle-class lifestyle, and maybe more" as a businessman. His plan is to carve out a niche for himself back in Omaha. He'll gather three or four colleagues and produce custom software for businesses in town, from hospitals and steakhouses to law firms. Omaha is plenty big, he says, for a good business, but it's remote enough to insulate his startup from offshore competition—and even from the bigger competitors in Chicago.

Stephen understands the threat posed by smart and hungry programmers in distant lands. He was once such a programmer himself. From his senior year in high school all the way through college, he worked as a freelancer for a New York software-development company, Beachead Technologies Inc. Geoff Brookins, Beachead's young founder, spotted Stephen's prize-winning entry in the 1999 Microsoft Web-site design contest. He called Nebraska, sent Stephen some work, and was blown away. "He did two months of work in three days," he recalls. Brookins quickly signed him on at $15 an hour, ultimately paying him $45 an hour. Like the Indians, Stephen provided a low-cost alternative to big-city programmers—but he had an advantage because he spoke American English and was only one time zone away from New York.

The job let Stephen work on projects that normally would have been far beyond the reach of a student. One was to create IBM's Web page for its Linux operating-system technology—a crucial arm of Big Blue's business.

"Stephen was lead engineer on that project," Brookins says. The student also got to spend much of the summer of 2001 working at Beachead's office in New York City. It was a fun contrast to Nebraska, he recalls. But he stopped working for Beachead after he moved to Pittsburgh last summer.

It was there that Stephen got a strong signal that the prospects were dimming for programmers. When his wife, Amy, a fellow computer-science student from Nebraska, began looking for programming work, she came back to their suburban apartment disheartened. The only available jobs, she says, "would have paid me interns' rates." She ditched the profession and is now writing a Christian-themed novel.

Then, Stephen's old boss hammered home the dangers of coding for a living in a wired world. Beachead's competitors were finding cheaper labor offshore, and Brookins, to win contracts, had to match them. Last fall, he logged on to a Web site, RentACoder, a matchmaking service between employers and some 30,000 programmers around the world. There, Brookins found a 27-year-old Romanian named Florentin Badea, a star from Bucharest's Polytechnic University and the 11th-ranked programmer on the whole site. Badea was willing to charge just $250 for a project that would have cost $2,000, Brookins estimates, if Stephen had done it.

Those same global forces, Stephen admits, could eventually hollow out his business in Omaha. Already, Indian tech-services outfits such as Infosys and Wipro are competing head-to-head with U.S. companies in this country. But Stephen is betting that by working closely with customers, he can whip bigger firms on quality and service. He says he'll give the venture six months to a year and then see what happens.

Ultrafast Track

Deepa sees a reverse image of Stephen's worldview. Where the prospects for U.S. tech grads seem to narrow as they peer into the future, she's looking down an eight-lane highway. Yet she faces her own set of challenges, she acknowledges, while sipping tea with her classmates in a breezy open-air cafeteria on the Indian Institute of Technology's Bombay campus. They don't want to be cogs in a software-programming factory—India's role to date. Instead, they want India to be a tech powerhouse in its own right. "Good Indian engineers can do good design work, but we need a venture industry" so Indians can start their own companies, says Deepa. Her pals nod in agreement.

Deepa is positioned on India's ultrafast track. The country pins high hopes on the 3,000 students in the six Institutes of Technology. Their alumni are stars locally and worldwide—including Yogen Dalal, a top venture capitalist at Mayfield, and Desh Deshpande, founder of Sycamore Networks and Cascade Communications. Within this elite, Deepa and her friends are a rarified breed. They aced the grueling national exams, ranking in the top 0.2% and winning places in the school of computer science. They're known as "toppers." The challenge for Deepa's small crowd is to move beyond the achievements of Dalal and Deshpande, who notched their successes for U.S. companies, and to make their mark with new Indian companies.

That means bypassing the bread-and-butter service giants, such as Tata, Infosys, and Wipro, that dominate the Indian stage. The jobs they offer, says Deepa, sound boring. To get their hands on exciting research and more creative programming, she and her friends are banking mostly on U.S. companies in India, including Intel, Texas Instruments, and Veritas. This summer, when Deepa graduates, she'll be a software engineer at the Pune operations of Veritas Software Corp., a Silicon Valley storage-software maker. Her pay will start at $10,620 a year—plenty for a comfortable middle-class life in India. "I'm living my dream," she says.

And thrilling her family. Her father, Arun Paranjpe, who grew up in Mhow, a tiny army-base town in central India, could afford only a bachelor's degree, which prepared him for work as an officer in India's railways. He regretted not advancing further and along with Deepa's homemaker mother, he pushed his two daughters toward advanced professional degrees. So while she studied Indian classical vocal music for nine years and escaped, when she could, to the cricket field, Deepa always finished at the top of her class in mathematics. That helped her land a plum spot in the computer-science program at Nagpur University.

Now Deepa is ITT-Bombay's star in search technology—and she's hoping that this specialty will be her ticket to a rip-roaring career. She routinely works till 3 a.m. in the department's new 20-pod computer lab, doing research on search engines. She admits the work at Veritas, at least initially, will involve more routine database tasks than the cutting-edge work she's hoping for. But if Veritas disappoints, a topper like Deepa will have plenty of other options. Both the search giant Google Inc. and the Web portal Yahoo! are setting up research and development centers in India this year. Deepa hopes to manage a research lab some day, and ultimately, she says, "I'd like to be an entrepreneur."

But she's an entrepreneurial revolutionary and family traditionalist at the same time. It's part of her balancing act. Consider her eventual marriage. As an attractive, professional woman, she'll make a prize catch in India's conservative marriage market. Deepa expects she will have an arranged marriage: Her parents will chose a suitable husband for her from within her own caste. But she is firm: Her husband would have to be an entrepreneur, or a tech whiz, and preferably in the same field, "so we can have a common platform and he can understand my work," she says.

Maybe one day the couple will be able to raise venture money together. While venture-capital investing didn't exist in India until a few years ago, the industry is starting to take root. In 2003, India's 85 venture-capital firms invested about $162 million in tech companies, according to estimates from the India trade group National Association of Software & Services Cos. That's up from zero in 1998. Still, it's miles short of the financial support available to Stephen and his classmates. The 700 U.S. venture firms poured $9.2 billion into tech startups last year, according to market researcher VentureOne.

Multicultural Edge

Diversity is another advantage the U.S. has over India. Take a stroll with Deepa through the leafy ITT campus, and practically everyone is Indian. Stephen's scene at CMU, by contrast, feels like the U.N. Classmates joke in Asian and European languages, and a strong smell of microwaved curry floats in the air. This atmosphere extends to American tech companies. With their diverse workforces, American companies can field teams that speak Mandarin, Hindi, French, Russian—you name it. As global software projects take shape, with development ceaselessly following the path of daylight around the globe, multicultural teams have a big edge. Who better than U.S.-based workers to stitch together these projects and manage them? "These people can act as bridges to the global economy," says Amar Gupta, a technology professor at Massachusetts Institute of Technology's Sloan School of Management.

The question is whether the technology industry can respond quickly enough to a revolution that's racing ahead on Internet time. Stephen's former boss, Brookins, frets that the pace could overwhelm the coming generation of U.S. programmers, including his former Nebraska star. "He's a genius. He's the future of the country. [But] if the question is whether there's going to be a happy ending for Stephen, there's a big question mark there," Brookins says. Stephen is betting that quality and customer service will offset the cost advantage of having computer programmers 10 time zones away. He still sees software in the U.S. as a path to wealth—"though I won't really know until I get out there," he says.

While Stephen is busy mounting his defenses, Deepa is setting out on the hard climb to build Silicon India. Much like their two countries, the leader is looking cautiously over his shoulder while the challenger is chugging single-mindedly ahead. No matter which way they may zig or zag, both of them are prepared to encounter rough competition from every corner of the globe. There's no such thing as a safe distance in software anymore.

Letter From Silicon Valley

By Rebecca Vesely

Ellen Chase never thought her life would be like this at age 52. More than a year ago, her husband, Russ, was laid off from his job as a quality assurance engineer in San Jose, California. Then last August, she lost her job as a secretary for a fruit labeling company that was relocating out of the area. They've both been looking for work ever since. Between paying monthly rent of $1,114 and shelling out nearly $600 a month for COBRA health insurance, the Chases are barely able to make ends meet. No other healthcare company will insure the couple because Russ, 57, had open-heart surgery—putting them in the dreaded category of "pre-existing condition." A few years ago, they brought in a combined annual income of $65,000 and were saving for retirement. Today, they live on unemployment benefits of less than $2,000 a month that will expire in May.

She describes herself as politically conservative, and yet Chase says that her plight has changed her views on issues like healthcare, workers' fights and government responsibility. She now believes that the United States needs "socialized medicine, like in England," and should offer more help to those who find themselves without a safety net. "I really feel that the government is not taking care of us," she says. "For people who have worked as long and as hard as we have, a married couple who pay their fair share of taxes, it's very upsetting."

In Silicon Valley, long synonymous with an entrepreneurial spirit, free-market capitalism and libertarianism, more and more workers are, like Chase, rethinking their political views. Not that people are trading in their computers for picket signs, but worker protection, universal healthcare, affordable housing and other traditionally liberal causes are gaining popularity. This shift became evident last November when California bucked a national voting trend that put control of both the US House and Senate into Republican hands. Despite Democratic Governor Gray Davis's low approval ratings, Californians elected Democrats to all eight of the top state positions for the first time since 1882. The California Congressional delegation is now overwhelmingly Democratic, and San Francisco Representative Nancy Pelosi reigns as House minority leader. Membership in the state Libertarian Party has dropped by about 5,500, from a high of nearly 95,000 in 2000, according to the party's website.

Peter Leyden, a former editor at *Wired* magazine and co-author of *The Long Boom*, once imagined twenty-five years of free market prosperity where government played only a supporting role. Today Leyden says that a backlash against globalization and corporate irresponsibility, coupled with terrorism and a Republican agenda that doesn't support technological innovation like stem-cell research, are responsible for the shift in the laissez-faire Valley credo. "I really believe that we are entering an era where we will see a rebalancing toward more government and a conscious effort to force corporations to take more responsibility," says Leyden, now a "knowledge developer" at Global Business Network and co-author of a new book, *What's Next?*

The sustained recession in Silicon Valley has challenged many residents. For ten consecutive months through February, San Jose has reported the nation's highest unemployment rate for metro areas with populations of more than 1 million. The jobless rate for San Jose in February was 8.5 percent—compared with 5.8 percent nationally and 6.6 percent statewide. Santa Clara County, the heart of Silicon Valley, lost 85,000 jobs between 2000 and 2002. The office vacancy rate in the Valley is 24 percent, compared with less than 2 percent in early 2000. In a Field Poll released on April 28, 82 percent of Bay Area residents surveyed said that jobs were scarce. And a first-quarter consumer confidence study of Silicon Valley by the Survey and Policy Research Institute found that the proportion of people who say their families are worse off now than a year ago grew to 41 percent—about 10 percent more than last year.

This growing lack of confidence can be partly attributed to joblessness, but it also reflects a widespread sentiment that the good life is out of reach. Despite the large number of people who have lost their sources of income, Santa Clara County remains one of the most expensive places to live in the country, with a one bedroom apartment renting for about $1,200 a month. Foreclosure proceedings in the county climbed 8.2 percent from the first quarter of 2002 to the first quarter of 2003, yet housing prices continued to rise. The median home price in the Bay Area last December was $416,000, up from $377,000 the previous December.

Business is booming among social services. The first statewide study of hunger, released by the University of California at Los Angeles last November, found that one in four low-income adults in Santa Clara County has trouble buying groceries. Just north of San Jose, in the affluent town of Sunnyvale, a nonprofit group called Sunnyvale Community Services gave out nearly $600,000 in the 2001-02 fiscal year to help people on a one-time basis pay their rent and electricity bills, an 88 percent increase over 1999–2000. Second Harvest Food Bank, which serves Silicon Valley, now feeds 167,200 people a month; one out of four has a college education. Jennifer Luciano, communications director for Second Harvest, says she is witnessing a rising level of anger among those in need and a greater willingness to talk publicly. "People are starting to feel that if speaking out will help educate public leaders about hunger and poverty and perhaps result in changes to the system, then they will talk," she says, "despite the dignity issue of coming forward."

People are also expressing their views through the ballot box. In the 2002 election, pro-labor candidates for San Jose City Council garnered 61 percent of the vote; moving an already moderate Democratic council farther to the left. The growing population of Latino and Asian immigrants is contributing to the rising support for such candidates, because of immigrant worker concerns about housing costs, wages and benefits. Santa Clara County has the highest number of immigrants in the Bay Area, according to US Census data. Some believe a wider workers' rights movement is brewing. "We are entering a more populist era," says Amy Dean, executive officer of the South Bay AFL-CIO Labor Council. "I've been in grassroots politics for twenty years, and what we are seeing today is not just that people want workers to have more power—in issues like a living wage, holding developers accountable and renters' rights—but we are seeing that people want unions to have more power."

A national survey conducted by Peter D. Hart Research Associates last August for the AFL-CIO suggests that union support is higher than at any time since the group began collecting data in 1984. Half of workers who don't already have a union say they would join one tomorrow if given the chance, compared with 42 percent in 2001, according to the report. Dean attributes this not just to the economic downturn but also to 9/11 and recent corporate scandals. "For the first time in decades, people are articulating positive views about the important role that government plays in their lives," she says. "They are yearning for protection from corporate interests and terrorism."

Those views are not confined to the working and middle class. "Companies today say, 'Let's hire people to meet investor needs, and then let's lay them off,'" says an unemployed telecom executive in Silicon Valley who once earned $160,000 a year. "I've never been a political person, but now I see that unions keep companies in line. We need unions to defend workers, because companies sure aren't thinking about them."

Pete Bennett, a 46-year-old former software developer, has launched his own workers' rights campaign. A father of two, Bennett says he folded his software development company in 2000 after being repeatedly underbid for contracts from companies in India. He looked for work at high-tech companies in the Valley, only to find, he says, that he was competing with Indian software developers here on H-1B visas, which allow employers to temporarily hire specialized foreign workers. "US citizens are getting a raw deal," Bennett says. "But the H-1B

workers are also being victimized by corporations because they aren't getting a fair wage." Bennett contends that soaring unemployment rates in Silicon Valley and other high-tech corridors are a direct result of a lack of worker protection in the United States and companies moving their software operations offshore. "It's like we've created our own recession," he says. "The damage has been done."

During the dot-com boom, high-tech companies clamored for an expansion of the H-1B visa program. Congress complied, raising the ceiling from 95,000 in 1998 to the current 195,000. Now labor groups have stepped up their efforts to limit the program.

A Forrester Research report released in December projects that companies will move 3.3 million white-collar jobs and $136 billion in wages overseas in the next fifteen years, with technology companies leading the way. Silicon Valley companies like Oracle and Nortel Networks have already moved software development jobs to India and other countries to cut costs. Hewlett-Packard services chief Ann Livermore told Wall Street analysts in the fourth quarter of last year, "We're trying to move everything we can offshore." This strategy includes adding more workers to the several thousand the company already employs in India.

Not everyone agrees that foreign workers are the Valley's problem. John Aaron Atkins, who was laid off from his job doing software quality assurance at Nortel Networks in November 2001, points out that some H-1B workers have lost their jobs, too. "It's the boom-and-bust cycle of the Valley. If you're going to live here, you have to get used to it," he says. Peter Leyden of the Global Business Network argues that the exodus of jobs involving tasks that will become more automated over time will, in the long term, be better for California workers. These workers should instead be looking toward more creative and higher-paying jobs, like those in biotechnology, nanotechnology, wireless and sophisticated security industries, he says. "I hate to stand back and be a hard ass about this because I know a lot of people are suffering right now," he says. "But I do think that things are picking up. Old Internet jobs are going offshore, but I don't think that will create a long term vacuum here."

President Bush stopped by Santa Clara in early May to push his $550 million tax-cut plan and pledge to bring jobs to the embattled region. He said "I know there's people hurting here in Silicon Valley." But this doesn't help the many people like the Chases get through the meantime, when unemployment benefits are running out and no jobs are in sight. Ellen Chase has been repeatedly rejected for retail jobs at Target, Starbucks and Barnes & Noble. Her husband, Russ—near retirement age and with a bad back—is looking for work as a day laborer, hoping to make $8 an hour. After years of living firmly in the middle class, the Chases face an uncertain future. And yet, they say, what else can they do but wait for the upside?

Rebecca Vesely is a healthcare reporter at the Oakland Tribune *and a former editor at* Business 2.0 *and* Wired News. *Her articles have appeared in* Wired, Mother Jones *and many other publications.*

When Long Hours at a Video Game Stop Being Fun

RANDALL STROSS

CHARLES DICKENS himself would shudder, I should think, were he to see the way young adults are put to work in one semi-modern corner of our economy. Gas lamps are long gone, and the air is free of soot. But you can't look at a place like **Electronic Arts,** the world's largest developer of entertainment software, and not think back to the early industrial age when a youthful work force was kept fully occupied during all waking hours to enrich a few elders.

Games for video consoles and PC's have become a $7 billion-a-year business. Based in Redwood City, Calif., Electronic Arts is the home of the game franchises for N.F.L. football, James Bond and "Lord of the Rings," among many others. For avid players with professional ambitions to develop games, E.A. must appear to be the best place in the world. Writing cool games and getting paid to boot: what more could one ask?

Yet there is unhappiness among those who are living that dream. Based on what can be glimpsed through cracks in E.A.'s front facade, its high-tech work force is toiling like galley slaves chained to their benches.

The first crack opened last summer, when Jamie Kirschenbaum, a salaried E.A. employee, filed a class-action lawsuit against the company, accusing it of failure to pay overtime compensation. He remains at the company, so I spoke with him by phone last week to get an update. He told me that since joining E.A. in June 2003 in the image production department, he has been working—at the company's insistence—around 65 hours a week, spread over six or seven days. Putting in long hours is what the industry calls "crunching." Once upon a time, the crunch came in the week or two before shipping a new release. Mr. Kirschenbaum's experience, however, has been a continuous string of crunches.

Crunches also once were followed by commensurate periods of time off. Mr. Kirschenbaum reports, however, that E.A. has scaled back informal comp time, never formally codified, to a token two weeks per project. He said his own promised comp time had disappeared altogether. At this point, he said he would be glad to enjoy a Labor Day without laboring, or eat a Fourth of July spread at some place other than his cubicle, pleasures he has not enjoyed for two years. The company said it had no comment on the lawsuit, but it is likely to argue that Mr. Kirschenbaum's image production position is exempt from the laws governing overtime compensation.

A few days ago, another crack opened—one large enough to fit a picture window. An anonymous writer who signed herself as "E.A. Spouse" posted on the Web a detailed account of hellish employer-mandated hours reaching beyond 80 hours a week for months. No less remarkable were the thousands of comments that swiftly followed in online discussion forums for gamers and other techies, providing volumes of similar stories at E.A. and at other game developers.

I learned the identity of the E.A. employee described in the anonymous account and spoke at length with him in person late one night, adding a third shift to the day's double that he'd already worked. He seemed credible in all respects, in his command of technical detail, in his unshakable enthusiasm for the games he works on—and in his pallor.

For around $60,000 a year in an area with a high cost of living, he had been set to work on a six-day-a-week schedule. On weekdays, his team worked from 9 to 10 (that is, 9 a.m. to 10 p.m.), and on Saturdays, a half-day (that means 9 to 6). Then Sundays were added—noon to 8 or 10 p.m. The weekly total was 82 to 84 hours.

By tradition, Silicon Valley employers have always offered their bleary-eyed employees lottery tickets in the form of stock options. E.A.'s option grants, however, offer little chance of a Google-like bonanza. An employee who started today with an options package like that of the E.A. worker just described (and who stayed with the company the four years required to fully vest) would get $120,000, for example, if the share price quadrupled—and proportionally less for more modest increases. The odds of a skyrocketing stock grew much longer this month, when the company said competition had forced it to cut prices on core sports titles.

Still, the company is a generous warden: free laundry service, free meals, free ice cream and snacks. The first month, the E.A. employee recalled, he and his colleagues were delighted by the amenities. But he said they soon came to feel that seeing the sun occasionally would have had more of a tonic effect.

This employee, who has not had a single day off in two months, is experienced in the game software business. But he said he had never before had to endure a death-march pace that begins many months before the beta testing phase that precedes the release of a project.

Jeff Brown, a company spokesman, declined to comment on E.A. Spouse's allegations. Mr. Brown did say that the company was interested in its employees' opinions, as illustrated by its employee survey, conducted every two years. This suggests that it needs to conduct a survey to learn whether a regular routine of 80-hour weeks is popular among the salaried rank and file.

Asked about reports of employees working long, uncompensated hours, Mr. Brown responded that "the hard work" entailed in writing games "isn't unique to E.A." He is correct; smaller studios demand it, too. The International Game Developers Association conducted an industrywide "quality of life" survey this year documenting that "crunch time is omnipresent." The study urged readers to tell "the young kids just starting out" in the industry to reject the hours that lock them into "an untenable situation once they start wanting serious relationships and families."

Electronic Arts' early history has none of the taint of present labor practices, and many who are acquainted with the old E.A. and the new E.A. have publicly lamented in Web forums the disappearance of the generosity practiced by Trip Hawkins, who founded the company in 1982. Mr. Hawkins, who has not been associated with E.A. for many years, said that he was not surprised by E.A. Spouse's story. He called today's E.A. a corporate "Picture of Dorian Gray," its attractive surface hiding a not-so-attractive reality.

INDEED, E.A. is noticeably young in appearance. After Randy Pausch, a computer science professor at Carnegie Mellon University, spent a sabbatical last spring as a researcher at the company, he wrote, "I am 43 and I felt absolutely ancient during my time there." He said the place felt to him like "Logan's Run," the 1976 science fiction movie in which no one is allowed to live past 30—and he felt even older when he realized that the 20-somethings were too young to know the reference.

The company has 3,300 employees in its studios developing game titles, and it hires 1,000 new people a year. (Company officials said voluntary turnover is about 10 percent annually.) In the past, it has hired only about 10 percent of new studio personnel directly from college; it has set a goal of increasing that to 75 percent, which would skew the median age still younger.

Professor Pausch listed cost savings from lower salaries as one reason E.A. wishes to shift hiring to a younger group. The company also recognizes that fresh graduates are the most suggestible; Professor Pausch said he heard managers say that "young kids don't know what's impossible." That, however, they will learn when they get their schedules.

Randall Stross *is a historian and author based in Silicon Valley. E-mail:ddomain@nytimes.com.*

The Computer Evolution

Rob Valletta, Research Advisor
and GeoffreyMacDonald, Research Associate

Since the introduction of the IBM PC in 1981, desktop computers have become a standard fixture in most workplaces. Through their ubiquity and impact on how work is done, personal computers (PCs) arguably have transformed the workplace. At the same time, the use and impact of PCs varies across worker groups with different educational and skill levels. As a result, an extensive body of research suggests that the spread of computers, or perhaps increased workplace emphasis on skills that are closely related to computer use, has altered the distribution of wages as well. This process has been marked not so much by abrupt change as by slow and steady change—it is an "evolution" rather than a "revolution."

In this *Economic Letter*, we use data from five special surveys, covering the period 1984–2001, to examine two key aspects of the computer evolution: the spread of PCs at work and the evolving wage differentials between individuals who use them and those who do not. Although the spread of computers has been relatively uniform across labor force groups, the wage returns associated with computers tilted sharply in favor of the highly educated at the end of our sample frame. This finding appears consistent with the increase in trend productivity growth that occurred around the same time.

Computers and workers

By the middle to late 1980s, the rapid expansion of computer power embodied in PCs, combined with software that enhanced the overall ease of PC use and application to common business tasks, suggested to researchers and casual observers alike that computers were playing an increasingly important role in the determination of worker productivity and wages. In the first systematic analysis of the impact of computer use on wages, Krueger (1993) used data for the years 1984 and 1989 to estimate standard wage regressions that included controls for computer use at work. As such his estimates reflect wage differences between workers who use and do not use computers, adjusted for other observable differences across such workers that are systematically related to wages as well (age, educational attainment, sex, etc.). His results suggested that workers who used computers earned about 10%–20% more than workers who did not. Moreover, Krueger found that differences between highly educated and less educated workers in the incidence of and returns to computer use could account for 40%–50% of the increased return to education during the 1980s.

Krueger's analysis tied in well with earlier work regarding the contribution of technological change to increased dispersion in the U.S. wage distribution. Since then, wage gaps have widened even further, intensifying the research focus on how equipment like computers can alter the wage distribution by altering the demand for workers with the skills to use such equipment effectively. In a notable recent piece, Autor, Levy, and Murnane (2003) argue that increased computer use can explain most of the increase in nonroutine job tasks, hence the advanced skill content of jobs, during the 1970s, 1980s, and 1990s, and as such can explain most of the increased relative demand for college-educated workers. Although Autor et al. do not directly address the question of computer effects on earnings, their results indirectly suggest that rising computer use also explains a substantial portion of the rising wage gaps between highly educated and less educated workers over these three decades.

PC diffusion and wage effects

Given these existing findings about computer use, skill demand, and wages, an updated assessment of the returns to computer use is in order. To do so, we use the School Enrollment and the Computer and Internet Use Supplements to the federal government's Current Population Survey (CPS). The CPS covers about 60,000 households each month; the resulting sample of individuals serves as a primary source of information on U.S. employment, unemployment, and income patterns. The supplements we use were conducted in 1984, 1989, 1993, 1997, and 2001 (Krueger's work relied on the first two of these). In these surveys, the respondents were asked about computer use at home, work, and school. Although the exact content of the supplements changed over time (for example, Internet use was first addressed in 1997), the question about computer use at work has been essentially unaltered. We rely on samples of about 60,000 employed individuals in each survey to calculate rates of computer use at work; of these, information on wages and related variables is provided for a bit under one-fourth of the sample (about 12,000–14,000 individuals). We restrict the analysis to individuals age 18 to 65.

Figure 1 shows the time series of computer use rates for college graduates, nongraduates, and the combined population. Although the level of computer use is significantly higher for workers with a bachelor's degree (82.3% in 2001) than for those without it (42.7%), the diffusion over time has been relatively uniform across these groups. Additional tabulations show a similar pattern of diffusion when the sample is broken down into narrower educational groups or by additional characteristics such as gender, race, age, geography, and occupation. In percentage terms, we find the sharpest

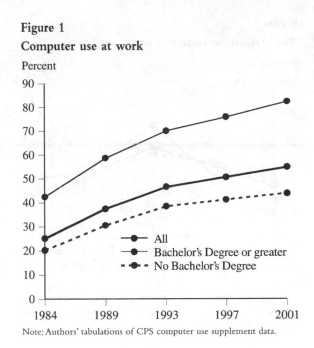

Figure 1

Computer use at work

Note: Authors' tabulations of CPS computer use supplement data.

increase in computer use at work for groups with low initial use, including older workers, part-time workers, blue-collar workers, and workers without a high school degree. Moreover, the diffusion of computer use at work slowed after 1993. These patterns are consistent with common models of technology diffusion, in which individuals and firms with the most to gain adopt the new technology first and the rate of diffusion slows as the group that has not yet adopted it shrinks.

To estimate the effect of computer use on wages, we use a regression model similar to Krueger's (1993). The model controls for observable characteristics that are systematically related to wages, including age, education, race, sex, marital status, veteran status, union status, part-time status, and geographic location (region and urban/rural residence), allowing us to isolate the effect of computer use on wages independent of the influence of these other characteristics. Given the potentially important interaction between computer use and education level, we also allow for separate estimates of the return to computer use for individuals who have attained at least a college degree versus those who have not. After applying an appropriate mathematical transformation based on the logarithmic regression function, we obtain the estimated percentage effect of computer use on wages.

Figure 2 plots how the estimated return to computer use at work has changed over time. For the full sample of workers, the return to computer use reached a peak in 1993, with a 24.2% wage advantage over otherwise similar workers. The estimated return to computer use for the full sample declined to 19.2% in 2001. However,

Figure 2

Wage returns to computer use

Percent

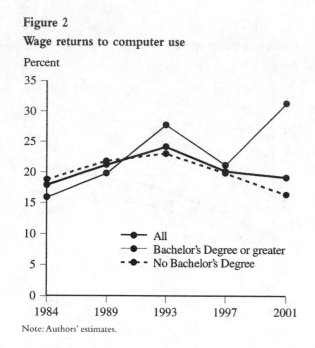

Note: Authors' estimates.

Legend:
— All
— Bachelor's Degree or greater
- - No Bachelor's Degree

Implications

Our findings confirm that workers who use computers earn more than otherwise similar workers who do not. We also find that this effect has been especially large for highly educated workers in recent years. Some researchers, however, have questioned whether the computer effect on wages is fundamentally meaningful in an economic sense. For example, DiNardo and Pischke (1997) have shown that workers who use simple office tools like pencils earn a wage premium similar to that estimated for computer users. This suggests the possibility that the estimated effect of computer use on wages reflects unobserved aspects of skilled workers and their jobs, such that these workers would earn higher wages even if they did not use computers. In other words, DiNardo and Pischke argue that computer use does not have an independent "causal" impact on wages but instead serves as a mediating or auxiliary factor, reflecting related skills that are more fundamental than the direct ability to use a computer.

Nevertheless, an abundance of evidence regarding close relationships among the use of advanced technology and the demand for and wages of skilled workers suggests an important causal role for computers and the skills needed to use them. In that regard, an emphasis on "causal" impacts may be misplaced. For many jobs, effective performance requires computer use, which suggests a close relationship between computer use and critical job skills. In technical parlance, the ability to use a computer probably is not a "sufficient" condition for earning high wages, but it is increasingly a "necessary" condition.

Overall, we interpret the evidence as suggesting that direct computer skills or skills that closely relate to computer use command a substantial premium in the labor market, especially in conjunction with a college degree. It remains to be seen whether the recent increase in returns to computer use for highly educated individuals will continue. However, the trend over the past few years suggests that U.S. productivity growth remains on (or even above) the accelerated growth path that was established during the late 1990s. Going forward, it is likely that these productivity gains will be largely reflected in wage gains for highly educated individuals who use computers, much as was the increase in the relative return to computer use for these individuals during the period 1997–2001.

the return for individuals with a college or graduate degree increased dramatically during the last period, reaching 31.4% in 2001. This sharp change is surprising, as it conflicts with the general expectation, based on economic reasoning, that the return to scarce skills (those needed for computer use) should decline as that skill becomes less scarce. As shown in Figure 1, only about one in five college-educated workers did not use computers at work in 2001, which suggests that the skills needed to use computers are far from scarce among the highly educated.

Although the spread of computer skills suggests that the wage returns to computer use should decline, this argument ignores the possibility that production technology is changing rapidly and in ways that support increased rewards for workers with the skills needed for effective use of critical technologies such as computers. Available evidence suggests that rapid expansion of information technology capital (mainly computers and software) in the workplace accounts for a substantial portion of the increased growth in labor productivity during the period 1996–2001 (see for example Oliner and Sichel 2003). While computers make some tasks easier and reduce required skill levels, many advances in computer technology have enabled increasingly sophisticated applications that require complex analytical and evaluative skills. A leading reason to attend college is to acquire such skills. It appears that these skills commanded an increasing premium as workplace computer use intensified between 1997 and 2001, enabling college-educated workers to capture the largest benefits from the spread of computers in the workplace during this period.

References

Autor, David H., Frank Levy, and Richard J. Murnane. 2003. "The Skill Content of Recent Technological Change: An

Empirical Exploration." *Quarterly Journal of Economics* 118(4) (November), pp. 1279–1333.

DiNardo, John, and Jörn-Steffen Pischke. 1997. "The Return to Computer Use Revisited: Have Pencils Changed the Wage Structure Too?" *Quarterly Journal of Economics* 112(1) (February), pp. 291–303.

Krueger, Alan. 1993. "How Computers Have Changed the Wage Structure: Evidence from Microdata, 1984–1989." *Quarterly Journal of Economics* 108(1) (February), pp. 33–60.

Oliner, Stephen D., and Daniel E. Sichel. 2003. "Information Technology and Productivity: Where Are We Now and Where Are We Going?" *Journal of Policy Modeling* 25(5) (July), pp. 477–503.

Reprinted with permission from the Federal Reserve Bank of San Francisco *FRBSF Economic Letter,* No. 2004-19, July 23, 2004, pp. 1-3. The opinions expressed in this article do not necessarily reflect the views of the management of the Federal Reserve Bank of San Francisco, or of the Board of Governors of the Federal Reserve System.

Making Yourself Understood

In an age of technology, writing skills are more important than ever.

Stuart Crainer and Des Dearlove

Business leaders have never had so many ways to communicate: e-mail, teleconferencing, text messaging, instant messaging, websites, weblogs, and satellite linkups—not to mention the old standbys. Your memos and directives and statements now can reach their intended recipients instantly, unfiltered by secretaries. You don't have to wait for a speech to be ghostwritten, scheduled, delivered, and reported; you don't have to wait for your annual-report opening statement to hit stockholders' desks; you don't have to wait for water-cooler gossip to distribute a new policy.

But there's a dark lining to the new media and easy communication: It's never been so easy to be misunderstood. Your messages can be overlooked, misinterpreted, misused. Messages and memos that don't make a clear, immediate impact are likely to be lost in the deluge of information flooding the nation's inboxes.

In short, this may be a digital world, but the written word remains the fundamental tool of communication, and being able to write effectively and persuasively—whether creating a business plan, e-mail, report, appraisal, or positioning statement—is a core executive skill. Sure, America's e-mailers routinely infuriate grammarians by omitting punctuation and capitalization, and "like" is pervading spoken English, but when it comes to making yourself understood, language is critical.

While the PR or corporate-communications department is on call to help draft public documents for external audiences, executives must rely on their own literary devices for the multitude of internal documents that are increasingly grist to the management mill. The decline in secretarial support also means that the person who once tweaked the executive's grammar has typically been replaced by dubious spell-checking software. Be it purple or otherwise, the full glory of an executive's prose is likely to be exposed to the organization. If you can barely string together a sentence—let alone construct a pithy argument—your subordinates will know.

"There's a growing misconception that the proliferation of multimedia technology has diminished the need for strong writing skills, and this is just plain false," says Don Spetner, senior VP for global marketing at recruitment firm Korn/Ferry International. "At the core of all communications is content, which is a fancy word for good old-fashioned storytelling or straightforward, concise writing. We take a very critical eye toward a candidate's ability to write, whether it's in their resume, their cover letter, or the various samples of work product that reflect the quality of their skills."

The reality is that executives are spending ever more time writing in one form or another. Literary purists may regard e-mail as writing's poor cousin, but it has become the dominant form of corporate communication. A 2003 survey by Clearswift, the American Management Association, and The ePolicy Institute found that the average U.S. employee spends about one hour and forty-seven minutes a day dealing with e-mail. A Goizueta Business School study puts this even higher: Research among 1,200 managers found that more than half spend at least two hours per day answering e-mail at work, with 30 percent clocking an additional hour or more at home.

As philanthropist and former eBay president Jeff Skoll told us: "It's funny that in an age when e-mail has become such a dominant form of communication, people are writing more than they ever have. They spend so much time in front of the computer these days with written communication, and yet it seems that the art of that communication has declined over the same time."

Managers must increasingly rely on persuasion—and inspiration.

Of course, it's not just e-mail. Techno-savvy executives may keep up their own online commentary/diary weblogs, commonly known as blogs. Blogdex.net, part of an MIT-sponsored research project, estimates the number of blogs at one million and rising fast. And instant messaging, once associated with teenagers and chat rooms, is also rapidly finding its way into corporations—as a business tool. A year ago, Forrester Research

The Good, the Bad, and the Ugly

Business writing is riddled with literary nightmares. Take this job ad—please:

"The Senior Business Analyst will have primary responsibility to elicit, analyze, validate, specify, verify, and manage the real needs of the project stakeholders, including customers and end users. He/she will take the role of functional area manager, where he/she is the primary conduit between the customer community (the functional areas) and the software development and implementation team through which requirements flow."

The classic writing-by-committee approach tends to produce lists of verbs covering every eventuality and to introduce buzzwords such as *stakeholders, customer community*, and *implementation* at every opportunity.

Jargon is endemic and can render straightforward statements completely meaningless. One organization pronounced: "We continually exist to synergistically supply value-added deliverables such that we may continue to proactively maintain enterprise-wide data to stay competitive in tomorrow's world."

Beware of synergy in its many guises and value in its confusing array of valueless forms.

Another common mistake is to completely overlook the audience. A food company's annual report contained the following paragraph: "With the continued growth of hand-held foods, the commercialization of our patented sauce filling cold forming extrusion technology has attracted industry-wide interest for appetiser, hand-held and centre-of-plate applications."

Unfortunately, the audience for the company's annual report—investors, analysts, reporters, and so on—were unlikely to be knowledgeable about extrusion technology, meaning that the impact was therefore less than desired.

And then there is the writing-by-dictation approach, exemplified by that of business guru Tom Peters. At his best, Peters is insightful and enthusiastic. At his worst, his writing practically transcribes his seminar rants word-for-word. Take this example:

"Never—ever!—neglect 'community building.' WOW Projects feed on a growing web of supporters. You must—always!—be in the 'hustling' (suck up!) mode. Sure, your 'substantive'/operational duties could absorb the energy of a platoon. No matter. Make-the-damn-time-to-do-community-building. It's called politics . . . Building Bridges . . . Forging Alliances. Making Friends. Neutralizing Enemies. It's called WOW Project success!"

This is the literary equivalent of shouting. After a while—a short while—its impact wanes.

Luckily, there are plenty of examples of good business writing. Consider the opening of Gary Hamel and C.K. Prahalad's bestseller *Competing for the Future*:

"Look around your company. Look at the high-profile initiatives that have been launched recently. Look at the issues that are preoccupying senior management. Look at the criteria and benchmarks by which progress is being measured. Look at the track record of new business creation. Look into the faces of your colleagues and consider their dreams and fears. Look toward the future and ponder your company's ability to shape that future and regenerate success again and again in the years and decades to come."

This leads off a book about *strategy*. Despite their unpromising subject matter, Hamel and Prahalad write clearly, concisely, and effectively. Note the short sentences, the direct, personal tone, and the accessible language.

Or think of corporate slogans that manage to motivate and drive entire organizations with a few well-chosen words, such as Microsoft's call to arms, "A computer on every desk and in every home."

The quintessence of effective business writing comes in advertising. Whether it is IBM's Think or Budweiser's King of Beers, great ad slogans distill complex messages down to a few well-chosen words. Indeed, the addition of a single word—*new*—before a product routinely boosts sales. Written words are powerful tools. Handle them with care.

—Stuart Crainer and Des Dearlove

estimated instant messaging's penetration in corporations at 45 percent, and the figure has certainly climbed since then. With IBM and Microsoft both adopting and pushing the technology, it is likely to become ubiquitous.

The Power of the Pen

The style of business writing is also changing. The rise of e-mail and other electronic channels has coincided with a growing need for executives to ensure that their communication is more direct, more personal. Flatter management structures mean that executives can no longer rely on hierarchical power to get things done. Issuing edicts is less often an option. Instead, managers must increasingly rely on persuasion—and inspiration. This requires a more sophisticated style of communication, one that is directed at the individual and imbued with emotional context as well as content. One survey of sixty executives found that the messages that get attention are those in which the message is personalized, evokes an emotional response, comes from a trustworthy or respected sender, and is concise.

Of course, great leaders have long been aware of this. They realize that while speeches can be inspirational, they are transient. At best, they are absorbed into an organization's oral history. But written communications—whether they boost morale, announce triumphs, acknowledge disasters, or spur employees to greater productivity—endure.

"Great business leaders, and those who aspire to the status, succeed in communicating well what is important," says Peter Knight, CEO of the London-based CEO Circle network. "Their writing stands out from the whirl of information. It memorably expresses the values, focuses, and thrusts necessary for their companies to prosper. It summarizes and reinforces the message of all their forms of communication."

The rise of instant messaging suggests that worse is to come.

Jack Welch habitually sent handwritten notes to GE workers at all levels, from part-time staff to inner-circle executives. Some even framed his letters, as tangible proof of their leader's appreciation.

From the handwritten to the homespun, Berkshire Hathaway CEO Warren Buffett is another exponent of the corporate missive. Each year, the sage of Omaha pens a letter that has become an annual media event, summarized in *Fortune* and dissected by stock analysts everywhere. Buffett's annual letter to his company's shareholders can move markets and make fortunes.

But it's not just the old guard that appreciates the power of writing. Jeff Skoll insists that writing laid the foundation of the eBay culture. When eBay was launched, many of its employees—in customer service, for example—were highly dispersed around the world, and communication was invariably by e-mail. "How do you build an organization, how do you build a culture, when your primary means of communication is written?" Skoll muses. "I guess the answer is that you have to be very thoughtful, and you have to be clear in your writing style. Both [founder] Pierre Omidyar and I put a lot of effort into getting our points across in writing."

The New Language of Business

While executives may recognize the importance of well-crafted writing, time pressures often conspire against quality. Jargon, obfuscation, poor punctuation, garbled syntax, and tortured grammar are facts of business life. Literary purists would be appalled to see much of what issues forth from executives' pens and keyboards.

Consultant and author Sam Hill, who has taught business-writing skills to fellow consultants at Booz Allen Hamilton and occasionally at Northwestern University, doesn't think business writing is necessarily getting worse. "I think it's always been terrible," he says. "But I do think tools like PowerPoint and e-mail, coupled with the organizational downsizing of secretaries, has given illiterate businesspeople the ability to send babble out unedited, and this has increased visibility of the problem."

E-mail hasn't improved matters. The medium that has done more than any other to elevate the importance of executive writing is often characterized by literary sloppiness and inattention to detail—a fact evidenced, painfully, by perhaps half of the messages currently in your Outlook inbox.

There are several reasons for this. E-mails are inherently more informal than letters, so the author tends to take less care with their construction and language. And dealing with an inbox full of e-mails is time-consuming, so executives, following the dubious example of the world's teenagers, take shortcuts. *Please* becomes *pls*, and it's a slippery slope down. Such linguistic contortions become trendy, and some e-mailers who adopt them out of convenience begin to do so self-consciously, to better appeal to Gen-X workers and managers.

If e-mail has corrupted the English language, the rise of instant messaging suggests that worse is to come. IM skips the drafting-and-rewriting stage that produces well-thought-out letters—indeed, that's the whole point. Together with texting, still a largely European phenomenon, it is the most lax of increasingly casual modes of communication.

"Most of us relax the rules of grammar and spelling when participating in a chat or instant-messaging situation, because the speed of this type of communication makes formatting difficult," observes Deborah Valentine of the Goizueta Business School Writing Center.

But despite the havoc wreaked on the conventions of writing—the use of the lowercase personal pronoun *i*, the wholesale omission of vowels, the mass abbreviation—does any of it really matter? Is this new writing *bad writing?*

John Patrick is president of Attitude LLC and former VP of Internet technology at IBM, where he worked for thirty-five years. Patrick, whose blogpatrickweb.com offers commentary on technology and its impact on business and society, believes effective writing to be a critical skill for the future—as it always has been. But he insists that we shouldn't blame the medium if the message is poorly constructed: "E-mail is a form of writing," he says. "Like with pen and paper, some people are good at it and some are not. Well-written e-mail is powerful and has numerous other positive attributes, including its ability to be sorted, archived, indexed, and

---

The Power Of Words

The wrong words in the wrong place can prove costly. In 1983, computer manufacturer Coleco wiped $35 million off its balance sheet in one quarter. How? Customers swamped the company with returns of a new product line. There was nothing wrong with the product—the problem was that the manuals were unreadable. The firm went bust.

In another example, a major oil company sank hundreds of thousands of dollars of R&D into developing a new pesticide only to find that one of its own employees had invented the same product some time ago. Why did no one know? Because the report in which the discovery was written up was such heavy going that no one had bothered to read it all the way through.

One study of military-personnel researchers noted that officers took up to 23 percent less time to read clearly written documents. The researchers concluded that the Navy alone could save over $26.5 million in wasted man-hours if documents were written in a plain, easy-to-understand style. True, the Navy is unlikely to collapse due to a poorly written manual, but last time we checked, $30 million was real money.   —*Stuart Crainer and Des Dearlove*

---

so on. I also think blogging is grossly underestimated by just about everyone."

The Return of the Punctuators

A panda goes into a bar and orders some food. After finishing its meal, the panda produces a pistol and fires a shot into the ceiling before heading to the door. The barman catches up with the panda outside and asks for an explanation. "A panda eats, shoots, and leaves," the panda replies, thereby illustrating the power of the humble comma.

There is a burgeoning back-to-basics movement. As we write, Lynne Truss's *Eats, Shoots & Leaves: The Zero Tolerance Approach to Punctuation* remains high on U.K. best-seller lists and is about to be published stateside. The book sold fifty thousand copies in the ten days after U.K. publication, and U.S. rights were sold for a six-figure sum. Proper punctuation is bizarrely fashionable these days.

Good writing, it seems, is reasserting itself. Sixty percent of Goizueta's surveyed executives claimed to prefer standard usage in business communication. This is, Valentine suggests, because traditional grammar and punctuation have developed over many centuries, and for a good reason: to guide the reader. "Paragraphs provide a visual break," she notes, "and punctuation slows or stops the reader at the appropriate place."

Valentine offers three reasons why the shortcuts characteristic of e-mail and instant messaging have little place in executive-level communication. First, not every recipient will understand the acronyms and abbreviations—time saved in the typing will likely be lost in the deciphering. Savvy executives, she says, write with their audiences' needs in mind. Second, clarity is essential and shortcuts can obscure meaning. (Warren Buffett has

opined that if he doesn't understand something, he assumes that someone is trying to fool him.) Finally, careless e-mails can prove costly, as brokerage firm Merrill Lynch learned recently: After e-mails revealed analysts offhandedly disparaging stocks they were talking up in public, the embarrassed firm agreed to adopt conflict-of-interest reforms—and to a $100 million fine. It is best to remember, Valentine advises, that e-mail is forever. Bad writing habits, however, needn't be.

The Opportunity

For linguistically challenged executives, help is at hand. Growing recognition among executives of the importance of good writing is manifest in the growth in business-writing instruction. Executives and consultants are increasingly turning to communications experts, including journalists, for help. Says Peter Knight: "The whole purpose of The CEO Circle is to assist CEOs to improve their performance, to achieve greater success. To find better ways of expressing this was why I attended a writing workshop, and it certainly helped me. All I write is colored by my belief that well-written communication of what really matters helps produce the performance that makes companies and leaders great."

There is a profusion of writing coaches, classes, and ghostwriters ready to make sure that the message, whatever it is, is finely phrased. "Our clients—senior executives at technology and financial-services firms—understand the increasing importance of clear, persuasive writing in internal and external communications. The explosion of electronic information distribution over the Internet provides enormous opportunity and an enormous amount of content to be digested," says Write Effect co-founder Lynn Kearney, who has consulted on communications and organizational issues

12 Habits of Effective Writers

1. Get real: Writing is something we do all the time, so don't be precious about it. Think practical rather than poetical.

2. Distill it: What is your message in a nutshell? Effective writers are masters of distillation. Think of advertising slogans and newspaper headlines.

3. Think reader: Know your audience. Tune into your readers' world. What matters to them?

4. Prepare to write: Think before you write rather than writing before you think. Effective writers don't use the writing process to discover what they want to say. They have thought about it already and know what their point is.

5. Find the story: Effective writers—whether composing an e-mail, a report, or a newspaper article—decide on the angle. If you're writing an e-mail, fill in the subject box before you begin.

6. Don't reinvent the wheel: Seek out templates, style guides, and anything else that will make your life easier. Most organizations have these, but employees often are unaware of their existence.

7. Map it out: Good writers start with a structure. They think and write in modules—from the Ten Commandments to the four Ps of marketing.

8. Keep it simple: Effective writers aim for clarity. They know that an average sentence length of about eight words is the most readable and understandable. At fifteen words a sentence, comprehension falls to about 90 percent. At twenty words, it drops to 75 percent. At twenty-five words, it drops to 62 percent.

9. Make an impact: The first line counts no matter what you are writing.

10. Stay fresh: The clearer your mind, the clearer your writing.

11. Make it fit: Edit to length, and ask: Does it meet the brief? Does it fulfill its purpose?

12. Deliver and follow through: Make sure that what you have written arrives safely. Otherwise you have wasted your time.

—Stuart Crainer and Des Dearlove

for more than two decades. "In years past, we have worked with corporate training and development managers to create business-writing courses. We now get calls directly from senior business-unit managers with specific requests for highly customized programs that include not just content but also guidance on how to package ideas that grab readers' attention. Increased competition for readers—clients—has alerted managers to the need for improved writing quality as a means to build and maintain client relationships."

Writer's block is a luxury that executives cannot afford.

Our own experience training executives and MBA students in effective business writing confirms that many veteran and fledgling managers recognize their deficiencies in this area. Many have similar issues and problems. For example, we are often asked about how to create effective messages for different audiences—say, internal and external stakeholders—and how to structure and present information in the most compelling way. Other requests include how to overcome blank-page syndrome or first-paragraph hell. Writer's block, we

helpfully tell course participants, is a luxury that executives cannot afford.

While most executives recognize the difference between good and bad writing, they tend to accept poor writing—including their own—as a fact of business life. Yet improving the quality of writing is actually much easier, and less time-consuming, than people imagine. "Great writing is a state of mind as much as anything," says Gerry Griffin of the London-based Business Communication Forum, a media training organization. "Once I was reminded of the basic characteristics of good and bad writing, my own writing improved. Instead of taking it for granted, I began to think about writing more carefully, to think about my audience and so on."

Self-awareness about writing makes a significant difference to the quality of written output—and, potentially, your career. "Good writing is a wonderful way to differentiate yourself inside a company," Sam Hill says. "Back when I was competing with all those other aggressive young associates at Booz Allen, all of us in the same charcoal-gray Jos. A. Bank suits and faux Hermes ties, I used the ability to express myself clearly to get myself noticed. I used to work for hours at home secretly writing and rewriting reports until they were logical and stylistic masterpieces. The next afternoon, I'd drop them on my partner's desk casually and do my best to create the implication that I'd just dashed them off—and hopefully create the impression in his mind that I was effortlessly brilliant. It must have worked: I made partner." The write stuff works.

STUART CRAINER and DES DEARLOVE are the founders of Suntop Media. Their last article was "Windfall Economics," the July/ August 2003 cover story.

UNIT 4

Computers, People, and Social Participation

Unit Selections

Key Points to Consider

- The Overview to this unit mentions de Tocqueville's observation that Americans tend to form civic associations and Putnam's argument that this tendency is declining. Do you think that computing has played any part in the decline? What does Putnam say? What do other scholars say about Putnam's work?

- "From Virtual Community to Smart Mobs" describes a helmet that will allow the wearer to filter out the "ever-greater intrusions by government and business" on your "personal space and freedom?" What else might it filter out? Would you wear this helmet? What is the cost?

- Christine Rosen in "New Technologies And Our Feelings" says that "our technologies enable and often promote two detrimental forces in modern relationships: the demand for total transparency and a bias toward the oversharing of personal information." This seems to run counter to the popular perception that honesty is the best policy in relationships. Is Rosen advocating dishonesty?

Student Website

www.mhcls.com/online

Internet References

Further information regarding these websites may be found in this book's preface or online.

Adoption Agencies
   http://www.amrex.org/

Alliance for Childhood: Computers and Children
   http://www.allianceforchildhood.net/projects/computers/index.htm

The Core Rules of Netiquette
   http://www.albion.com/netiquette/corerules.html

How the Information Revolution Is Shaping Our Communities
   http://www.plannersweb.com/articles/bla118.html

SocioSite: Networks, Groups, and Social Interaction
   http://www2.fmg.uva.nl/sociosite/topics/interaction.html

That early and astute observer of American culture, Alexis de Tocqueville (1805-1859), had this to say about the proclivity of Americans to form civic associations:

Americans of all ages, all conditions, and all dispositions constantly form associations....The Americans make associations to give entertainments, to found seminaries, to build inns, to construct churches, to diffuse books, to send missionaries to the antipodes; in this manner they found hospitals, prisons, and schools. If it is proposed to inculcate some truth or to foster some feeling by the encouragement of a great example, they form a society. Wherever at the head of some new undertaking you see the government in France, or a man of rank in England, in the United States you will be sure to find an association.... The first time I heard in the United States that a hundred thousand men had bound themselves publicly to abstain from spriritous liquors, it appeared to me more like a joke than a serious engagement, and I did not at once perceive why these temperate citizens could not content themselves with drinking water by their own firesides.... Nothing, in my opinion is more deserving of our attention than the intellectual and moral associations of America....In democratic countries the science of association is the mother of science; the progress of all the rest depends upon the progress it has made (v. 2, pp. 114-118)[1]

De Tocqueville laid this tendency squarely at the feet of democracy. If all men—we're talking about the first half of the 19th century here—are equal before the law, then to do any civic good requires that these equal, but individually powerless, men band together.

A century and a half later, we have the technical means to communicate almost instantly, almost effortlessly across great distances. Yet in 1995, Robert D. Putnam, made the news with an article, later expanded into a book, called *Bowling Alone*. He argued that the civil associations de Tocqueville had noticed so long ago were breaking down. Americans were not joining the PTA, the Boy Scouts, the local garden club, or bowling leagues in their former numbers. Putnam discovered that although more people are bowling than ever, participation in leagues was down by 40% since 1980.[2] The consequences for a functioning democracy are severe.

Although the articles in this Unit do not directly address the idea of civic participation, that question is the necessary glue that holds them together. Do computers assist or detract from civic life? Another French social observer, Emile Durkheim (1858-1917), argued that a vital society must have members who feel a sense of community. Community is easily evident in pre-industrial societies where kinship ties, shared religious belief, and custom reinforce group identity and shared values. Not so in modern societies, particularly the United States, where a mobile population commutes long distances and retreats each evening to the sanctity and seclusion of individual homes. Contemporary visitors to the United States are struck by the cultural cafeteria available to Americans. They find a dizzying array of religions beliefs, moral and philosophical perspectives, modes of

social interaction, entertainment venues and, now, networked computers. One need only observe a teenager frantically "instant-messaging" her friends from a darkened bedroom to know that while computer technology has surely given us great things, it has taken away something as well. The capacity to maintain friendships without face-to-face contact, the ability to construct a computer profile that edits anything not in line with one's interests, seems to push society a step closer to self-interested individualism.

On the other hand, one can argue that the new communications technologies permit relationships that were never before possible. To cite a large example, the organization moveon.org, organized many thousands of people, in a matter of weeks, entirely over the Internet, to oppose the invasion of Iraq in the spring of 2003. Or a smaller one, immigration, always a wrenching experience, is less wrenching now, since immigrants to the United States can be in daily touch with their families across the globe. Or consider how the virtual bazaar, eBay, surely one of the extraordinary aspects of the Internet, puts Americans in touch with Japanese, Latvians, Montenegrans, peoples whom we might never have known. Recall Postman: "technology giveth and technology taketh away."

What technology seems to have been giving this past year or two, is the capacity to display one's every thought and emotion to the world. Blogs, or Web Logs, on-line diaries made possible by the Web, are too new to have attracted much sociological attention, though rumor has it that the machinery of academic research is on their trail. It should surprise no one that entering freshman, who grew up using the Internet, should turn to university-sponsored blogs to ease the transition to college life. "Back-to-School Blogging" tells the story of blogs at Davidson College and Washington University. Here's a sample posting that some faculty might take issue with:

Squirrelhanded (August 15, 10:18 p.m.): here's a piece of advice…

If you have a choice between having an incredible talk with a good friend in the hallway or getting 3 extra hours of sleep … take the talk. If it's between ANOTHER 5-point math assignment and a midnight magical mystery trek through town… go crazy. Have a good time. Don't get me wrong, academics are priority. They're the reason we're all here in the first place….but choose your memories. Make them lasting ones.

An early indicator of academic interest into blogging is "Structure and Evolution of Blogspace." Here we learn that bloggers in the 19-21 age group tend to be interested in "dorm life, frat parties, college life, my tattoo, pre-med," while their parents in the 46-57 year old age group tend to blog about "science fiction, wine, walking, travel, cooking, politics, history, poetry, jazz, writing, reading, hiking." Once they pass 57, however, their interests turn toward cats, poetry, and death.

Related to the self-revealing blogosphere is on-line dating. Christine Rosen's "New Technologies and Our Feelings," provides a critical look at a practice that is not only becoming common but lucrative, as well. Revenues from online dating services exceeded $302 million in 2002 with sites like Jdate.com (for Jewish dates), CatholicSingles.com and HappyBuddhist.com.

From a blogger's point of view, the audience for his or her interior life cannot be too large. But there are only so many hours in a day and only so many blogs, on-line magazines, and email messages that can be read. What's a Web surfer to do? If you are a reader of the on-line editions of the *Wall Street Journal, the Los Angeles Times*, the *Christian Science Monitor,* you can tailor the offerings to your own tastes. Whether this is an instance of technology giving or technology taking away is a matter of opinion. An extreme version of filtering is described in a review culled from *The Futurist,* "From Virtual Communities to Smart Mobs." Here we learn about a professor from the University of Toronto who wears a helmet that mediates the reality he experiences. According to the writer, he "considers his computer helmet self-defense against what he sees as ever-greater intrusions by government and business on his personal space and freedom."

On the other hand, information technology has even made it possible to attend to one of our social networks while we are immersed in another. Go to a large conference these days, and you will surely notice the number of attendees typing on their laptops, sending instant messages, doing what has come to be called multitasking. But the data has begun to suggest that "business people who multitask 'are making themselves worse business people.'"

Finally, what is a unit on social participation without at least a nod to Google, reference librarian of first resort to so many of us. "You don't get to be a verb unless you're doing something right," says linguist Geoffrey Nunberg in "Making Meaning." Google has been in the news ever since its 2004 stock offering. This particular piece argues that the social network reflected in the Google database "is less like a piazza than a souk—a jumble of separate spaces, each with its own isolated chatter." Has technology given or taken away?

The final article in this unit is the story of an especially rarefied species of social interaction: literary snobbery. Now, it seems, that the Author, Author quiz of the *Times Literary Supplement* is falling prey to the power of Google. But the *Times*, according to one editor, has shut its "eyes to the whole Google phenomenon and carried on as if it made no difference."

---

1. Tocqueville, Alexis de. Democracy in America. New York: Vintage Books, 1945.
2. Putnam, Robert D. Bowling Alone: The Collapse and Revival of American Community. New York: Simon & Schuster, 2000.

Back-to-School Blogging

Web logs help new students prepare for campus life

Brock Read

LIKE ALMOST ANY STUDENT preparing to move into a freshman dormitory, Nora Goldberger spent much of the summer batting around questions about college life: Would she struggle to make friends? Which courses should she take, and which ones should she avoid? How would she get her laundry done?

Such concerns are the stuff that precollege apprehension is made of. But Ms. Goldberger, a Philadelphia native who is beginning her studies at Davidson College, says she feels more at ease than most of her friends. Credit for that, she says, goes to her computer.

Throughout the summer she joined her peers in posting questions on a Web log, or blog, for students at the North Carolina college. Using the informal discussion forum, maintained by students at Davidson, she chatted with her soon-to-be-classmates and hit up wizened upperclassmen for advice on the coming year.

When Ms. Goldberger wondered if she could trust the university's laundry service—which collects students' dirty clothes and washes them at no cost—she asked her fellow bloggers. Within a day, several upperclassmen had given her a consensus opinion: Don't be afraid to use the service, but wash delicate items yourself.

When she wanted to know how much she should expect to pay for a semester's worth of textbooks, she quickly got a number of estimates. And after she mentioned offhand-edly that she'd been listening to a song by the band Sister Hazel, she compared notes with two other students who owned all of the cult group's albums.

The popularity of blogs is helping students across the country meet their dorm mates, form study groups, and make friends before they set foot on their new campuses.

Free, Web-based tools like Xanga and LiveJournal, which allow users to easily create their own blogs, have attracted a large following among high-school and college students. At institutions like Davidson, enterprising students have used the popularity of the medium to create thriving communities in which incoming freshmen meet to exchange practical questions, personal information, movie recommendations, and jokes.

Administrators say the sites constitute an important new trend: Students who grow up using the Web as a social tool can now ask their peers, instead of college officials, for counseling on the process of preparing for college. The colleges aren't about to get rid of their orientation sessions, but officials say freshmen who use the Internet for college planning may become more self-reliant students.

Meanwhile, students like Ms. Goldberger relish the chance to get a head start on college socializing. "This has definitely made me feel more excited and better about coming here," she says. "I have friendly faces and people to look out for, and I'm just a little bit better informed."

FLOOD OF QUESTIONS

The success of the Davidson students' Web log (http://www.livejournal.com/community/davidson college) has exceeded the expectations of its creator, Emily McRae, a sophomore.

Ms. McRae started the site—a group journal that allows anyone to post comments—this summer after speaking to an incoming freshman who found her own blog inundated with questions about Davidson from people she'd never met.

The flood of questions, Ms. McRae says, proves that first-year students are eager to touch base with their peers—and that information travels quickly among bloggers. A Web log, she reasoned, would let incoming freshmen share questions about Davidson among a broad pool of college-age bloggers.

The blog is hosted on LiveJournal, a free service. Anyone can see the postings, but only those who have signed up with the service can contribute. On pages that resemble discussion boards, users with pseudonymous screen names like "onenoisygirl" and "atrain14" post questions or comments, and others respond.

At first the site was popular with freshmen who logged on to do little more than introduce themselves and post their course schedules. But soon upperclassmen happened onto the Web log and made their presence known. Students began asking about cafeteria food, required courses, dorm-room accouterments, and other concerns of campus life, and the community took off.

"I think freshmen became really interested when there were upperclassmen giving sage advice on classes, orientation, and living in Davidson," says Peter Benbow, a sophomore who regularly contributes to the site as "crazydcwildcat7."

"We know what it's like to come wide-eyed and mystified onto a college campus," he says.

The site now has almost 80 users, including alumni and prospective students. "The alumni get to reconnect, the freshmen get to ask advice, the upperclassmen get to consult one another, and the prospectives get lots of answers for 'Why did you come to Davidson?'" says Ms. McRae.

The site has a generally earnest tone, with posts that range from informational to motivational. During the week before freshmen headed to campus for orientation activities in August, students sought tips for decorating their rooms and updated classmates on their packing progress. One first-year student tried to set up a knitting party, a sophomore offered an inspirational poem, another student asked her classmates for help in choosing a gym class, and an alumnus reminded frantic packers to bring cold medicine.

The site has caught on with upperclassmen and alumni because they remember how daunting the transition to dormitory life can be, says Rachel Andoga, a sophomore who helps run the LiveJournal blog and posts regularly under the name "rachigurl5." "I imagine that if I'd had something like this when I came to college, I wouldn't have been as insanely nervous about starting out," she says. "Everyone's so friendly on the site."

Ms. Andoga hopes that the blog will survive the start of the academic year and become an informal bulletin board where first-year students can organize study sessions and publicize extracurricular activities. The bonds that students have formed on the site are real, she says. She expects to drop in on several freshman bloggers to see how they are adjusting to college, and she is helping to plan a party for all the Davidson students who joined the LiveJournal community.

LURKING ADMINISTRATORS

Davidson administrators, too, have been tuning in to the blog—even though they had no part in its creation—in an effort to determine what issues freshmen are most worried about.

"I think I've spent as much time on the site as the students have," jokes Leslie Marsicano, director of residence life at the college. "It's been riveting and addicting for me."

She has recommended the site to students and parents who called her office with niggling questions about bedsheets and laundry arrangements. Some students have speculated that she had recruited upperclassmen to log on and serve as mentors to incoming students.

To the contrary, she says: She's strictly a watcher of the blog. "I think if we tried to encourage the site we'd spoil it," she says. "It works so much better because it comes from the grass roots, and there's no administration figures for students to be suspicious of."

But Davidson officials do have a vested interest in the online gathering. For many prospective students, Ms. Marsicano says, the Web log may be a more effective form of advertisement than a glossy brochure or even a college visit. High-school students choosing between Davidson and its competitors are adept at tracking down student Web logs and are likely to trust them to provide an unfiltered view of college life, she says.

Davidson is lucky: The blog has been consistently cheery and cordial. But Ms. Marsicano says she'd be unhappy if she felt that students were misrepresenting the institution. "When parents call me to ask how long the beds are, they're really asking if there's some nice person who will look after their baby," she says. "I'd like to be able to keep pointing to this site to say, 'The kids can take care of each other.'"

Chemistry 115, Midnight Treks, and Knitting:
Online Reassurance at Davidson College

Users who post messages on Davidson College's student-run Web log, or blog, discuss a wide range of topics, including course schedules, extracurricular activities, and their views of college life. A sampling of comments:

sleeprocker (August 13, 1:27 a.m.): I signed up for Organic Chemistry, but now I think I want to drop back to Chem 115. The course schedule says that all the sections are full right now. How likely is it that I can make the switch?

nayetter (August 13, 7:17 a.m.): Go to the 115 class on the first day (or both 115 classes, if you can) and talk to the professor, and explain your situation to him. He won't be able to raise the ceiling beyond how many students can fit in the lab at once, but if you talk to him then he'll do his best to accommodate your needs.

Also, watching the "add/drop" page like a hawk is a good idea.

squirrelhanded (August 15, 10:18 p.m.): here's a piece of advice. . . . if you have the choice between having an incredible talk with a good friend in the hallway or getting 3 extra hours of sleep . . . take the talk. if it's between ANOTHER 5-point math assignment and a midnight magical mystery trek through town. . . . go crazy. have a good time.

don't get me wrong, academics are priority. they're the reason we're all here in the first place.... but choose your memories. make them lasting ones.

rachigurl5 (August 16, 8:28 a.m.): Exactly. Education isn't limited to the classroom . . . God, if I had a nickel for every Great Thing I've learned from long midnight talks . . . le sigh!

superluci (August 18, 3:23 a.m.): I haven't been able to find out anything about this online. I'm a knitter, and I'm looking for yarn stores in the Davidson area. Are there any stores selling yarn and knitting supplies near the college? I'm stocked up reasonably well coming in but I doubt my supply will last long. I love knitting with other people so if anybody wants to knit with me or have stitch & bitch parties that would be awesome! See you all. . . . TODAY! :) Belk 243, come by and chat!

advice_and_ice (August 18, 6:51 a.m.): There's a knitting store on main street. would a crocheter be welcome occasionally? ;-)

BONDING ONLINE

Blogs are not the only online forums that have developed to help incoming students break the ice with classmates. Many students are using e-mail lists and social-networking sites like Friendster and Thefacebook to make bonds before arriving on the campus.

For Anna Dinndorf, a freshman at Washington University in St. Louis, a personal Web log and an online discussion group led to romance. Last spring she mentioned her early-admission acceptance in her online journal, a daily blog she maintains on the popular Web site Diaryland. Another blogger who had been admitted to Washington spotted the entry and invited Ms. Dinndorf to join a growing group of incoming students in a discussion forum that makes use of a free service by Yahoo, the popular search site.

"I had never spoken to her before, and I never spoke to her after that, but she clued me in, and for that I'm very thankful," Ms. Dinndorf says.

In the Yahoo group, users not only post questions about courses and dorm preparations at Washington, but contribute to a database of students' contact information, exchange screen names so they can chat on instant-messaging software, and create informal polls that ask their peers to comment on matters both political and personal. For example, almost none of the incoming freshmen approve of the Bush administration's proposed Constitutional amendment to ban gay marriage. On a lighter note, most students said they order soft drinks by asking for "soda" instead of "pop" or "Coke."

CHATTIER COMMENTS

With more than 200 students registered, the discussion at Washington is chattier and less focused than the Davidson blog. It's also a bit franker: Some students grouse about their housing assignments or other matters. But the incoming students, by and large, seem to have few quibbles with Washington, and administrators surfing the site would find little to worry about.

For most students, the site is more about socializing than it is for airing serious concerns. Ms. Dinndorf says she's spent much of her time on the site just meeting people, including a fellow freshman whom she now calls her boyfriend. The pair, it turns out, have met only once in real life, but they've gotten to know each other through posts on the discussion board and on AOL Instant Messenger chats.

"We started out talking online and things developed, and then we met in person when I went to Washington for a weekend in July," says Ms. Dinndorf. "It's so great to be going down to school and already have all these connections."

The connections, she says, are forged by jokes and gossip as much as by serious conversations. Some students took notice when a rumor popped up on the board that the radio "shock jock" Howard Stern's daughter would be part of the Class of 2008 at Washington, but, ultimately, the claim was debunked.

For Ms. Dinndorf, that light touch is a welcome distraction from the often tense process of preparing to move away from home. "Basically, the site has been like a sounding board for all the precollege jitters and worries and questions and everything that everyone goes through at this point," she says. "And I'm really addicted to it."

STRUCTURE AND EVOLUTION OF
Blogspace

RAVI KUMAR, JASMINE NOVAK, PRABHAKAR RAGHAVAN, AND ANDREW TOMKINS

A critical look at more than one million bloggers and the individual entries of some 25,000 blogs reveals blogger demographics, friendships, and activity patterns over time.

*B*logs constitute a remarkable artifact of the Web. Most people think of them as Web pages with reverse chronological sequences of dated entries, usually with sidebars of profile information and usually maintained and published with the help of a popular blog authoring tool. They tend to be quirky, highly personal, typically read by repeat visitors, and interwoven into a network of tight-knit but active communities. We refer to the collection of blogs and all their links as blogspace. By analyzing the structure and content of more than one million blogs worldwide, we've now unearthed some fascinating insights into blogger behavior.

An analysis of blogspace must reflect at least two distinct perspectives: the temporal (how it evolves over time) and the spatial (how bloggers congregate in terms of interests and demographics). Studying them requires data sets with distinctive characteristics; in particular, the temporal needs a time-dependent history of a collection of blogs. Here, we describe how we've studied these interests and demographics, eliciting some striking correlations in the friendships among bloggers and their interests, as well as the temporal, based on a set of blogs we've analyzed over time.

Who are these bloggers? We've studied the profile pages of 1.3 million bloggers at livejournal.com, one of the world's most popular blogging sites. Each live-journal blogger has a self-reported profile of basic personal information, including name, geographic location, date of birth, interests, friends, and other bloggers listing this blogger as a friend. Bloggers may opt not to specify or even expose certain fields; for example, only 52% of the livejournal entries (investigated February 2004) included age information. Geographic information is specified by selecting a country and optionally a U.S. state from a drop-down menu, then optionally entering an arbitrary city and an arbitrary state/province/territory for non-U.S. bloggers. Thus, geographic information is a combination of structured and unstructured data entry. Additionally, bloggers manually specify interests based on specific instructions regarding proper formulation; as a result, they share many interests, resulting in informal interest groups. There are roughly 850,000 interest groups listed at livejournal.com, 15% with only a single member. Approximately 68% of live journal bloggers express at least one interest, with some expressing many more. Interests are wide-ranging, including, for example, vegetarianism, parenting, witchcraft, and catnip.

Where do these bloggers come from? Blogging is a global phenomenon; our data includes blogs from all seven continents, including Antarctica. But certain regions have large numbers of bloggers. As expected, centers of computing activity (such as California, Florida, New York, and Michigan) are strongly represented, as are Canada, England, Russia, and Australia.

What can be said about their ages and their interests? Table 1 lists the fraction of bloggers (whose profiles included age information) that fall into each age group, along with representative interests for each group.

Three out of four live journal bloggers are between 16 and 24 years of age. Their interests (and friendships) are highly correlated with age. The surprising category of 1–3 year olds consists of individuals creating blogs for their pets and newborn children. The age-correlated interest groups showed a steady progression from early high school (MTV's Fuse network, rocker Adam Carson, drama club) through college (dorm life, frat parties), to 20-something lifestyle (Long Island iced tea, Liquid Television, bar hopping, grad school), into a more refined 30s (my kids, parenting, Doctor Who, and Bloom County), a somewhat conflicted 40s (Society for Creative Anachronism, Babylon 5, gardening), and even into later life (wine, cooking, travel). Many of the strongly age-correlated interests are completely unfamiliar to most people outside the age group; for us, exploring them has been a source of accelerated extracurricular learning. Bloggers do not express their interests randomly; certain interests

Table 1. Percentage of bloggers might themselves be world-wide in different age groups and representative interests for each (Original data source: www.livejournal.com)

Age	%	Representative Interests
1-3	0.5	treats, catnip, daddy, mommy, purring, mice, playing, napping, scratching, milk
13-15	3.5	Web designing, Jeremy Sumpter, Chris Wilson, Emma Watson,TV, Tom Felton, FUSE, Adam Carson, Guyz, Pac Sun, mall, going online
16-18	25.2	198(6, 7, 8), class of 200(4, 5), Dream Street, drama club, band trips, 16, Brave New Girl, drum major, talking on the phone, high school, Junior Reserve Officers' Training Corps
19-21	32.8	198(3, 5), class of 2003, dorm life, frat parties, college life, my tattoo, pre-med
22-24	18.7	198(1, 2), Dumbledore's army, Midori sours, Long Island iced tea, Liquid Television, bar hopping, disco house, Sam Adams, fraternity, He-Man, She-Ra
25-27	8.4	1979, Catherine Wheel, dive bars, grad school, preacher, Garth Ennis, good beer, public radio
28-30	4.4	Hal Hartley, geocaching, Camarilla, Amtgard,Tivo, Concrete Blonde, motherhood, SQL, TRON
31-33	2.4	my kids, parenting, my daughter, my wife, Bloom County, Doctor Who, geocaching, the prisoner, good eats, herbalism
34-36	1.5	Cross Stitch,Thelema,Tivo, parenting, cubs, role-playing games, bicycling, shamanism, Burning Man
37-45	1.6	SCA, Babylon 5, pagan, gardening, Star Trek, Hogwarts, Macintosh, Kate Bush, Zen, tarot
46-57	0.5	science fiction, wine, walking, travel, cooking, politics, history, poetry, jazz, writing, reading, hiking
>57	0.2	death, cheese, photography, cats, poetry

Table 2. Sample "interest clusters" among bloggers worldwide. (Original data source: livejournal.com)

Cluster Label	Interests Expressed	Age Group	Location
Existentialism	Dostoevsky, Sartre, Kafka, Camus	25-29	NY
Coastal Preppies	Burberry, Diesel, Coach, Mark Jacobs, New York, Starbucks		NY, CA
Toddlers	Puppies, kitties, bunnies, sparkles, doggies	1-3	North America
New age	Zen, metaphysics, Nietzsche, quantum physics, Buddhism, philosophy, theology	25-36	Seattle
Harry Potter	Hogwarts, Slytherin, Quidditch, Ravenclaw, Gryffindor	43-48	U.K.
Coffee	Coffee, caffeine, espresso	28-30	Seattle
Outdoor activities	Kayaking, backpacking, hiking, rock climbing, mountain biking	25-36	WA
Fast food	Burger King,Wendys, Subway	16-18	FL
Vegans	Vegan, tofu, soy, PETA		
Body art	Tattoos, body art, body piercing	25-39	Australia
Russian hackers	Java, programming, Linux, php, FreeBSD, hacking, open source	22-39	Russia

tend to occur together in user profiles. By building clusters around pairs of co-occurring interests, we distilled 300 densely connected "interest clusters" (see Table 2). The first column of the table includes a label we assigned to each cluster. The second column lists representative interests from that cluster. The third and fourth columns (if reported) list the age groups and locations most strongly associated with the cluster.

Though we assigned the labels in the first column manually, the cleanliness of the clusters suggests we could do so almost automatically from the interests in the second column, then with recourse to a semantic network (such as WordNet) [2].

The locations, ages, and interests of individual bloggers paint an intriguing picture of the constituents of blogspace. But to complete this picture, we need to understand the interconnections among bloggers, or who is a friend of whom? On average, each live journal blogger profile explicitly names 14 other bloggers as friends. In 80% of these cases, the expression of friendship is mutual; if Bob names Sally as a friend, then Sally names Bob as a friend.

Are these friendships located randomly throughout the worldwide blogger community? Are they more clustered? Researchers studying the theory of social networks calculate the "clustering coefficient" of a network of friends, defined as the chance that two of my friends are themselves friends. Previous studies [8] have typically covered much smaller networks, with clustering coefficient values ranging from 0.1 to 0.2. For our extremely large network of bloggers, the clustering coefficient is 0.2, meaning that a remarkable 20% of the time, two friends of the same blogger are themselves friends.

One possible reason for friends to be clustered so tightly is that friendships result from commonalities (such as being from the same town, being the same age, or sharing an interest in a particular topic). If two of my friends share my interest in snorkeling, they might themselves be friends due to their own shared interest. Since we know interests, ages, and locations of the bloggers (as they've reported them), we can ask how many friendships are "explained" by these commonalities (see Figure 1). We present them as a Venn diagram to show that certain friendships might be between individuals who share an interest and are the same age.

Surprisingly, over 70% of friendships among live-journal.com bloggers can be explained by these three factors, so fewer than 30% of friendships are between bloggers of different ages, from different locations, and with no expressed shared interests. Age is the weakest explanation for friendships, while location and interest are roughly equivalent. Interest alone explains 45% of friendships, while location alone explains 55%; together these two factors explain 70% of friendships, and 92% of friends of the same age also share an interest or location.

Evolution of Blogspace

The culture of blogspace focuses on local community interactions among a small number of bloggers, from, say, three to 20. Members of such an informal community might list one another's blogs in a "blogroll" (a sidebar within a particular blog listing the other blogs the blogger frequents) and might read, link to, and respond to content in other community members' blogs. These sequences of responses often take place during a brief burst of activity as an interesting topic arises, jumps prominence, then recedes. We observed and modeled this highly dynamic, temporal community structure in order to reveal the evolution of blog-space over time.

To do so, we considered each blogger as more than a static object, extending our view of the individual blog to include a temporal component, reflecting the fact that blog entries are posted over time. It is difficult to capture the particular topics covered by each entry, as the entries lack structure; even the definition of a topic is subjective. However, we've observed that bloggers in a community often link to and cross-reference one another's postings, so we can infer community structure by analyzing the linkage patterns among blog entries.

In this view of the worldwide blogging network, a "community" is a set of blogs linking back and forth to one another's postings while discussing common topics. Each community may exhibit different levels of activity over particular periods of time; for example, a community may show a burst of rapid-fire discussion during a three-week period, then lie dormant for several more weeks before the next burst of activity.

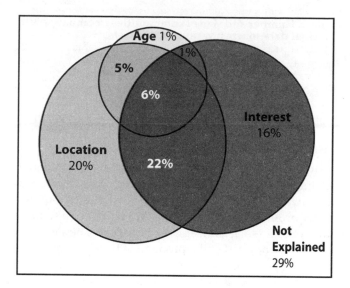

Figure 1. Explaining friendships through age, interests, and locations. (Original data source: www.livejournal.com)

For our study, we collected blog postings from seven popular blog sites: blogger.com, memepool.com, globeofblogs.com, metafilter.com, blogs.salon.com, blogtree.com, and Yahoo blogs. In January 2003, we crawled approximately 25,000 blogs from these sites, including all current and archived entries. Analyzing individual blogger data, we found three quarters of a million links from one of these blogs to another of these blogs, of which about 10% were distinct.

We then sought to study communities of blogs in the data to identify bursts of activity taking place in them, as illustrated in the following example. In Seattle, a group of local artists formed a blogging community around a particular blogger we call Jane. Jane was involved in fringe theater. Some of the other community members were in a band. Several events reflected the burst of activity that occurred in the community during the four months from June to October 2002. Jane decided to connect with old high-school friends, asking two members of the community to set up blogs for them. The event generated a mini-burst of blogging activity. She then convinced two high-school friends to visit Seattle on two different weekends. Lots of blogging then covered what to show them when they would visit, along with picking them up at the airport, their reaction to Jane's theater performance, and more. A third event during the same period occurred when two members of the community got engaged to be married, prompting another mini-bursts of blogging activity about the engagement and the beautiful children they would have.

We detected this community and the bursts within it automatically through a two-step process: extracting the communities themselves, then analyzing each community for bursts of activity.

We extracted the communities by identifying collections of blogs that frequently link back and forth to one another. Table 3 outlines the number of communities re-

Table 3. Number and size of communities in January 2003. (Original data sources: various blog sites)

Size	3	4	5	6	7	8	9
No.	143	165	79	14	2	1	5

sulting from this extraction; for instance, the table reports that we found 79 communities in which a community consisted of five blogs.

Given these communities, how might social network researchers identify bursty periods of high interlinking activity? An algorithm presented in [5] identifies bursts of activity around certain words or expressions in a sequence of documents (such as an email repository). The same algorithm can be applied to the problem of finding bursts of activity in blog communities by treating each hyperlink between blogs in a community as a "word." Figure 2 shows the burstiness of communities from January 1999 to January 2003. The x axis specifies the number of months following January 1999, and the y axis specifies the number of communities worldwide displaying bursty activity.

The figure indicates an interesting pattern of behavior. The early history of blogspace—through 1999 and most of 2000—was characterized by little noticeable bursty community activity. However, there was sudden rapid growth in this activity toward the end of 2001, continuing to the beginning of 2003, the limit of the data we collected.

Interestingly, the increase in the number of bursts was not explained by the increase in the number of communities alone. Not only did the number of communities in blogspace increase over this period, the burstiness of typical communities also increased. This data suggests a change in the behavior of the bloggers themselves toward more community-oriented activity. (For more on the size and structure of blogspace, see blogcount.com; for more on the structure and dynamics of blogspace, see [1, 3, 4, 7].)

Conclusion

Blogspace is a rich and complex social environment that admits study at many levels. Our experiments are based on the profiles of more than one million livejournal.com bloggers in February 2004 and on the individual entries of some 25,000 blogs drawn from a variety of worldwide sources. A view of blogspace emerges in three layers: At the bottom is the individual blogger, who can be defined in terms of age, geography, and interests. These characteristics interact, resulting in clusters of interest groups, often with geographic or demographic correlations. In the middle is a web of friendships between pairs of bloggers. They are frequent and important and are usually explained in terms of shared locations and/or shared interests. Finally, at the top is the evolution of blog communities. They show identifiable bursts of activity that can be tracked over time. The magnitude of burstiness in communities appears to be increasing, suggesting that lo-

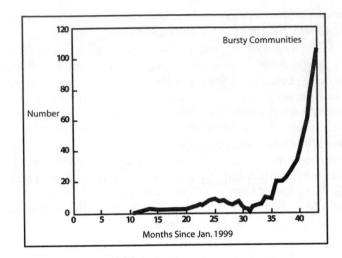

Figure 2. Burstiness of communities. (Original data sources: various blog sites)

cal community structure and community-level interactions are being reinforced as blogspace grows.

We expect blogs to remain a pervasive phenomenon on the Web, and fascinating insights into the sociology of bloggers can be divined from the analysis of the structure and content of blogspace.

References

1. Adar, E., Zhang, L., Adamic, L., and Lukose, R. Implicit structure and the dynamics of blogspace. Presented at the Workshop on the Weblogging Ecosystem at the 13th International World Wide Web Conference (New York, May 18, 2004); www.sims.berkeley.edu/~dmb/blogging.html.

2. Fellbaum, C. WordNet: An Electronic Lexical Database. MIT Press, Cambridge, MA, 1998.

3. Gill, K. How can we measure the influence of the blogosphere? Presented at the Workshop on the Weblogging Ecosystem at the 13th International World Wide Web Conference (New York, May 18, 2004); faculty.washington.edu/kegill/pub/www2004_blogosphere_gill.pdf.

4. Gruhl, D., Guha, R., Liben-Nowell, D., and Tomkins, A. Information diffusion through blogspace. In Proceedings of the 13th International World Wide Web Conference (New York, May 17–22). ACM Press, New York, 2004, 491–501.

5. Kleinberg, J. Bursty and hierarchical structure in streams. In Proceedings of the Eighth ACM SIGKDD International Conference on Knowledge Discovery and Data Mining (Edmonton, Canada, July 23–26). ACM Press, New York, 2002, 91–101.

6. Kumar, R., Novak, J., Raghavan, P., and Tomkins, A. On the bursty evolution of blogspace. In Proceedings of the 12th International World Wide Web Conference (Budapest, Hungary, May 20–24). ACM Press, New York, 2003, 568–576.

7. Lin, J. and Halavais, A. Mapping the blogosphere in America. Presented at the Workshop on the Weblogging Ecosystem at the 13th International World Wide Web Conference (New

York, May 18, 2004); `www.blogpulse.com/papers/`
`www2004linhalavais.pdf`.

8. Newman, M. The structure and function of complex networks. *SIAM Review 45*, 2 (2003).

Ravi Kumar (ravi@almaden.ibm.com) is a research staff member in the Computer Science Principles and Methodologies Department at the IBM Almaden Research Center, San Jose, CA.

Jasmine Novak (jnovak@almaden.ibm.com) is a software engineer on the WebFountain team at the IBM Almaden Research Center, San Jose, CA.

Prabhakar Raghavan (pragh@verity.com) is the chief technology officer of Verity, Inc., Sunnyvale, CA.

Andrew Tomkins (tomkins@almaden.ibm.com) is a manager in the Computer Science Principles and Methodologies Department at the IBM Almaden Research Center, San Jose, CA.

NEW TECHNOLOGIES AND OUR FEELINGS

Romance
on the
Internet

Christine Rosen

When Samuel F. B. Morse sent his first long-distance telegraph message in 1844, he chose words that emphasized both the awe and apprehension he felt about his new device. "What hath God wrought?" read the paper tape message of dots and dashes sent from the U.S. Capitol building to Morse's associates in Baltimore. Morse proved prescient about the potential scope and significance of his technology. In less than a decade, telegraph wires spread throughout all but one state east of the Mississippi River; by 1861, they spanned the continent; and by 1866, a transatlantic telegraph cable connected the United States to Europe.

The telegraph, and later, the telephone, forever changed the way we communicate. But the triumph wrought by these technologies was not merely practical. Subtly and not so subtly, these technologies also altered the range of ways we reveal ourselves. Writing in 1884, James Russell Lowell wondered a bit nervously about the long-term consequences of the "trooping of emotion" that the electric telegraph, with its fragmented messages, encouraged. Lowell and others feared that the sophisticated new media we were devising might alter not just how we communicate, but how we feel.

Rapid improvement in communication technologies and the expansion of their practical uses continue unabated. Today, of course, we are no longer tethered to telegraph or telephone wires for conversation. Cell phones, e-mail, Internet chatrooms, two-way digital cameras—we can talk to anyone, anywhere, including those we do not know and never see. The ethical challenges raised by these new communication technologies are legion, and not new. Within a decade of the invention of the telephone, for example, we had designed a way to wiretap and listen in on the private conversations flourishing there. And with the Internet, we can create new or false identities for ourselves, mixing real life and personal fantasy in unpredictable ways. The "confidence man" of the nineteenth century, with his dandified ruses, is replaced by the well-chosen screen name and false autobiography of the unscrupulous Internet dater. Modern philosophers of technology have studied the ethical quandaries posed by communication technologies—questioning whether our view of new technologies as simply means to generally positive ends is naïve, and encouraging us to consider whether our many devices have effected subtle transformations on our natures.

But too little consideration has been given to the question of how our use of these technologies influences our emotions. Do certain methods of communication flatten emotional appeals, promote immediacy rather than thoughtful reflection, and encourage accessibility and transparency at the expense of necessary boundaries? Do our technologies change the way we feel, act, and think?

Love and E-Mail

There is perhaps no realm in which this question has more salience than that of romantic love. How do our ubiquitous technologies—cell phones, e-mail, the Internet—impact our ability to find and experience love? Our technical devices are of such extraordinary practical use that we forget they are also increasingly the primary medium for our emotional expression. The technologies we use on a daily basis do not merely change the ways, logistically, we pursue love; they are in some cases transforming the way we think and feel about what, exactly, it is we should be pursuing. They change not simply how we find our beloved, but the kind of beloved we hope to find. In a world where men and women still claim to want to find that one special person—a "soul mate"—to spend their life with, what role can and should we afford technology and, more broadly, science, in their efforts?

Love After Courtship

The pursuit of love in its modern, technological guise has its roots in the decline of courtship and is indelibly marked by that loss. Courtship as it once existed—a practice that assumed adherence to certain social conventions, and recognition of the differences, physical and emotional, between men and women—has had its share of pleased obituarists. The most vigorous have been feminists, the more radical of whom appear to take special delight in quelling notions of romantic love. Recall Andrea Dworkin's infamous equation of marriage and rape, or Germaine Greer's terrifying rant in *The Female Eunuch*: "Love, love, love—all the wretched cant of it, masking egotism, lust, masochism, fantasy under a mythology of sentimental postures, a welter of self-induced miseries and joys, blinding and masking the essential personalities in the frozen gestures of courtship, in the kissing and the dating and the desire, the compliments and the quarrels which vivify its barrenness." Much of this work is merely an unpersuasive attempt to swaddle basic human bitterness in the language of female empowerment. But such sentiments have had their effect on our culture's understanding of courtship.

More thoughtful chroniclers of the institution's demise have noted the cultural and technological forces that challenged courtship in the late nineteenth and early twentieth century, eroding the power of human chaperones, once its most effective guardians. As Leon Kass persuasively argued in an essay in *The Public Interest*, the obstacles to courtship "spring from the very heart of liberal democratic society and of modernity altogether." The automobile did more for unsupervised sexual exploration than many technologies in use today, for example, and by twentieth century's end, the ease and availability of effective contraceptive devices, especially the birth control pill, had freed men and women to pursue sexual experience without the risk of pregnancy. With technical advances came a shift in social mores. As historian Jacques Barzun has noted, strict manners gave way to informality, "for etiquette is a barrier, the casual style an invitation."

Whether one laments or praises courtship's decline, it is clear that we have yet to locate a successful replacement for it—evidently it is not as simple as hustling the aging coquette out the door to make way for the vigorous debutante. On the contrary, our current courting practices—if they can be called that—yield an increasing number of those aging coquettes, as well as scores of unsettled bachelors. On college campuses, young men and women have long since ceased formally dating and instead participate in a "hooking up" culture that favors the sexually promiscuous and emotionally disinterested while punishing those intent on commitment. Adults hardly fare better: as the author of a report released in January by the Chicago Health and Social Life Survey told CNN, "on average, half your life is going to be in this single and dating state, and this is a big change from the 1950s." Many men and women now spend the decades of their twenties and thirties sampling each other's sexual wares and engaging in fits of serial out-of-wedlock domesticity, never finding a marriageable partner.

In the 1990s, books such as *The Rules*, which outlined a rigorous and often self-abnegating plan for modern dating, and observers such as Wendy Shalit, who called for greater modesty and the withholding of sexual favors by women, represented a well-intentioned, if doomed, attempt to revive the old courting boundaries. Cultural observers today, however, claim we are in the midst of a new social revolution that requires looking to the future for solutions, not the past. "We're in a period of dramatic change in our mating practices," Barbara Dafoe Whitehead told a reporter for *U.S. News & World Report* recently. Whitehead, co-director of the National Marriage Project at Rutgers University, is the author of *Why There are No Good Men Left*, one in a booming mini-genre of books that offer road maps for the revolution. Whitehead views technology as one of our best solutions—Isolde can now find her Tristan on the Internet (though presumably with a less tragic finale). "The traditional mating system where people met someone in their neighborhood or college is pretty much dead," Whitehead told CBS recently. "What we have is a huge population of working singles who have limited opportunities to go through some elaborate courtship."

Although Whitehead is correct in her diagnosis of the problem, neither she nor the mavens of modesty offer a satisfactory answer to this new challenge. A return to the old rules and rituals of courtship—however appealing in theory—is neither practical nor desirable for the majority of men and women. But the uncritical embrace of technological solutions to our romantic malaise—such as Internet dating—is not a long-term solution either. What we need to do is create new boundaries, devise better guideposts, and enforce new mores for our technological age. First, however, we must understand the peculiar challenges to romantic success posed by our technologies.

Full Disclosure

Although not the root cause of our romantic malaise, our communication technologies are at least partly culpable, for they encourage the erosion of the boundaries that are necessary for the growth of successful relationships. Our technologies enable and often promote two detrimental forces in modern relationships: the demand for total transparency and a bias toward the over-sharing of personal information.

To Google or not to google

With the breakdown of the old hierarchies and boundaries that characterized courtship, there are far fewer opportunities to glean information about the vast world of strangers we encounter daily. We can little rely on town gossips or networks of extended kin for background knowledge; there are far fewer geographic boundaries marking people from "the good part of town"; no longer can we read sartorial signals, such as a well-cut suit or an expensive shoe, to place people as in earlier ages. This is all, for the most part, a good thing. But how, then, do people find out about each other? Few self-possessed people with an Internet connection could resist answering that question with one word: Google. "To google"—now an acceptable if ill-begotten verb—is the practice of typing a person's name into an Internet search engine to find out what the world knows and says about him or her. As one writer confessed in the *New York Observer*, after meeting an attractive man at a midtown bar: "Like many of my twenty-something peers in New York's dating jungle, I have begun to use Google.com, as well as other online search engines, to perform secret background checks on potential mates. It's not perfect, but it's a discreet way of obtaining important, useless and sometimes bizarre information about people in Manhattan—and it's proven to be as reliable as the scurrilous gossip you get from friends."

That is—not reliable at all. What Google and other Internet search engines provide is a quick glimpse—a best and worst list—of a person, not a fully drawn portrait. In fact, the transparency promised by technologies such as Internet search engines is a convenient substitute for something we used to assume would develop over time, but which fewer people today seem willing to cultivate patiently: trust. As the single Manhattanite writing in the *Observer* noted, "You never know. He seemed nice that night, but he could be anyone from a rapist or murderer to a brilliant author or championship swimmer."

In sum, transparency does not guarantee trust. It can, in fact, prove effective at eroding it—especially when the expectation of transparency and the available technological tools nudge the suspicious to engage in more invasive forms of investigation or surveillance. One woman I interviewed, who asked that her name not be revealed, was suspicious that her live-in boyfriend of two years was unfaithful when her own frequent business trips took her away from home. Unwilling to confront him directly with her doubts, she turned to a technological solution. Unbeknownst to him, she installed a popular brand of "spyware" on his computer, which recorded every keystroke he made and took snapshots of his screen every three minutes—information that the program then e-mailed to her for inspection. "My suspicions were founded," she said, although the revelation was hardly good news. "He was spending hours online looking at porn, and going to 'hook-up' chatrooms seeking sex with strangers. I even tracked his ATM withdrawals to locations near his scheduled meetings with other women."

She ended the relationship, but remains unrepentant about deploying surveillance technology against her mate. Considering the amount of information she could find out about her partner by merely surfing the Internet, she rationalized her use of spyware as just one more tool—if a slightly more invasive one—at the disposal of those seeking information about another person. As our technologies give us ever-greater power to uncover more about each other, demand for transparency rises, and our expectations of privacy decline.

The other destructive tendency our technologies encourage is over-sharing—that is, revealing too much, too quickly, in the hope of connecting to another person. The opportunities for instant communication are so ubiquitous—e-mail, instant messaging, chatrooms, cell phones, Palm Pilots, BlackBerrys, and the like—that the notion of making ourselves unavailable to anyone is unheard of, and constant access a near-requirement. As a result, the multitude of outlets for expressing ourselves has allowed the level of idle chatter to reach a depressing din. The inevitable result is a repeal of the reticence necessary for fostering successful relationships in the long term. Information about another person is best revealed a bit at a time, in a give-and-take exchange, not in a rush of overexposed feeling.

The Bachelor

Perhaps the best example of this tendency is reality TV and its spawn. Programs like *The Bachelor* and *The Bachelorette*, as well as pseudo-documentary shows such as *A Dating Story* (and *A Wedding Story* and *A Baby Story*) on The Learning Channel, transform the longings of the human heart into top Nielsen ratings by encouraging the lovelorn to discuss in depth and at length every feeling they have, every moment they have it, as the cameras roll. Romances begin, blossom, and occasionally end in the space of half an hour, and audiences—privy to even the most excruciatingly staged expressions of love and devotion—nevertheless gain the illusion of having seen "real" examples of dating, wedding, or marriage.

On the Internet, dating blogs offer a similar sophomoric voyeurism. One dating blogger, who calls himself Quigley, keeps a dreary tally of his many unsuccessful attempts to meet women, peppering his diary with adolescent observations about women he sees on television. Another dating blogger, who describes herself as an "attractive 35-year old," writes "A Day in the Life of Jane," a dating diary about her online dating travails. Reflecting on one of her early experiences, she writes: "But what did I learn from Owen? That online dating isn't so different from regular dating. It has its pros and cons: Pros—you learn a lot more about a person much more quickly, that a person isn't always what they seem or what you believe them to be, that you have to be really honest with yourself and the person you are communicating with; Cons—uh, same as the pros!"

BadXPartners.com

Successful relationships are not immune to the over-sharing impulse, either; a plethora of wedding websites such as SharetheMoments.com and TheKnot.com offer up the intimate details of couples' wedding planning and ceremonies—right down to the brand of tie worn by the groom and the "intimate" vows exchanged by the couple. And, if things go awry, there are an increasing number of revenge websites such as BadXPartners.com, which offers people who've been dumped an opportunity for petty revenge. "Create a comical case file of your BadXPartners for the whole world to see!" the website urges. Like the impulse to Google, the site plays on people's fears of being misled, encouraging people to search the database for stories of bad exes: "Just met someone new? Think they are just the one for you? Well remember, they are probably someone else's X .... Find out about Bill from Birmingham's strange habits or Tracy from Texas' suspect hygiene. Better safe than sorry!"

Like the steady work of the wrecking ball, our culture's nearly-compulsive demand for personal revelation, emotional exposure, and sharing of feelings threatens the fragile edifice of newly-forming relationships. Transparency and complete access are exactly what you want to avoid in the early stages of romance. Successful courtship—even successful flirtation—require the gradual peeling away of layers, some deliberately constructed, others part of a person's character and personality, that make us mysteries to each other.

Among Pascal's minor works is an essay, "Discourse on the Passion of Love," in which he argues for the keen "pleasure of loving without daring to tell it." "In love," Pascal writes, "silence is of more avail than speech…there is an eloquence in silence that penetrates more deeply than language can." Pascal imagined his lovers in each other's physical presence, watchful of unspoken physical gestures, but not speaking. Only gradually would they reveal themselves. Today such a tableau seems as arcane as Kabuki theater; modern couples exchange the most intimate details of their lives on a first date and then return home to blog about it.

"It's difficult," said one woman I talked to who has tried—and ultimately soured on—Internet dating. "You're expected to be both informal and funny in your e-mails, and reveal your likes and dislikes, but you don't want to reveal so much that you appear desperate, or so little so that you seem distant." We can, of course, use these technologies appropriately and effectively in the service of advancing a relationship, but to do so both people must understand the potential dangers. One man I interviewed described a relationship that began promisingly but quickly took a technological turn for the worse. After a few successful dates, he encouraged the woman he was seeing, who lived in another city, to keep in touch. Impervious to notions of technological etiquette, however, she took this to mean the floodgates were officially open. She began telephoning him at all hours, sending overly-wrought e-mails and inundating him with lengthy, faxed letters—all of which had the effect not of bringing them closer together, which was clearly her hope, but of sending him scurrying away as fast as he could. Later, however, he became involved in a relationship in which e-mail in particular helped facilitate the courtship, and where technology—bounded by a respect on the part of both people for its excesses—helped rather than harmed the process of learning about another person. Technology itself is not to blame; it is our ignorance of its potential dangers and our unwillingness to exercise self-restraint in its use that makes mischief.

The Modern-Day Matchmaker

Internet dating offers an interesting case study of these technological risks, for it encourages both transparency and oversharing, as well as another danger: it insists that we reduce and market ourselves as the disembodied sum of our parts. The woman or man you might have met on the subway platform or in a coffee shop—within a richer context that includes immediate impressions based on the other person's physical gestures, attire, tone of voice, and overall demeanor—is instead electronically embalmed for your efficient perusal online.

And it is a booming business. Approximately forty percent of American adults are single, and half of that population claims to have visited an online dating site. Revenue for online dating services exceeded $302 million in 2002. There is, not surprisingly, something for the profusion of tastes: behemoth sites such as Match.com, Flirt.com, Hypermatch.com, and Matchmaker.com traffic in thousands of profiles. Niche sites such as Dateable.org for people with disabilities, as well as sites devoted to finding true love for foot fetishists, animal lovers, and the obese, cater to smaller markets. Single people with religious preferences can visit Jdate.com (for Jewish dates), CatholicSingles.com, and even HappyBuddhist.com to find similarly-minded spiritual singles. As with any product, new features are added constantly to maintain consumer interest; even the more jaded seekers of love might quail at Match.com's recent addition to its menu of online options: a form of "speed dating" that offers a certain brutal efficiency as a lure for the time-challenged modern singleton.

A Case Study

One woman I interviewed, an attractive, successful consultant, tried online dating because her hectic work schedule left her little time to meet new people. She went to Match.com, entered her zip code, and began perusing profiles. She quickly decided to post her own. "When you first put your profile on Match.com," she said, "it's like walking into a kennel with a pork chop around your neck. You're bombarded with e-mails from men." She received well over one hundred solicitations. She responded to a few with a "wink," an electronic gesture that allows another person to know you've seen their profile and are interested—but not interested enough to commit to sending an e-mail message. More alluring profiles garnered an e-mail introduction.

After meeting several different men for coffee, she settled on one in particular and they dated for several months. The vagaries of online dating, however, quickly present new challenges to relationship etiquette. In her case, after several months of successful dating, she and her boyfriend agreed to take their Match.com profiles down from the site. Since they were no longer "single and looking," but single and dating, this seemed to make sense—at least to her. Checking Match.com a week later, however, she found her boyfriend's profile still up and actively advertising himself as available. They are still together, although she confesses to a new wariness about his willingness to commit.

The rapid growth of Internet dating has led to the erosion of the stigma that used to be attached to having "met someone on the Internet" (although none of the people I interviewed for this article would allow their names to be used). And Internet dating itself is becoming increasingly professionalized—with consultants, how-to books, and "expert" analysis crowding out the earlier generation of websites. This February, a "commonsense guide to successful Internet dating" entitled *I Can't Believe I'm Buying This Book* hit bookstores. *Publishers Weekly* describes the author, an "Internet dating consultant," as "a self-proclaimed online serial dater" who "admits he's never sustained a relationship for more than seven months," yet nevertheless "entertainingly reviews how to present one's self on the Web."

Designing the "dating software" that facilitates online romance is a science all its own. *U.S. News & World Report* recently described the efforts of Michael Georgeff, who once designed software to aid the space shuttle program, to devise similar algorithms to assess and predict people's preferences for each other. "Say you score a 3 on the introvert scale, and a 6 on touchy-feely," he told a reporter. "Will you tend to like somebody who's practical?" His weAttract.com software purports to provide the answer. On the company's website, amid close-ups of the faces of a strangely androgynous, snuggling couple, weAttract—whose software is used by Match.com—encourages visitors to "Find someone who considers your quirks adorable." Fair enough. But the motto of weAttract—"Discover your instinctual preferences"—is itself a contradiction. If preferences are instinctual, why do you need the aid of experts like weAttract to discover them?

We need them because we have come to mistrust our own sensibilities. What is emerging on the Internet is a glorification of scientific and technological solutions to the challenge of finding love. The expectation of romantic happiness is so great that extraordinary, scientific means for achieving it are required—or so these companies would have you believe. For example, Emode, whose pop-up ads are now so common that they are the Internet equivalent of a swarm of pesky gnats, promotes "Tickle Matchmaking," a service promising "accurate, Ph.D. certified compatibility scores with every member!"

EHarmony.com

The apotheosis of this way of thinking is a site called eHarmony.com, whose motto, "Fall in love for the right reasons," soothes prospective swains with the comforting rhetoric of professional science. "Who knew science and love were so compatible?" asks the site, which is rife with the language of the laboratory: "scientifically-proven set of compatibility principles," "based on 35 years of empirical and clinical research," "patent-pending matching technology," "exhaustively researched" methods, and "the most powerful system available." As the founder of eHarmony told *U.S. News & World Report* recently, we are all too eager—desperate, even—to hustle down the aisle. "In this culture," he said, "if we like the person's looks, if they have an ability to chatter at a cocktail party, and a little bit of status, we're halfway to marriage. We're such suckers." EHarmony's answer to such unscientific mating practices is a trademarked "Compatibility Matching System" that promises to "connect you with singles who are compatible with you in 29 of the most important areas of life." As the literature constantly reminds the dreamy romantics among us, "Surprisingly, a good match is more science than art."

EHarmony's insistence that the search for true love is no realm for amateurs is, of course, absurdly self-justifying. "You should realize," their website admonishes, after outlining the "29 dimensions" of personality their compatibility software examines, "that it is still next to impossible to correctly evaluate them on your own with each person you think may be right for you." Instead you must pay eHarmony to do it for you. As you read the "scientific" proof, the reassuring sales pitch washes over you: "Let eHarmony make sure that the next time you fall in love, it's with the right person."

In other words, don't trust your instincts, trust science. With a tasteful touch of contempt, eHarmony notes that its purpose is not merely dating, as it is for megasites such as Match.com. "Our goal is to help you find your soul mate." Four pages of testimonials on the website encourage the surrender to eHarmony's expertise, with promises of imminent collision with "your" soul mate: "From the minute we began e-mailing and talking on the phone, we knew we had found our soul mate," say Lisa and Darryl from Dover, Pennsylvania. "It took some time," confessed Annie of Kansas City, Missouri, "but once I met John, I knew that they had made good on their promise to help me find my soul mate."

Some observers see in these new "scientific" mating rituals a return to an earlier time of courtship and chaperoned dating. *Newsweek* eagerly described eHarmony as a form of "arranged marriage for the digital age, without the all-powerful parents," and Barbara Dafoe Whitehead argues that the activities of the Internet love seeker "reflect a desire for more structured dating." Promoters of these services see them as an improvement on the mere cruising of glossy photos encouraged by most dating sites, or the unrealistic expectations of "finding true love" promoted by popular culture. Rather, they say, they are like the chaperones of courtship past—vetting appropriate candidates and matching them to your specifications.

Not Real Matchmakers

As appealing as this might sound, it is unrealistic. Since these sites rely on technological solutions and mathematical algorithms, they are a far cry from the broader and richer knowledge of the old-fashioned matchmaker. A personality quiz cannot possibly reveal the full range of a person's quirks or liabilities. More importantly, the role of the old-fashioned matchmaker was a social one (and still is in certain communities). The matchmaker was embedded within a community that observed certain rituals and whose members shared certain assumptions. But technological matchmaking allows courtship to be conducted entirely in private, devoid of the social norms (and often the physical signals) of romantic success and failure.

Finally, most Internet dating enthusiasts do not contend with a far more alarming challenge: the impact such services have on our idea of what, exactly, it is we should be seeking in another person. Younger men and women, weaned on the Internet and e-mail, are beginning to express a preference for potential dates to break down their vital stats for pre-date perusal, like an Internet dating advertisement. One 25-year old man, a regular on Match.com, confessed to *U.S. News & World Report* that he wished he could have a digital dossier for all of his potential dates: "It's, 'OK, here's where I'm from, here's what I do, here's what I'm looking for. How about you?'" One woman I spoke to, who has been Internet dating for several years, matter-of-factly noted that even a perfunctory glance at a potential date's résumé saves valuable time and energy. "Why trust a glance exchanged across a crowded bar when you can read a person's biography in miniature before deciding to strike up a conversation?" she said. This intolerance for gradual revelation increases the pace of modern courtship and erodes our patience for many things (not the least of which is commencement of sexual relations). The challenge remains the same—to find another person to share your life with—but we have allowed the technologies at our disposal to alter dramatically, even unrecognizably, the way we go about achieving it.

The Science of Feeling

This impulse is part of a much broader phenomenon—the encroachment of science and technology into areas once thought the province of the uniquely intuitive and even the ineffable. Today we program computers to trounce human chess champions, produce poetry, or analyze works of art, watching eagerly as they break things down to a tedious catalog of techniques: the bishop advances, the meter scans, the paintbrush strokes across the canvas. But by enlisting machines to do what once was the creative province of human beings alone, we deliberately narrow our conceptions of genius, creativity, and art. The *New York Times* recently featured the work of Franco Moretti, a comparative literature professor at Stanford, who promotes "a more rational literary history" that jettisons the old-fashioned reading of texts in favor of statistical models of literary output. His dream, he told reporter Emily Eakin, "is of a literary class that would look more like a lab than a Platonic academy."

Yet this "scientific" approach to artistic work yields chillingly antiseptic results: "Tennyson's mind is to be treated like his intestines after a barium meal," historian Jacques Barzun noted with some exasperation of the trend's earlier incarnations. Critic Lionel Trilling parodied the tendency in 1950 in his book, *The Liberal Imagination*. By this way of thinking, Trilling said, the story of Romeo and Juliet is no longer the tragic tale of a young man and woman falling in love, but becomes instead a chronicle of how, "their libidinal impulses being reciprocal, they activated their individual erotic drives and integrated them within the same frame of reference."

What Barzun and Trilling were expressing was a distaste for viewing art as merely an abstraction of measurable, improvable impulses. The same is true for love. We can study the physiological functions of the human heart with echocardiograms, stress tests, blood pressure readings, and the like. We can examine, analyze, and investigate ad nauseum the physical act of sex. But we cannot so easily measure the desires of the heart. How do you prove that love exists? How do we know that love is "real"? What makes the love of two lovers last?

There is a danger in relying wholly or even largely on science and technology to answer these questions, for it risks eroding our appreciation of the ineffable things—intuition and physical attraction, passion and sensibility—by reducing these feelings to scientifically explained physiological facts. Today we catalog the influence of hormones, pheromones, dopamine, and serotonin in human attraction, and map our own brains to discover which synapses trigger laughter, lying, or orgasm. Evolutionary psychology explains our desire for symmetrical faces and fertile-looking forms, even as it has little to tell us about the extremes to which we are taking its directives with plastic surgery. Scientific study of our communication patterns and techniques explains why it is we talk the way we do. Even the activities of the bedroom are thoroughly analyzed and professionalized, as women today take instruction from a class of professionals whose arts used to be less esteemed. Prostitutes now run sex seminars, for example, and a recent episode of Oprah featured exotic pole dancers who teach suburban housewives how to titillate their husbands by turning the basement rec room into a simulacrum of a Vegas showgirl venue.

Science continues to turn sex (and, by association, love and romance) into something quantifiable and open to manipulation and solution. Science and technology offer us pharmaceuticals to enhance libido and erectile function, and popular culture responds by rigorously ranking and discussing all matters sexual—from the disturbingly frank talk of female characters on Sex and the City to the proliferation of "blind date" shows which subject hapless love-seekers to the withering gaze of a sarcastic host and his viewing audience. "What a loser!" cackled the host of the reality television program Blind Date, after one ignominious bachelor botched his chance for a good night kiss. "The march of science," Barzun wrote, "produces the feeling that nobody in the past has ever done things right. Whether it's teaching or copulation, it has 'problems' that 'research' should solve by telling us just how, the best way."

Test-Driving Your Soul Mate

Why is the steady march of science and technology in these areas a problem? Shouldn't we be proud of our expanding knowledge and the tools that knowledge gives us? Not necessarily. Writing recently in the journal Techné, Hector Jose Huyke noted the broader dangers posed by the proliferation of our technologies, particularly the tendency to "devalue the near." "When a technology is introduced it, presumably, simply adds options to already existing options," he writes. But this is not how technology's influence plays out in practice. In fact, as Huyke argues, "as what is difficult to obtain becomes repeatedly and easily accessible, other practices and experiences are left out—they do not remain unchanged." The man who sends an e-mail to his brother is not merely choosing to write an e-mail and thus adding to his range of communication options; he is choosing not to make a phone call or write a letter. A woman who e-mails a stranger on the Internet is choosing not to go to a local art exhibit and perhaps meet someone in person. "Communications technologies indeed multiply options," says Huyke. "An increase in options, however, does not imply or

even serve an advance in communications." Technologies, in other words, often make possible "what would otherwise be difficult to obtain." But they do so by eliminating other paths.

Personal Ads

Love and genuine commitment have always been difficult to attain, and they are perhaps more so today since it is the individual bonds of affection—not family alliance, property transfer, social class, or religious orthodoxy—that form the cornerstone of most modern marriages. Yet there remains a certain grim efficiency to the vast realm of love technologies at our disposal. After a while, perusing Internet personal ads is like being besieged by an aggressive real estate agent hoping to unload that tired brick colonial. Each person points out his or her supposedly unique features with the same banal descriptions ("adventurous," "sexy," "trustworthy") never conveying a genuine sense of the whole. Machine metaphors, tellingly, crop up often, with women and men willingly categorizing themselves as "high maintenance" or "low maintenance," much as one might describe a car or small kitchen appliance. As an executive of one online dating service told a reporter recently, "If you want to buy a car, you get a lot of information before you even test-drive. There hasn't been a way to do that with relationships."

But we have been "test driving" something: a new, technological method of courtship. And although it is too soon to deliver a final verdict, it is clear that it is a method prone to serious problems. The efficiency of our new techniques and their tendency to focus on people as products leaves us at risk of understanding ourselves this way, too—like products with certain malfunctioning parts and particular assets. But products must be constantly improved upon and marketed. In the pursuit of love, and in a world where multiple partners are sampled before one is selected, this fuels a hectic culture of self-improvement—honing the witty summary of one's most desirable traits for placement in personal advertisements is only the beginning. Today, men and women convene focus groups of former lovers to gain critical insights into their behavior so as to avoid future failure; and the perfection of appearance through surgical and non-surgical means occupies an increasing amount of people's time and energy.

Our new technological methods of courtship also elevate efficient communication over personal communication. Ironically, the Internet, which offers many opportunities to meet and communicate with new people, robs us of the ability to deploy one of our greatest charms—nonverbal communication. The emoticon is a weak substitute for a coy gesture or a lusty wink. More fundamentally, our technologies encourage a misunderstanding of what courtship should be. Real courtship is about persuasion, not marketing, and the techniques of the laboratory cannot help us translate the motivations of the heart.

The response is not to retreat into Luddism, of course. In a world where technology allows us to meet, date, marry, and even divorce online, there is no returning to the innocence of an earlier time. What we need is a better understanding of the risks of these new technologies and a willingness to exercise restraint in using them. For better or worse, we are now a society of sexually liberated individuals seeking "soul mates"—yet the privacy, gradualism, and boundaries that are necessary for separating the romantic wheat from the chaff still elude us.

Alchemy

Perhaps, in our technologically saturated age, we would do better to rediscover an earlier science: alchemy. Not alchemy in its original meaning—a branch of speculative philosophy whose devotees attempted to create gold from base metals and hence cure disease and prolong life—but alchemy in its secondary definition: "a power or process of transforming something common into something precious." From our daily, common interactions with other people might spring something precious—but only if we have the patience to let it flourish. Technology and science often conspire against such patience. Goethe wrote, "We should do our utmost to encourage the Beautiful, for the Useful encourages itself." There is an eminent usefulness to many of our technologies—e-mail and cell phones allow us to span great distances to communicate with family, friends, and lovers, and the Internet connects us to worlds unknown. But they are less successful at encouraging the flourishing of the lasting and beautiful. Like the Beautiful, love occurs in unexpected places, often not where it is being sought. It can flourish only if we accept that our technologies and our science can never fully explain it.

Christine Rosen is a senior editor of *The New Atlantis* and resident fellow at the Ethics and Public Policy Center. Her book *Preaching Eugenics: Religious Leaders and the American Eugenics Movement* was just published by Oxford University Press.

From Virtual Communities to Smart Mobs

Wearable computers and phones offer a transparent future. Should we trust it?

by Lane Jennings

$\mathcal{S}$ome futures have a way of coming back.

Well before the Internet took off, Howard Rheingold, former editor of *The Whole Earth Review* and author of *The Virtual Community* (Perseus, 1993), envisioned computer bulletin boards evolving into planet-spanning voluntary networks of individuals, formed for commercial exchange and mutual support—in short, a radical transformation of society, where "neighbors" would be people who shared common goals and interests, not geography.

Now, a decade later, social transformation via the machine seems at hand once more. In his latest book, *Smart Mobs*, Rheingold explores how handheld wireless phones, linked to the Internet and capable of transmitting images and printed text, can radically transform the way groups and individuals relate to one another and get things done.

Cell phones have already changed the lives of many teenagers and young adults in Scandinavia and Japan—technologically advanced urban centers where wireless phones and service are relatively cheap but privacy at home and places to hang out in public are often hard to find. Cell phones made it possible for kids to congregate, exchange news, and share personal experiences in real time without physically meeting. As the phenomenon spreads, Rheingold notes, many young cell phone users come to consider anyone they are connected to by phone as being present, and even prefer phone exchanges to live conversation.

As psychologists discovered when computer chat was new, text messaging often feels somehow safer than speaking aloud. Adolescents in particular are liable to express emotions and share intimate details of their lives more freely in printed messages—even to relative strangers—than talking face to face with adult advisers, family members, or close friends.

Wireless phone connections can help individuals make sense of what is going on around them, even in chaotic situations. One dramatic example occurred on September 11, 2001, when passengers aboard United Flight 93, using their cell phones, learned about the other hijackings and decided to take action. In January of that same year, relayed waves of cell phone text messages guided thousands of otherwise unconnected citizens to join the spontaneous street demonstrations that forced Philippine President Joseph Estrada from office.

From Portable to Wearable

Handheld wireless is only one technology driving the social revolution Rheingold sees ahead. Other elements include computers and video gear designed to be worn like clothing or jewelry, and microchips, equipped with sensors and communications devices, built into cars, buildings, and objects of every kind.

Already, a few individuals make small computers and video cameras routine parts of the clothing they wear every day. One such self-styled cyborg (cybernetic organism) is Steve Mann, a professor at the University of Toronto. Since the early 1990s, when he was a graduate student at MIT's Media Lab, Mann has worn ever more refined versions of a computer helmet equipped with video cameras. Video feed from these cameras—the only images that reach Mann's eyes—are all filtered through computer circuits. This enables him to mediate reality on command—for example, by making selected objects stand out from their background or disappear entirely from view. Walking the streets of Manhattan, Mann can instruct his helmet cameras to blank out all the billboards or placards he approaches, immunizing himself to commercial advertising.

Mann considers his computer helmet self-defense against what he sees as ever-greater intrusions by government and business on his personal space and freedom. He distrusts efforts to create a smart environment, where buildings and machines have built-in microchips that detect the presence of human beings and react to commands or even anticipate them. Rather than accept such a world of electronic control, with "cameras and microphones everywhere in the environment watching and listening to us in order to be 'helpful,'" Mann wants tomorrow's wearable computers to function exclusively under the wearer's control, in order to "create and foster independence and community interaction."

One example of what Mann calls community interaction, also known as peer-to-peer (P2P) computing, is Napster, the notorious Web site that helped users exchange recorded music over the Internet without paying royalties. Another is SETI@home, the project by which PC users permit remote access to otherwise inactive circuits in their machines. Linking up small amounts of unused processing capacity from thousands—even millions—of individual PCs creates the functional equivalent of a supercomputer. And this enables radio astronomers engaged in the search for extraterrestrial intelligence to sift rapidly through mountains of raw data for possible evidence of advanced civilizations among the stars.

But P2P applications go far beyond looking for messages from outer space and trading hit recordings. P2P has become a cause—a seemingly all-win approach to problem solving, where many individuals cooperate in projects that cost each one very little. Because the cost is low, and so little conscious effort is required, people feel free to risk impulsively enlisting in projects of many kinds, whether to potentially benefit humanity or just make someone smile.

Millions of people allow the use of the background space on their personal computers for advancing cancer research, finding prime numbers, forecasting weather, designing synthetic molecules to produce new drugs, and generally tackling problems and simulations so complex that researchers could never attempt them before. But this sort of cooperation requires trust. From blind dates to global diplomacy, people tend to cooperate only when they have reason to believe they can trust each other.

Commercial transactions on the Internet at major sites like eBay are made easier and less risky by the use of buyer/seller rating systems that establish a personal track record or reputation for participants based on their past behavior. One more important aspect of the social revolution that Rheingold looks for in the next few years is that wireless cell phones and wearable computer gear will give people meeting for the first time face-to-face anywhere in the world power to instantly verify each other's identity and check one another's background using online sources.

Transparency, Trust, And Treachery

Providing a reasonable basis for trust in real-world situations could go far toward making a true global village out of what has come to seem more like an overcrowded global subway car crammed with mutually suspicious and menacing strangers.

But the impending era of wireless computing and communication has its dark side, too. Rheingold's own ambivalent feelings are revealed in his book's title. "Smart mobs" suggests both new opportunities for strangers to increase their collective intelligence by rapidly exchanging information and the ominous new power that anonymous masses on the move, linked by mobile communications and able to tap the vast resources of the Internet, will gain for committing violent and disruptive acts.

That swarm of eager adolescents in the streets of Tokyo or Stockholm chatting and texting on their cell phones could soon just as easily be a gang of toughs in Hamburg or New York City stalking potential victims to mug or rape. The same technology that helped Philippine crowds turn out en masse to topple a corrupt politician in 2001 also helped violent demonstrators evade police and coordinate acts of vandalism two years earlier in Seattle during protests against the World Trade Organization. The line between democracy in action and irresponsible disruption is unclear at best, and new technologies are never guaranteed to serve the public interest.

Permitting outside access to memory space in your computer can involve the harmless swapping of tunes among music fans, but it can also enable unscrupulous hackers or criminals to secretly store their stashes of pornography or stolen business files on your hard drive without your knowledge. The same distributed processing through multiple PCs that helps legitimate scientists distinguish radio signals from background radiation can just as easily be used by terrorists to help design a bomb or calculate the most destructive way to spread biotoxins through a city subway system. The smart devices promised for the coming generation of appliances and buildings to ensure comfort and convenience in our homes and public places could conceivably be turned into an inescapable net of surveillance cameras and hidden microphones directed by some Big Brother agency in government or business, or perhaps simply vulnerable to savvy hackers and voyeurs.

Howard Rheingold and Steve Mann offer alternate ways of dealing with the social implications of new wireless technology. Mann sees wearable computers as a kind of body armor—an equalizer that individuals can use to defend their independence in an age of big government and giant corporations. Rheingold looks rather to the opportunity that wireless communication offers for an individual to locate and cooperate with others to achieve desirable outcomes great and small.

Both men underscore the need for caution. However fast wireless Internet and P2P communications spread, we clearly need to do some serious futures thinking. As we enact new laws and set binding universal standards for cell phones, distributed processing, wearable computers, and smart buildings, governments and private citizens alike will need to clarify their vision of a desirable future world.

Now more than ever, technology has the potential to dictate the pace and define the norms of daily life for decades to come. It may be hard for many of us to imagine a world where mutual benefit beats out greed as the driving force determining individual behavior. But the potential for such change does exist, and if consumers and regulators alike begin to ask more questions and become more proactively involved in setting goals and limits, there is still time to shape a humane and sustainable communications environment.

Source: *Smart Mobs: The Next Social Revolution* by Howard Rheingold. Perseus Publishing. 2002. 266 pages. $26. Visit www.smartmobs.com for background on the book, related articles, and links to a host of other sites and sources.

Originally published in the May/June 2003 issue of *The Futurist*. Used with permission from the World Future Society, 7910 Woodmont Avenue, Suite 450, Bethesda, MD 20814. Telephone: 301/656-8274; Fax: 301/951-0394; http://www.wfs.org. © 1999.

Making Meaning: As Google Goes, So Goes the Nation

By GEOFFREY NUNBERG

YOU don't get to be a verb unless you're doing something right. Do a Google search on "ford," for example, and the first batch of results includes the pages for the Ford Motor Company, the Ford Foundation, the Betty Ford Center, Harrison Ford and Gerald R. Ford—all good guesses at what a user would be looking for, particularly considering that Google estimates its index holds more than 16 million pages including the word.

Google now conducts 55 percent of all searches on the World Wide Web. People have come to trust the service to act as a digital bloodhound. Give it a search term to sniff, and it disappears into the cyber wilderness, returning a fraction of a second later with the site you were looking for in its mouth.

A high place in Google's rankings can have a considerable value for commercial sites. Some go so far as to pay other sites to link to them to raise their standing.

And a high Google ranking can also have a lot of clout in the marketplace of ideas. It seems to confer "ownership" on a particular word or phrase—deciding, in effect, who gets to define it. It's easy to read these results as reflecting the consensus of an extended Internet community, with the power to shape opinion and events. As James F. Moore, a fellow at the Berkman Center for Internet and Society at Harvard Law School, wrote in an article on his blog posted March 31, the Internet has become a "shared collective mind" that is coming to figure as a "second superpower."

Sometimes, though, the deliberations of the collective mind seem to come up short. Take Mr. Moore's use of "second superpower" to refer to the Internet community. Not long ago, an article on the British technology site The Register (theregister.com) accused Mr. Moore of "googlewashing" that expression—in effect, hijacking the the expression and giving it a new meaning.

It had actually originated in a Feb. 17 article by Patrick E. Tyler in The New York Times that referred to the United States and world public opinion as the "two superpowers on the planet." Shortly after that, the phrase "second superpower" was adopted by organizations like Greenpeace and was used by Kofi Annan, the United Nations secretary general, to refer to antiwar opinion. But Mr. Moore's article was linked to by a number of bloggers sympathetic to his ideas, and quickly became the first hit returned when someone searches Google for "second superpower."

There was nothing underhanded in Mr. Moore's ability to co-opt ownership of the phrase in the rankings; it follows from the way Google works. Its algorithms rank results both by looking at how prominently the search terms figure in the pages that include them and by taking advantage of what Google calls "the uniquely democratic nature of the Web" to estimate the popularity of a site. It gives a higher rank to pages that are linked to by a number of other pages, particularly if the referring pages themselves are frequently linked to. (The other major search engines have adopted similar techniques.)

When you search for a common item like "ford" or "baseball," the engines naturally give the highest rankings to major sites that are linked to by hundreds or thousands of other pages. But when searches are more specific—whether "second superpower" or "Sinatra arrangers"—the rankings will mirror the interests of the groups that aggregate around particular topics: the bloggers, experts, hobbyists and, often, the crackpots.

Not long ago a German friend of mine went to Google for help in refuting a colleague who maintained that American authorities engineered the attacks of Sept. 11, 2001, citing as evidence, among other things, the delay in sending American fighter jets aloft that morning. My friend did searches on a number of obvious strings, like "9/11 scramble jets intercept." But almost all the pages that came up were the work of conspiracy theorists, with titles like "Guilty for 9-11: Bush, Rumsfeld, Myers" and "Pentagon surveillance videos—where are the missing frames?"

"To judge from the Google results, there's plenty of evidence for a conspiracy and little to the contrary," my friend said.

That's the sort of result that often leads people to complain that the Web is full of junk or that the search engines aren't working as they should. From the standpoint of the search engines, however, this is all as it should be. The beauty of the Web, after all, is that it enables us to draw on the expertise of people who take a particular interest in a topic and are willing to take the trouble to set down what they think about it. In that sense, the Web is a tool that enables people who have a life to benefit from the efforts of those who don't.

In the marketplace of ideas, an Internet search engine is becoming a dominant voice.

But given the "uniquely democratic" nature of the Web, it shouldn't be surprising that the votes reported by the search engines have many of the deficiencies of plebiscites in the democracies on the other side of the screen. On topics of general interest, the rankings tend to favor the major sites and marginalize the smaller or newer ones; here, as elsewhere, money and power talk.

And when it comes to more specialized topics, the rankings give disproportionate weight to opinions of the activists and enthusiasts that may be at odds with the views of the larger public. It's as if the United Nations General Assembly made all its decisions by referring the question to whichever nation cares most about the issue: the Swiss get to rule on watchmaking, the Japanese on whaling.

THE outcomes of Google's popularity contests can be useful to know, but it's a mistake to believe they reflect the consensus of the "Internet community," whatever that might be, or to think of the Web as a single vast colloquy—the picture that's implicit in all the talk of the Internet as a "digital commons" or "collective mind."

Seen from a Google's eye view, in fact, the Web is less like a piazza than a souk—a jumble of separate spaces, each with its own isolated chatter. The search engines cruise the alleyways to listen in on all of these conversations, locate the people who are talking about the subject we're interested in, and tell us which of them has earned the most nods from the other confabulators in the room. But just because someone is regarded as a savant in the barbershop doesn't mean he'll pass for wise with the people in the other stalls.

Geoffrey Nunberg, a Stanford linguist, is heard regularly on NPR's "Fresh Air" and is the author of "The Way We Talk Now."

Conquered by Google: A Legendary Literature Quiz

NOAM COHEN

THE Author, Author quiz in the Times Literary Supplement has pleasurably tortured British readers for many years, inducing them to put their intellectual self-respect at risk in return for minor celebrity among literary scholars and pedants. But now, Google and other Internet search engines can help even the virtually illiterate find many of the answers.

Each week, Author, Author offers three thematically linked, stunningly obscure quotations and asks who wrote them. Bernard Knox, the eminent scholar of ancient Greek, writing in The New York Review of Books in 1995, happily called the quiz an "infuriating competition," concocted by "fiends" who "ransacked their authors' lesser-known works for texts innocent of such clues as proper names, dates, or allusions to historical events."

Q. Can any arcane quotation be identified?
A. Almost.

The first contest, on Nov. 23, 1979, had no winner—a prophetic result. The £10 prize was shared by the two competitors who came closest: J. W. Thirsk of Headington, Oxford, and G. K. Pechey of St. Albans. (The prize is now £25, or about $50.)

Twenty-five years later, textual scholarship, like almost everything else, has been colonized by Google and the collective wisdom of the World Wide Web. Plug part of the quotation into the search engine, and it's likely a variety of Web sites can place it in its proper context. Not every T.L.S. contest yields completely to the power of the search engine (to see where Google failed, look at the right-hand column of test questions), but rarely does the Web fail to identify at least one, and more often two, of the three quotations.

Look, for example, at the Author, Author published on April 8: A patch of Latin, a soupçon of French and some English iambic verse. "Res gerere et captos ostendere civibus hostis . . . ," comes from the letters of Horace; "Je me fais veix, j'ai soixante ans ..." is a line in the song "Carcasonne," by George Brassens; and "the finger-post says Mamble . . ." is a line from a poem by John Drinkwater. Five minutes of Internet searching was all it took.

A typical quiz rarely gets more than 50 or 60 correct entries, said Mick Imlah, the editor responsible for Author, Author since the early 1990's. Usually there are significantly fewer. Mr. Imlah did say in an e-mail message that "there are two regular entrants I've got down, fairly or not, as Google players—one in New York, one in Oxford—because they enter so often, and because they don't seem to know the answers they give, if you see what I mean."

Meanwhile, Mr. Imlah said that the people involved with Author, Author "have shut their eyes to the whole Google phenomenon and carried on as if it made no difference."

Each week, the Author, Author quiz in the *Times Literary Supplement* provides obscure selections of prose or poetry and asks readers to name the texts in which they appear.

Author, Author quiz of Feb. 11, 2005, solved using Google searches:

1. "She who raised these questions in D-D's mind was occupied in gambling: not in the open air under a southern sky, tossing coppers on a ruined wall, with rags about her limbs; but in one of those splendid resorts which the enlightenment of ages has prepared for the same species of pleasure at a heavy cost of gilt mouldings, dark-toned colour and chubby nudities, all correspondingly heavy-forming a suitable condenser for human breath belonging, in great part, to the highest fashion, and not easily procur-able to be breathed in else-where in the like proportion, at least by persons of little fashion."
   Daniel Deronda, by George Eliot.

2. "Inside, D-D pours himself some more / And holds a cinder to his clay with tongs / Belching out smoke."
   "The Card-Players," by Philip Larkin. D-D is Dirk Dogstoerd.

3. "An' they're hangin' D- D- in the mornin'."
   "Danny Deever," by Rudyard Kipling.

Recent Author, Author quotations that Google searches could not identify:

From Jan. 28:
"Yahya!"
"Wazi jahm?"
"Ah didadidacti, didadidacti."
"Kataka mukha?
"Ah mawardi, mawardi."
"Jelly."
"Valmouth," by Ronald Firbank

From Feb. 18:
"Say what you will, 'the naked feet' is disgusting more so in Scotland than in Germany, from the tawdry or squalid appearance of the bare-footed // In Germany there is a uniform Dress in the Class that go bare-footed & they always have their Shoes in their Hands or on their Heads / In Scotland Cabin Gowns, white Petticoat, all tawdry fine, & naked Legs, & naked Splaidfeet, & gouty ancles."
   Notebooks of Samuel T. Coleridge, Aug. 18, 1803.

From March 11:
"Halford has been with me this morning gossiping (which he likes); he gave me an account of the discovery of Charles I's head, to which he was directed by Wood's account in the 'Athenae Oxonienses.' . . . He says Charles's head was exactly as Vandyke had painted him."
   Memoirs of Charles Greville, July 20, 1831.

UNIT 5

Societal Institutions: Law, Politics, Education, and the Military

Unit Selections

Key Points to Consider

- The Overview to this unit mentions that civil institutions were overlooked in the excitement after the collapse of the former Soviet Union. Find on the Internet and read Francis Fukuyama's essay, "The End of History." Do you agree with his arguments? Does computing have any role to play in the development of civil institutions?
- File sharing software has been much in the news lately? Do you agree with the recording industry's position that downloading music is copyright infringement?
- What parts of the Internet are necessary to regulate? Who should regulate them?
- At least one state has replaced polling places with mail-in voting. The next step would be to replace mail-in voting with the Internet. How would this affect democracy in the United States?
- Several articles in the unit are about technologically-based warfare. Use the Internet to find out if commentators have anything to say about the difficulty of managing complex weaponry in outposts around the globe.

Student Website

www.mhcls.com/online

Internet References

Further information regarding these websites may be found in this book's preface or online.

ACLU: American Civil Liberties Union
   http://www.aclu.org

Information Warfare and U.S. Critical Infrastructure
   http://www.twurled-world.com/Infowar/Update3/cover.htm

Living in the Electronic Village
   http://www.rileyis.com/publications/phase1/usa.htm

Patrolling the Empire
   http://www.csrp.org/patrol.htm

United States Patent and Trademark Office
   http://www.uspto.gov/

World Intellectual Property Organization
   http://www.wipo.org/

After the collapse of the former Soviet Union, many Americans believed that democracy and a market economy would develop in short order. Commentators seemed to have taken a cue from Francis Fukuyama's imposingly entitled essay, "The End of History," that appeared in *The National Interest* in 1989. "What we may be witnessing," he wrote, "is not just the end of the Cold War, or the passing of a particular period of post-war history, but ...the universalization of Western liberal democracy as the final form of human government." Fukuyama, deputy director of the State Department's planning staff in the elder Bush administration, hedged a bit. He was careful to argue that the victory of liberal capitalism "has occurred primarily in the realm of ideas or consciousness and is as yet incomplete in the real or material world."

We have grown wiser since those heady times. The events of September 11 showed Americans, in the most brutal fashion, that not everyone shares their values. More importantly, the political and economic chaos that has been so much a part of Russian life for the past decade, has led many commentators to conclude that liberal democracy and a market economy require more than "the realm of ideas or consciousness." They need, above all else, institutions that govern political and economic relationships. They require mechanisms for business contracts and land use, courts to adjudicate disputes, government agencies to record titles and regulate resources, and, not just a mechanism but a tradition of representative government. In a phrase, democracy and a market economy require the institutions of civil society.

We in the United States and Western Europe have long traditions of civil society, in some cases reaching back hundreds of years. The French sociologist, Emile Durkheim (1858-1917), hoped that as traditional societies gave way to urban industrial societies, rule by contract and law would provide the glue for social cohesion. To a very large extent this has been the case in the United States. The room in which I am writing is part of a house that sits on a small piece of property that belongs to me. I am confident that my title to this property is part of the public record. Were someone to appear on my doorstep with a claim to my property, a procedure exists to adjudicate our dispute. If I do not personally understand the rule, I can hire a lawyer, a specialist in civil procedures, to make my case before an independent judiciary.

But the rapid introduction of information technology over the past decade has proven problematic for the orderly resolution of disputes. It has been difficult for legislators to formulate laws for a set of relationships—those mediated by a computer—that are not well understood. Even if laws are successfully enacted, their existence does not guarantee compliance, especially in the absence of an enforcement mechanism. As Jonathan Band points out in "The Copyright Paradox," "the problem with piracy is not the inadequacy of existing laws, but high cost of enforcing any law against the large universe of infringers." Still, the computer and recording industry tries. The Digital Millennium Copyright Act of 1998 provides severe penalties for both piracy and for publicizing ways to circumvent security mechanisms. Despite difficulties in enforcing such transgressions, industry is pushing its control over its products a step further. Edward Tenner reports ("You Bought It. Who Controls It?") that "Senator Fritz Hollings (D-South Carolina) has introduced a bill that would require all electronic devices...to have built into them some sort of ... security software that would limit users' rights to inspect and modify them."

The civil institution most sacred in any democracy is the right to vote. Until the Florida voting disaster during the 2000 Presidential Election, most Americans paid little attention to how votes were actually cast and counted. The emphasis throughout American history has always been on extending the franchise, not the nuts and bolts of counting the votes. Now, prodded by the federal government that is spending billions to improve the voting process, many jurisdictions are moving to computerized voting systems. This all seemed fine until William O'Dell, CEO of one of the largest suppliers of touch-screen voting machines, composed a letter inviting friends to a Republican fund raiser. The letter included these lines: "I am committed to helping Ohio deliver its electoral votes to the president next year." To be fair, computer scientists are finding more wrong with computer-based voting than the political loyalties of Mr. O'Dell. Two articles in this unit look at some of the issues surrounding electronic voting machines.

Another social institution vital to a democracy is education. The contribution of computing—if not always uncontroversial—has been substantial. From educational software, to wired college campuses, to Internet-mediated distance education, computing has been a part of education since the introduction of personal computers in the early eighties. If you throw in mass standardized testing, an enterprise nearly unthinkable without computers, computing has been a part of American education since the fifties. Two articles in this unit take a look at the use of the Internet on college campuses. It might surprise contemporary students to know that the kind of Internet college-shopping that all college-bound high schoolers engage in is a recent phenomenon. Recent or not, competition among colleges to produce flashy websites is intense. Another locus of intensity is the president's office. Never an easy job, leading a college in the age of the Internet requires sifting through email, reading blogs, and fending off criticism whose volume would be inconceivable without networked computers.

Strictly speaking, the military is not part of civil society. Yet since the U.S. military is constitutionally mandated to be under civilian control, we can consider it a civil institution without stretching the meaning of the term terribly. As of this writing (August, 2005), the war in Iraq is front page news every day. On the eve of war, the media focused its attention on the changing U.S. military. *BusinessWeek*, in a pair of articles, examines changes in the U.S. military. "Point, Click...Fire," lets us see the new military technology in action. The authors explain that "in many cases, the same servers, satellites and fiber-optic networks, as well as software that major corporations routinely use, can be pressed into service to link images from Global Hawk unmanned aircraft with commanders and shooters on the ground." The closing words of "The Doctrine of Digital War," seem eerily prescient: "And now, as high-tech dreams meet low-tech tactics in the barren landscape of Iraq, [computer-based weaponry] is facing its first big test."

THE Copyright Paradox

Fighting Content Piracy in the Digital Era

by Jonathan Band

The Internet has given rise to a puzzling copyright paradox. To hear the recording industry tell it, the copyright world as we know it is coming to an end. Between Gnutella and Napster-like sites, fans can easily exchange music files over the Internet, sending CD sales plummeting. Copyright law is powerless to halt the onslaught of Internet piracy, which will soon remove any economic incentive for creative activity.

At the same time, libraries, universities, and content user groups, voicing their helplessness before ever-strengthening copyright legal protections, insist that the content provider community is better positioned than ever to eliminate traditional user privileges. Historically, for example, the fair use doctrine has allowed academic users to reproduce without payment parts of copyrighted works for purposes such as criticism and classroom use. But, say these users, the new Uniform Computer Information Transactions Act (UCITA), adopted by the National Conference of Commissioners on Uniform State Laws in 1999, and the technological measures protected by the 1998 Digital Millennium Copyright Act (DMCA) will soon enable content providers to create the "pay-per-use" environment they have long sought.

Who's Right?

At first blush, it would seem that the content providers and the content users—the Recording Industry Association of America and the libraries and universities (hereafter the library community)—can't both be right. We can't possibly be living in both the best of times and the worst of times for copyright protection. One of these two communities must be exaggerating.

Indeed, the available facts suggest that the recording industry may be overstating the harm caused by Napster and Gnutella. Although CD sales in record stores near university campuses have fallen (college students are among the biggest users of Napster and Gnutella), CD sales overall have grown 8 percent since last year. The group 'N Sync recently broke the one-week record for CD sales, ringing up more than 2.5 million. Beyond these hard numbers, anecdotal evidence suggests that people sample music on Napster and then buy the higher-quality CD if they like what they hear. So Napster-like sites may actually spur CD sales.

Moreover, the content community seems to be on a winning streak. The recording industry secured a preliminary injunction against Napster (at this writing, the injunction was stayed pending appeal). A judge imposed the largest amount of statutory damages in copyright history—more than $100 million—on MP3.com. The major sports leagues shut down IcraveTV. And the motion picture studios won an injunction against DeCSS, software that unlocks the encryption protecting DVDs.

Still, there is no question that the Internet facilitates piracy by allowing the widespread dissemination of lawful copies with no degradation in quality. Further, technologies like Gnutella do not require a central server, as does Napster or a typical pirate web site, making it hard to detect infringers. In short, the Internet does seem to pose an increasing threat to providers of copyrighted content.

At the same time, technological measures like encryption or copy controls encoded in software will prevent a teacher from making digital copies of an article for classroom use, and the DMCA has banned devices that enable users to circumvent such measures. The net effect will be less fair use, and the de facto extension of the copyright term, as works remain technologically protected long after the copyright expires. (This assumes, of course, that the DMCA will survive the constitutional challenges now being mounted against it.)

> # The content community fears too little copyright protection; the library community fears too much. How can this be?

Similarly, UCITA validates the enforceability of shrink-wrap licenses (which appear on software packages) and click-on licenses (which appear on screen and which users must click to install software or access a web site) and will accelerate their use to prohibit fair use by contract. The circuit courts are split as to whether such license terms are preempted by federal law, and it may take years for the Supreme Court to resolve the issue. And if the Supreme Court decides that federal law does not preempt such license terms, licensees will be at the mercy of the licensors.

Which brings us back to the copyright paradox: both the content community and the library community appear to have legitimate, yet opposite, concerns about the future of copyright in the digital era. The content community fears too little protection, the library community too much. How can this be?

Of Ends and Means

The paradox is rooted in a mismatch between the stated ends of the content community and the means employed to reach them. The content industries have responded to the threat of Internet piracy by pushing for more legislation, such as the DMCA and UCITA. But although new legislation is the most expedient response to the threats posed by new technologies, it probably will not hinder Internet piracy because the problem with piracy is not the inadequacy of existing laws, but the high cost of enforcing any law against the large universe of infringers. Each of the hundreds of millions of computers attached to the Internet is a potential distributor of unlawful copies. Although of limited use against this large universe of potential individual pirates,

the new legislation ensnares the libraries—the most public of our institutions.

The following examples demonstrate the disparate impact of UCITA and the DMCA. A software firm markets a CD-ROM subject to a shrink-wrap license that prohibits the further distribution of the CD-ROM or its contents. If a consumer acquires the CD-ROM, copies it onto his hard drive, and e-mails it to a dozen friends, the publisher is unlikely to find out about the breach of contract, much less prosecute it. If, however, a library acquires the CD-ROM and lends it out in accordance with copyright's first-sale doctrine, the publisher almost certainly will sue the library for breach of contract. While the shrink-wrap license (validated by UCITA) cannot stop infringing activity by the consumer, it can stop otherwise legitimate lending activity by the library.

Similarly, the DMCA probably would not discourage a college student from finding a circumvention utility somewhere on the Internet and using it to elude the technological protection on his favorite CD so that he could make the sound recordings on it available to his friends. But the DMCA would prevent a library from acquiring the utility through legitimate channels to make a preservation copy permitted under Section 108 of the Copyright Act. The DMCA flatly bans almost all circumvention devices, even those capable of noninfringing uses. Put differently, the DMCA would do little to deter unlawful conduct, but much to deter conduct that is otherwise lawful.

In short, libraries (and other high-profile entities such as universities and large corporations) are likely to obey the laws and contractual terms that apply to them

because they are law-abiding institutions and because they know they probably would be sued if they did not follow the law. In contrast, individual infringers are not likely to obey the law because they are not law-abiding and because they know they are unlikely to get caught. Seen in this light, the copyright paradox makes sense. Because the new laws do not meaningfully address Internet piracy, the content community remains vulnerable to piracy, but libraries are kept from engaging in historic library activities. The new laws also interfere with legitimate corporate activities. UCITA, for example, allows a software company to prohibit a business from selling copies of software when it sells a subsidiary even though copyright's first-sale doctrine permits the transfer.

The logical next question is whether this discontinuity between means and ends, and the resultant collateral damage, is inadvertent or intentional. The charitable view is that the content community really believes that this legislation will help reduce piracy and has no intention of stifling library and educational activities. A more cynical perspective is that the content community pursued this legislation in part because it allowed the rollback of fair use, first-sale, and other user privileges the content community has always opposed. Indeed, conspiracy theorists believe that the libraries were the real target of the legislation, and Internet piracy served as a convenient pretext. Although generally I am not a conspiracy theorist, I am reminded of the following aphorism: "Just because you're paranoid doesn't mean they're not out to get you." ∎

You bought it.
Who controls it?

A LEADING THINKER ON THE IRONIES OF TECHNOLOGY ARGUES THAT MACHINES
MEANT TO LIBERATE US ARE INSTEAD PUTTING CONSUMERS IN A STRAITJACKET—
AND STIFLING VITAL INNOVATION IN THE PROCESS.

BY EDWARD TENNER

The personal-computing revolution began with a promise: after decades of submission to centralized mainframes, ordinary users were now in control. Buttoned-up IBM loosened its collar, opened its new PC to accommodate hardware and software from a variety of suppliers, and even bought its operating system from a couple of Harvard University dropouts. To reinforce this message, IBM chose as its marketing emblem a look-alike of Charlie Chaplin—timeless hero of the harried underdog. It was a clever choice, and not inappropriate: the PC and other machines like it really did confer upon users a degree of control over information never before available. Twenty years later, technology industries are still promising us autonomy and independence.

But that promise is falling flat. Asserting an unprecedented degree of control over their goods, even once they are in the customers' hands, technology producers are moving to circumscribe the freedom that technology users have long taken for granted. The same powerful trends that have brought leaps in performance—ubiquitous microprocessors, cheap digital storage, and virtually free data transmission—are making possible new ways for technology makers to control users' behavior. These developments reek more of Big Brother than the Little Tramp.

It's not that companies have ill intent. Manufacturers are offering hardware and code they claim will release the full potential of information technology: promoting creativity and productivity while making computing and the Internet secure and reliable at last. Their products address real problems—from brand counterfeiting and piracy, which cost billions, to malfunctioning equipment. But despite the benign intent, some features built into

new generations of devices, like the Greek infiltrators in the belly of the Trojan horse, provide openings for intrusion and even conquest. Call it the Trojan mouse.

Measures to control behavior can depend on either accountability or incapacitation. Think of automotive traffic control. Until recently, most communities tried to control speeding with radar-equipped patrol cars. More recently, some towns have shifted to a strategy of incapacitation: they are making speeding physically difficult with increasing use of "traffic-calming" devices such as speed bumps. Police radar is a technology of accountability; it needs the courts to be effective and can be defeated at least some of the time by sensitive detectors. Traffic-calming structures, by contrast, are technologies of incapacitation: they limit passively what people can do with their vehicles.

Technology makers increasingly prefer incapacitation as a strategy of control. The software industry, for example, once used a double standard for enforcing its licenses: companies vigorously regulated software usage by commercial establishments while pretty much letting individual consumers do as they pleased. But as the distinction between home and office blurs, consumers now find themselves wrestling with the sort of constraints once intended mainly for corporate users. Microsoft is leading the way by beginning to license its Windows operating system for household use in much the way it deals with businesses: each machine must have its own paid upgrade to the next version. Users do have the right to continue running older versions of Windows, but they may find that new programs they want or need run only on the latest release. The result is "forced migration," to use a stark metaphor dating from the mainframe era.

MEASURES TO CONTROL BEHAVIOR CAN DEPEND EITHER ON ACCOUNTABILITY (THINK TRAFFIC COPS) OR INCAPACITATION (SPEED BUMPS). MAKERS OF TECHNOLOGY ARE TURNING MORE AND MORE TO THE STRATEGY OF INCAPACITATION.

Other technology and entertainment companies are also cracking down through incapacitation. Instead of paying more patent and copyright lawyers to take alleged infringers to court, they are modifying their products so that the user is physically barred from using them in unsanctioned ways. The traffic cop is giving way to the speed bump.

Information Lockdown

In the early days of the PC software industry, elaborate anti-copying systems blocked users from duplicating programs for use by friends or colleagues. By the 1990s, consumer resistance had restricted copy protection to niche products such as computer-assisted-design programs. But now, companies are reimposing such limits. Here again, technology producers are displaying a taste for incapacitation.

Yes, copyright owners have tried using accountability—they took Napster to court and brought the file-sharing service down with a lawsuit. But that was a victory in one battle of what has become a widening war; a new file-sharing network seems to rise from the ashes of each defeated one. Individual songs and entire movies are now routinely available on the Web weeks before their official release. While the music industry is beginning to introduce its own download sites online and, soon, in retail stores, it is also alarmed by peer-to-peer exchange among friends. Soon, even entry level personal computers will have the capability to record CDs and DVDs, and enough disk space for hours of music and video. The consumer, in other words, is becoming a low-cost rival manufacturer and, through Internet file sharing, an essentially zero-cost rival distributor. The strategy of accountability, it seems, is losing the war.

Companies have already begun to limit movements of data. Sony, a leading audio and video company and copyright owner, may be offering a preview of controls to come. Some of its computers already use proprietary software to encrypt digital music, limiting the number of times a song can be downloaded ("checked out," in Sony's parlance) to an external device. After three downloads, a song must be "checked in" to the original device before it can be checked out again. While the aim is protection of copyrighted material, the program makes it difficult to duplicate any CD at all—including one that contains music created and recorded by the owner.

Such schemes will of course have little effect against the greatest economic threats to the copyright holders: the pirate factories of eastern Europe and Asia. These illicit operations can pay technical experts to defeat protection, or bribe insiders for unprotected copies of source material. Whether intentionally or not, therefore, Sony is targeting the controls at the less serious losses from sharing among friends.

Why should a legitimate owner of a CD or DVD object to such copy protection? These schemes do, after all, permit backups and second copies for use in other machines, such as portable or automobile CD players. But the controls can also degrade the quality of the product. Even some electrical engineers who believe that sophisticated copy protection is undetectable to most listeners acknowledge that because music and videos already make use of data compression algorithms that take advantage of the limits of human senses, a few people with especially discerning ears may indeed be able to tell the difference. Moreover, copy control often works by weakening the error correction schemes in the stored data—an alteration that may wash out subtleties of performance or make discs less scratch resistant.

Last October, *Audio Revolution* magazine reported that DVD players constructed without the normally mandated series of internal conversions between digital and analog formats—circuits included by industry agreement purely to foil piracy—produce "stunning" images compared to those from conventional players. The British organization Campaign for Digital Rights has denounced copy protection as an unacceptably blunt weapon against piracy: determined outlaws can still find computers that will allow the CDs to be ripped for MP3s, while honest consumers receive what many audio and video enthusiasts consider musically compromised products.

Despite the complaints, past experience has shown that what technology *can* control, the law *will* control—or at least try to. That's exactly what has happened here, as constraints on data copying draw strength and legitimacy from the force of the Digital Millennium Copyright Act of 1998. This legislation provides harsh penalties not only for piracy but also for publicizing ways to circumvent security. So far, however, the law appears not to have slowed the diffusion of control-evading techniques: the anarchical impulse of technology users is not easily suppressed.

Security vs. Freedom

In the most thorough form of incapacitation, technology makers are building their products to resist any form of alteration once they leave the factory. The paradox here is that while many technology users resent such control, they also need it. A computer network that

THE TAMPERPROOFING THAT SOME TECHNOLOGY COMPANIES ARE NOW PUTTING IN PLACE THREATENS A TRADITION OF USER-CENTERED INNOVATION. INCAPACITATING DESIGNS WILL SLAM THE DOOR ON THESE VITAL SUPERTINKERERS.

is truly open, for example, is also dangerously vulnerable to attack by viruses.

Not surprisingly, these days the computer industry is giving higher priority to security than openness. Take, for example, the controversial Microsoft project originally known as Palladium and recently renamed Next-Generation Secure Computing Base for Windows. This effort involves the development of a set of secure features for a new generation of computers. The goal: let users such as banks communicate in ways that prevent disclosure of information to unauthorized persons, using stronger hardware as well as software protection. The system would protect the privacy of medical and financial data far more effectively than today's security software, and Microsoft insists that it will not restrict the rights of most computer owners; machines will be shipped with the new capabilities turned off.

A computer built on the new specification could run existing software like any other. But the Secure Computing Base could give Microsoft or other vendors the power to disable third-party software on their customers' computers, if they believe it circumvents rights management. Vendors could also detect and disable user hardware modifications that, as judge, jury, and executioner, they deem a threat to the security of their programs. As evidence of this intent, critics point to phrases in the user license agreements of Microsoft's Windows Media Player that seem to allow the program's security updates to disable other programs. "The keys will be kept in tamper-resistant hardware rather than being hidden in software," contends Ross Andersen, a University of Cambridge computer scientist. "There will be lots of bugs and workarounds that people discover, but eventually they will get fixed up, and it will be progressively harder to break."

Paul England, a software architect at Microsoft familiar with the system, considers such fears unwarranted. There is, he says, "no a priori remote control" that it will impose or let others impose on a user's applications. Copyright owners would not, he insists, be able to use the system to inactivate other programs that could capture their data and store it in different file formats.

This blanket of security can smother as well as protect. Web businesses and software vendors will have the option of offering their products only to "trusted" machines—that is, those in which the protection system has been activated. Most content companies would probably begin to restrict compatibility to trusted machines. Downloading a magazine article or a song, for example, might require a machine in which the Microsoft technology was present and activated.

Such measures can prevent hackers and unethical companies from stealing personal information and hijacking personal machines for nefarious purposes. But tamperproofing technology also allows companies, while flying the banner of fighting piracy, to take steps that degrade the performance that law-abiding consumers get from their computers.

Critics argue that Microsoft's Secure Computing Base comes at too high a price. Princeton computer scientist Edward W. Felten warns that if technology vendors "exploit Palladium fully to restrict access to copyrighted works, education and research will suffer." Scientists, he points out, must be able to inspect and modify electronic technology, just as automotive engineers and designers must be able to take vehicles apart and tweak components.

Indeed, the kinds of tamperproofing now being put in place threaten the individual tinkering upon which so much innovation is based. They would deprive people of their long-standing right to improve on products they lawfully own—even when they are not violating copyrights or creating hazards. Such user-centered innovation has a long history in the United States. Henry Ford's Model T and tractor, for example, were made for resourceful country people who constantly found new uses for them: once the drive axle was lifted and a wheel removed, the hub could drive tools and farm equipment. It was a mini power station on wheels, its variations and applications limited only by the user's imagination.

Some contend that the freedom users have to modify a system and its software is worth the risk. As John Gilmore, a cofounder of the Electronic Frontier Foundation, a Washington, DC-based civil-liberties organization, has written, "Be very glad that your PC is insecure—it means that after you buy it, you can break into it and install what software you want. What *you* want, not what Sony or Warner or AOL wants."

The Cost of Control

Legislation now pending would make tamperproofing the law of the land. Senator Fritz Hollings (D-South Carolina) has introduced a bill that would require all electronic devices—from computers to Furby toys—to have built into them some form of rights-management or security software that would limit users' rights to inspect and modify them. According to Hollings's office, the measure is intended to prod the electronics and media industries to come to an agreement on security standards.

Some information technology experts remain sanguine. Even if the Hollings bill becomes law, they contend, competition and market pressures will preserve people's freedom to modify the technological products they buy. Mark Granovetter, a professor of sociology at Stanford University, says that a massive public backlash would prevent Microsoft from implementing the Secure Computing Base.

Others, however, are more pessimistic. Jonathan Zittrain, a professor of information law at Harvard, foresees the introduction of "closed, appliance-like devices as substitutes for the general PC." Such appliances would be more reliable than PCs but would offer their owners less control. Zittrain fears the end of what will be seen, in retrospect, as a fleeting era of computer freedom. "A diverse and vibrant community of independent software developers and vendors," he says, may have been "a transitory phenomenon of the 1980s and 1990s."

If Zittrain's prophecy proves correct, the locked-down landscape of technology will disappoint its architects. First, incapacitation will not eliminate the costs of accountability but rather shift them. A regime of constraints depends on laws banning technologies that would defeat or circumvent the control schemes, and those bans will need to be enforced. Second, protection may degrade data, if only subtly, and introduce bugs that may stain a brand's reputation and compromise its market share.

Most seriously, forms of control that work through incapacitation will undermine the chaotic, dynamic society that made the personal-computing revolution possible in the first place. Powerless against determined pirates, they would strike hardest at creative customers, such as the chip-modifying fans who have breathed new life into moribund computer games—the very people whose ideas could help develop new generations of lucrative products. As MIT management professor Eric von Hippel wrote in 2001 in the *Sloan Management Review*, "innovations that only a few leaders use today may be in general demand tomorrow"—especially, he says, if early adopters "have a chance to innovate, to learn by doing, and to develop the general utility of their innovations." Incapacitating designs will slam the door in the faces of these vital supertinkerers.

Incapacitation would also limit the academic training of companies' future technical staff. Freedom to tinker—defined by Felten as "your freedom to understand, discuss, repair, and modify the technological devices that you own"—benefits technology industries most of all. Even the film industry needs young people who have had free access to the nuts and bolts of digital graphics and special effects, and I'll bet that Microsoft doesn't make its young Xbox game-programming recruits sign an affidavit that they have never violated an end-user license agreement. New hardware security is manifestly a good idea for servers with sensitive information. There is a good case for new levels of protection, like the Microsoft scheme, for these vulnerable sites. But if they extend incapacitation too far, the builders of the Trojan mouse may find themselves caught in their own trap.

Edward Tenner is author of Why Things Bite Back: Technology and the Revenge of Unintended Consequences *and the forthcoming* Our Own Devices: The Past and Future of Body Technology *(Knopf).*

Electronic Voting Systems:
the Good, the Bad, and the Stupid

Is it true that politics and technology don't mix?

Barbara Simons

As a result of the Florida 2000 election fiasco, some people concluded that paper ballots simply couldn't be counted. Instead, paperless computerized voting systems (known as direct recording electronic systems, or DREs) were touted as the solution to "the Florida problem." Replacing hanging chads with 21st century technology, proponents claimed, would result in accurate election counts and machines that were virtually impossible to rig. Furthermore, with nothing to hand-count and no drawn-out recounts to worry about, computerized voting systems were expected to enable the reporting of results shortly after the polls had closed.

Many election officials loved the idea, believing the new machines would also prove cheaper and more reliable than the old systems. That enthusiasm was reinforced by the promise of nearly $4 billion in federal funds for the purchase of DREs, courtesy of the Help America Vote Act (HAVA), passed in 2002.

The idea of computerized voting systems drew advocates from many sectors. Among the most outspoken advocates of paperless DREs is Jim Dickson, vice-president of the American Association of People with Disabilities. The League of Women Voters has also lobbied on behalf of paperless DREs (though the national office retracted its support when members revolted at the recent LWV convention).

Yet now, just two years after the passage of HAVA, voter-verifiable paper trails are being demanded by numerous public interest groups, computing professionals, and members of Congress. Where did things go wrong?

For starters, software for electronic voting machines is proprietary, the certification testing process is both secret and incomplete, and the test results are secret. (Note to system designers: this is *not* a good formula for building trust.) To cap things off, the COTS (commercial off-the-shelf) software contained in voting systems is not examined in any of the testing, simply because FEC (Federal Election Commission) guidelines don't require it.

For years, prominent computer security experts have been arguing that paperless DRE machines present major security problems, including buggy software and the risk of malicious code affecting the outcome of an election. But the warnings of experts such as Rebecca Mercuri (http://www.notablesoftware.com/evote.html) and Peter Neumann (http://www.csl.sri.com/users/neumann/neumann.html#5) went largely unheeded by election officials and the public until David Dill created a petition (http://www.verifiedvoting.org/index.asp) calling for voter-verifiable audit trails. The core idea behind the Dill petition is that voters should be able to verify that their ballots have been correctly recorded; also, it should be possible to conduct a meaningful recount. To avoid the risk that the machine prints the correct result while storing an incorrect result in computer memory, it should be possible to manually recount some number of randomly selected paper ballots as a check on the machine-generated results.

A FEW HORROR STORIES

Because of the secrecy surrounding almost every aspect of e-voting—along with a lack of public incident reporting—independent computing technologists can provide only limited analyses of problems related to electronic voting system hardware, software, testing, security, and human factors. Nonetheless, evidence of problems is widespread. A few examples follow.

In January 2004, a special election was held in Broward County, Florida. Only one contest was included on the ballot. Yet, of the 10,844 votes cast on ES&S (Election Systems & Software) paperless touch-screen voting machines, 134 were . . . for no one at all. Since the winning candidate won by only 12 votes, people understandably wondered what had become of those 134 votes; there was no way of telling if some had been lost by the computer. County officials are now calling for paper ballots.

In November 2003, in Boone County, Indiana, more than 144,000 votes were cast—even though Boone County contains fewer than 19,000 registered voters, and, of those, only 5,532 actually voted. The county clerk stated the problem had been caused by a "glitch in the software." Updated results then were obtained that were consistent with the number of people who had actually voted, and the public was assured that the new electronic tally was accurate. Still, because the county used paperless MicroVote DREs, it was impossible to verify independently that the updated results were indeed correct.

> An attacker with access to the source code would have the ability to modify voting and auditing records.

When the polls opened in Hinds County, Mississippi, in November 2003, voters arrived to find that the WIN-vote DREs were down. Worse yet, no paper ballots were available. By mid-morning, some machines were still down. Voters complained about waiting in long lines and how they had been required to complete makeshift paper ballots—some being nothing more than scraps of paper—without adequate privacy. At 8 p.m., voters were still standing in line. One report claimed the machines had overheated. Subsequently, the Mississippi State Senate declared the results in that district invalid and scheduled a new election.

SERIOUS SECURITY CONCERNS

Diebold, one of the major DRE vendors, has been at the center of a political maelstrom because of intemperate remarks made in 2003 by its CEO, Walden O'Dell. But that little PR problem pales in comparison to the security problems uncovered when Bev Harris (http://www.scoop.co.nz/mason/stories/HL0302/S00036.htm) announced in February 2003 that she had discovered Diebold voting machine software on an open FTP Web site.

Computer science professors Aviel Rubin (Johns Hopkins University) and Dan Wallach (Rice University), and their students Tadayoshi Kohno and Adam Stubblefield, subsequently analyzed some of that software and published their findings in a paper, sometimes referred to as the "Hopkins paper," presented at the May 2004 IEEE Symposium on Security and Privacy (http://avirubin.com/vote/analysis/index.html). One of the more shocking revelations made in that paper is that Diebold uses a single DES key to encrypt all of the data on a storage device. Consequently, an attacker with access to the source code would have the ability to modify voting and auditing records.

Perhaps even more surprising, Diebold had been warned in 1997 about its sloppy key management by

Douglas Jones, a professor of computer science at the University of Iowa and a member of the Iowa Board of Examiners for Voting Machines and Electronic Voting Equipment (http://www.cs.uiowa.edu/~jones/voting/dieboldftp.html):

> [N]either the technical staff nor salespeople at Global Election Systems [purchased by Diebold in 2001] understood cryptographic security. They were happy to assert that they used the federally approved data encryption standard, but nobody seemed to understand key management; in fact, the lead programmer to whom my question was forwarded, by cellphone, found the phrase key management to be unfamiliar and he needed explanation. On continued questioning, it became apparent that there was only one key used, companywide, for all of their voting products. The implication was that this key was hard-coded into their source code!

Because of the security issues raised in the Hopkins paper, the State of Maryland, which had just committed to purchasing Diebold DREs, commissioned a study of Diebold machines by Science Applications International Corporation (SAIC). The SAIC report (http://www.dbm.maryland.gov/dbm_publishing/public_content/dbm_search/technology/toc_voting_system_report/votingsystemreportfinal.pdf) is a very fast read, since only about one-third of it was made public. (According to Frank Schugar, project manager for SAIC, the report was redacted by Maryland, not by SAIC. The Electronic Privacy Information Center has submitted a public records request to obtain the unredacted version.) Even the limited amount of information that was released in the report, however, is quite damning. For example, the report states that the Diebold system is so complicated that even if all of the problems were fixed, there still could be security risks because of poorly trained election officials.

In November 2003, the Maryland Department of Legislative Services commissioned yet another study of Diebold machines by RABA Technologies (http://www.raba.com/press/TA_Report_AccuVote.pdf). The Trusted Agent report, released in January 2004, based on a "red team" effort to hack Diebold voting systems, revealed physical security problems such as the use of identical keys on security panels covering PCMCIA and other sockets on the machines—as well as locks that could be picked in a few seconds.

Unfortunately, when DRE vendors tout the virtues of DREs to election officials, they tend to gloss over security issues related to short- and long-term storage of the machines, as well as machine access control before and after elections.

Meanwhile, the State of Ohio, which had been considering the purchase of Diebold DREs for the entire state, hired Compuware to test hardware and software and InfoSentry to conduct a security assessment. The Compuware study uncovered yet another hardwired password, this time involving the supervisor's card, used to start up each voting machine on Election Day as well as to terminate the voting process at the end of the day. When the card is inserted into the DRE, the election official must enter the same password or PIN that has been hardwired into the card—but not into the voting software. Consequently, anyone who is able to obtain a supervisor's card, or who manages to create a fake card with a different password, would be able to conduct a denial-of-service attack by prematurely halting the voting machines, thereby denying some voters the opportunity to vote.

A SOFTWARE BUG THAT PREVENTS AUDITS

Concerns have also been raised about ES&S, another major player in the DRE market (altogether, DREs and optical scan voting systems manufactured by Diebold and ES&S are expected to count something between two-thirds and 80 percent of the ballots cast in the November 2004 election; see the attachments in http://www.election dataservices.com/EDSInc_DREoverview.pdf for a detailed breakdown by machine type). That's because a software bug had corrupted the audit log and vote image report in ES&S machines used in Miami-Dade County and many other parts of the country. (For a detailed discussion of the ES&S bug, see http://www.cs. uiowa.edu/~jones/voting/miami.pdf.)

An internal memo written in June 2003 by Orlando Suarez, division manager of the county's enterprise technology services department, describes a discrepancy in the internal auditing mechanism of the ES&S machines that make the audit reports "unusable for the purpose that we were considering (audit an election, recount an election, and if necessary, use these reports to certify an election)."

The audit log contained results for some nonexistent machines, and it also failed to report all the results for the machines that were in operation. According to Doug Jones, there were actually two bugs. One—triggered by a low battery condition—caused corruption in the event log; the second caused the election management system to misread the machine's serial number in the face of this corruption. Although the true vote count was not affected, the problems uncovered are symptomatic of the kinds of anomalies that are not tested for under the current certification process. "As of midsummer," explained Jones, "the State of Florida has approved a fix to the two bugs that caused this problem and, in the pre-election testing conducted on August 13, the event records extracted from compact flash cards showed correct reports of low battery conditions without any corruption of serial numbers. Curiously, it was a member of the Miami-Dade [Election Reform] Coalition who found this evidence as

she went over printouts of the event logs generated from the compact flash cards."

On July 27, 2004, the Miami-Dade Election Reform Coalition announced that audit data it had requested revealed that computer crashes had deleted all the election results from the September 2002 gubernatorial race in Miami-Dade, as well as from several more recent municipal elections. It appeared that no backups had been made, leading to speculation that the loss of the ballot images could be a violation of Florida law regarding the retention of ballots. (Amazingly, Miami-Dade officials chose to ignore a memo sent before the crashes occurred in which Cathy Jackson of the county's audit and management services department warned of the lack of backups and suggested that all data should be burned to CD-ROMs following each election.)

After spending a few embarrassing days trying to explain how election officials might have lost critical voting records, Miami-Dade County Elections Supervisor Constance Kaplan announced that her secretary had located a computer disk containing the missing data in the conference room next to her office. According to Jones, "The disk was a CD-R in a file folder. The county had only begun making archival CD-R copies of the data after the county audit and management department suggested that they do so that summer. Apparently, although this was being done, there was as yet no institutional memory of where these disks were being put."

CERTIFICATION FLAWS

The first FEC standard for electronic voting machines, issued in 1990, was replaced in 2002 (http://www.fec.gov/pages/vssfinal/vss.html). Still, many voting systems in use today were certified according to the 1990 standards.

Machines are tested and certified by three private companies—Ciber, Wyle, and SysTest—which are referred to as ITAs (independent testing authorities). The ITAs themselves are certified by the National Association of State Election Directors, but are not subject to any government oversight. Vendors pay for all testing.

One of the bizarre aspects of the certification process is that it distinguishes between firmware and software, with *firmware* being defined as the software that runs in the actual voting machines, while *software* is used to refer to the code used by the election management system. Wyle certifies only firmware, while Ciber certifies only software. SysTest certifies overall systems.

Rather than checking the software for security flaws and attacking the software to see if it can be compromised, the ITAs limit their tests strictly to items specifically required by the FEC standards. Particularly prominent among these are control-flow requirements, with Do-While (False) constructs and the use of intentional exceptions used as GoTos being explicitly prohibited. The 2002 FEC standards also call for "effective password management," but the phrase is not defined. We can certainly infer from the Diebold results, however, that no one is checking to see if encryption keys have been hardwired into the code. The testing also fails to check for exceptions, and there are no provisions for the inspection of COTS code.

Then there's the matter of BDFs (ballot definition files), which contain the candidates and issues information for each election. (For a detailed discussion of BDFs, see http://www.votersunite.org/info/BallotProgramming.pdf.) Clearly, these files are critical to the whole electronic voting process, yet they are never independently inspected by an ITA. Also, pre-election BDF testing is not routine in many jurisdictions.

When BDF errors do occur—leading, for example, to votes for one candidate being credited to a different candidate—they can be detected with optical scan voting systems simply because anomalous computer-reported results can be discovered through manual recounts of paper ballots. With paperless DREs, however, there is no way to perform such a recount.

ALTERNATIVE VOTING MACHINE DESIGNS

Diebold, Sequoia, ES&S, and Hart InterCivic are the major manufacturers of paperless DREs. Most DREs use touch screens as inputs, though Hart InterCivic uses a dial for candidate selection. DREs also can be equipped with earphones and various devices, typically handheld, that allow voters with vision impairments to vote independently. DREs do not allow voters to select more candidates than allowed (overvotes), and they alert voters to any omitted votes (undervotes). DREs also allow voters to review their ballots before submitting them (second-chance voting).

DREs that produce voter-verifiable paper ballots. Accu-Poll and Avante produce DRE voting systems that print out ballots that voters can check to ensure that an accurate paper record of their votes exists. Avante also manufactures a model that prints optical scan ballots that sighted voters can mark, along with an "accessible" optical voting system that allows vision-impaired voters to print out optical scan ballots marked to reflect their choices.

Optical scan voting machines. Besides avoiding many of the security problems associated with paperless DREs, optical scan systems are less expensive. Typically, these systems require the voter to mark the ballot in much the same way that students taking standardized tests make computer-readable marks by using number 2 pencils to fill in ovals.

Precinct-based optical scanners require the voter to "test" the ballot by submitting it to the scanner to determine whether or not the ballot contains overvotes. This will also alert the voter should the ballot be discovered to be blank. Ideally, at the end of Election Day—after all the ballots have been initially tallied in the precinct—all the ballots, together with the results, can then be forwarded to the tabulation center. (The chance of ballot boxes or tabulation sheets being illegally manipulated is reduced if the local results are posted locally.) Note that optical scan voting systems by definition create voter-verified paper ballots.

Hybrid models. Ballot-marking systems are a cross between DREs and optical scan systems. One, made by Vogue Election Systems (VES) and currently marketed by ES&S, offers a touch screen like a DRE. The voter simply inserts a blank optical scan ballot into the machine and then proceeds as if interacting with a DRE. Once the voter has entered all of his or her choices, the machine marks the optical scan ballot accordingly, avoiding overvotes and raising alerts to undervotes in the process. This also serves to eliminate any stray pencil marks that could otherwise confuse the scanner. Attached headphones, meanwhile, provide an option that allows blind voters to vote without any assistance.

Another system, produced by Populex, includes a screen that operates with an attached stylus. The system also prints out a completed ballot once the voter has entered all of his or her choices. For human perusal, the ballot uses numbers to represent voter choices, along with corresponding bar codes for the optical scanner's benefit. Like the Vogue system, attached headphones can be provided for blind voters. For both systems headphones attached to the scanner would make it possible for vision-impaired voters, as well as the sighted, to verify their ballots, but this option is not currently available.

Cryptographic voting systems. Both VoteHere (http://www.votehere.net/) and David Chaum (http://www.seas.gwu.edu/~poorvi/Chaum/chaum.pdf) have developed voting systems that provide an encrypted receipt that voters can use to verify that their ballots have been accurately counted. Chaum's system is not currently being manufactured, however. A problem common to both of these systems is that they offer no way to conduct a recount should it be determined that a ballot tabulation problem has occurred, although individual ballots can be corrected. Also, neither scheme is particularly easy for voters to understand.

Open source. The OVC (Open Voting Consortium, http://www.openvotingconsortium.org/) is a non-profit group of software engineers and computer scientists working to build an open source voting system that will run on PC hardware and produce a voter-verifiable paper ballot. The group also hopes to provide a general standard for interoperable open source voting software.

PRUDENT PRECAUTIONARY MEASURES FOR DREs

Because paperless DREs provide no audit trail, it's imperative that they be extensively tested before, during, and after each election. DREs must also be securely stored *between* elections, as well as at polling sites before and during Election Day.

Similarly, all of the ballot definition files should always be scrupulously tested—with all test results (not just the BDF tests) not only made public but also archived in a central repository. In addition, there should also be a national repository of DRE problems, just as is the case with aircraft.

Finally, paper ballots should be made available at every polling location that uses DREs, both as backup in the case of failures of the DREs and to provide voters with the option of voter-verifiable paper ballots.

None of these steps can ensure that DRE software is free of malicious code and potentially damaging bugs. The best we can do is attempt to reduce the risks associated with these machines.

CONCLUSION

The issue of e-voting should have been primarily a technological issue—one that involves computer security, human factors, reliability, and efficiency. Unfortunately, within the political sphere, things are rarely quite so simple.

Election officials have had to endure a painful learning experience. Having been told that DREs were inexpensive to operate and were extensively tested and certified to ensure reliable and secure service, they've since learned that the costs associated with testing and securely storing DREs are high, the testing and certification processes are suspect, and the software is far from bug-free.

The education process continues as technologists make concerted efforts to inform both policy makers and the public about the risks associated with paperless DREs. It is critical for the continued health of democracy that we succeed.

ACKNOWLEDGMENTS

Thanks to Dan Wallach, Tracy Volz, Laura Gould, Lynn Landes, Rebecca Mercuri, and Doug Jones for their very useful comments.

BARBARA SIMONS earned her Ph.D. from U.C. Berkeley and was a computer science researcher at IBM Research, where she worked on compiler optimization, algorithm analysis, and scheduling theory. A former president of ACM, Simons co-chairs the ACM's U.S. Public Policy Committee (USACM). She served on the National Science Foundation panel on Internet Voting, the security peer review group for the Department of Defense's Internet voting project (SERVE), the President's Export Council's Subcommittee on Encryption, and the President's Council on the Year 2000 Conversion. She is a Fellow of ACM and the American Association for the Advancement of Science.

Small VOTE MANIPULATIONS
Can Swing Elections

Considering the effects and implications of changing only a single vote per machine.

Anthony Di Franco, Andrew Petro, Emmett Shear, *AND* Vladimir Vladimirov

UNDER THE MANDATE OF THE HELP AMERICA Vote Act, precincts across the U.S. are upgrading their polling processes. Some precincts are choosing to purchase electronic voting machines, and some commentators advocate using e-voting machines as the standard. The use of direct-recording electronic voting machines (DREs), or more generally, any electronic means of vote tabulation and reporting, raises the concern that a single, simple, subtle fraudulent change to the system software can take effect everywhere these machines are deployed.

We attempted to determine the influence a hypothetical adversary might have had on the outcome of the 2000 U.S. Presidential election. Our adversary is able to select and change a small fixed number of votes per machine, representing the effect of modifying the voting software to misreport the results from each machine. A seemingly insignificant action on every voting machine, multiplied by the large number of machines required across the country, gives the adversary considerable influence. We calculate the number of states and electoral votes such an adversary might change, and conclude that the outcome of the election can be changed by manipulating one vote per voting machine. Furthermore, changing a few more votes can establish, or overcome, a considerable margin of victory.

Method

We examine a hypothetical electronically balloted version of the 2000 election, assuming that 90% of the total votes are cast by means of e-voting machines. The remaining 10% are assumed to be cast in some other way (hand-counted paper ballots, lever machines, and so forth) and do not contribute to the number of e-voting machines required. In essence, we ask: What if e-voting advocates [9] succeed in making DREs universal?

We suppose an adversary favoring candidate B who selects from each voting machine m ballots containing votes for candidate A and changes them to votes for candidate B. We then assume one e-voting machine is re-

quired for every v votes to be cast by machine. The number of voting machines required is thus (90% × total votes cast) / v. We use $v = 200$ in our calculations. We believe this is reasonable given the recent e-voting machine purchases of the states of Georgia and Maryland.[1] A voting machine serving 200 voters in a 14-hour election day serves one voter every 4.2 minutes on average.

In any case, our results are not particularly sensitive to the exact value of v or the proportion of votes cast electronically. For instance, the adversary remains effective even under conservative assumptions where each machine serves 500 voters and 5/6 of votes are cast electronically.[2] Even then, a manipulation of one vote per machine would be enough to overcome the margin for both Florida and New Mexico, and two votes per machine adds Wisconsin and Iowa in the 2000 election.

There were 184,394 voting precincts in the 2000 election [2], for an average of 572 votes cast per precinct. If the adversary is only able to change votes on a per-precinct basis,[3] the outcomes in Florida, New Mexico, and Iowa, and thus the outcome of the election, are still reversed by two vote changes per precinct.

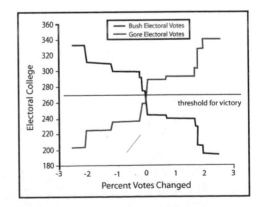

Electoral college votes changed versus percent popular vote changed.

State	Electoral votes	Vote count		Winning Margin		
		Bush	Gore	Total	Absolute	Percent of total
FL	25	**2,912,790**	2,912,253	5,963,110	537	0.009%
NM	5	286,417	**286,783**	598,605	366	0.061%
WI	11	1,237,279	**1,242,987**	2,598,607	5,708	0.220%
IA	7	624,373	**638,517**	1,315,563	4,144	0.315%
OR	7	713,577	**720,342**	1,533,968	6,765	0.441%

Table 1. Five closest-margin states [3–5].

m votes manipulated per machine	States swung		
	Count	Electoral votes	Percentage of total electoral votes
1	1	25	4.6%
4	2	29	5.3%
8	5	65	12.1%

Table 2. States swung from Bush to Gore by manipulating m votes per machine.

m votes manipulated per machine	States swung		
	Count	Electoral votes	Percentage of total electoral votes
1	4	30	5.6%
4	4	30	5.6%
8	5	40	7.4%

Table 3. States swung from Gore to Bush by manipulating m votes per machine.

Results

The data given in Table 1 shows statistics for the five closest-margin 2000 presidential election states. These states were all decided by margins of less than half of one percent of votes cast. The figure here shows the number of electoral votes changed versus the percent of the popular vote changed in favor of each candidate. Note that less than a small fraction of one percent of votes needed to be modified to change the winner to Gore, due to the very small margin in Florida, though changing about two percent of popular votes would give either candidate a large margin in the electoral college.

Tables 2 and 3 show the capacity of the adversary to direct the manipulation to the benefit of a particular candidate. In particular, Table 2 indicates that an adversary capable of changing one vote per voting machine could have swung 25 electoral votes from Bush to Gore. This would have made the final electoral college totals 246 votes for Bush versus 291

votes for Gore, rather than the actual 271 votes for Bush versus 266 votes for Gore. Thus, an adversary with the ability to manipulate one vote per machine could have changed the outcome of the 2000 U.S. Presidential election.

Conclusion

E-voting machines potentially make electoral fraud unprecedentedly simple. An election saboteur need only introduce a small change in the master copy of the voting software to be effective. As Mercuri noted, "Whereas earlier technologies required that election fraud be perpetrated at one polling place or machine at a time, the proliferation of similarly programmed e-voting systems invites opportunities for large-scale manipulation of elections" [8]. Our analysis demonstrates that even a trivial example of this kind of fraud can be effective.

We have shown that changing just one vote per voting machine is enough to allow an adversary to control the result of this election. Moreover, an adversary able to change a few more votes can swing states with much wider margins, which may be effective in changing the outcome of an election with wider margins overall than those of the 2000 election, or in establishing wider margins for other purposes, such as avoiding recounts and revotes or establishing a mandate beyond merely winning the election.

Such slight manipulations, despite significantly changing the outcome of the election, are small enough that they might plausibly evade detection entirely, be dismissed as random noise if detected, be obscured by noise inherent in the voting and auditing process, or fail to prompt a recount if they are detected but their significance is underestimated or misunderstood.

E-VOTING MACHINES POTENTIALLY MAKE ELECTORAL FRAUD UNPRECEDENTEDLY SIMPLE. AN ELECTION SABOTEUR NEED ONLY INTRODUCE A SMALL CHANGE IN THE MASTER COPY OF THE VOTING SOFTWARE TO BE EFFECTIVE.

This emphasizes the importance of a voter-verified audit trail as protection against this sort of pervasive, subtle manipulation. To guard against such an attack, the correspondence between each voter's intentions and the tally reported by the system must be made absolute by such means as the Mercuri method [8], where each voter personally verifies a machine-produced paper ballot that is then counted by machine in a reliable, repeatable manner, but can nonetheless still be counted manually.

Notes

[1]Georgia purchased 19,015 [6] voting machines to serve the entire state. If these machines had been used to collect the 2,596,804 votes cast in Georgia in the 2000 Presidential election, then 136 votes would have been cast per machine. Georgia does not have absentee voting. Maryland recently purchased 11,000 [7] machines. In the 2000 Presidential election, there were 2,025,480 [3] votes cast in Maryland. If those 11,000 machines had been used to collect the votes cast in 2000, 186 votes would have been cast per machine. We adopt the more conservative figure of $v = 200$, providing the adversary fewer opportunities to manipulate the election.

[2]See the recent article in *The Nation* by R. Dugger: www.thenation.com/docprint.mhtml?i=20040816&s=dugger.

[3]Scenarios in which the precinct rather than the machine is the relevant unit of manipulation include manipulating in-precinct optical-scan ballot talliers and realizing some unanticipated efficiency of e-voting technologies that makes only one e-voting machine necessary per precinct.

References

1. Di Franco, A., Petro, A., Vladimirov, V., and Shear, E. *Tiny Systematic Vote Manipulations Can Swing Elections*. Yale University Department of Computer Science, Tech. Rep. YALEU/DCS/TR-1285; ftp.cs.yale.edu/ pub/TR/tr1285.pdf.

2. Election Data Services. New study shows 50 million voters will use electronic voting systems, 32 million still with punch cards in 2004 (Feb. 12, 2004); www.electiondataservices.com/EDSInc_VEstudy2004.pdf.

3. Federal Election Commission. *2000 Official Presidential General Election Results*. Updated: December 2001; www.fec.gov/pubrec/2000presgeresults. htm.

4. Federal Election Commission. *2000 General Election Votes Cast for U.S. President, Senate and House*. June 2001, Updated December 2001; www.fec.gov/pubrec/fe2000/gevotes.htm.

5. Federal Election Commission. *2000 Presidential General Election Result*; www.fec.gov/pubrec/fe2000/2000presge.htm.

6. Georgia Secretary of State. *Georgia Counts! Voting Project— Frequently Asked Questions*, 2002; www.georgiacounts.com/faqs.htm.

7. Kohno, T., Stubblefield, A., Rubin, A.D., and Wallach, D.S. Analysis of an electronic voting system. In *Proceedings of the IEEE Symposium on Security and Privacy* (May 2004); avirubin.com/vote.pdf.

8. Mercuri, R. A better ballot box? *IEEE Spectrum 39*, 10 (Oct. 2002); www.spectrum.ieee.org/WEBONLY/publicfeature/oct02/evot.html.

9. Miller, H. Electronic voting is solution. *USA Today* (Feb. 4, 2004), 14A.

Anthony Di Franco (anthony.difranco@yale.edu), Andrew Petro (microcline@gmail.com), Emmett emmett.shear@yale.edu), and Vladimir Vladimirov (vladimir.vladimirov@yale.edu) are undergraduates at or recent graduates of Yale University. This article is based on a technical report [1] the authors produced while undergraduates.

From *Communications of the ACM*, Vol. 47, No. 10, October 2004, pp. 43-45. Copyright © 2004 by Association for Computing Machinery, Inc. Reprinted by permission.

To Size Up Colleges, Students Now Shop Online

Institutions pep up their Web sites with flashy graphics, podcasts, and blogs

Dan Carnevale

The same high-school students who think nothing of going to J. Crew's Web site to order the right pair of jeans—sifting through the plethora of styles that seem to change by the week—are turning out to be equally sophisticated online consumers of college information.

Take Gina M. Antonini, who is set to graduate from Thomas A. Edison High School, in Virginia. After spending much of her spare time in high school working to become a singer-songwriter, she wanted a college with a strong music program.

She turned to a Web site called Destination-U, which is just one of many online services—some for profit, some not—that allow students to learn about various colleges and universities before setting foot on any of their campuses. And colleges themselves are working hard to make sure that students see, and relate to, their official Web sites.

But selling colleges online is more difficult than selling boot-fit jeans. The competition from other institutions is stiff and getting more so, leading to a kind of online arms race that pits splashy Flash graphics against the latest interactive features, like admissions blogs and podcasts.

"This is a response to the consumer culture, and it really does benefit the institution," says Shelley Rodgers, director of government relations and communications at the American Association of Collegiate Registrars and Admissions Officers. "These students that we are seeing today are very Internet savvy."

First Contact

Admissions officials know their Web sites are the first point of contact for many prospective students, says Judy Hingle, director for professional development at the National Association for College Admission Counseling. The association has created a list of Internet services that help high-school students search for and apply to colleges (http://www.nacac.com/w_general.html).

"It has changed from the Internet being a supplement to the Internet being the first source," Ms. Hingle says. "For a great majority of students, this is going to be their first impression. This is going to be their handshake."

With that in mind, Drexel University's admissions office provides e-mail addresses of current students who have agreed to respond to questions from prospective students. The biggest challenge is making sure replies come quickly, says Joan T. McDonald, vice president for enrollment management at Drexel.

"They do expect pretty much instantaneous responses," Ms. McDonald says. "The use of technology is terrific in recruiting students, but you have to have the staff to be there to respond."

Starting in September, Drexel plans to make its Web presence even more personalized for interested applicants. Potential students will each be given a Web page on the university's server. The pages will highlight campus information in which applicants have expressed an interest.

For example, if a potential student is considering majoring in biology, the university's biology information will be front and center. And as announcements are made about research projects or events surrounding a topic of interest to that student, the student's personal Web page will be updated with that information.

"It's really customized or tailored information for a student," Ms. McDonald says. "Students want to know that their specific interests are going to be met."

Drexel officials have also worked to make sure the institution's Web site appears at the top of as many Google queries involving colleges as possible. The university surveys incoming students and asks them how they used the Internet to search for information about Drexel and other institutions and what terms they plugged into search engines. Then the university tweaks its Web site and its meta tags—the hidden descriptive information about Web pages that search engines use.

"You want to make sure you're monitoring that activity as much as possible, so that you come to the top of Web searches," says Ms. McDonald.

Rensselaer Polytechnic Institute started a student blog this spring, featuring three university students who post messages once a week about their lives on the campus (http://polyblogs.rpi.edu).

"I write about how exams went, how much homework I have," says one of the bloggers, Bryan Knight, a senior studying computer-systems engineering and computer science. "One night I wrote about how I went on a date with a girl I met online and how it was a complete disaster."

Glenna L. Ryan, director of enrollment services at Rensselaer, says the blogs have proved popular with parents as well as high-school students. The bloggers receive about one e-mail message per week from students and parents, asking about such topics as campus housing or what novels they're reading.

"It's really been a great way to connect students to the campus in a virtual format," Ms. Ryan says. "It's really about the student-to-student contact."

While the blogs take an informal tone, they are tamer than many unofficial student blogs at other institutions, which favor swear words and feature tales of drunkenness and emotional breakdowns. The student representatives are handpicked by Rensselaer, but Ms. Ryan says the university has never censored anything that the students have written for their blogs.

PROFESSIONAL HELP

As colleges try to serve up information on the Web to parents and students, a multitude of online businesses are trying to guide students to colleges that can match their interests and abilities. And those businesses have found numerous ways to cash in on guiding students through the dizzying college-application process. For every step in the process, there is an online service out there promising to make it easier.

Among the most popular college-match services is one offered by the College Board. Since so many students are already visiting the College Board Web site to gather information about the SAT and check their scores, they also use the organization's Web services, which are free to the public.

More than one million students use the organization's college-search service (http://collegeboard.com/csearch) every month on average, officials say. Students fill out a questionnaire, explaining what kinds of colleges they are looking for. The survey allows students to choose among specific criteria, such as how close a college is to a city, what kinds of sports and activities are available, and enrollment.

The search then provides a number of colleges that match the student's preferences, with several pages of information collected from the College Board's annual survey, such as what percentage of students are admitted, what factors colleges consider when admitting students, and freshman retention.

When a student expresses interest in a particular college, the student will also be given names of other institutions reviewed by students with similar interests—similar to Amazon.com's feature displaying other products that shoppers with similar interests bought.

Laura Barnes, product director for CollegeBoard.com, says the search feature helps students find colleges they might not otherwise be aware of. "That's definitely one of the goals of the College Board, to expand their opportunities," Ms. Barnes says. "We try to be an objective and trusted source of the information."

Destination-U, which charges students a one-time fee of $49.95, provides a similar service.

Greg Waldorf, chief executive officer of the company, likens the service to a personal guidance counselor on the Internet. "Choosing a college is a really complex decision," he says. "For the cost of about one application, isn't it worth having good advice going in?"

Mr. Waldorf says the company's service is different than the College Board's—instead of asking students to describe their ideal colleges, students are asked to describe themselves and their learning styles. They are then matched with appropriate colleges.

"We still haven't given up on what I call the personal touch. But we're using the Internet pretty extensively."

"We think one of the reasons that the four-year graduation rate isn't very good is because kids are going to the wrong school," he says. "If kids apply to schools where they're

well matched, they have a better chance of getting in, and more importantly they have a better chance of graduating on time."

In addition, Destination-U offers a planning service that lets students know when they have to turn in the different components of their applications, such as their test scores and their essays.

Ms. Antonini, who will graduate from her Virginia high school in June, says the system at Destination-U is simple to use, although she felt the initial survey, which takes about 15 minutes to complete, was a bit long. But she liked how the Web site lists several matching institutions, labeling them as "reach," "target," and "safety," depending on how likely she would be to get accepted. Destination-U also provided information about admissions, enrollment, graduation rates, and cost for each institution.

After she got her list of institutions, Ms. Antonini also searched through each college's Web site to get more information, such as how close the campus was to a major city, the male-to-female ratio of the students, and how close it was to her home. "I don't want to be too far," she says. "And I don't want to be too close."

One of the suggestions on her list was an institution she had never heard of: Middle Tennessee State University.

"It's kind of an out-there school," she says. "I don't think I would have come across it. It was a rare gem, I guess you would say."

For Ms. Antonini, the university seemed to harmonize perfectly with her music interests. It is located just outside of Nashville, and its curriculum includes music production, so she can fulfill her goal of becoming a producer. She is set to start classes there in the fall.

However, not everything about the university is perfect—Ms. Anto-

nini is a big pop-music fan, and she expects to do some adjusting to live near the country-music Mecca. "I'm not so much a country fan," she says. "But I'm getting used to it now."

SURPRISE VISITS

Gregory A. Pyke, senior associate dean of admission for Wesleyan University, says he can tell that applicants are using new online resources to discover the university—but he isn't always sure which tools. More and more students are arriving at Wesleyan for visits without making any official contact beforehand, and he doubts that is by accident.

"If you're showing up on our campus, I suspect you're doing some research to get here—you weren't just wandering around in your car," Mr. Pyke says. "It means we have to be ready."

Technology generally supplements the traditional outreach methods, college officials say, but it does not replace them. Colleges still mail glossy brochures, and students still visit campuses to get a feel for colleges. And name recognition still goes a long way in selling a student on a particular university.

J. James Wager, assistant vice provost for enrollment management and university registrar at Pennsylvania State University at University Park, says Internet tools help the university reach out to students, but that officials still rely on old-fashioned methods to attract applicants.

"We still haven't given up on what I call the personal touch," Mr. Wager says. "But we're using the Internet pretty extensively."

Besides, although students depend on the Web to conduct research about colleges, they don't always buy what the institution is trying to sell them. Britni E. Wilcher, a graduating senior at Claremont High

School, in California, says she bypasses much of a college Web site's bells and whistles, like blogs and podcasts, for the important information, such as what courses are available and who the professors are.

"I just look for the information I'm interested in," she says. "On the Internet, you can mold your own perspective of a college."

Facing Down the E-Maelstrom

When every campus dispute has the potential to explode—thanks to e-mail and blogs—presidents are never off the hot seat

Jeffrey Selingo

BY SAN FRANCISCO STATE UNIVERSITY STANDARDS, it was a small protest. Early last month some 100 students turned out at a campus career fair to demonstrate against the presence of military recruiters. A few protesters were removed by university police officers for allegedly violating the student-conduct code on rallies.

Ten years ago such an incident might have received a mention in the student newspaper, and that would have been that. But times have changed. Within hours of the protest, the university's president, Robert A. Corrigan, had received two dozen e-mail messages, mostly from people off the campus, criticizing the administration for allowing students to march against the military. Then, about a week later, while Mr. Corrigan was traveling, his in-box was flooded with about 200 more messages, many from out of state, demanding that he not censure the students involved.

The deluge of messages left Mr. Corrigan wondering how so many people had found out about such a small skirmish on his campus. So his

assistant poked around on the Web and discovered that six days after the protest, a liberal blog (http://sf.indymedia.org) run by the San Francisco Independent Media Center had posted an article headlined "Defend Free Speech Rights at San Francisco State University" that included Mr. Corrigan's e-mail address.

It was not the first time that Mr. Corrigan has been electronically inundated after a campus incident. Three years ago he received 3,000 e-mail messages after a pro-Israel rally was held at the university.

"Every time something happens on campus, an organized group goes after you," he says. "The president becomes the conduit for all this hate stuff, for the political polarization in this country, and electronic communication spreads it everywhere."

Among college leaders, Mr. Corrigan is hardly alone in his frustration. It used to take days or weeks, if ever, for an incident simmering on a campus to ignite into a full-fledged controversy. But now, thanks to e-mail—and, more recently, blogs—news about even minor campus dust-ups is disseminated much more

quickly, and well beyond the bounds of the college or local community. The president, as the institution's public face, must deal with the resulting flood of interest in his campus's doings.

Compounding the problem of dealing with the sheer volume of responses is the fact that the e-mail or blog reports of the initial clash are frequently taken out of context or just plain wrong—often purposely so, to advance political agendas.

"Campuses are no longer places for civil public discourse," says Robert Zemsky, chairman of the Learning Alliance for Higher Education, a think tank at the University of Pennsylvania that advises college leaders on management issues. "They've become places for political campaigns that are getting sourer and sourer. People are no longer willing to fight their battles without trying to muster allies outside of campus."

For campus CEO's accustomed to responding to nearly everything that happens at their institutions, this new environment has left them not only fatigued, but also wondering how best to handle a situation before they become the next Lawrence H. Summers or Elizabeth Hoffman.

Few campus leaders have figured out how to manage the huge volume of e-mail they receive when their campuses are thrust into the spotlight. Presidents who pick and choose which messages to respond to know that they do so at their own peril, since they never can be sure which dispute will draw the attention of well-to-do donors or influential politicians.

And the many leaders who have just given up and pushed the situation off on assistants face another danger: "There is something about having as many tentacles out there as possible," says Mr. Corrigan, of San Francisco State. "The notion that you are available to lots of people can help you manage the enterprise better. It's too bad if we're forced to cut ourselves off."

EVERYONE HAS A BEEF

Conflicts on campuses are nothing new, of course. But colleges today are no longer viewed as ivory towers. Institutions of all sizes and types are under greater scrutiny than ever before from lawmakers, parents, taxpayers, students, alumni, and especially political partisans. Empowered by their position or by the fact that they sign the tuition checks, they do not hesitate to use any available forum to complain about what is happening at a particular institution.

In this Internet age, information travels quickly and easily, and colleges have become more transparent, says Collin G. Brooke, an assistant professor of writing at Syracuse University, who studies the intersection between rhetoric and technology. Many universities' Web sites list the e-mail addresses of every employee, from the president on down, enabling unencumbered access to all of them.

"That was not possible 10 years ago," Mr. Brooke says. "Maybe I'd go to a library, find a college catalog, and get an address. Then I'd have to write a letter. Now it's easy to whip off a couple of sentences in an e-mail when it takes only a few seconds to find that person's address."

And no subject is off limits. Last year the Board of Trustees of Rice University was blitzed with hundreds of e-mail messages by alumni and others as it weighed a decision on downgrading its athletics program from the National Collegiate Athletic Association's top tier, Division I-A. The messages flooded in even though the university had set up a Web site for just such input. The volume of e-mail was such that the trustees did not even attempt to respond (most of the messages were against the move, and the trustees eventually decided to stay put).

E-mail is just one part of the growing communications nightmare facing presidents. In the past year or so, a new electronic tool has accelerated the flow of information from campuses: blogs. There are now an estimated 10 million Web logs in cyberspace, many with loyal followings and widespread readership. E-mail messages about campus contretemps that once got forwarded to maybe a dozen people now get posted on blogs for anyone to see. Blogs link to other blogs and get picked up by popular group blogs like Metafilter. In the blogosphere "there is no gatekeeper," says Barry Toiv, director of communications and public affairs at the Association of American Universities.

"Now everybody and anybody with a keyboard in front of them has the ability to have his reporting or his views or some combination heard or read," says Mr. Toiv, who worked in the White House press office during the Clinton administration. "As soon as higher education became a vehicle for partisan politics, this became inevitable. Nonevents become problems, and problems become crises."

A HATE-MAIL FOLDER

Take an incident at Tufts University in October 2001, less than a month after the September 11 terrorist attacks. Editors of a conservative campus magazine decided to paint an American flag on a cannon in the middle of the campus. (It is a Tufts tradition for students to redecorate the cannon, often nightly, with birthday wishes, promotions for sporting events, or political statements.) One of the editors ended up getting into a tussle with three peace activists. The editor filed a complaint with the judicial-affairs office at Tufts, and the three pacifists were eventually sentenced to probation by a student judicial board.

The university's president, Lawrence S. Bacow, says the panel's decision should have been the end of the story. But one of the magazine editors wrote an article about the confrontation, saying conservative students at Tufts were under assault. It was posted on a conservative Web site (http://www.frontpagemag.com) run by David Horowitz, president of the Los Angeles-based Center for the Study of Popular Culture.

Almost immediately, Mr. Bacow's e-mail box started filling up with messages from off-campus sources attacking him for the light sentence given to the three peace activists. Liberals also weighed in. Over the course of the next few weeks, the president says he received hundreds of e-mail messages. He saved some of them in a file called "hate mail."

The subject lines include "American Flag disgraced," "What Kind of Left Wing Show Are You People Running," and "The endless and continuing sixties—another bubba legacy." One message promised that Republicans would "cut off all tax money to leftist universities like yours." Another wondered when Tufts would be moving to another country, "more friendly to its 'America is always wrong' viewpoint." Some writers were personal, calling Mr. Bacow a "coward" with "no common sense."

In the end, the e-mail barrage did nothing to change the outcome of the judicial hearing. But Mr. Bacow says the constant flow of messages was disruptive: "It makes it all that much more difficult to pay attention to legitimate events." The president eventually answered the most thoughtful and courteous messages, he says, although he never received any responses in return. (He objects to form responses because, he says, they tend to stimulate yet another round of e-mail.)

LIKE A NEVER-ENDING CAMPAIGN

The conservatives, liberals, and activists of every kind who publicize political controversies like those at Tufts and San Francisco State rarely do so because they have any affinity for the institution in question. More often they do it for their own purposes, particularly fund raising. The result, college administrators say, is that the ideological and scholarly debates that were once a mainstay of campus classrooms and academic quads have largely turned into a partisan free-for-all that at times feels like a grueling election-year campaign. When yet another issue on another campus pops up, the outsiders move on.

"The others who enter the fray have absolutely no interest long term in the civility of the debate," Mr. Bacow says. "We are a community, and what kind of community we are when this is done depends on how we treat this issue and each other. People on campus understand that. Those from the outside have no such interest."

One of those outsiders is Mr. Horowitz, who is leading a national campaign to get state legislatures and Congress to adopt an "academic bill of rights." It enumerates several principles that colleges should follow in making tenure decisions, developing course curricula, and selecting campus speakers in order to foster a variety of political and religious beliefs.

While Mr. Horowitz laughs at the suggestion that he is the root cause of the e-mail traffic to college administrators in response to postings on his Web site, he says that if presidents are complaining, then those who write to them are indeed making a difference. "They deserve all the criticism they can get," he says. "These people are not hired to disrespect their conservative students. They pay $40,000 a year at some of these universities, and they are second-class citizens."

How much longer people either off campus or on will be able to quickly reach a college's president by e-mail, though, is unclear. While some presidents, like Mr. Bacow and Mr. Corrigan, still have just one e-mail address, many others have added a second address that is not publicly available. It wasn't just the political e-mail that was getting out of hand. Presidents were fielding suggestions from boosters about how to improve the football team, complaints from students about tuition increases, and pleas from parents for more financial aid. At many of those colleges, messages now sent to the president's public e-mail address are read by an assistant or the public-affairs office.

Since 2001 Graham B. Spanier, president of Pennsylvania State University, has had his public-affairs staff send him summaries of the e-mail in his public in-box (occasionally he asks to see certain messages). The change was prompted by a surge of messages, up to 500 on some days. "We'd have thousands of people writing telling him how to change the BCS formula," says Stephen J. MacCarthy, vice president for university relations. (Mr. Spanier is a conference representative in college football's Bowl Championship Series.)

NO SINGLE STRATEGY

In an era when news of campus incidents spreads so quickly that another dispute may erupt before campus leaders have had a chance to respond to the first, there seems to be no single, agreed-upon strategy for helping presidents cope.

For years, college leaders dealing with a crisis have followed a script borrowed from their days as academics: Examine the incident, talk to all sides, develop a response, and then vet that statement with other administrators. Such an approach would sometimes take days or even weeks. Now a response from the university is needed immediately, says Christopher Simpson, president of Simpson Communications, a public-relations firm in Williamsburg, Va., that works with colleges.

"If you subscribe to the theory that you can wait to gather all the facts, the opposition will eat your lunch," says Mr. Simpson, who was recently hired by the University of Colorado System to repair its public image in the wake of recent scandals. "You need to be able to work in minutes and hours, not in days and weeks, to resolve these issues."

But speed should not always be the first priority in putting out a response, says Terry Shepard, vice president for public affairs at Rice University. It's more important, he says, to get the facts right. "Given that the folks attacking you can say what they want, the only thing we have is our credibility," he says. "If your credibility starts crumbling under your desire to act quickly, then you lose the higher ground."

A response is sometimes necessary even if the issue at hand seems too ridiculous to warrant one, public-relations experts say. San Francisco State, for example, sent form responses to many of the people who e-mailed the president after the military-recruiting protest.

One reason to respond is that college officials never know which cyberspace rumor will gain traction. Last fall, using blogs and e-mail, conservative groups took aim at universities that offered speaking engagements to the controversial filmmaker Michael Moore. At Penn State, Mr. Moore was invited by the College Democrats, who also paid for his appearance, but the story making the rounds over the Internet was that the university was sponsoring the event. Penn State officials acted quickly to refute that account; Mr. MacCarthy says he spent three weeks doing little else but replying to e-mail messages about Michael Moore. "If we didn't address the facts in the minds of angry alumni," he says, "conservative donors would walk away from the university, and we can't let that happen."

Correcting such inaccuracies, however, is usually difficult because the source of the information is so often unknown, he adds. "In the days when you got your news from three networks, if something was wrong, you could go to the source and get it fixed quickly," he says. "Now there are thousands of sources."

And with advances in technology, campus officials fear that the problems they face today are only going to get worse.

"If there is a saturation point," says Mr. Toiv, of the Association of American Universities, "we haven't reached it yet."

Point, Click...Fire

Awesome technology gets a helluva field test

By John Carey, Spencer E. Ante, Frederik Balfour, Laura Cohn, Stan Crock

As the tanks and artillery of the U.S. 3rd Infantry Division converge on Baghdad to confront the troops and armor of Saddam Hussein's Republican Guard, they're following the metaphorical footsteps of legendary Chinese tactician Sun Tzu. "Know the enemy and know yourself," he advised in the 6th century B.C. If that is done, "In a hundred battles, you will never know peril." Modern warriors haven't yet figured out how to read the enemy's mind. But on the shifting sands of Iraq, the powerful U.S.-led force is attempting to do the next best thing: harness America's edge in information technology, sophisticated networking, and precision weapons to give the U.S. military an unprecedented view of the battlefield—and a decisive edge.

This strategy is achieving some remarkable successes, such as the surgical destruction of government buildings in Baghdad. But strains are already evident, including tragic glitches in the technology used to distinguish friend from foe and the problems posed by a persistent enemy whose low-tech ruses have unexpectedly disrupted the coalition's long, vulnerable supply chain. It goes to show that all the high-tech gear in the world is no guarantee of an easy victory.

The problems haven't yet dimmed the Pentagon's faith in the new digital war strategy, though. And glimpses of the new face of technology are everywhere on the battlefield. Inside the tanks and Bradley Fighting Vehicles of the 3ID are computers linked to a sophisticated network. As the units maneuver across the desert, commanders and their troops see blue dots on the computer screens that representing U.S. units. Red dots show the positions of Iraqi troops. A yellow diamond would mark fallout zones in the case of a chemical or biological attack. Planes, helicopters, and circling Predator drones spot Iraqi troops and vehicles—providing intelligence that is relayed almost instantly to commanders so that satellite-guided bombs can be dropped swiftly, while the information is still current.

The result: precision targeting on a scale unknown in modern warfare. On Mar. 25, in a blinding sandstorm, units of the 3ID fought a pitched battle with Iraqi defenses for control of crossings over the Euphrates River near Najaf. The sophisticated networks enabled U.S. troops to "see" each other in the poor visibility—as well as to call in precision airstrikes to beat back Iraqi attacks.

The fight was more than just a convincing display of firepower under harsh conditions, though. It was a small example of how the new type of network-driven warfare championed by Defense Secretary Donald H. Rumsfeld is supposed to work. The 1991 Gulf War spotlighted high-tech weaponry. What's different now is that the military's sensors, weapons, communications systems, commanders, and soldiers are linked into a giant computing grid that gives U.S. troops the clearest picture of the battlefield warriors have ever known—an attempt to lift the fog of war. In theory, this could be a profound leap, comparable to past advances such as the longbow at Agincourt in 1415 or the repeating rifle in the Civil War. Both forever altered how conflicts are waged. "Long-term, more and more warfare is about pushing photons around on the battlefield rather than men and machines," says Loren B. Thompson, an analyst at the Lexington Institute, a public policy think tank.

Yet even as the high-tech legions lay siege to Baghdad, disturbing questions are emerging about the wisdom of relying so heavily on technology to do the work of war. Machines make mistakes. Already, there have been several friendly-fire incidents that should not have happened. While seven Iraqi surface-to-surface missiles have been knocked down by U.S. Patriot missiles, a technical glitch may have been responsible for the accidental downing of a British Tornado jet by one of the Patriot batteries—and a subsequent attack by an F-16 on another Patriot installation. And on Mar. 25, Iraqi officials claim bombs struck a Baghdad market, killing 15 civilians. "As you've seen just recently, technology doesn't always work perfectly," sighs Air Commodore Andy Warnes, Britain's commander for communications systems in Doha, Qatar.

Moreover, as coalition forces enter a second phase of fighting in Iraq's cities, high-tech gear will no longer give them such an overwhelming edge. The best sensors and precision weapons don't help as much against an elusive foe that fights from building to building and blends in with the civilian population. And weapons of mass destruction remain a giant wild card. Technology should allow U.S. soldiers to react more quickly if chemical or biological weapons are unleashed, but it can't stop those attacks from being carried out.

While the Pentagon plays up the new technology, a fully networked military is still a distant dream. Many U.S. troops have not yet been outfitted with the latest high-tech gear, sometimes with tragic consequences. One example so far: the tragedy of the lost maintenance convoy. On Mar. 23, a group of U.S. soldiers made a wrong turn into an Iraqi ambush. The route was changed at the last minute, but these troops didn't have the advanced technology that would have alerted them to the change, according to sources in the 3ID.

Some of the 3ID's supply troops have been forced to communicate via ordinary off-the-shelf Motorola walkie-talkies, which have a range of a mere 5 miles. In fact, one supply convoy Humvee driver had to shout from the window to pass along an order to douse headlights, because he didn't know the frequencies for the radios being used by the drivers behind him. "We're not the digitized division," Colonel Steven Lyons of the supply brigade complains. "When it comes to reality, we're one of the more starved outfits in the army."

Pentagon leaders acknowledge that digitization of the military is a work in progress, but they insist it is already giving them crucial advantages. They're belatedly tapping into the latest Internet technology—the way corporations did in 1990s—to become nimbler and more efficient. It's an all-out effort to harness the power of the Web and other cutting-edge information technologies. That means tearing down virtual walls and building lightning-fast links between the armed services so that these onetime rivals can collaborate more. "We look to the business community for inspiration," says John Arquilla, an associate professor at the Naval Postgraduate School. "Networked organizational forms are highly efficient, and we like to emulate that."

Rumsfeld's bold vision represents a remarkable shift in attitude toward information technology, too. The basic idea: Since the private sector has already figured out how to manage, integrate, and analyze huge amounts of information on networks, why not tap into the same hardware, software, and expertise? In many cases, the same servers, satellites, and fiber-optic networks, as well as software that major corporations routinely use, can be pressed into service to link images from Global Hawk unmanned aircraft with commanders and shooters on the ground.

These new technologies have enabled fresh military tactics, some of which are already visible in tank tracks in the Iraqi sands. In the 1991 war, U.S. forces advanced in a largely unbroken line. Now, the allies swarm across the desert with far more widely dispersed units, counting on help from the air that's just an e-mail or satellite phone call away.

Experts believe that the tactics of urban warfare may undergo a shift, too. Because sensors and precision weapons don't help much against an elusive foe that blends in with the civilian population, General Tommy R. Franks, head of

U.S. Central Command, is expected to try a new strategy—a combination of siege and quick surgical strikes—to take Baghdad. The idea is to send small teams in and out fast, taking out key targets, rather than laboriously storming the city street by street a la Stalingrad. The latest technology and communications gear should help. Soldiers equipped with night-vision goggles stay in touch with each other and commanders in real time while on missions. They can call in air strikes so precise that they can take out one building at a time—although the ability to do so may be limited by Iraqi willingness to locate troops or targets in civilian structures. So, while the situation isn't ideal, having the technology edge is still better than not having it.

Ditto when it comes to chemical and biological warfare. Gear that protects against biological and chemical attacks has improved dramatically in the past few years. One significant new innovation is the Fox Nuclear-Biological-Chemical Reconnaissance System, an armored vehicle equipped with sensors that can detect contaminants and instantly transmit alert information to commanders. If such attacks occur, soldiers will don the latest protective garb, a full-body suit that soaks up chemicals with a layer of charcoal lining and lasts for up to 45 days.

While many of the technologies in use in Iraq have been available for years, it is only now that a critical mass of them have come together to create a truly networked battlefield. The glue that binds the system is the so-called tactical Internet. Deployed in Afghanistan for the first time, the tactical Net is the computer interface used by soldiers to communicate and share information. Special Operations Forces in Afghanistan logged on to a Web page and could read battlefield reports and view video feeds downloaded from the surveillance cameras in Predator drones flying overhead.

Certainly, the scene at coalition Central Command in Doha, Qatar, represents a dramatic change from the command centers of wars past. Instead of relying on maps with pins to mark troop locations, Franks watches the battle unfold in real time on seven 60-inch plasma screens—and he can react on the spot. "The Joint Operations Center is light years ahead of the way we used to process and manage information during the Gulf War," says a senior military official in Doha. "By sharing information across the board—service to service, country to country—we're a much more efficient and potent fighting force."

It helps that all four armed services are represented in the Joint Operations Center. Plus, all of the communications and data links between them happen automatically, so not collaborating isn't an option. Military people working at the JOC say that while the historic tensions and rivalries between the services still exist, they're less intense.

The first key to making the digital war vision pay off is an array of ever-more-sophisticated eyes in the sky and on the ground. Spy satellites can read a newspaper from their perches 200 miles to 400 miles high. In the joint surveillance target attach radar system (JSTARS), circling Boeing 707s are fitted with sophisticated radar that can keep track of traffic in the air and movement on the ground. Unmanned Predators and Global Hawks bristle with TV cameras and sensors capable of spotting heat rising from missiles, tank engines, or troops. In one of the apparent successes of the war so far, the Defense Dept. says Iraqi missile launches have been spotted quickly enough for improved Patriot III missiles to intercept and destroy seven of them so far. In addition, two landed harmlessly in the desert, and one landed in the gulf. That's a huge improvement over the largely ineffectual Gulf War Patriot. A General Accounting Office report later concluded the Patriot did its job only four out of 47 times in that conflict.

Individual bits of data aren't of much use by themselves. The big advance since the Kosovo conflict is being able to merge information from multiple sources. By combining the radar image of a moving vehicle from JSTARS with video from a Predator and infrared data from a Global Hawk, analysts at the command center can quickly determine if a suspect blip on the ground is a tank rather than a civilian bus. That's helping to cut the "kill time"—the time from spotting a potential target to taking it out—from more than an hour to less than a minute. But that carries potential perils as well. If targeting errors occur, there is little time to correct them before bombs are launched.

The eyes in the sky perform another invaluable function as well. Whether it's Sun Tzu or Stonewall Jackson, battles have been won by knowing the terrain better than the enemy does. Now, U.S. troops in Iraq are using detailed maps to reveal where enemy troops may be hiding and to determine where best to put fuel dumps and resupply points. When fighting starts in Baghdad, the ability to chart the constantly changing urban landscape, as buildings fall and streets are blown up, will offer a valuable advantage.

But armies that live by technology can also be vulnerable to a curse of modern computing—hack attacks by a determined enemy. Jamming communications or taking down wireless networks can paralyze a digital foe. Even when everyone is on the network, savvy enemies can still attack at numerous vulnerable points. Precision weapons and position sensors on tanks and troops depend on receiving signals from the satellites of the so-called global positioning system. Block those signals—as the Iraqis attempted to do with inexpensive Russian GPS jammers—and bombs miss their mark: The fog of war begins to return. Indeed, on Mar. 25, U.S. Air Force Major General Victor E. Renuart Jr. announced that his forces had found and destroyed six GPS jammers used by Iraqi units.

As with corporations, the effectiveness of high-tech military technology can be hobbled by incompatibility problems. From command and control all the way down to the grunts fighting on the field, lack of interoperability is slowing down decision-making. The 3ID, for instance, has several different tanks with varied communications and logistics systems that don't talk to one another. And only one person in the logistics arm of the division, Colonel Jim Hodge, is outfitted with the newest battlefield-communications system. Among the 70 other support vehicles, only three are even equipped with a more primitive communications and logistics system. Worse, during the long trek toward Baghdad on Mar. 24, those vehicles were in a part of the convoy that got split off, leaving the front section without any way of tracking them. When technologies aren't up to snuff for corporations—which is often—it's frustrating. But with the military, it can be a life-and-death matter.

Whatever the problems, however, the move to automate war has become an irreversible force. Plans are under way to network practically every piece of the military machine, from front line troops to logistics to the healthcare system. The Army's Land Warrior project, for instance, encompasses everything worn, carried, or consumed by soldiers: It calls for a wearable computer, helmet-mounted information display, and wireless network system. Because so much computer smarts will be embedded in new weapons, personal-communications gear, and targeting systems that pinpoint locations for artillery and air strikes, power and weight are seen as limiting factors. On the Army's drawing board are such futuristic concepts as lightweight chameleon body armor that senses its surroundings and changes color to blend in—and also reacts to outside temperature to keep the soldier comfortable.

As tempting as some of this high-tech gear sounds, planners and soldiers alike understand the limits of technology. Troops on the ground in Iraq have the latest chemical-weapons protection equipment, but they still carry pigeons as an early-warning system. You always need a fallback. Many Marines have personal digital assistants, "but we still have our little green notebook as well," says Lieutenant Colonel Steven H. Mattos, director of the technology division at the Marine Corps Warfighting Laboratory in Quantico, Va. "If you put a hole in a paper map, you have a map with a hole in it. You put a bullet through a computer screen, what do you have? A piece of junk."

Still, the dream of reshaping the battlefield with technology burns bright. The initial step, which we're now witnessing in this first digital war, is knowing the positions of friend and foe. The coming next step is knowing that a particular enemy vehicle is a certain kind of tank with specific firepower. And ultimately, the U.S. military wants to know what the enemy has been trained to do, so that U.S. commanders can predict how foes will react as American forces approach. If the Pentagon succeeds in getting there, they will be as close as warriors can come to Sun Tzu's vision of fighting a hundred battles and never knowing peril.

By John Carey in Washington and Spencer E. Ante in New York, with Frederik Balfour with the 3ID, Laura Cohn in Doha, Qatar, Stan Crock in Washington, and bureau reports.

The Doctrine of Digital War

How high tech is shaping America's military strategy: the pros and cons

By Stan Crock, Paul Magnusson, Lee Walczak, and Frederik Balfour

When Defense Secretary Donald H. Rumsfeld, mindful of America's two-month rout of the Taliban regime in Afghanistan, sat down with war planners to prepare for a U.S.-led thrust into Iraq, he had a vision of how the unfolding conflict would play out. A devotee of a new theory of warfare that places enormous stress on air power, computer communications, and small, agile ground forces, the Pentagon chief began work on a battle plan that was a marvel of technological prowess.

Ever since he joined the Administration, fresh from a second career as a successful CEO, Rumsfeld had been fighting skirmishes with his military brass. His notion of "transformation"—Rumspeak for a leaner, more technologically driven force that leapfrogs generations of Cold War weaponry—met with resistance from generals and congressional porkmeisters alike. Defenders of the status quo insisted that future wars would be won the old-fashioned way—with lethal firepower and plenty of U.S. grunts on the ground. The debates intensified as the prospect of war in Iraq drew nearer and Commander-in-Chief George W. Bush signaled his determination to oust Saddam Hussein.

The blueprint Rumsfeld wound up with is a blend of his ideas for War Lite and the more traditional desires of Tommy Franks, the tough-talking general who heads the U.S. Central Command. Franks argued successfully for a large conventional force of up to 250,000 combat and support troops. In return, Rumsfeld got Franks to agree to deploying the troops in phases, rather than all at once. And Rumsfeld also prevailed on a strategy built around simultaneous air and land strikes, a rapid advance to Baghdad, and extensive use of special-operations units. Their assignment: to go behind enemy lines to knock out targets, thus lessening the need, Rumsfeld argued, for more frontal assault troops.

Whatever the compromises, there is little doubt the plans Rumsfeld finally signed off on were designed to showcase many of the reformers' theories. Some nine days into the assault, this new-wave warfare is being put to the test in the harsh sands of Iraq, and not everything is going with clockwork precision. True, it is early in the fight, and what looks like a series of initial glitches could be overcome by future breakthroughs. For instance, if the coalition secures its southern flank, it would fare better in the assault on Baghdad.

Still, it's undeniable that the first week of "shock and awe" did not go as the Pentagon had hoped. As U.S. forces gather for a climactic battle for Baghdad, they have been hobbled by sandstorms, guerrilla strikes by *fedayeen* irregulars, stretched supply lines, friendly fire incidents, and signs that the Iraqis may use chemical and nerve agents. As a result, Rumsfeld and Franks face increasing flak. The most frequently heard charge: that the U.S. lacks the ground troops for what may turn into a tough, protracted fight in Iraq.

That wasn't how things were supposed to play out. Pentagon planners had hoped that a blitz of precision bombing and cruise-missile strikes would sever Saddam Hussein's ability to communicate with his commanders. A simultaneous land assault would arrive on Saddam's doorstep with unnerving speed. Isolated and surrounded, Iraqi soldiers were expected to surrender en masse.

There was one more thing: Strict targeting restrictions would minimize civilian casualties to help the Americans and British be perceived as liberators by a skeptical Arab world.

Rumsfeld's strategy lends itself to caricature by critics, in part because of the Pentagon chief's unwavering confidence in all things Rumsfeldian. But in fact, it represents the culmination of years of thinking by hawkish policy advisers who advocate a preemptive tack toward America's enemies in an era of proliferating weapons of mass destruction. In these encounters, the U.S. would bring to the battle advantages drawn from the nation's edge in high technology. Advances in communications, stealth technology, robotics, and precision targeting would act as "force multipliers" that lessen the need for lumbering land armies and big cannons.

But with military analysts questioning whether the U.S. has sent enough troops for the task, some wonder if, just like some '90s dot-com visionary, Rumsfeld oversold techno-war. One example: Despite disruption to Saddam's communications, Iraqi soldiers and irregulars have still found ways to harass the coalition advance. "We're bogged down in a low-intensity conflict like we would find in any Third World country," Major William Gillespie of the 3rd Infantry told *BusinessWeek*. "Guys in civilian clothes in pickup trucks are taking shots at us."

And, as widely predicted, even vaunted three-dimensional views of the battlefield cannot prevent friendly fire accidents or mistaken attacks on civilian cars, buses, and houses. With the Republican Guards preparing for a fight to the finish in Baghdad, some analysts suggest that without the missing 4th Infantry Division—a unit that was supposed to move into Northern Iraq from Turkey but now faces a lengthy detour to Kuwait—U.S. armor may be too thin for the coming showdown.

Amid the haze of war, it's still unclear whether the skeptics will be proved right. But one thing is certain: What's being tested in Iraq is not just the mettle of the U.S. military but an entire philosophy of warfare. The Rumsfeld approach is in sharp contrast with the "overwhelming force" doctrine outlined by then-Chairman of the Joint Chiefs of Staff Colin L. Powell prior to the 1991 Gulf War. A former artillery officer whose views were shaped by Vietnam, Powell stated that barring a mandate from the American people, a clear objective, and a force advantage of at least three times the enemy's troop strength, America should steer clear of wars. That's why Powell insisted on a U.S.-led invasion force of 550,000 during Operation Desert Storm.

Rumsfeld's new-wavers think massing huge numbers of land troops isn't always needed in an era when powerful networked-computing systems and unerringly accurate munitions can do much of the dirty work. "There's a substitution of information for mass," says retired Vice-Admiral Arthur K. Cebrowski, a key Rumsfeld adviser on transformation.

The outcome of the Iraq war could determine the fate of Rumsfeld's vision, which has run into spirited resistance from entrenched military chiefs. If the U.S. wins a quick victory, it will accelerate moves to modernize U.S. forces and make them more reliant on high-tech wizardry. And it would be a boon to the still reeling high-tech industry. But if the Iraq intervention bogs down amid costly street fighting, the Pentagon chief would face a major setback.

Rumsfeld seems stung by the potshots, but he's determined to prove that technology and speed will prevail over crude mass in Iraq. "It is a good plan," he insisted on Mar. 25. "Wars are unpredictable, and there's lots of difficulties." In the end, says Rumsfeld, the coalition will roll up Baghdad sooner rather than later, and with far fewer casualties than pessimists envision.

Still, Rumsfeld has been sketchy on the details of his promised tech and strategic revolution. With the exception of axing the 70-ton Crusader howitzer, he hasn't killed any major weapons programs that were envisioned for Cold War conflicts. The current Pentagon arsenal is in reality just a better-funded version of what the Clinton Administration crafted.

What's more, top military officials are still scrambling to figure out ways to tackle the 21st Century challenges the Pentagon foresees. Some of those threats are hardly distant, from the risks of urban warfare—which U.S. troops face in Baghdad—to the lack of access to bases near a newly menacing North Korea.

Indeed, to some analysts, Rumsfeld's Pentagon is acting much as Sears, Roebuck did when it saw Wal-Mart Stores making inroads in rural retail markets. Sears responded by making its catalog business more efficient. In the same way, instead of changing, the U.S. military is more efficient at doing what it always did. It's "much better at waging the kind of war we did in 1991 in the Persian Gulf," says Andrew F. Krepinevich, executive director of the Center for Strategic & Budgetary Assessments, a Washington think tank.

If the U.S. manages to extricate itself more or less intact from Iraq, that may be all that's needed this time around. And in the end, the vaunted Rumsfeld Doctrine may be perceived as little more than a flexible road map for doing whatever is needed to win wars in the future. But to Rumsfeld, it's much more than that. The nation's chief war planner wants nothing less than to create a new military strategy that makes America's technological might the ultimate weapon. And now, as high-tech dreams meet low-tech tactics in the barren landscape of Iraq, it is facing its first big test.

By Stan Crock, Paul Magnusson, and Lee Walczak in Washington, with Frederik Balfour with the 3rd Infantry Division in Iraq

UNIT 6
Risk

Unit Selections

Key Points to Consider

- The Overview to this unit mentions Michael Crichton's latest novel, *Prey*. The physicist Freeman Dyson reviews this novel in the February 13, 2002 issue of The New York Review of Books. Do you agree with what he has to say about the threats that technology holds for us?

- Who is Kevin Mitnick? Where does he work now? What does this say about the way we view white-collar crime in the United States?

- Use the Internet to find out more about Robert Tappan Morris, mentioned in the Overview to this unit. His family history is interesting. Why?

- Do you feel safe giving your credit card number to merchants over the Web? Find out how (or if) your number is protected from criminals who might intercept traffic between you and the merchants.

- The problems confronting government archivists in "The Fading Memory of State," are also faced by librarians across the country. Interview librarians in your school. How are they contending with disintegrating media and changing file formats?

Student Website
www.mhcls.com/online

Internet References
Further information regarding these websites may be found in this book's preface or online.

AntiOnline: Hacking and Hackers
http://www.antionline.com/index.php

Copyright & Trademark Information for the IEEE Computer Society
http://computer.org/copyright.htm

Electonic Privacy Information Center (EPIC)
http://epic.org

Internet Privacy Coalition
http://www.epic.org/crypto/

Center for Democracy and Technology
http://www.cdt.org/crypto/

Survive Spyware
http://www.cnet.com/internet/0-3761-8-3217791-1.html

An Electronic Pearl Harbor? Not Likely
http://www.nap.edu/issues/15.1/smith.htm

If literature and film are guides, we in the United States and Western Europe have tangled feelings about technology. On the one hand, we embrace each technical marvel that enters the market place. On the other, a world in which machines have gained the upper hand is a cultural staple. Not long ago, Michael Crichton's novel, *Prey*, frightened us with killer robots that evolved by natural selection to inhabit bodies, snatch souls, and take over the world. Teenagers around the country are still watching the handsome couple from *The Matrix*, Neo and Trinity, once again take on technology run amuck. This time our creations farm humankind and harvest their capacity to produce energy.

As it happens, we have good reason to worry about technology, especially computer technology, but the risks are more prosaic. They include privacy intrusions, software that cannot be made error free, and deliberate sabotage. We even have grounds to fear that much of our cultural heritage, now digitized, will be inaccessible when the software used to encode it becomes obsolete. These are issues that concern practicing computer scientists and engineers. *The Communications of the*

ACM, the leading journal in the field, has run a column in recent years called "Inside Risks," dedicated to exploring the unintended consequences of computing. Another ACM journal, *Software Engineering Notes*, devotes a large part of each issue to chronicling software failures.

It should not be surprising to anyone that networked computers offer new opportunities to criminals. Though actual data is lacking, perhaps due to concerns about publicity, cyber extortion appears to be growing. Anyone who uses the Internet is surely familiar with the barrage of spam offering discount drugs. Once again, it would be surprising if criminals had not found their way into this growing market. The Federal Trade Commission estimates that identity theft costs $53 billon each year, only a bit less than the estimated annual cost of the war in Iraq.

Though less dramatic than identity theft, spyware—software downloaded unknowingly—is receiving increasing attention. According to a recent piece in the *Communications of the ACM* ("Why Spyware Poses Multiple Threats to Security"), an important computer science journal, harm caused by spyware ranges from gobbling up computer speed on your PC to enlisting your machine in attacks that can disrupt major businesses or the government.

Yet another unintended consequence of networked computers is the use of the Net by terrorist organizations. David Talbot ("Terror's Server") tells us that "most experts agree that the Internet is not just a tool of terrorist organizations, but is central to their operations. This article leads naturally to a long and fascinating profile ("Homeland Insecurity") of Bruce Schneier, once a prominent writer on cryptography—his *Applied Cryptography* (Wiley, 1996) is a standard reference—and now the owner of a computer security firm that brings a common-sense, low-tech approach to computer crime. Schneier believes that current approaches to network security, emphasizing technical cure-alls, are, at best, wrong. Some will even make us less safe. Though not about information technology, a story from the automobile industry illustrates the problem. In the 1990's car companies began to make the ignitions of expensive cars hard to hot-wire, and so more difficult to steal. The technical fix worked. It reduces the likelihood that a car would be stolen from a parking lot. It seems also to have contributed to the invention of car-jacking, a more dangerous crime.

Ever since a Cornell graduate student, Robert Tappan Morris, released a worm onto the fledgling Internet in 1988, computer experts and users alike have been aware of computer network vulnerability. An increasingly common type in the world of hacking is the insider working for the good guys. The web site www.happyhacker.org, for example, offers this advice from someone who calls himself "Agent Steal," writing, he says, from an unnamed federal prison: "let me tell you what this all means. You're going to get busted, lose everything you own, not get out on bail, snitch on your enemies, get even more time than you expected and have to put up with a bunch of idiots in prison. Sounds fun? Keep hacking." Good advice, of course.

For a more personal view of Agent Steal and his friends, we offer a long piece from *The New York Times Magazine*, "The Virus Underground." The second paragraph begins with these words: "When Mario is bored—and out here in the countryside, surrounded by soaring snowcapped mountains and little else, he's bored a lot—he likes to sit at his laptop and create computer viruses and worms."

Yet another risk associated with computer technology is implicit in the title of a piece from *Technology Review*: "The Fading Memory of the State." Government documents, from the 38 million emails generated by the Clinton administration to electronic records of the 1989 invasion of Panama, are on disintegrating electronic media, stored using now obsolete formats. In the worst scenario, they have been simply discarded. The reasons are legion, but one is sheer volume. One expert quoted in the article "says that in the next three years, humanity will generate more data—from websites to digital photos and video—than it generated in the previous 1000 years."

Anyone who has spent time looking at Internet news sources, knows that they can sometimes be unreliable. Paul Hitlin's "False Reporting on the Internet and the Spread of Rumors," examines Internet coverage of the Vince Foster suicide along with other stories to understand just why this is so.

In July of 2005, problems with the space shuttle were again in the news. Insulating foam came loose during the launch, the very cause of the 2003 Columbia Space Shuttle disaster. The next-to-last piece in this unit finds a less obvious culprit. "The Level of Discourse Continues to Slide," begins like this: "Is there anything so deadening to the soul as a PowerPoint presentation." As it happens, not only our souls are in danger. John Schwartz tells us that at least one expert on visual communication claims that the shuttle Columbia's explosion might have been due, in part, to a badly prepared PowerPoint slide. Is technology neutral? In this case, was PowerPoint misused or is there something about PowerPoint itself that encourages misuse?

"Technology giveth and technology taketh away," said Neil Postman, or, as the title of a book on technology puts it: *Why Things Bite Back* (Edward Tenner, Knopf, 1996). Along with the ability to communicate effortlessly around the globe, we must contend with cyber crime, spyware, data extinction, and PowerPoint fever, all concerns that barely existed five years ago and not at all a generation ago. As always, Shakespeare says it best: "O brave new world…."

WHY SPYWARE POSES MULTIPLE Threats to Security

ROGER THOMPSON

Spyware is becoming a relentless onslaught from those seeking to capture and use private information for their own ends. Spyware is annoying and negatively impacts the computing experience. Even worse, there are real and significant threats to corporate and even national security from those who use and abuse spyware.

There is much debate in Congress, state legislatures, and industry about what constitutes spyware. While that debate is an important one in terms of possible remedies, we can count the cost that unfettered spyware is having on individual users as well as on corporate networks. Regardless of whether we agree to divide the term spyware into various subsets such as adware or malware, the truth is any software application, if downloaded unknowingly or unwittingly, and without full explanation, is unacceptable and unwelcome.

With that understanding as a backdrop, the following is a working definition of spyware: Any software intended to aid an unauthorized person or entity in causing a computer, without the knowledge of the computer's user or owner, to divulge private information. This definition applies to legitimate business as much as to malicious code writers and hackers who are taking advantage of spyware to break into users' PCs.

Theft through spyware could be the most important and LEAST UNDERSTOOD ESPIONAGE TACTIC IN USE TODAY.

Many PC users have unwittingly loaded, or unknowingly had spyware downloaded onto their computers. This happens when a user clicks "yes" in response to a lengthy and often extremely technical or legalistic end user licensing agreement. Or it happens when a user simply surfs the Web, where self-activating code is simply dropped onto their machines in what is known as a "drive-by download."

SPYWARE DANGERS REAL AND PERVASIVE

The dangers of spyware are not always known and are almost never obvious. Usually, you know when you have a virus or worm—they are quite obvious. Spyware silently installs itself on a PC, where it might start to take any number of different and unwanted actions, including:

- "Phone home" information about an individual, their computer, and their surfing habits to a third party to use to spam a computer user or push pop-up ads to their screen;
- Open a computer to a remote attacker using a Remote Access Trojan (RAT) to remotely control a computer;
- Capture every keystroke a user types—private or confidential email, passwords, bank account information—and report it back to a thief or blackmailer;
- Allow a computer to be hijacked and used to attack a third party's computers in a denial-of-service attack that can cost enterprises millions and expose them to legal liability; and
- Probe a system for vulnerabilities that can enable a hacker to steal files or otherwise exploit a computer system.

SPYWARE HARMS COMPUTER PERFORMANCE

The misuse of technology and hijacking of spyware is a real and present danger to security and privacy. The ill effects of spyware do not stop there. Spyware seriously degrades computer performance and productivity.

Testing at our company's research laboratory earlier this year revealed that the addition of just one adware pest slowed a computer's boot time by 3.5 minutes. Instead of just under two minutes to perform this operation, it took the infected PC close to seven minutes. Multiply that by a large number of PCs and you have a huge productivity sinkhole. Add another pest and the slowdown doubles again.

We also tested Web page access, and again it took much longer once a pest was added to a clean machine. Almost five times longer in fact for a Web page to load on an infected PC. The pest also caused three Web sites to be accessed, rather than the one requested, and caused the PC to transmit and receive much greater amounts of unknown data—889 bytes transmitted compared to 281 transmitted from the clean machine, and 3,086 bytes received compared to 1,419 bytes received by the clean machine. This translates into significant increases in bandwidth utilization. Managing bandwidth costs money.

Increased costs due to unnecessary consumption of bandwidth on individual PCs, and the necessary labor costs in rebuilding systems to ensure they are no longer corrupt are virtually unquantifiable. System degradation is time consuming for the individual PC user and even more so for network administrators managing corporate networks. Even new PCs straight from the factory come loaded with thousands of pieces of spyware, all busy "phoning home" information about the user and slowing down computing speeds.

NATIONAL SECURITY THREATS

As noted here, keystroke loggers and other programs embedded with spyware can be used to steal critical data. Literally thousands of spyware applications are downloaded every day in large organizations whose employees use the Internet. The probability is high that at least some of those applications are designed to steal passwords and other critical data. Theft through spyware could be the most important and least understood espionage tactic in use today.

Another disturbing threat posed by spyware goes directly to the ability of terrorists or others to disable computer networks in times of crisis. In the past year, spyware has been used to essentially hijack large numbers of personal computers and organize them into "Bot Armies." Some of the organizers of these armies use them to send millions of spam email messages without user knowledge. Advertisements offering this service have even appeared in Europe and Asia.

The potential exists to move beyond annoyance to something much worse—targeted distributed denial-of-service (DDoS) attacks aimed at disrupting major business or government activity. A DDoS attack coordinated through thousands of individual PCs, owned by innocent and even unwitting users, could be a very difficult threat to address quickly, effectively, and fairly.

Individual PC users are never aware their machine is being used to disrupt Internet traffic. There is currently little or no recourse to a legal solution even if the occurrence can be monitored.

POSSIBLE SOLUTIONS

Only a combination of education and protection, disclosure through legislation, active prosecution, and plan-

ning will provide the answer needed to address the spyware threat. None of these solutions by themselves is enough.

The first line of defense is education and protection. Any individual, business, or government agency currently connected to the Internet must realize they are part of a complex network that is inextricably intertwined. Creators of spyware take advantage of that fact, plus the knowledge that most PC users are not sophisticated technologists. The technology industry has begun to make computer users aware of the spyware threat by the creation of and active outreach by several groups and organizations, including the Consortium of Anti-Spyware Technology (COAST).

Consumer education about spyware and promotion of comprehensive anti-spyware software aimed at detecting and removing unwanted pests is fundamental to this outreach, which is modeled after the decade-long effort by anti-virus software companies to raise awareness about virus threats. However, individual computer users, precisely because of the insidious nature of spyware, can only do so much to protect themselves, and are not personally responsible for controlling the spread of spyware.

Which brings us to the second line of defense—disclosure legislation. All applications, including those bundled and downloaded along with free software and with legitimate commercial applications, should be readily identifiable by users prior to installation and made easy to remove or uninstall. It is this transparent disclosure, and the ability of individual users to decide what does and does not reside on their systems, that must be legislated. Individuals should have the ability to make fully informed decisions about what they choose to download onto their machines, while understanding the implications of doing so.

The third line of defense is aggressive prosecution. The deceptive practices employed by many spyware developers are already illegal under existing laws against consumer fraud and identity theft. Law enforcement agencies at the federal and state level should be encouraged to aggressively pursue and prosecute those who clandestinely use spyware to disrupt service, steal data, or engage in other illegal activity. Appropriate agencies should work closely with their counterparts in other countries to address this issue.

The final line of defense is planning. A spyware Bot Army DDoS targeted at key federal, state, or local agencies is well within the realm of possibility. Such an attack could be very damaging, especially if it was designed to conceal a more conventional attack, or disrupt a response to such an attack. Overcoming this type of DDoS attack could itself be highly disruptive to both individuals and businesses. It is critical that responsible bodies plan for both spyware-related DDoS attacks and responses to those attacks. If necessary, those plans should be coordinated with businesses and others. Again, this coordination should include working with responsible bodies in other countries.

Spyware is a significant threat to the effective functioning and continued growth of the Internet. It also poses threats to national security. Given the dangers it represents, it is important that business and government work together to address the issue and safeguard the productivity and security of the Internet computing environment.

Roger Thompson is director of malicious content research at Computer Associates.

Terrors Server

Fraud, gruesome propaganda, terror planning: the Net enables it all.
The online industry can help fix it.

David Talbot

Two hundred two people died in the Bali, Indonesia, disco bombing of October 12, 2002, when a suicide bomber blew himself up on a tourist-bar dance floor, and then, moments later, a second bomber detonated an explosives-filled Mitsubishi van parked outside. Now, the mastermind of the attacks—Imam Samudra, a 35-year-old Islamist militant with links to al-Qaeda—has written a jailhouse memoir that offers a primer on the more sophisticated crime of online credit card fraud, which it promotes as a way for Muslim radicals to fund their activities.

Law enforcement authorities say evidence collected from Samudra's laptop computer shows he tried to finance the Bali bombing by committing acts of fraud over the Internet. And his new writings suggest that online fraud—which in 2003 cost credit card companies and banks $1.2 billion in the United States alone—might become a key weapon in terrorist arsenals, if it's not already. "We know that terrorist groups throughout the world have financed themselves through crime," says Richard Clarke, the former U.S. counterterrorism czar for President Bush and President Clinton. "There is beginning to be a reason to conclude that one of the ways they are financing themselves is through cyber-crime."

Online fraud would thereby join the other major ways in which terrorist groups exploit the Internet. The September 11 plotters are known to have used the Internet for international communications and information gathering. Hundreds of jihadist websites are used for propaganda and fund-raising purposes and are as easily accessible as the mainstream websites of major news organizations. And in 2004, the Web was awash with raw video of hostage beheadings perpetrated by followers of Abu Musab al-Zarqawi, the Jordanian-born terror leader operating in Iraq. This was no fringe phenomenon. Tens of millions of people downloaded the video files, a kind of vast medieval spectacle enabled by numberless Web hosting companies and Internet service providers, or ISPs. "I don't know where the line is. But certainly, we have passed it in the abuse of the Internet," says Gabriel Weimann, a professor of communications at the University of Haifa, who tracks use of the Internet by terrorist groups.

Meeting these myriad challenges will require new technology and, some say, stronger self-regulation by the online industry, if only to ward off the more onerous changes or restrictions that might someday be mandated by legal authorities or by the security demands of business interests. According to Vinton Cerf, a founding father of the Internet who codesigned its protocols, extreme violent content on the Net is "a terribly difficult conundrum to try and resolve in a way that is constructive." But, he adds, "it does not mean we shouldn't do anything. The industry has a fair amount of potential input, if it is to try to figure out how on earth to discipline itself. The question is, which parts of the industry can do it?" The roadblocks are myriad, he notes: information can literally come from anywhere, and even if major industry players agree to restrictions, Internet users themselves could obviously go on sharing content. "As always, the difficult question will be, Who decides what is acceptable content and on what basis?"

Some work is already going on in the broader battle against terrorist use of the Internet. Research labs are developing new algorithms aimed at making it easier for investigators to comb through e-mails and chat-room dialogue to uncover criminal plots. Meanwhile, the industry's anti-spam efforts are providing new tools for authenticating e-mail senders using cryptography and other methods, which will also help to thwart fraud; clearly, terrorist exploitation of the Internet adds a national-security dimension to these efforts. The question going forward is whether the terrorist use of the medium, and the emerging responses, will help usher in an era in which the distribution of online content is more tightly controlled and tracked, for better or worse.

The Rise of Internet Terror

Today, most experts agree that the Internet is not just a tool of terrorist organizations, but is central to their operations*. Some say that al-Qaeda's online presence has become more potent and pertinent than its actual physical presence since the September 11 attacks. "When we say al-Qaeda is a global ideology, this is where it existson the Internet," says Michael Doran, a Near East scholar and terrorism expert at Princeton University. "That, in itself, I find absolutely amazing. Just a few years ago, an organization like this would have been more cultlike in nature. It wouldn't be able to spread around the world the way it does with the Internet."

The universe of terror-related websites extends far beyond al-Qaeda, of course. According to Weimann, the number of such websites has leapt from only 12 in 1997 to around 4,300 today. (This includes sites operated by groups like Hamas and Hezbollah, and others in South America and other parts of the world.) "In seven years it has exploded, and I am quite sure the number will grow next week and the week after," says Weimann, who described the trend in his report "How Modern Terrorism Uses the Internet," published by the United States Institute of Peace, and who is now at work on a book, *Terrorism and the Internet*, due out later this year.

These sites serve as a means to recruit members, solicit funds, and promote and spread ideology. "While the [common] perception is that [terrorists] are not well educated or very sophisticated about telecommunications or the Internet, we know that that isn't true," says Ronald Dick, a former FBI deputy assistant director who headed the FBI's National Infrastructure Protection Center. "The individuals that the FBI and other law enforcement agencies have arrested have engineering and telecommunications backgrounds; they have been trained in academic institutes as to what these capabilities are." (Militant Islam, despite its roots in puritanical Wahhabism, taps the well of Western liberal education: Khalid Sheikh Mohammed, the principal September 11 mastermind, was educated in the U.S. in mechanical engineering; Osama bin Laden's deputy Ayman al-Zawahiri was trained in Egypt as a surgeon.)

The Web gives jihad a public face. But on a less visible level, the Internet provides the means for extremist groups to surreptitiously organize attacks and gather information. The September 11 hijackers used conventional tools like chat rooms and e-mail to communicate and used the Web to gather basic information on targets, says Philip Zelikow, a historian at the University of Virginia and the former executive director of the 9/11 Commission. "The conspirators used the Internet, usually with coded messages, as an important medium for international communication," he says. (Some aspects of the terrorists' Internet use remain classified; for example, when asked whether the Internet played a role in recruitment of the hijackers, Zelikow said he could not comment.)

Finally, terrorists are learning that they can distribute images of atrocities with the help of the Web. In 2002, the Web facilitated wide dissemination of videos showing the beheading of *Wall Street Journal* reporter Daniel Pearl, despite FBI requests that websites not post them. Then, in 2004, Zarqawi made the gruesome tactic a cornerstone of his terror strategy, starting with the murder of the American civilian contractor Nicholas Berg—which law enforcement agents believe was carried out by Zarqawi himself. From Zarqawi's perspective, the campaign was a rousing success. Images of orange-clad hostages became a headline-news staple around the world—and the full, raw videos of their murders spread rapidly around the Web. "The Internet allows a small group to publicize such horrific and gruesome acts in seconds, for very little or no cost, worldwide, to huge audiences, in the most powerful way," says Weimann.

And there's a large market for such material. According to Dan Klinker, webmaster of a leading online gore site, Ogrish.com, consumption of such material is brisk. Klinker, who says he operates from offices in Western and Eastern Europe and New York City, says his aim is to "open people's eyes and make them aware of reality." It's clear that many eyes have taken in these images thanks to sites like his. Each beheading video has been downloaded from Klinker's site several million times, he says, and the Berg video tops the list at 15 million. "During certain events (beheadings, etc.) the servers can barely handle the insane bandwidths—sometimes 50,000 to 60,000 visitors an hour," Klinker says.

Avoiding the Slippery Slope

To be sure, Internet users who want to block objectionable content can purchase a variety of filtering-software products that attempt to block sexual or violent content. But they are far from perfect. And though a hodgepodge of Web page rating schemes are in various stages of implementation, no universal rating system is in effect—and none is mandated—that would make filters chosen by consumers more effective.

But passing laws aimed at allowing tighter filtering—to say nothing of actually mandating filtering—is problematical. Laws aimed at blocking minors access to pornography, like the Communications Decency Act and Childrens Online Protection Act, have been struck down in the courts on First Amendment grounds, and the same fate has befallen some state laws, often for good reason: the filtering tools sometimes throw out the good with the bad. "For better or worse, the courts are more concerned about protecting the First Amendment rights of adults than protecting children from harmful material," says Ian Ballon, an expert on cyberspace law and a partner at Manatt, Phelps, and Phillips in Palo Alto, CA. Pornography access, he says, "is something the courts have been more comfortable regulating in the physical world than on the Internet." The same challenges pertain to images of extreme violence, he adds.

The Federal Communications Commission enforces "decency" on the nation's airwaves as part of its decades-old mission of licensing and regulating television and radio stations. Internet content, by contrast, is essentially unregulated. And so, in 2004, as millions of people watched video of beheadings on their computers, the FCC fined CBS $550,000 for broadcasting the exposure of singer Janet Jacksons breast during the Super Bowl halftime show on television.

"While not flatly impossible, [Internet content] regulation is hampered by the variety of places around the world at which it can be hosted," says Jonathan Zittrain, codirector of the Berkman Center for Internet and Society at Harvard Law School—and thats to say nothing of First Amendment concerns. As Zittrain sees it, "its a gift that the sites are up there, because it gives us an opportunity for counterintelligence."

Industry adoption of tighter editorial controls would be a matter of good taste and of supporting the war on terror, says Richard Clarke.

As a deterrent, criminal prosecution has also had limited success. Even when those suspected of providing Internet-based assistance to terror cells are in the United States, obtaining convictions can be difficult. Early last year, under provisions of the Patriot Act, the U.S. Department of Justice charged Sami Omar al-Hussayen, a student at the University of Idaho, with using the Internet to aid terrorists. The government alleged that al-Hussayen maintained websites that promoted jihadist-related activities, including funding terrorists. But his defense argued that he was simply using his skills to promote Islam and wasn't responsible for the sites radical content. The judge reminded the jury that, in any case, the Constitution protects most speech. The jury cleared al-Hussayen on the terrorism charges but deadlocked on visa-related charges; al-Hussayen agreed to return home to his native Saudi Arabia rather than face a retrial on the visa counts.

Technology and ISPs

But the government and private-sector strategy for combatting terrorist use of the Internet has several facets. Certainly, agencies like the FBI and the National Security Agency—and a variety of watchdog groups, such as the Site Institute, a nonprofit organization based in an East Coast location that it asked not be publicized—closely monitor jihadist and other terrorist sites to keep abreast of their public statements and internal communications, to the extent possible.

It's a massive, needle-in-a-haystack job, but it can yield a steady stream of intelligence tidbits and warnings. For example, the Site Institute recently discovered, on a forum called the Jihadi Message Board, an Arabic translation of a U.S. Air Force Web page that mentioned an American airman of Lebanese descent. According to Rita Katz, executive director of the Site Institute, the jihadist page added, in Arabic, "This hypocrite will be going to Iraq in September of this year [2004]—I pray to Allah that his cunning leads to his slaughter. I hope that he will be slaughtered the Zarqawi's way, and then [go from there] to the lowest point in Hell." The Site Institute alerted the military. Today, on one if its office walls hangs a plaque offering the thanks of the Air Force Office of Special Investigations.

New technology may also give intelligence agencies the tools to sift through online communications and discover terrorist plots. For example, research suggests that people with nefarious intent tend to exhibit distinct patterns in their use of e-mails or online forums like chat rooms. Whereas most people establish a wide variety of contacts over time, those engaged in plotting a crime tend to keep in touch only with a very tight circle of people, says William Wallace, an operations researcher at Rensselaer Polytechnic Institute.

This phenomenon is quite predictable. "Very few groups of people communicate repeatedly only among themselves," says Wallace. "It's very rare; they don't trust people outside the group to communicate. When 80 percent of communications is within a regular group, this is where we think we will find the groups who are planning activities that are malicious." Of course, not all such groups will prove to be malicious; the odd high-school reunion will crop up. But Wallaces group is developing an algorithm that will narrow down the field of so-called social networks to those that warrant the scrutiny of intelligence officials. The algorithm is scheduled for completion and delivery to intelligence agencies this summer.

And of course, the wider fight against spam and online fraud continues apace. One of the greatest challenges facing anti-fraud forces is the ease with which con artists can doctor their e-mails so that they appear to come from known and trusted sources, such as colleagues or banks. In a scam known as "phishing," this tactic can trick recipients into revealing bank account numbers and passwords. Preventing such scams, according to Clarke, "is relevant to counterterrorism because it would prevent a lot of cyber-crime, which may be how [terrorists] are funding themselves. It may also make it difficult to assume identities for one-time-use communications."

A Window on Online Fraud

In 2003, 124,509 complaints of Internet fraud and crime were made to the U.S. Internet Crime Complaint Center, an offshoot of the FBI that takes complaints largely from the United States. The perpetrators' reported home countries broke down as follows:

Rank	Country	Reports
1	United States	76.4%
2	Canada	3.3%
3	Nigeria	2.9%
4	Italy	2.5%
5	Spain	2.4%
6	Romania	1.5%
7	Germany	1.3%
8	United Kingdom	1.3%
9	South Africa	1.1%
10	Netherlands	0.9%

Technology Review, February 2005

New e-mail authentication methods may offer a line of defense. Last fall, AOL endorsed a Microsoft-designed system called Sender ID that closes certain security loopholes and matches the IP (Internet Protocol) address of the server sending an inbound e-mail against a list of servers authorized to send mail from the message's purported source. Yahoo, the world's largest e-mail provider with some 40 million accounts, is now rolling out its own system, called Domain Keys, which tags each outgoing e-mail message with an encrypted signature that can be used by the recipient to verify that the message came from the purported domain. Google is using the technology with its Gmail accounts, and other big ISPs, including Earthlink, are following suit.

Finally, the bigger ISPs are stepping in with their own reactive efforts. Their "terms of service" are usually broad enough to allow them the latitude to pull down objectionable sites when asked to do so. "When you are talking about an online community, the power comes from the individual," says Mary Osako, Yahoo's director of communications. "We encourage our users to send [any concerns about questionable] content to us—and we take action on every report."

Too Little, or Too Much

But most legal, policy, and security experts agree that these efforts, taken together, still don't amount to a real solution. The new anti-spam initiatives represent only the latest phase of an ongoing battle. "The first step is, the industry has to realize there is a problem that is bigger than they want to admit," says Peter Neumann, a computer scientist at SRI International, a nonprofit research institute in Menlo Park, CA. "There's a huge culture change that's needed here to create trustworthy systems. At the moment we dont have anything I would call a trustworthy system."

Even efforts to use cryptography to confirm the authenticity of e-mail senders, he says, are a mere palliative. There are still lots of problems with online security, says Neumann. "Look at it as a very large iceberg. This shaves off one-fourth of a percent, maybe 2 percent—but its a little bit off the top."

But if it's true that existing responses are insufficient to address the problem, it may also be true that we're at risk of an overreaction. If concrete links between online fraud and terrorist attacks begin emerging, governments could decide that the Internet needs more oversight and create new regulatory structures. "The ISPs could solve most of the spam and phishing problems if made to do so by the FCC," notes Clarke. Even if the Bali bombers writings don't create such a reaction, something else might. If no discovery of a strong connection between online fraud and terrorism is made, another trigger could be an actual act of "cyberterrorism"—the long-feared use of the Internet to wage digital attacks against targets like city power grids and air traffic control or communications systems. It could be some online display of homicide so appalling that it spawns a new drive for online decency, one countenanced by a newly conservative Supreme Court. Terrorism aside, the trigger could be a pure business decision, one aimed at making the Internet more transparent and more secure.

Zittrain concurs with Neumann but also predicts an impending overreaction. Terrorism or no terrorism, he sees a convergence of security, legal, and business trends that will force the Internet to change, and not necessarily for the better. "Collectively speaking, there are going to be technological changes to how the Internet functions—driven either by the law or by collective action. If you look at what they are doing about spam, it has this shape to it," Zittrain says. And while technological change might improve online security, he says, "it will make the Internet less flexible. If its no longer possible for two guys in a garage to write and distribute killer-app code without clearing it first with entrenched interests, we stand to lose the very processes that gave us the Web browser, instant messaging, Linux, and e-mail."

The first needed step: a culture change in the industry, to acknowledge a problem bigger than they want to admit, says Peter Neumann.

A concerted push toward tighter controls is not yet evident. But if extremely violent content or terrorist use of the Internet might someday spur such a push, a chance for preemptive action may lie with ISPs and Web hosting companies. Their efforts need not be limited to fighting spam and fraud. With respect to the content they publish, Web hosting companies could act more like their older cousins, the television broadcasters and newspaper and magazine editors, and exercise a little editorial judgment, simply by enforcing existing terms of service.

Is Web content already subject to any such editorial judgment? Generally not, but sometimes, the hopeful eye can discern what appear to be its consequences. Consider the mysterious inconsistency among the results returned when you enter the word "beheading" into the major search engines. On Google and MSN, the top returns are a mixed bag of links to responsible news accounts, historical information, and ghoulish sites that offer raw video with teasers like "World of Death, Iraq beheading videos, death photos, suicides and crime scenes." Clearly, such results are the product of algorithms geared to finding the most popular, relevant, and well-linked sites.

But enter the same search term at Yahoo, and the top returns are profiles of the U.S. and British victims of beheading in Iraq. The first 10 results include links to biographies of Eugene Armstrong, Jack Hensley, Kenneth Bigley, Nicholas Berg, Paul Johnson, and Daniel Pearl, as well as to memorial websites. You have to load the second page of search results to find a link to Ogrish.com. Is this oddly tactful ordering the aberrant result of an algorithm as pitiless as the ones that churn up gore links elsewhere?

Or is Yahoo, perhaps in a nod to the victims' memories and their families' feelings, making an exception of the words "behead" and "beheading," treating them differently than it does thematically comparable words like "killing" and "stabbing?"

Yahoo's Osako did not reply to questions about this search-return oddity; certainly, a technological explanation cannot be excluded. But it's clear that such questions are very sensitive for an industry that has, to date, enjoyed little intervention or regulation. In its response to complaints, says Richard Clarke, "the industry is very willing to cooperate and be good citizens in order to stave off regulation." Whether it goes further and adopts a stricter editorial posture, he adds, "is a decision for the ISP [and Web hosting company] to make as a matter of good taste and as a matter of supporting the U.S. in the global war on terror." If such decisions evolve into the industrywide assumption of a more journalistic role, they could, in the end, be the surest route to a more responsible medium—one that is less easy to exploit and not so vulnerable to a clampdown.

David Talbot is Technology Review's *chief correspondent.*

HOMELAND INSECURITY

A top expert says America's approach to protecting itself will only make matters worse.
Forget "foolproof" technology—we need systems designed to fail smartly.

- *To stop the rampant theft of expensive cars, manufacturers in the 1990s began to make ignitions very difficult to hot-wire. This reduced the likelihood that cars would be stolen from parking lots—but apparently contributed to the sudden appearance of a new and more dangerous crime, carjacking.*

- *After a vote against management Vivendi Universal announced earlier this year that its electronic shareholder-voting system, which it had adopted to tabulate votes efficiently and securely, had been broken into by hackers. Because the new system eliminated the old paper ballots, recounting the votes—or even independently verifying that the attack had occurred—was impossible.*

- *To help merchants verify and protect the identity of their customers, marketing firms and financial institutions have created large computerized databases of personal information: Social Security numbers, credit-card numbers, telephone numbers, home addresses, and the like. With these databases being increasingly interconnected by means of the Internet, they have become irresistible targets for criminals. From 1995 to 2000 the incidence of identity theft tripled.*

BY CHARLES C. MANN

As was often the case, Bruce Schneier was thinking about a really terrible idea. We were driving around the suburban-industrial wasteland south of San Francisco, on our way to a corporate presentation, while Schneier looked for something to eat not purveyed by a chain restaurant. This was important to Schneier, who in addition to being America's best-known ex-cryptographer is a food writer for an alternative newspaper in Minneapolis, where he lives. Initially he had been sure that in the crazy ethnic salad of Silicon Valley it would be impossible not to find someplace of culinary interest—a Libyan burger stop, a Hmong bagelry, a Szechuan taco stand. But as the rented car swept toward the vast, amoeboid office complex that was our destination, his faith slowly crumbled. Bowing to reality, he parked in front of a nondescript sandwich shop, disappointment evident on his face.

Schneier is a slight, busy man with a dark, full, closely cropped beard. Until a few years ago he was best known as a prominent creator of codes and ciphers; his book *Applied Cryptography* (1993) is a classic in the field. But despite his success he virtually abandoned cryptography in 1999 and co-founded a company named Counterpane Internet Security. Counterpane has spent considerable sums on advanced engineering, but at heart the company is dedicated to bringing one of the oldest forms of policing—the cop on the beat—to the digital realm. Aided by high-tech sensors, human guards at Counterpane patrol

computer networks, helping corporations and governments to keep their secrets secret. In a world that is both ever more interconnected and full of malice, this is a task of considerable difficulty and great importance. It is also what Schneier long believed cryptography would do—which brings us back to his terrible idea.

"Pornography!" he exclaimed. If the rise of the Internet has shown anything, it is that huge numbers of middle-class, middle-management types like to look at dirty pictures on computer screens. A good way to steal the corporate or government secrets these middle managers are privy to, Schneier said, would be to set up a pornographic Web site. The Web site would be free, but visitors would have to register to download the naughty bits. Registration would involve creating a password—and here Schneier's deep-set blue eyes widened mischievously.

People have trouble with passwords. The idea is to have a random string of letters, numbers, and symbols that is easy to remember. Alas, random strings are by their nature hard to remember, so people use bad but easy-to-remember passwords, such as "hello" and "password." (A survey last year of 1,200 British office workers found that almost half chose their own name, the name of a pet, or that of a family member as a password; others based their passwords on the names Darth Vader and Homer Simpson.) Moreover, computer users can't keep different passwords straight, so they use the same bad passwords for all their accounts.

Many of his corporate porn surfers, Schneier predicted, would use for the dirty Web site the same password they used at work. Not only that, many users would surf to the porn site on the fast Internet connection at the office. The operators of Schneier's nefarious site would thus learn that, say, "Joesmith," who accessed the Web site from Anybusiness.com, used the password "JoeS." By trying to log on at Anybusiness.com as "Joesmith," they could learn whether "JoeS" was also the password into Joesmith's corporate account. Often it would be.

The way people think about security, especially security on computer networks, is almost always wrong. All too often planners seek cures, magic bullets to make problems vanish. Most of the security measures envisioned after September 11 will be ineffective—and some will even make Americans less safe than they would be without them.

"In six months you'd be able to break into Fortune 500 companies and government agencies all over the world," Schneier said, chewing his nondescript meal. "It would work! It would work—that's the awful thing."

During the 1990s Schneier was a field marshal in the disheveled army of computer geeks, mathematicians, civil-liberties activists, and libertarian wackos that—in a series of bitter lawsuits that came to be known as the Crypto Wars—asserted the right of the U.S. citizenry to use the cryptographic equivalent of kryptonite: ciphers so powerful they cannot be broken by any government, no matter how long and hard it tries. Like his fellows, he believed that "strong crypto," as these ciphers are known, would forever guarantee the privacy and security of information—something that in the Information Age would be vital to people's lives. "It is insufficient to protect ourselves with laws" he wrote in *Applied Cryptography*. "We need to protect ourselves with mathematics."

Schneier's side won the battle as the nineties came to a close. But by that time he had realized that he was fighting the wrong war. Crypto was not enough to guarantee privacy and security. Failures occurred all the time—which was what Schneier's terrible idea demonstrated. No matter what kind of technological safeguards an organization uses, its secrets will never be safe while its employees are sending their passwords, however unwittingly, to pornographers—or to anyone else outside the organization.

The Parable of the Dirty Web Site illustrates part of what became the thesis of Schneier's most recent book, *Secrets and Lies* (2000): The way people think about security, especially security on computer networks, is almost al-

ways wrong. All too often planners seek technological cure-alls, when such security measures at best limit risks to acceptable levels. In particular, the consequences of going wrong—and all these systems go wrong sometimes—are rarely considered. For these reasons Schneier believes that most of the security measures envisioned after September 11 will be ineffective, and that some will make Americans *less* safe.

It is now a year since the World Trade Center was destroyed. Legislators, the law-enforcement community, and the Bush Administration are embroiled in an essential debate over the measures necessary to prevent future attacks. To armor-plate the nation's security they increasingly look to the most powerful technology available: retina, iris, and fingerprint scanners; "smart" driver's licenses and visas that incorporate anti-counterfeiting chips; digital surveillance of public places with face-recognition software; huge centralized databases that use data-mining routines to sniff out hidden terrorists. Some of these measures have already been mandated by Congress, and others are in the pipeline. State and local agencies around the nation are adopting their own schemes. More mandates and more schemes will surely follow.

Schneier is hardly against technology—he's the sort of person who immediately cases public areas for outlets to recharge the batteries in his laptop, phone, and other electronic prostheses. "But if you think technology can solve your security problems," he says, "then you don't understand the problems and you don't understand the technology." Indeed, he regards the national push for a high-tech salve for security anxieties as a reprise of his own early and erroneous beliefs about the transforming power of strong crypto. The new technologies have enormous capacities, but their advocates have not realized that the most critical aspect of a security measure is not how well it works but how well it fails.

THE CRYPTO WARS

If mathematicians from the 1970s were suddenly transported through time to the present, they would be happily surprised by developments such as the proofs to Kepler's conjecture (proposed in 1611, confirmed in 1998) and to Fermat's last theorem (1637, 1994). But they would be absolutely astonished by the RSA Conference, the world's biggest trade show for cryptographers. Sponsored by the cryptography firm RSA Security, the conferences are attended by as many as 10,000 cryptographers, computer scientists, network managers, and digital-security professionals. What would amaze past mathematicians is not just the number of conferences but that they exist at all.

Cryptology is a specialized branch of mathematics with some computer science thrown in. As recently as the 1970s there were no cryptology courses in university mathematics or computer-science departments; nor were there crypto textbooks, crypto journals, or crypto software. There was no private crypto industry, let alone venture-capitalized crypto start-ups giving away key rings at trade shows (*crypto key* rings—techno-humor). Cryptography, the practice of cryptology, was the province of a tiny cadre of obsessed amateurs, the National Security Agency, and the NSA's counterparts abroad. Now it is a multibillion-dollar field with applications in almost every commercial arena.

As one of the people who helped to bring this change about, Schneier is always invited to speak at RSA conferences. Every time, the room is too small, and overflow crowds, eager to hear their favorite guru, force the session into a larger venue, which is what happened when I saw him speak at an RSA conference in San Francisco's Moscone Center last year. There was applause from the hundreds of seated cryptophiles when Schneier mounted the stage, and more applause from the throng standing in the aisles and exits when he apologized for the lack of seating capacity. He was there to talk about the state of computer security, he said. It was as bad as ever, maybe getting worse.

In the past security officers were usually terse ex-military types who wore holsters and brush cuts. But as computers have become both attackers' chief targets and their chief weapons, a new generation of security professionals has emerged, drawn from the ranks of engineering and computer science. Many of the new guys look like people the old guard would have wanted to arrest, and Schneier is no exception. Although he is a co-founder of a successful company, he sometimes wears scuffed black shoes and pants with a wavering press line; he gathers his thinning hair into a straggly ponytail. Ties, for the most part, are not an issue. Schneier's style marks him as a true nerd—someone who knows the potential, both good and bad, of technology, which in our technocentric era is an asset.

Schneier was raised in Brooklyn. He got a B.S. in physics from the University of Rochester in 1985 and an M.S. in computer science from American University two years later. Until 1991, he worked for the Department of Defense, where he did things he won't discuss. Lots of kids are intrigued by codes and ciphers, but Schneier was surely one of the few to ask his father, a lawyer and a judge, to write secret messages for him to analyze. On his first visit to a voting booth, with his mother, he tried to figure out how she could cheat and vote twice. He didn't actually want her to vote twice—he just wanted, as he says, to "game the system."

Unsurprisingly, someone so interested in figuring out the secrets of manipulating the system fell in love with the systems for manipulating secrets. Schneier's childhood years, as it happened, were a good time to become intrigued by cryptography—the best time in history, in fact. In 1976 two researchers at Stanford University invented an entirely new type of encryption, public-key encryption, which abruptly woke up the entire field.

Public-key encryption is complicated in detail but simple in outline. All ciphers employ mathematical proce-

WHY THE MAGINOT LINE FAILED

In fact, the Maginot Line, the chain of fortifications on France's border with Germany, was indicative neither of despair about defeating Germany nor of thought mired in the past. It was instead evidence of faith that technology could substitute for manpower. It was a forerunner of the strategic bomber, the guided missile, and the "smart bomb." The same faith led to France's building tanks with thicker armor and bigger guns than German tanks had, deploying immensely larger quantities of mobile big guns, and above all committing to maintain a continuous line—that is, advancing or retreating in such coordination as to prevent an enemy from establishing a salient from which it could cut off a French unit from supplies and reinforcements. (Today, military strategists call this "force protection.") But having machines do the work of men and putting emphasis on minimal loss of life carried a price in slowed-down reaction times and lessened initiative for battlefield commanders.

—Ernest R. May, *Strange Victory: Hitler's Conquest of France* (2000)

dures called algorithms to transform messages from their original form into an unreadable jumble. (Cryptographers work with ciphers and not codes, which are spy-movie-style lists of prearranged substitutes for letters, words, or phrases—"meet at the theater" for "attack at nightfall.") Most ciphers use secret keys: mathematical values that plug into the algorithm. Breaking a cipher means figuring out the key. In a kind of mathematical sleight of hand, public-key encryption encodes messages with keys that can be published openly and decodes them with different keys that stay secret and are effectively impossible to break using today's technology. (A more complete explanation of public-key encryption is on *The Atlantic's* Web site, www.theatlantic.com.)

The best-known public-key algorithm is the RSA algorithm, whose name comes from the initials of the three mathematicians who invented it. RSA keys are created by manipulating big prime numbers. If the private decoding RSA key is properly chosen, guessing it necessarily involves factoring a very large number into its constituent primes, something for which no mathematician has ever devised an adequate shortcut. Even if demented government agents spent a trillion dollars on custom factoring computers, Schneier has estimated, the sun would likely go nova before they cracked a message enciphered with a public key of sufficient length.

Schneier and other technophiles grasped early how important computer networks would become to daily life. They also understood that those networks were dreadfully insecure. Strong crypto, in their view, was an answer of almost magical efficacy. Even federal officials believed that strong crypto would Change Everything Forever—except they thought the change would be for

The Worm in the Machine

Buffer overflows (sometimes called *stack smashing*) are the most common form of security vulnerability in the last ten years. They're also the easiest to exploit; more attacks are the result of buffer overflows than any other problem…

Computers store everything, programs and data, in memory. If the computer asks a user for an 8-character password and receives a 200-character password, those extra characters may overwrite some other area in memory. (They're not supposed to—that's the bug.) If it is just the right area of memory, and we overwrite it with just the right characters, we can change a "deny connection" instruction to an "allow access" command or even get our own code executed.

The Morris worm is probably the most famous overflow-bug exploit. It exploited a buffer overflow in the UNIX fingerd program. It's supposed to be a benign program, returning the identity of a user to whomever asks. This program accepted as input a variable that is supposed to contain the identity of the user. Unfortunately, the fingerd program never limited the size of the input. Input larger than 512 bytes overflowed the buffer, and Morris wrote a specific large input that allowed his rogue program to [install and run] itself… Over 6,000 servers crashed as a result; at the time [in 1988] that was about 10 percent of the Internet.

Skilled programming can prevent this kind of attack. The program can truncate the password at 8 characters, so those extra 192 characters never get written into memory anywhere… The problem is that with any piece of modern, large, complex code, there are just too many places where buffer overflows are possible… It's very difficult to guarantee that there are no overflow problems, even if you take the time to check. The larger and more complex the code is, the more likely the attack.

Windows 2000 has somewhere between 35 and 60 million lines of code, and no one outside the programming team has ever seen them.

—Bruce Schneier, *Secrets and Lies: Digital Security in a Networked World* (2000)

the worse. Strong encryption "jeopardizes the public safety and national security of this country," Louis Freeh, then the director of the (famously computer-challenged) Federal Bureau of Investigation, told Congress in 1995. "Drug cartels, terrorists, and kidnappers will use telephones and other communications media with impunity knowing that their conversations are immune" from wiretaps.

The Crypto Wars erupted in 1991, when Washington attempted to limit the spread of strong crypto. Schneier testified before Congress against restrictions on encryption, campaigned for crypto freedom on the Internet, co-wrote an influential report on the technical snarls awaiting federal plans to control cryptographic protocols, and rallied 75,000 crypto fans to the cause in his free monthly e-mail

newsletter, *Crypto-Gram* (www.counterpane.com/crypto-gram.html). Most important, he wrote *Applied Cryptography*, the first-ever comprehensive guide to the practice of cryptology.

Washington lost the wars in 1999, when an appellate court ruled that restrictions on cryptography were illegal, because crypto algorithms were a form of speech and thus covered by the First Amendment. After the ruling the FBI and the NSA more or less surrendered. In the sudden silence the dazed combatants surveyed the battleground. Crypto had become widely available, and it had indeed fallen into unsavory hands. But the results were different from what either side had expected.

As the crypto aficionados had envisioned, software companies inserted crypto into their products. On the "Tools" menu in Microsoft Outlook, for example, "encrypt" is an option. And encryption became big business, as part of the infrastructure for e-commerce—it is the little padlock that appears in the corner of Net suffers' browsers when they buy books at Amazon.com, signifying that credit-card numbers are being enciphered. But encryption is rarely used by the citizenry it was supposed to protect and empower. Cryptophiles, Schneier among them, had been so enraptured by the possibilities of uncrackable ciphers that they forgot they were living in a world in which people can't program VCRs. Inescapably, an encrypted message is harder to send than an unencrypted one, if only because of the effort involved in using all the extra software. So few people use encryption software that most companies have stopped selling it to individuals.

Among the few who do use crypto are human-rights activists living under dictatorships. But, just as the FBI feared, terrorists, child pornographers, and the Mafia use it too. Yet crypto has not protected any of them. As an example, Schneier points to the case of Nicodemo Scarfo, who the FBI believed was being groomed to take over a gambling operation in New Jersey. Agents surreptitiously searched his office in 1999 and discovered that he was that rarity, a gangster nerd. On his computer was the long-awaited nightmare for law enforcement: a crucial document scrambled by strong encryption software. Rather than sit by, the FBI installed a "keystroke logger" on Scarfo's machine. The logger recorded the decrypting key—or, more precisely, the passphrase Scarfo used to generate that key—as he typed it in, and gained access to his incriminating files. Scarfo pleaded guilty to charges of running an illegal gambling business on February 28 of this year.

Schneier was not surprised by this demonstration of the impotence of cryptography. Just after the Crypto Wars ended, he had begun writing a follow-up to *Applied Cryptography*. But this time Schneier, a fluent writer, was blocked—he couldn't make himself extol strong crypto as a security panacea. As Schneier put it in *Secrets and Lies*, the very different book he eventually did write, he had been portraying cryptography—in his speeches, in his congressional testimony, in *Applied Cryptography*—as "a kind of magic security dust that [people] could sprinkle over their software and make it secure." It was not. Nothing could be. Humiliatingly, Schneier discovered that, as a friend wrote him, "the world was full of bad security systems designed by people who read *Applied Cryptography*."

In retrospect he says, "Crypto solved the wrong problem." Ciphers scramble messages and documents, preventing them from being read while, say, they are transmitted on the Internet. But the strongest crypto is gossamer protection if malevolent people have access to the computers on the other end. Encrypting transactions on the Internet, the Purdue computer scientist Eugene Spafford has remarked, "is the equivalent of arranging an armored car to deliver credit-card information from someone living in a cardboard box to someone living on a park bench."

To effectively seize control of Scarfo's computer, FBI agents had to break into his office and physically alter his machine. Such black-bag jobs are ever less necessary, because the rise of networks and the Internet means that computers can be controlled remotely, without their operators' knowledge. Huge computer databases may be useful, but they also become tempting targets for criminals and terrorists. So do home computers, even if they are connected only intermittently to the Web. Hackers look for vulnerable machines, using software that scans thousands of Net connections at once. This vulnerability, Schneier came to think, is the real security issue.

With this realization he closed Counterpane Systems, his five-person crypto-consulting company in Chicago, in 1999. He revamped it and reopened immediately in Silicon Valley with a new name, Counterpane Internet Security, and a new idea—one that relied on old-fashioned methods. Counterpane would still keep data secret. But the lessons of the Crypto Wars had given Schneier a different vision of how to do that—a vision that has considerable relevance for a nation attempting to prevent terrorist crimes.

Where Schneier had sought one overarching technical fix, hard experience had taught him the quest was illusory. Indeed, yielding to the American penchant for all-in-one high-tech solutions can make us *less* safe—especially when it leads to enormous databases full of confidential information. Secrecy is important, of course, but it is also a trap. The more secrets necessary to a security system, the more vulnerable it becomes.

To forestall attacks, security systems need to be small-scale, redundant, and compartmentalized. Rather than large, sweeping programs, they should be carefully crafted mosaics, each piece aimed at a specific weakness. The federal government and the airlines are spending millions of dollars, Schneier points out, on systems that screen every passenger to keep knives and weapons out

of planes. But what matters most is keeping dangerous passengers out of airline cockpits, which can be accomplished by reinforcing the door. Similarly, it is seldom necessary to gather large amounts of additional information, because in modern societies people leave wide audit trails. The problem is sifting through the already existing mountain of data. Calls for heavy monitoring and record-keeping are thus usually a mistake. ("Broad surveillance is a mark of bad security," Schneier wrote in a recent *Crypto-Gram*.)

To halt attacks once they start, security measures must avoid being subject to single points of failure. Computer networks are particularly vulnerable: once hackers bypass the firewall, the whole system is often open for exploitation. Because every security measure in every system can be broken or gotten around, failure must be incorporated into the design. No single failure should compromise the normal functioning of the entire system or, worse, add to the gravity of the initial breach. Finally, and most important, decisions need to be made by people at close range—and the responsibility needs to be given explicitly to people, not computers.

The moral, Schneier came to believe, is that security measures are characterized less by their success than by their manner of failure. All security systems eventually miscarry in one way or another. But when this happens to the good ones, they stretch and sag before breaking, each component failure leaving the whole as unaffected as possible.

Unfortunately, there is little evidence that these principles are playing any role in the debate in the Administration, Congress, and the media about how to protect the nation. Indeed, in the argument over policy and principle almost no one seems to be paying attention to the practicalities of security—a lapse that Schneier, like other security professionals, finds as incomprehensible as it is dangerous.

STEALING YOUR THUMB

A couple of months after September 11, I flew from Seattle to Los Angeles to meet Schneier. As I was checking in at Sea-Tac Airport, someone ran through the metal detector and disappeared onto the little subway that runs among the terminals. Although the authorities quickly identified the miscreant, a concession stand worker, they still had to empty all the terminals and re-screen everyone in the airport, including passengers who had already boarded planes. Masses of unhappy passengers stretched back hundreds of feet from the checkpoints. Planes by the dozen sat waiting at the gates. I called Schneier on a cell phone to report my delay. I had to shout over the noise of all the other people on their cell phones making similar calls. "What a mess" Schneier said. "The problem with airport security, you know, is that it fails badly."

For a moment I couldn't make sense of this gnomic utterance. Then I realized he meant that when something goes wrong with security, the system should recover well. In Seattle a single slip-up shut down the entire airport, which delayed flights across the nation. Sea-Tac, Schneier told me on the phone, had no adequate way to contain the damage from a breakdown—such as a button installed near the x-ray machines to stop the subway, so that idiots who bolt from checkpoints cannot disappear into another terminal. The shutdown would inconvenience subway riders, but not as much as being forced to go through security again after a wait of several hours. An even better idea would be to place the x-ray machines at the departure gates, as some are in Europe, in order to scan each group of passengers closely and minimize inconvenience to the whole airport if a risk is detected—or if a machine or a guard fails.

Schneier was in Los Angeles for two reasons. He was to speak to ICANN, the Internet Corporation for Assigned Names and Numbers, which controls the "domain name system" of Internet addresses. It is Schneier's belief that attacks on the address database are the best means of taking down the Internet. He also wanted to review Ginza Sushi-Ko, perhaps the nation's most exclusive restaurant, for the food column he writes with his wife, Karen Cooper.

The government has been calling for a new security infrastructure: iris, retina, and fingerprint scanners; hand-geometry assayers; face-recognition software; smart cards with custom identification chips. Their use may on the whole make Americans less safe, because many of these tools fail badly—they're "brittle," in engineering jargon.

Minutes after my delayed arrival Schneier had with characteristic celerity packed himself and me into a taxi. The restaurant was in a shopping mall in Beverly Hills that was disguised to look like a collection of nineteenth-century Italian villas. By the time Schneier strode into the tiny lobby, he had picked up the thread of our airport discussion. Failing badly, he told me, was something he had been forced to spend time thinking about.

In his technophilic exuberance he had been seduced by the promise of public-key encryption. But ultimately Schneier observed that even strong crypto fails badly. When something bypasses it, as the keystroke logger did with Nicodemo Scarfo's encryption, it provides no protection at all. The moral, Schneier came to believe, is that security measures are characterized less by their manner

of success than by their manner of failure. All security systems eventually miscarry. But when this happens to the good ones, they stretch and sag before breaking, each component failure leaving the whole as unaffected as possible. Engineers call such failure-tolerant systems "ductile." One way to capture much of what Schneier told me is to say that he believes that when possible, security schemes should be designed to maximize ductility, whereas they often maximize strength.

Since September 11 the government has been calling for a new security infrastructure—one that employs advanced technology to protect the citizenry and track down malefactors. Already the USA PATRIOT Act, which Congress passed in October, mandates the establishment of a "cross-agency, cross-platform electronic system… to confirm the identity" of visa applicants, along with a "highly secure network" for financial-crime data and "secure information sharing systems" to link other, previously separate databases. Pending legislation demands that the Attorney General employ "technology including, but not limited to, electronic fingerprinting, face recognition, and retinal scan technology." The proposed Department of Homeland Security is intended to oversee a "national research and development enterprise for homeland security comparable in emphasis and scope to that which has supported the national security community for more than fifty years"—a domestic version of the high-tech R&D juggernaut that produced stealth bombers, smart weapons, and anti-missile defense.

Iris, retina, and fingerprint scanners; hand-geometry assayers; remote video-network surveillance; face-recognition software; smart cards with custom identification chips; decompressive baggage checkers that vacuum-extract minute chemical samples from inside suitcases; tiny radio implants beneath the skin that continually broadcast people's identification codes; pulsed fast-neutron analysis of shipping containers ("so precise," according to one manufacturer, "it can determine within inches the location of the concealed target"); a vast national network of interconnected databases—the list goes on and on. In the first five months after the terrorist attacks the Pentagon liaison office that works with technology companies received more than 12,000 proposals for high-tech security measures. Credit-card companies expertly manage credit risks with advanced information-sorting algorithms, Larry Ellison, the head of Oracle, the world's biggest database firm, told *The New York Times* in April; "We should be managing security risks in exactly the same way." To "win the war on terrorism," a former deputy undersecretary of commerce, David J. Rothkopf, explained in the May/June issue of *Foreign Policy*, the nation will need "regiments of geeks"—"pocket-protector brigades" who "will provide the software, systems, and analytical resources" to "close the gaps Mohammed Atta and his associates revealed."

Such ideas have provoked the ire of civil-liberties groups, which fear that governments, corporations, and

GUMMI FINGERS

Tsutomu Matsumoto, a Japanese cryptographer, recently decided to look at biometric fingerprint devices. These are security systems that attempt to identify people based on their fingerprint. For years the companies selling these devices have claimed that they are very secure, and that it is almost impossible to fool them into accepting a fake finger as genuine. Matsumoto, along with his students at the Yokohama National University, showed that they can be reliably fooled with a little ingenuity and $10 worth of household supplies.

Matsumoto uses gelatin, the stuff that Gummi Bears are made out of. First he takes a live finger and makes a plastic mold. (He uses a free-molding plastic used to make plastic molds, and is sold at hobby shops.) Then he pours liquid gelatin into the mold and lets it harden. (The gelatin comes in solid sheets, and is used to make jellied meats, soups, and candies, and is sold in grocery stores.) This gelatin fake finger fools fingerprint detectors about 80% of the time…

There's both a specific and a general moral to take away from this result. Matsumoto is not a professional fake-finger scientist; he's a mathematician. He didn't use expensive equipment or a specialized laboratory. He used $10 of ingredients you could buy, and whipped up his gummy fingers in the equivalent of a home kitchen. And he defeated eleven different commercial fingerprint readers, with both optical and capacitive sensors, and some with "live finger detection" features… If he could do this, then any semiprofessional can almost certainly do much more.

—Bruce Schneier, *Crypto-Gram*, May 15, 2002

the police will misuse the new technology. Schneier's concerns are more basic. In his view, these measures can be useful, but their large-scale application will have little effect against terrorism. Worse, their use may make Americans less safe, because many of these tools fail badly—they're "brittle," in engineering jargon. Meanwhile, simple, effective, ductile measures are being overlooked or even rejected.

The distinction between ductile and brittle security dates back, Schneier has argued, to the nineteenth-century linguist and cryptographer Auguste Kerckhoffs, who set down what is now known as Kerckhoffs's principle. In good crypto systems, Kerckhoffs wrote, "the system should not depend on secrecy, and it should be able to fall into the enemy's hands without disadvantage." In other words, it should permit people to keep messages secret even if outsiders find out exactly how the encryption algorithm works.

At first blush this idea seems ludicrous. But contemporary cryptography follows Kerckhoffs's principle closely. The algorithms—the scrambling methods—are openly revealed; the only secret is the key. Indeed, Schneier says,

Kerckhoffs's principle applies beyond codes and ciphers to security systems in general: every secret creates a potential failure point. Secrecy, in other words, is a prime cause of brittleness—and therefore something likely to make a system prone to catastrophic collapse. Conversely, openness provides ductility.

From this can be drawn several corollaries. One is that plans to add new layers of secrecy to security systems should automatically be hewed with suspicion. Another is that security systems that utterly depend on keeping secrets tend not to work very well. Alas, airport security is among these. Procedures for screening passengers, for examining luggage, for allowing people on the tarmac, for entering the cockpit, for running the autopilot software—all must be concealed, and all seriously compromise the system if they become known. As a result, Schneier wrote in the May issue of *Crypto-Gram*, brittleness "is an inherent property of airline security."

Few of the new airport-security proposals address this problem. Instead, Schneier told me in Los Angeles, they address problems that don't exist. "The idea that to stop bombings cars have to park three hundred feet away from the terminal, but meanwhile they can drop off passengers right up front like they always have…" He laughed. "The only ideas I've heard that make any sense are reinforcing the cockpit door and getting the passengers to fight back." Both measures test well against Kerckhoffs's principle: knowing ahead of time that law-abiding passengers may forcefully resist a hijacking en masse, for example, doesn't help hijackers to fend off their assault. Both are small-scale, compartmentalized measures that make the system more ductile, because no matter how hijackers get aboard, beefed-up doors and resistant passengers will make it harder for them to fly into a nuclear plant. And neither measure has any adverse effect on civil liberties.

Evaluations of a security proposal's merits, in Schneier's view, should not be much different from the ordinary cost-benefit calculations we make in daily life. The first question to ask of any new security proposal is, What problem does it solve? The second: What problems does it cause, especially when it fails?

Failure comes in many kinds, but two of the more important are simple failure (the security measure is ineffective) and what might be called subtractive failure (the security measure makes people less secure than before). An example of simple failure is face-recognition technology. In basic terms, face-recognition devices photograph people; break down their features into "facial building elements"; convert these into numbers that, like fingerprints, uniquely identify individuals; and compare the results with those stored in a database. If someone's facial score matches that of a criminal in the database, the person is detained. Since September 11 face-recognition technology has been placed in an increasing number of public spaces: airports, beaches, nightlife districts. Even visitors to the Statue of Liberty now have their faces scanned.

Face-recognition software could be useful. If an airline employee has to type in an identifying number to enter a secure area, for example, it can help to confirm that someone claiming to be that specific employee is indeed that person. But it cannot pick random terrorists out of the mob in an airline terminal. That much-larger-scale task requires comparing many sets of features with the many other sets of features in a database of people on a "watch list." Identix, of Minnesota, one of the largest face-recognition-technology companies, contends that in independent tests its FaceIt software has a success rate of 99.32 percent—that is, when the software matches a passenger's face with a face on a list of terrorists, it is mistaken only 0.68 percent of the time. Assume for the moment that this claim is credible; assume, too, that good pictures of suspected terrorists are readily available. About 25 million passengers used Boston's Logan Airport in 2001. Had face-recognition software been used on 25 million faces, it would have wrongly picked out just 0.68 percent of them—but that would have been enough, given the large number of passengers, to flag as many as 170,000 innocent people as terrorists. With almost 500 false alarms a day, the face-recognition system would quickly become something to ignore.

The potential for subtractive failure, different and more troublesome, is raised by recent calls to deploy biometric identification tools across the nation. Biometrics—"the only way to prevent identity fraud," according to the former senator Alan K. Simpson, of Wyoming—identifies people by precisely measuring their physical characteristics and matching them up against a database. The photographs on driver's licenses are an early example, but engineers have developed many high-tech alternatives, some of them already mentioned: fingerprint readers, voiceprint recorders, retina or iris scanners, face-recognition devices, hand-geometry assayers, even signature-geometry analyzers, which register pen pressure and writing speed as well as the appearance of a signature.

Appealingly, biometrics lets people be their own ID cards—no more passwords to forget! Unhappily, biometric measures are often implemented poorly. This past spring three reporters at C'T, a German digital-culture magazine, tested a face-recognition system, an iris scanner, and nine fingerprint readers. All proved easy to outsmart. Even at the highest security setting, Cognitec's FaceVACS-Logon could be fooled by showing the sensor a short digital movie of someone known to the system—the president of a company, say—on a laptop screen. To beat Panasonic's Authenticam iris scanner, the German journalists photographed an authorized user, took the photo and created a detailed, life-size image of his eyes, cut out the pupils, and held the image up before their faces like a mask. The scanner read the iris, detected the

presence of a human pupil—and accepted the imposture. Many of the fingerprint readers could be tricked simply by breathing on them, reactivating the last user's fingerprint. Beating the more sophisticated Identix Bio-Touch fingerprint reader required a trip to a hobby shop. The journalists used graphite powder to dust the latent fingerprint—the kind left on glass—of a previous, authorized user; picked up the image on adhesive tape; and pressed the tape on the reader. The Identix reader, too, was fooled. Not all biometric devices are so poorly put together, of course. But all of them fail badly.

"Okay, somebody steals your thumbprint," Schneier says. "Because we've centralized all the functions, the thief can tap your credit, open your medical records, start your car, any number of things. Now what do you do? With a credit card, the bank can issue you a new card with a new number. But this is your *thumb*—you can't get a new one."

Consider the legislation introduced in May by Congressmen Jim Moran and Tom Davis, both of Virginia, that would mandate biometric data chips in driver's licenses—a sweeping, nationwide data-collection program, in essence. (Senator Dick Durbin, of Illinois, is proposing measures to force states to use a "single identifying designation unique to the individual on all driver's licenses"; President George W. Bush has already signed into law a requirement for biometric student visas.) Although Moran and Davis tied their proposal to the need for tighter security after last year's attacks, they also contended that the nation could combat fraud by using smart licenses with bank, credit, and Social Security cards, and for voter registration and airport identification. Maybe so, Schneier says. "But think about screw-ups, because the system will screw up."

Smart cards that store non-biometric data have been routinely cracked in the past, often with inexpensive oscilloscope-like devices that detect and interpret the timing and power fluctuations as the chip operates. An even cheaper method, announced in May by two Cambridge security researchers, requires only a bright light, a standard microscope, and duct tape. Biometric ID cards are equally vulnerable. Indeed, as a recent National Research Council study points out, the extra security supposedly provided by biometric ID cards will raise the economic incentive to counterfeit or steal them, with potentially disastrous consequences to the victims. "Okay, somebody steals your thumbprint," Schneier says. "Because we've centralized all the functions, the thief can tap your credit, open your medical records, start your car, any number of things. Now what do you do? With a credit card, the bank can issue you a new card with a new number. But this is your *thumb*—you can't get a new one."

The consequences of identity fraud might be offset if biometric licenses and visas helped to prevent terrorism. Yet smart cards would not have stopped the terrorists who attacked the World Trade Center and the Pentagon. According to the FBI, all the hijackers seem to have been who they said they were; their intentions, not their identities, were the issue. Each entered the country with a valid visa, and each had a photo ID in his real name (some obtained their IDs fraudulently, but the fakes correctly identified them). "What problem is being solved here?" Schneier asks.

Good security is built in overlapping, cross-checking layers, to slow down attacks; it reacts limberly to the unexpected. Its most important components are almost always human. "Governments have been relying on intelligent, trained guards for centuries," Schneier says. "They spot people doing bad things and then use laws to arrest them. All in all, I have to say, it's not a bad system."

THE HUMAN TOUCH

One of the first times I met with Schneier was at the Cato Institute, a libertarian think tank in Washington, D.C., that had asked him to speak about security. Afterward I wondered how the Cato people had reacted to the speech. Libertarians love cryptography, because they believe that it will let people keep their secrets forever, no matter what a government wants. To them, Schneier was a kind of hero, someone who fought the good fight. As a cryptographer, he had tremendous street cred: he had developed some of the world's coolest ciphers, including the first rigorous encryption algorithm ever published in a best-selling novel (*Cryptonomicon*, by Neal Stephenson) and the encryption for the "virtual box tops" on Kellogg's cereals (children type a code from the box top into a Web site to win prizes), and had been one of the finalists in the competition to write algorithms for the federal government's new encryption standard, which it adopted last year. Now, in the nicest possible way, he had just told the libertarians the bad news: he still loved cryptography for the intellectual challenge, but it was not all that relevant to protecting the privacy and security of real people.

In security terms, he explained, cryptography is classed as a protective countermeasure. No such measure can foil every attack, and all attacks must still be both detected and responded to. This is particularly true for digital security, and Schneier spent most of his speech evoking the staggering insecurity of networked computers. Countless numbers are broken into every year, including machines in people's homes. Taking over computers is simple with the right tools, because software is so often misconfigured or flawed. In the first five months of this year, for example, Microsoft released five "critical" security patches for Internet Explorer, each intended to rectify lapses in the original code.

How Insurance Improves Security

Eventually, the insurance industry will subsume the computer security industry. Not that insurance companies will start marketing security products, but rather that the kind of firewall you use—along with the kind of authentication scheme you use, the kind of operating system you use, and the kind of network monitoring scheme you use—will be strongly influenced by the constraints of insurance.

Consider security, and safety, in the real world. Businesses don't install building alarms because it makes them feel safer; they do it because they get a reduction in their insurance rates. Building-owners don't install sprinkler systems out of affection for their tenants, but because building codes and insurance policies demand it. Deciding what kind of theft and fire prevention equipment to install are risk management decisions, and the risk taker of last resort is the insurance industry...

Businesses achieve security through insurance. They take the risks they are not willing to accept themselves, bundle them up, and pay someone else to make them go away. If a warehouse is insured properly, the owner really doesn't care if it burns down or not. If he does care, he's underinsured...

What will happen when the CFO looks at his premium and realizes that it will go down 50% if he gets rid of all his insecure Windows operating systems and replaces them with a secure version of Linux? The choice of which operating system to use will no longer be 100% technical. Microsoft, and other companies with shoddy security, will start losing sales because companies don't want to pay the insurance premiums. In this vision of the future, how secure a product is becomes a real, measurable, feature that companies are willing to pay for... because it saves them money in the long run.

—Bruce Schneier, *Crypto-Gram*, March 15, 2001

Computer crime statistics are notoriously sketchy, but the best of a bad lot come from an annual survey of corporations and other institutions by the FBI and the Computer Security Institute, a research and training organization in San Francisco. In the most recent survey, released in April, 90 percent of the respondents had detected one or more computer-security breaches within the previous twelve months—a figure that Schneier calls "almost certainly an underestimate." His own experience suggests that a typical corporate network suffers a serious security breach four to six times a year—more often if the network is especially large or its operator is politically controversial.

Luckily for the victims, this digital mayhem is mostly wreaked not by the master hackers depicted in Hollywood techno-thrillers but by "script kiddies"—youths who know just enough about computers to download and run automated break-in programs. Twenty-four hours a day, seven days a week, script kiddies poke and prod at computer networks, searching for any of the thousands of known security vulnerabilities that administrators have not yet patched. A typical corporate network, Schneier says, is hit by such doorknob-rattling several times an hour. The great majority of these attacks achieve nothing, but eventually any existing security holes will be found and exploited. "It's very hard to communicate how bad the situation is," Schneier says, "because it doesn't correspond to our normal intuition of the world. To a first approximation, bank vaults are secure. Most of them don't get broken into, because it takes real skill. Computers are the opposite. Most of them get broken into all the time, and it takes practically no skill." Indeed, as automated cracking software improves, it takes ever less knowledge to mount ever more sophisticated attacks.

Given the pervasive insecurity of networked computers, it is striking that nearly every proposal for "homeland security" entails the creation of large national databases. The Moran-Davis proposal, like other biometric schemes, envisions storing smart-card information in one such database; the USA PATRIOT Act effectively creates another; the proposed Department of Homeland Security would "fuse and analyze" information from more than a hundred agencies, and would "merge under one roof" scores or hundreds of previously separate databases. (A representative of the new department told me no one had a real idea of the number. "It's a lot," he said.) Better coordination of data could have obvious utility, as was made clear by recent headlines about the failure of the FBI and the CIA to communicate. But carefully linking selected fields of data is different from creating huge national repositories of information about the citizenry, as is being proposed. Larry Ellison, the CEO of Oracle, has dismissed cautions about such databases as whiny cavils that don't take into account the existence of murderous adversaries. But murderous adversaries are exactly why we should ensure that new security measures actually make American life safer.

Any new database must be protected, which automatically entails a new layer of secrecy. As Kerckhoffs's principle suggests, the new secrecy introduces a new failure point. Government information is now scattered through scores of databases; however inadvertently, it has been compartmentalized—a basic security practice. (Following this practice, tourists divide their money between their wallets and hidden pouches; pickpockets are less likely to steal it all.) Many new proposals would change that. An example is Attorney General John Ashcroft's plan, announced in June, to fingerprint and photograph foreign visitors "who fall into categories of elevated national security concern" when they enter the United States ("approximately 100,000" will be tracked this way in the first year). The fingerprints and photographs will be compared with those of "known or suspected terrorists" and "wanted criminals." Alas, no such database of

terrorist fingerprints and photographs exists. Most terrorists are outside the country, and thus hard to fingerprint, and latent fingerprints rarely survive bomb blasts. The databases of "wanted criminals" in Ashcroft's plan seem to be those maintained by the FBI and the Immigration and Naturalization Service. But using them for this purpose would presumably involve merging computer networks in these two agencies with the visa procedure in the State Department—a security nightmare, because no one entity will fully control access to the system.

Equivalents of the big, centralized databases under discussion already exist in the private sector: corporate warehouses of customer information, especially credit-card numbers. The record there is not reassuring. "Millions upon millions of credit-card numbers have been stolen from computer networks," Schneier says. So many, in fact, that Schneier believes that everyone reading this article "has, in his or her wallet right now, a credit card with a number that has been stolen," even if no criminal has yet used it. Number thieves, many of whom operate out of the former Soviet Union, sell them in bulk: $1,000 for 5,000 credit-card numbers, or twenty cents apiece. In a way, the sheer volume of theft is fortunate: so many numbers are floating around that the odds are small that any one will be heavily used by bad guys.

Large-scale federal databases would undergo similar assaults. The prospect is worrying, given the government's long-standing reputation for poor information security. Since September 11 at least forty government networks have been publicly cracked by typographically challenged vandals with names like "CriminalS," "S4t4n1c SOuls," "cr1m3 Org4n1z4dO," and "Discordian Dodgers." Summing up the problem, a House subcommittee last November awarded federal agencies a collective computer-security grade of F. According to representatives of Oracle, the federal government has been talking with the company about employing its software for the new central databases. But judging from the past, involving the private sector will not greatly improve security. In March, CERT/CC, a computer-security watchdog based at Carnegie Mellon University, warned of thirty-eight vulnerabilities in Oracle's database software. Meanwhile, a centerpiece of the company's international advertising is the claim that its software is "unbreakable." Other software vendors fare no better: CERT/CC issues a constant stream of vulnerability warnings about every major software firm.

Schneier, like most security experts I spoke to, does not oppose consolidating and modernizing federal databases per se. To avoid creating vast new opportunities for adversaries, the overhaul should be incremental and small-scale. Even so, it would need to be planned with extreme care—something that shows little sign of happening.

One key to the success of digital revamping will be a little-mentioned, even prosaic feature: training the users not

REMEMBER PEARL HARBOR

Surprise, when it happens to a government, is likely to be a complicated, diffuse, bureaucratic thing... It includes gaps in intelligence, but also intelligence that, like a string of pearls too precious to wear, is too sensitive to give to those who need it. It includes the alarm that fails to work, but also the alarm that has gone off so often it has been disconnected. It includes the unalert watchman, but also the one who knows he'll be chewed out by his superior if he gets higher authority out of bed. It includes the contingencies that occur to no one, but also those that everyone assumes somebody else is taking care of. It includes straightforward procrastination, but also decisions protracted by internal disagreement. It includes, in addition, the inability of individual human beings to rise to the occasion until they are sure it *is* the occasion—which is usually too late. (Unlike movies, real life provides no musical background to tip us off to the climax.) Finally, as at Pearl Harbor, surprise may include some measure of genuine novelty introduced by the enemy, and possibly some sheer bad luck.

The results, at Pearl Harbor, were sudden, concentrated, and dramatic. The failure, however, was cumulative, widespread, and rather drearily familiar. This is why surprise, when it happens to a government, cannot be described just in terms of startled people. Whether at Pearl Harbor or at the Berlin Wall, surprise is everything involved in a government's (or in an alliance's) failure to anticipate effectively.

—Foreword by Thomas C. Schelling to *Pearl Harbor: Warning and Decision* (1962) by Roberta Wohlstetter

---

to circumvent secure systems. The federal government already has several computer networks—INTELINK, SIPR-NET, and NIPRNET among them—that are fully encrypted, accessible only from secure rooms and buildings, and never connected to the Internet. Yet despite their lack of Net access the secure networks have been infected by e-mail perils such as the Melissa and I Love You viruses, probably because some official checked e-mail on a laptop, got infected, and then plugged the same laptop into the classified network. Because secure networks are unavoidably harder to work with, people are frequently tempted to bypass them—one reason that researchers at weapons labs sometimes transfer their files to insecure but more convenient machines.

Schneier has long argued that the best way to improve the very bad situation in computer security is to change software licenses. If software is blatantly unsafe, owners have no such recourse, because it is licensed rather than bought, and the licenses forbid litigation. It is unclear whether the licenses can legally do this (courts currently disagree), but as a practical matter it is next to impossible to win a lawsuit against a software firm. If some big software companies lose product-liability suits, Schneier believes, their confreres will begin to take security seriously.

Computer networks are difficult to keep secure in part because they have so many functions, each of which must be accounted for. For that reason Schneier and other experts tend to favor narrowly focused security measures—more of them physical than digital—that target a few precisely identified problems. For air travel, along with reinforcing cockpit doors and teaching passengers to fight back, examples include armed uniformed— *not* plainclothes—guards on select flights; "dead-man" switches that in the event of a pilot's incapacitation force planes to land by autopilot at the nearest airport; positive bag matching (ensuring that luggage does not get on a plane unless its owner also boards); and separate decompression facilities that detonate any altitude bombs in cargo before takeoff. None of these is completely effective; bag matching, for instance, would not stop suicide bombers. But all are well tested, known to at least impede hijackers, not intrusive to passengers, and unlikely to make planes less secure if they fail.

"The trick is to remember that technology can't save you," Schneier says. "We know this in our own lives. For real safety we park on nice streets where people notice if somebody smashes the window. Or we park in garages, where somebody watches the car. In both cases people are the essential security element. You always build the system around people."

It is impossible to guard all potential targets, because anything and everything can be subject to attack. Palestinian suicide bombers have shown this by murdering at random the occupants of pool halls and hotel meeting rooms. Horrible as these incidents are, they do not risk the lives of thousands of people, as would attacks on critical parts of the national infrastructure: nuclear-power plants, hydroelectric dams, reservoirs, gas and chemical facilities. Here a classic defense is available: tall fences and armed guards. Yet this past spring the Bush Administration cut by 93 percent the funds requested by the Energy Department to bolster security for nuclear weapons and waste; it denied completely the funds requested by the Army Corps of Engineers for guarding 200 reservoirs, dams, and canals, leaving fourteen large public-works projects with no budget for protection. A recommendation by the American Association of Port Authorities that the nation spend a total of $700 million to inspect and control ship cargo (today less than two percent of container traffic is inspected) has so far resulted in grants of just $92 million. In all three proposals most of the money would have been spent on guards and fences.

The most important element of any security measure, Schneier argues, is people, not technology—and the people need to be at the scene. Recall the German journalists who fooled the fingerprint readers and iris scanners.

139

None of their tricks would have worked if a reasonably attentive guard had been watching. Conversely, legitimate employees with bandaged fingers or scratched corneas will never make it through security unless a guard at the scene is authorized to overrule the machinery. Giving guards increased authority provides more opportunities for abuse, Schneier says, so the guards must be supervised carefully. But a system with more people who have more responsibility "is more robust," he observed in the June *Crypto-Gram*, "and the best way to make things work. (The U.S. Marine Corps understands this principle; it's the heart of their chain of command rules.)"

"The trick is to remember that technology can't save you," Schneier says. "We know this in our own lives. We realize that there's no magic anti-burglary dust we can sprinkle on our cars to prevent them from being stolen. We know that car alarms don't offer much protection. The Club at best makes burglars steal the car next to you. For real safety we park on nice streets where people notice if somebody smashes the window. Or we park in garages, where somebody watches the car. In both cases people are the essential security element. You always build the system around people."

LOOKING FOR TROUBLE

After meeting Schneier at the Cato Institute, I drove with him to the Washington command post of Counterpane Internet Security. It was the first time in many months that he had visited either of his company's two operating centers (the other is in Silicon Valley). His absence had been due not to inattentiveness but to his determination to avoid the classic high-tech mistake of involving the alpha geek in day-to-day management. Besides, he lives in Minneapolis, and the company headquarters are in Cupertino, California. (Why Minneapolis? I asked. "My wife lives there," he said. "It seemed polite.") With his partner, Tom Rowley, supervising day-to-day operations, Schneier constantly travels in Counterpane's behalf, explaining how the company manages computer security for hundreds of large and medium-sized companies. It does this mainly by installing human beings.

The command post was nondescript even by the bland architectural standards of exurban office complexes. Gaining access was like a pop quiz in security: How would the operations center recognize and admit its boss, who was there only once or twice a year? In this country requests for identification are commonly answered with a driver's license. A few years ago Schneier devoted considerable effort to persuading the State of Illinois to issue him a driver's license that showed no picture, signature, or Social Security number. But Schneier's license serves as identification just as well as a license showing a picture and a signature—which is to say, not all that well. With or without a picture, with or without a biometric chip, licenses cannot be more than state-issued cards with peo-

ple's names on them: good enough for social purposes, but never enough to assure identification when it is important. Authentication, Schneier says, involves something a person knows (a password or a PIN, say), has (a physical token, such as a driver's license or an ID bracelet), or is (biometric data). Security systems should use at least two of these; the Counterpane center employs all three. At the front door Schneier typed in a PIN and waved an iButton on his key chain at a sensor (iButtons, made by Dallas Semiconductor, are programmable chips embedded in stainless-steel discs about the size and shape of a camera battery). We entered a waiting room, where Schneier completed the identification trinity by placing his palm on a hand-geometry reader.

Beyond the waiting room, after a purposely long corridor studded with cameras, was a conference room with many electrical outlets, some of which Schneier commandeered for his cell phone, laptop, BlackBerry, and battery packs. One side of the room was a dark glass wall. Schneier flicked a switch, shifting the light and theatrically revealing the scene behind the glass. It was a Luddite nightmare: an auditorium-like space full of desks, each with two computer monitors; all the desks faced a wall of high-resolution screens. One displayed streams of data from the "sentry" machines that Counterpane installs in its clients' networks. Another displayed images from the video cameras scattered around both this command post and the one in Silicon Valley.

On a visual level the gadgetry overwhelmed the people sitting at the desks and watching over the data. Nonetheless, the people were the most important part of the operation. Networks record so much data about their usage that overwhelmed managers frequently turn off most of the logging programs and ignore the others. Among Counterpane's primary functions is to help companies make sense of the data they already have. "We turn the logs back on and monitor them," Schneier says. Counterpane researchers developed software to measure activity on client networks, but no software by itself can determine whether an unusual signal is a meaningless blip or an indication of trouble. That was the job of the people at the desks.

Highly trained and well paid, these people brought to the task a quality not yet found in any technology: human judgment, which is at the heart of most good security. Human beings do make mistakes, of course. But they can recover from failure in ways that machines and software cannot. The well-trained mind is ductile. It can understand surprises and overcome them. It fails well.

When I asked Schneier why Counterpane had such Darth Vaderish command centers, he laughed and said it helped to reassure potential clients that the company had mastered the technology. I asked if clients ever inquired how Counterpane trains the guards and analysts in the command centers. "Not often," he said, although that training is in fact the center of the whole system. Mixing long stretches of inactivity with short bursts of frenzy, the work rhythm of the Counterpane guards would have been familiar to police officers and firefighters everywhere. As I watched the guards, they were slurping soft drinks, listening to techno-death metal, and waiting for something to go wrong. They were in a protected space, looking out at a dangerous world. Sentries around Neolithic campfires did the same thing. Nothing better has been discovered since. Thinking otherwise, in Schneier's view, is a really terrible idea.

FURTHER READING

For clear primers on modern cryptography and on network security, it is hard to do better than Bruce Schneier's *Applied Cryptography* (1993) and *Secrets and Lies* (2000), respectively; these books (especially the latter) render technological arcana comprehensible to even the willfully Luddite.

The consensus classic in the field of cryptology remains *The Codebreakers: The Story of Secret Writing* (1967), by David Kahn. Kahn spent four years working on a book that sought, in his words, "to cover the entire history of cryptology." (That is in fact a modest description of a 1,200-page book that begins with a chapter called "The First 3,000 Years" and closes, twenty-five chapters later, with "Messages From Outer Space.") All subsequent chroniclers of cryptography unavoidably stand on Kahn's shoulders. But *The Codebreakers* nearly died aborning: reportedly, the Pentagon tried to suppress its publication; only after Kahn agreed to delete three passages was the book finally published. Kahn issued a new edition of the book in 1996, bringing his history nearly up to the century's end. Two of the most relevant books on the subject of homeland security, both published in 1998, were also the most prescient. *Terrorism and America: A Commonsense Strategy for a Democratic Society,* by Philip B. Heymann, and *America's Achilles' Heel: Nuclear, Biological, and Chemical Terrorism and Covert Attack*, by Richard A. Falkenrath, Robert D. Newman, and Bradley A. Thayer, warned of the imminent danger of a major terrorist attack on American soil.

Although the proposed Department of Homeland Security was hastily thrown together, the idea for such an entity had circulated within the government for years. Some of the proposals can be found in the excellent compilation of disparate reports that the U.S. Senate Committee on Foreign Relations put together last fall, when it was preparing for hearings on the subject of national security. The compilation is called **Strategies for Homeland Defense** and is available on the Internet at purl.access. gpo.gov/GPO/LPS15541.

Charles C. Mann, an Atlantic *correspondent, has written for the magazine since 1984. He is at work on a book based on his March 2002* Atlantic *cover story, "1491."*

The Virus Underground

Philet0ast3r, Second Part to Hell, Vorgon and guys like them around the world spend their Saturday nights writing fiendishly contagious computer viruses and worms. Are they artists, pranksters or techno-saboteurs?

By Clive Thompson

This is how easy it has become.

Mario stubs out his cigarette and sits down at the desk in his bedroom. He pops into his laptop the CD of Iron Maiden's "Number of the Beast," his latest favorite album. "I really like it," he says. "My girlfriend bought it for me." He gestures to the 15-year-old girl with straight dark hair lounging on his neatly made bed, and she throws back a shy smile. Mario, 16, is a secondary-school student in a small town in the foothills of southern Austria. (He didn't want me to use his last name.) His shiny shoulder-length hair covers half his face and his sleepy green eyes, making him look like a very young, languid Mick Jagger. On his wall he has an enormous poster of Anna Kournikova—which, he admits sheepishly, his girlfriend is not thrilled about. Downstairs, his mother is cleaning up after dinner. She isn't thrilled these days, either. But what bothers her isn't Mario's poster. It's his hobby.

When Mario is bored—and out here in the countryside, surrounded by soaring snowcapped mountains and little else, he's bored a lot—he likes to sit at his laptop and create computer viruses and worms. Online, he goes by the name Second Part to Hell, and he has written more than 150 examples of what computer experts call "malware": tiny programs that exist solely to self-replicate, infecting computers hooked up to the Internet. Sometimes these programs cause damage, and sometimes they don't. Mario says he prefers to create viruses that don't intentionally wreck data, because simple destruction is too easy. "Anyone can rewrite a hard drive with one or two lines of code," he says. "It makes no sense. It's really lame." Besides which, it's mean, he says, and he likes to be friendly.

But still—just to see if he could do it—a year ago he created a rather dangerous tool: a program that autogenerates viruses. It's called a Batch Trojan Generator, and anyone can download it freely from Mario's Web site. With a few simple mouse clicks, you can use the tool to create your own malicious "Trojan horse." Like its ancient namesake, a Trojan virus ar-

rives in someone's e-mail looking like a gift, a JPEG picture or a video, for example, but actually bearing dangerous cargo.

Mario starts up the tool to show me how it works. A little box appears on his laptop screen, politely asking me to name my Trojan. I call it the "Clive" virus. Then it asks me what I'd like the virus to do. *Shall the Trojan Horse format drive C:?* Yes, I click. *Shall the Trojan Horse overwrite every file?* Yes. It asks me if I'd like to have the virus activate the next time the computer is restarted, and I say yes again.

Then it's done. The generator spits out the virus onto Mario's hard drive, a tiny 3k file. Mario's generator also displays a stern notice warning that spreading your creation is illegal. The generator, he says, is just for educational purposes, a way to help curious programmers learn how Trojans work.

But of course I could ignore that advice. I could give this virus an enticing name, like "britney_spears_wedding_clip.mpeg," to fool people into thinking it's a video. If I were to e-mail it to a victim, and if he clicked on it—and didn't have up-to-date anti-virus software, which many people don't—then disaster would strike his computer. The virus would activate. It would quietly reach into the victim's Microsoft Windows operating system and insert new commands telling the computer to erase its own hard drive. The next time the victim started up his computer, the machine would find those new commands, assume they were part of the normal Windows operating system and guilelessly follow them. Poof: everything on his hard drive would vanish—e-mail, pictures, documents, games.

I've never contemplated writing a virus before. Even if I had, I wouldn't have known how to do it. But thanks to a teenager in Austria, it took me less than a minute to master the art.

Mario drags the virus over to the trash bin on his computer's desktop and discards it. "I don't think we should touch that," he says hastily.

COMPUTER EXPERTS CALLED 2003 "the Year of the Worm." For 12 months, digital infections swarmed across the Internet with the intensity of a biblical plague. It began in January, when the Slammer worm infected nearly 75,000 servers in 10 minutes, clogging Bank of America's A.T.M. network and causing sporadic flight delays. In the summer, the Blaster worm struck, spreading by exploiting a flaw in Windows; it carried taunting messages directed at Bill Gates, infected hundreds of thousands of computers and tried to use them to bombard a Microsoft Web site with data. Then in August, a worm called Sobig.F exploded with even more force, spreading via e-mail that it generated by stealing addresses from victims' computers. It propagated so rapidly that at one point, one out of every 17 e-mail messages traveling through the Internet was a copy of Sobig.F. The computer-security firm mi2g estimated that the worldwide cost of these attacks in 2003, including clean-up and lost productivity, was at least $82 billion (though such estimates have been criticized for being inflated).

The pace of contagion seems to be escalating. When the Mydoom.A e-mail virus struck in late January, it spread even faster than Sobig.F; at its peak, experts estimated, one out of every five e-mail messages was a copy of Mydoom.A. It also carried a nasty payload: it reprogrammed victim computers to attack the Web site of SCO, a software firm vilified by geeks in the "open source" software community.

You might assume that the blame—and the legal repercussions—for the destruction would land directly at the feet of people like Mario. But as the police around the globe have cracked down on cybercrime in the past few years, virus writers have become more cautious, or at least more crafty. These days, many elite writers do not spread their works at all. Instead, they "publish" them, posting their code on Web sites, often with detailed descriptions of how the program works. Essentially, they leave their viruses lying around for anyone to use.

Invariably, someone does. The people who release the viruses are often anonymous mischief-makers, or "script kiddies." That's a derisive term for aspiring young hackers, usually teenagers or curious college students, who don't yet have the skill to program computers but like to pretend they do. They download the viruses, claim to have written them themselves and then set them free in an attempt to assume the role of a fearsome digital menace. Script kiddies often have only a dim idea of how the code works and little concern for how a digital plague can rage out of control.

<The modern virus epidemic is born of a symbiotic relationship between the people smart enough to write a virus and the people dumb enough—or malicious enough—to spread it.>

Our modern virus epidemic is thus born of a symbiotic relationship between the people smart enough to write a virus and the people dumb enough—or malicious enough—to spread it. Without these two groups of people, many viruses would never see the light of day. Script kiddies, for example, were responsible for some of the damage the Blaster worm caused. The original version of Blaster, which struck on Aug. 11, was clearly written by a skilled programmer (who is still unknown and at large). Three days later, a second version of Blaster circulated online, infecting an estimated 7,000 computers. This time the F.B.I. tracked the release to Jeffrey Lee Parson, an 18-year-old in Minnesota who had found, slightly altered and re-released the Blaster code, prosecutors claim. Parson may have been seeking notoriety, or he may have had no clue how much damage the worm could cause: he did nothing to hide his identity and even included a reference to his personal Web site in the code. (He was arrested and charged with intentionally causing damage to computers; when his trial begins, probably this spring, he faces up to 10 years in jail.) A few weeks later, a similar scene unfolded: another variant of Blaster was found in the wild. This time it was traced to a college student in Romania who had also left obvious clues to his identity in the code.

This development worries security experts, because it means that virus-writing is no longer exclusively a high-skill profession. By so freely sharing their work, the elite virus writers have made it easy for almost anyone to wreak havoc online. When the damage occurs, as it inevitably does, the original authors just shrug. *We may have created the monster*, they'll say, *but we didn't set it loose*. This dodge infuriates security professionals and the police, who say it is legally precise but morally corrupt. "When they publish a virus online, they *know* someone's going to release it," says Eugene Spafford, a computer-science professor and security expert at Purdue University. Like a collection of young Dr. Frankensteins, the virus writers are increasingly creating forces they cannot control—and for which they explicitly refuse to take responsibility.

"WHERE'S THE BEER?" Philet0ast3r wondered.

An hour earlier, he had dispatched three friends to pick up another case, but they were nowhere in sight. He looked out over the controlled chaos of his tiny one-bedroom apartment in small-town Bavaria. (Most of the virus writers I visited live in Europe; there have been very few active in the United States since 9/11, because of fears of prosecution.) Philet0ast3r's party was crammed with 20 friends who were blasting the punk band Deftones, playing cards, smoking furiously and arguing about politics. It was a Saturday night. Three girls sat on the floor, rolling another girl's hair into thick dreadlocks, the hairstyle of choice among the crowd. Philet0ast3r himself—a 21-year-old with a small silver hoop piercing his lower lip—wears his brown hair in thick dreads. (Philet0ast3r is an online handle; he didn't want me to use his name.)

Philet0ast3r's friends finally arrived with a fresh case of ale, and his blue eyes lit up. He flicked open a bottle using the edge of his cigarette lighter and toasted the others. A tall blond friend in a jacket festooned with anti-Nike logos put his arm around Philet0ast3r and beamed.

"This guy," he proclaimed, "is the *best* at Visual Basic."

In the virus underground, that's love. Visual Basic is a computer language popular among malware authors for its simplicity; Philet0ast3r has used it to create several of the two dozen viruses he's written. From this tiny tourist town, he works as an assistant in a home for the mentally disabled and in his spare time runs an international virus-writers' group called the "Ready Rangers Liberation Front." He founded the group three years ago with a few bored high-school friends in his even tinier hometown nearby. I met him, like everyone profiled in this article, online, first e-mailing him, then chatting in an Internet Relay Chat channel where virus writers meet and trade tips and war stories.

Philet0ast3r got interested in malware the same way most virus authors do: his own computer was hit by a virus. He wanted to know how it worked and began hunting down virus-writers' Web sites. He discovered years' worth of viruses online, all easily downloadable, as well as primers full of coding tricks. He spent long evenings hanging out in online chat rooms, asking questions, and soon began writing his own worms.

One might assume Philet0ast3r would favor destructive viruses, given the fact that his apartment is decorated top-to-bottom with anticorporate stickers. But Philet0ast3r's viruses, like those of many malware writers, are often surprisingly mild things carrying goofy payloads. One worm does nothing but display a picture of a raised middle finger on your computer screen, then sheepishly apologize for the gesture. ("Hey, this is not meant to you! I just wanted to show my payload.") Another one he is currently developing will install two artificial intelligence chat-agents on your computer; they appear in a pop-up window, talking to each other nervously about whether your antivirus software is going to catch and delete them. Philet0ast3r said he was also working on something sneakier: a "keylogger." It's a Trojan virus that monitors every keystroke its victim types—including passwords and confidential e-mail messages—then secretly mails out copies to whoever planted the virus. Anyone who spreads this Trojan would be able to quickly harvest huge amounts of sensitive personal information.

Technically, "viruses" and "worms" are slightly different things. When a virus arrives on your computer, it disguises itself. It might look like an OutKast song ("hey_ya.mp3"), but if you look more closely, you'll see it has an unusual suffix, like "hey_ya.mp3.exe." That's because it isn't an MP3 file at all. It's a tiny program, and when you click on it, it will reprogram parts of your computer to do something new, like display a message. A virus cannot kick-start itself; a human needs to be fooled into clicking on it. This turns virus writers into armchair psychologists, always hunting for new tricks to dupe someone into activating a virus. ("All virus-spreading," one virus writer said caustically, "is based on the idiotic behavior of the users.")

Worms, in contrast, usually do not require any human intervention to spread. That means they can travel at the breakneck pace of computers themselves. Unlike a virus, a worm generally does not alter or destroy data on a computer. Its danger lies in its speed: when a worm multiplies, it often generates enough traffic to brown out Internet servers, like air-conditioners bringing down the power grid on a hot summer day. The most popular worms today are "mass mailers," which attack a victim's computer, swipe the addresses out of Microsoft Outlook (the world's most common e-mail program) and send a copy of the worm to everyone in the victim's address book. These days, the distinction between worm and virus is breaking down. A worm will carry a virus with it, dropping it onto the victim's hard drive to do its work, then e-mailing itself off to a new target.

< Computer code blurs the line between speech and act. // Posting a virus on a Web site, one expert says, is 'like taking a gun and sticking bullets in it and sitting it on the counter and saying, "Hey, free gun!"' >

The most ferocious threats today are "network worms," which exploit a particular flaw in a software product (often one by Microsoft). The author of Slammer, for example, noticed a flaw in Microsoft's SQL Server, an online database commonly used by businesses and governments. The Slammer worm would find an unprotected SQL server, then would fire bursts of information at it, flooding the server's data "buffer," like a cup filled to the brim with water. Once its buffer was full, the server could be tricked into sending out thousands of new copies of the worm to other servers. Normally, a server should not allow an outside agent to control it that way, but Microsoft had neglected to defend against such an attack. Using that flaw, Slammer flooded the Internet with 55 million blasts of data per second and in only 10 minutes colonized almost all vulnerable machines. The attacks slowed the 911 system in Bellevue, Wash., a Seattle suburb, to such a degree that operators had to resort to a manual method of tracking calls.

Philet0ast3r said he isn't interested in producing a network worm, but he said it wouldn't be hard if he wanted to do it. He would scour the Web sites where computer-security professionals report any new software vulnerabilities they discover. Often, these security white papers will explain the flaw in such detail that they practically provide a road map on how to write a worm that exploits it. "Then I would use it," he concluded. "It's that simple."

Computer-science experts have a phrase for that type of fast-spreading epidemic: "a Warhol worm," in honor of Andy Warhol's prediction that everyone would be famous for 15 minutes. "In computer terms, 15 minutes is a really long time," says Nicholas Weaver, a researcher at the International Computer Science Institute in Berkeley, who coined the Warhol term. "The worm moves faster than humans can respond." He suspects that even more damaging worms are on the way. All a worm writer needs to do is find a significant new flaw in a Microsoft product, then write some code that exploits it. Even Microsoft admits that there are flaws the company doesn't yet know about.

Virus writers are especially hostile toward Microsoft, the perennial whipping boy of the geek world. From their (somewhat self-serving) point of view, Microsoft is to blame for the worm epidemic, because the company frequently leaves flaws in its products that allow malware to spread. Microsoft markets its products to less expert computer users, cultivating precisely the sort of gullible victims who click on disguised virus attachments. But it is Microsoft's success that really makes it such an attractive target: since more than 90 percent of desktop computers run Windows, worm writers target Microsoft in order to hit the largest possible number of victims. (By relying so exclusively on Microsoft products, virus authors say, we have created a digital monoculture, a dangerous thinning of the Internet's gene pool.)

Microsoft officials disagree that their programs are poor quality, of course. And it is also possible that their products are targeted because it has become cool to do so. "There's sort of a natural tendency to go after the biggest dog," says Phil Reitinger, senior security strategist for Microsoft. Reitinger says that the company is working to make its products more secure. But Microsoft is now so angry that it has launched a counterattack. Last fall, Microsoft set up a $5 million fund to pay for information leading to the capture of writers who target Windows machines. So far, the company has announced $250,000 bounties for the creators of Blaster, Sobig.F and Mydoom.B.

THE MOTIVATIONS OF the top virus writers can often seem paradoxical. They spend hours dreaming up new strategies to infect computers, then hours more bringing them to reality. Yet when they're done, most of them say they have little interest in turning their creations free. (In fact, 99 percent of all malware never successfully spreads in the wild, either because it expressly wasn't designed to do so or because the author was inept and misprogrammed his virus.) Though Philet0ast3r is proud of his keylogger, he said he does not intend to release it into the wild. His reason is partly one of self-protection; he wouldn't want the police to trace it back to him. But he also said he does not ethically believe in damaging someone else's computer.

So why write a worm, if you're not going to spread it?

For the sheer intellectual challenge, Philet0ast3r replied, the fun of producing something "really cool." For the top worm writers, the goal is to make something that's brand-new, never seen before. Replicating an existing virus is "lame," the worst of all possible insults. A truly innovative worm, Philet0ast3r said, "is like art." To allow his malware to travel swiftly online, the virus writer must keep its code short and efficient, like a poet elegantly packing as much creativity as possible into the tight format of a sonnet. "One condition of art," he noted, "is doing good things with less."

When he gets stuck on a particularly thorny problem, Philet0ast3r will sometimes call for help from other members of the Ready Rangers Liberation Front (which includes Mario). Another friend in another country, whom Philet0ast3r has never actually met, is helping him complete his keylogger by writing a few crucial bits of code that will hide the tool from its victim's view. When they're done, they'll publish their invention in their group's zine, a semi-annual anthology of the members' best work.

The virus scene is oddly gentlemanly, almost like the amateur scientist societies of Victorian Britain, where colleagues presented papers in an attempt to win that most elusive of social currencies: street cred. In fact, I didn't meet anyone who gloated about his own talent until I met Benny. He is a member of 29A, a super-elite cadre within the virus underground, a handful of coders around the world whose malware is so innovative that even antivirus experts grudgingly admit they're impressed. Based in the Czech Republic, Benny, clean-cut and wide-eyed, has been writing viruses for five years, making him a veteran in the field at age 21. "The main thing that I'm most proud of, and that no one else can say, is that I always come up with a new idea," he said, ushering me into a bedroom so neat that it looked as if he'd stacked his magazines using a ruler and level. "Each worm shows something different, something new that hadn't been done before by anyone."

Benny—that's his handle, not his real name—is most famous for having written a virus that infected Windows 2000 two weeks before Windows 2000 was released. He'd met a Microsoft employee months earlier who boasted that the new operating system would be "more secure than ever"; Benny wrote (but says he didn't release) the virus specifically to humiliate the company. "Microsoft," he said with a laugh, "wasn't enthusiastic." He also wrote Leviathan, the first virus to use "multithreading," a technique that makes the computer execute several commands at once, like a juggler handling multiple balls. It greatly speeds up the pace at which viruses can spread. Benny published that invention in his group's zine, and now many of the most virulent bugs have adopted the technique, including last summer's infamous Sobig.F.

For a virus author, a successful worm brings the sort of fame that a particularly daring piece of graffiti used to produce: the author's name, automatically replicating itself in cyberspace. When antivirus companies post on their Web sites a new "alert" warning of a fresh menace, the thrill for the author is like getting a great book review: something to crow about and e-mail around to your friends. Writing malware, as one author e-mailed me, is like creating artificial life. A virus, he wrote, is "a humble little creature with only the intention to avoid extinction and survive."

Quite apart from the intellectual fun of programming, though, the virus scene is attractive partly because it's very social. When Philet0ast3r drops by a virus-writers chat channel late at night after work, the conversation is as likely to be about music, politics or girls as the latest in worm technology. "They're not talking about viruses—they're talking about relationships or ordering pizza," says Sarah Gordon, a senior research fellow at Symantec, an antivirus company, who is one of the only researchers in the world who has interviewed hundreds of virus writers about their motivations. Very occasionally, malware authors even meet up face to face for a party; Philet0ast3r once took a road trip for a beer-addled weekend of coding, and when I visited Mario, we met up with another Austrian virus writer and discussed code for hours at a bar.

The virus community attracts a lot of smart but alienated young men, libertarian types who are often flummoxed by the social nuances of life. While the virus scene isn't dominated by those characters, it certainly has its share—and they are often the ones with a genuine chip on their shoulder.

"I am a social reject," admitted Vorgon (as he called himself), a virus writer in Toronto with whom I exchanged messages one night in an online chat channel. He studied computer science in college but couldn't find a computer job after sending out 400 résumés. With "no friends, not much family" and no girlfriend for years, he became depressed. He attempted suicide, he said, by walking out one frigid winter night into a nearby forest for five hours with no jacket on. But then he got into the virus-writing scene and found a community. "I met a lot of cool people who were interested in what I did," he wrote. "They made me feel good again." He called his first virus FirstBorn to celebrate his new identity. Later, he saw that one of his worms had been written up as an alert on an antivirus site, and it thrilled him. "Kinda like when I got my first girlfriend," he wrote. "I was god for a couple days." He began work on another worm, trying to recapture the feeling. "I spent three months working on it just so I could have those couple of days of godliness."

Vorgon is still angry about life. His next worm, he wrote, will try to specifically target the people who wouldn't hire him. It will have a "spidering" engine that crawls Web-page links, trying to find likely e-mail addresses for human-resource managers, "like careers@microsoft.com, for example." Then it will send them a fake résumé infected with the worm. (He hasn't yet decided on a payload, and he hasn't ruled out a destructive one.) "This is a revenge worm," he explained—for "not hiring me, and hiring some loser that is not even half the programmer I am."

MANY PEOPLE MIGHT wonder why virus writers aren't simply rounded up and arrested for producing their creations. But in most countries, writing viruses is not illegal. Indeed, in the United States some legal scholars argue that it is protected as free speech. Software is a type of language, and writing a program is akin to writing a recipe for beef stew. It is merely a bunch of instructions for the computer to follow, in the same way that a recipe is a set of instructions for a cook to follow. A virus or worm becomes illegal only when it is activated—when someone sends it to a victim and starts it spreading in the wild, and it does measurable damage to computer systems. The top malware authors are acutely aware of this distinction. Most every virus-writer Web site includes a disclaimer stating that it exists purely for educational purposes, and that if a visitor downloads a virus to spread, the responsibility is entirely the visitor's. Benny's main virus-writing computer at home has no Internet connection at all; he has walled it off like an airlocked biological-weapons lab, so that nothing can escape, even by accident.

Vorgon is angry about life. His next worm, he says, will try to specifically target the people who wouldn't hire him. 'This is a revenge worm,' he explained.

Virus writers argue that they shouldn't be held accountable for other people's actions. They are merely pursuing an interest in writing self-replicating computer code. "I'm not responsible for people who do silly things and distribute them among their friends," Benny said defiantly. "I'm not responsible for those. What I like to do is programming, and I like to show it to people—who may then do something with it." A young woman who goes by the handle Gigabyte told me in an online chat room that if the authorities wanted to arrest her and other virus writers, then "they should arrest the creators of guns as well."

One of the youngest virus writers I visited was Stephen Mathieson, a 16-year-old in Detroit whose screen name is Kefi. He also belongs to Philet0ast3r's Ready Rangers Liberation Front. A year ago, Mathieson became annoyed when he found members of another virus-writers group called Catfish_VX plagiarizing his code. So he wrote Evion, a worm specifically designed to taunt the Catfish guys. He put it up on his Web site for everyone to see. Like most of Mathieson's work, the worm had no destructive intent. It merely popped up a few cocky messages, including: *Catfish_VX are lamers. This virus was constructed for them to steal.*

Someone did in fact steal it, because pretty soon Mathieson heard reports of it being spotted in the wild. To this day, he does not know who circulated Evion. But he suspects it was probably a random troublemaker, a script kiddie who swiped it from his site. "The kids," he said, shaking his head, "just cut and paste."

Quite aside from the strangeness of listening to a 16-year-old complain about "the kids," Mathieson's rhetoric glosses over a charged ethical and legal debate. It is tempting to wonder if the leading malware authors are lying—whether they do in fact circulate their worms on the sly, obsessed with a desire to see whether they will really work. While security officials say that may occasionally happen, they also say the top virus writers are quite likely telling the truth. "If you're writing important virus code, you're probably well trained," says David Perry, global director of education for Trend Micro, an antivirus company. "You know a number of tricks to write good code, but you don't want to go to prison. You have an income and stuff. It takes someone unaware of the consequences to release a virus."

But worm authors are hardly absolved of blame. By putting their code freely on the Web, virus writers essentially dangle temptation in front of every disgruntled teenager who goes online looking for a way to rebel. A cynic might say that malware authors rely on clueless script kiddies the same way that a drug dealer uses 13-year-olds to carry illegal goods— passing the liability off to a hapless mule.

"You've got several levels here," says Marc Rogers, a former police officer who now researches computer forensics at Purdue University. "You've got the guys who write it, and they know they shouldn't release it because it's illegal. So they put it out there knowing that some script kiddie who wants to feel like a big shot in the virus underground will put it out. They know these neophytes will jump on it. So they're grinning ear to ear, because their baby, their creation, is out there. But they didn't officially release it, so they don't get in trouble." He says he thinks that the original authors are just as blameworthy as the spreaders.

Sarah Gordon of Symantec also says the authors are ethically naïve. "If you're going to say it's an artistic statement, there are more responsible ways to be artistic than to create code that costs people millions," she says. Critics like Reitinger, the Microsoft security chief, are even harsher. "To me, it's online arson," he says. "Launching a virus is no different from burning down a building. There are people who would never toss a Molotov cocktail into a warehouse, but they wouldn't think for a second about launching a virus."

What makes this issue particularly fuzzy is the nature of computer code. It skews the traditional intellectual question about studying dangerous topics. Academics who research nuclear-fission techniques, for example, worry that their research could help a terrorist make a weapon. Many publish their findings anyway, believing that the mere knowledge of how fission works won't help Al Qaeda get access to uranium or rocket parts.

But computer code is a different type of knowledge. The code for a virus is itself the weapon. You could read it in the same way you read a book, to help educate yourself about malware. Or you could set it running, turning it instantly into an active agent. Computer code blurs the line between speech and act. "It's like taking a gun and sticking bullets in it and sitting it on the counter and saying, 'Hey, free gun!'" Rogers says.

Some academics have pondered whether virus authors could be charged under conspiracy laws. Creating a virus, they theorize, might be considered a form of abetting a crime by providing materials. Ken Dunham, the head of "malicious code intelligence" for iDefense, a computer security company, notes that there are certainly many examples of virus authors assisting newcomers. He has been in chat rooms, he says, "where I can see people saying, 'How can I find vulnerable hosts?' And another guy says, 'Oh, go here, you can use this tool.' They're helping each other out."

There are virus writers who appreciate these complexities. But they are certain that the viruses they write count as protected speech. They insist they have a right to explore their interests. Indeed, a number of them say they are making the world a better place, because they openly expose the weaknesses of computer systems. When PhiletOast3r or Mario or Mathieson finishes a new virus, they say, they will immediately e-mail a copy of it to antivirus companies. That way, they explained, the companies can program their software to recognize and delete the virus should some script kiddie ever release it into the wild. This is further proof that they mean no harm with their hobby, as Mathieson pointed out. On the contrary, he said, their virus-writing strengthens the "immune system" of the Internet.

These moral nuances fall apart in the case of virus authors who are themselves willing to release worms into the wild. They're more rare, for obvious reasons. Usually they are overseas, in countries where the police are less concerned with software crimes. One such author is Melhacker, a young man who reportedly lives in Malaysia and has expressed sympathy for Osama bin Laden. Antivirus companies have linked him to the development of several worms, including one that claims to come from the "Qaeda network." Before the Iraq war, he told a computer magazine that he would release a virulent worm if the United States attacked Iraq—a threat that proved hollow. When I e-mailed him, he described his favorite type of worm payload: "Stolen information from other people." He won't say which of his viruses he has himself spread and refuses to comment on his connection to the Qaeda worm. But in December on Indovirus.net, a discussion board for virus writers, Melhacker urged other writers to "try to make it in the wild" and to release their viruses in cybercafes, presumably to avoid detection. He also told them to stop sending in their work to antivirus companies.

Mathieson wrote a critical post in response, arguing that a good virus writer shouldn't need to spread his work. Virus authors are, in fact, sometimes quite chagrined when someone puts a dangerous worm into circulation, because it can cause a public backlash that hurts the entire virus community. When the Melissa virus raged out of control in 1999, many Internet service providers immediately shut down the Web sites of malware creators. Virus writers stormed online to pillory the Melissa author for turning his creation loose. "We don't need any more grief," one wrote.

IF YOU ASK cyberpolice and security experts about their greatest fears, they are not the traditional virus writers, like Mario or Philet0ast3r or Benny. For better or worse, those authors are a known quantity. What keeps antivirus people awake at night these days is an entirely new threat: worms created for explicit criminal purposes. These began to emerge last year. Sobig in particular alarmed virus researchers. It was released six separate times throughout 2003, and each time the worm was programmed to shut itself off permanently after a few days or weeks. Every time the worm appeared anew, it had been altered in a way that suggested a single author had been tinkering with it, observing its behavior in the wild, then killing off his creation to prepare a new and more insidious version. "It was a set of very well-controlled experiments," says Mikko Hypponen, the director of antivirus research at F-Secure, a computer security company. "The code is high quality. It's been tested well. It really works in the real world." By the time the latest variant, Sobig.F, appeared in August, the worm was programmed to install a back door that would allow the author to assume control of the victim's computer. To what purpose? Experts say its author has used the captured machines to send spam and might also be stealing financial information from the victims' computers.

No one has any clue who wrote Sobig. The writers of this new class of worm leave none of the traces of their identities that malware authors traditionally include in their code, like their screen names or "greetz," shout-out hellos to their cyberfriends. Because criminal authors actively spread their creations, they are cautious about tipping their hand. "The F.B.I. is out for the Sobig guy with both claws, and they want to make an example of him," David Perry notes. "He's not going to mouth off." Dunham of iDefense says his online research has turned up "anecdotal evidence" that the Sobig author comes from Russia or elsewhere in Europe. Others suspect China or other parts of Asia. It seems unlikely that Sobig came from the United States, because American police forces have been the most proactive of any worldwide in hunting those who spread malware. Many experts believe the Sobig author will release a new variant sometime this year.

Sobig was not alone. A variant of the Mimail worm, which appeared last spring, would install a fake pop-up screen on a computer pretending to be from PayPal, an online e-commerce firm. It would claim that PayPal had lost the victim's credit-card or banking details and ask him to type it in again. When he did, the worm would forward the information to the worm's still-unknown author. Another worm, called Bugbear.B, was programmed to employ sophisticated password-guessing strategies at banks and brokerages to steal personal information. "It was specifically designed to target financial institutions," said Vincent Weafer, senior director of Symantec.

The era of the stealth worm is upon us. None of these pieces of malware were destructive or designed to cripple the Internet with too much traffic. On the contrary, they were designed to be unobtrusive, to slip into the background, the better to secretly harvest data. Five years ago, the biggest danger was the "Chernobyl" virus, which deleted your hard drive. But the prevalence of hard-drive-destroying viruses has steadily declined to almost zero. Malware authors have learned a lesson that biologists have long known: the best way for a virus to spread is to ensure its host remains alive.

"It's like comparing Ebola to AIDS," says Joe Wells, an antivirus researcher and founder of WildList, a long-established virus-tracking group. "They both do the same thing. Except one does it in three days, and the other lingers and lingers and lingers. But which is worse? The ones that linger are the ones that spread the most." In essence, the long years of experimentation have served as a sort of Darwinian evolutionary contest, in which virus writers have gradually figured out the best strategies for survival.

Given the pace of virus development, we are probably going to see even nastier criminal attacks in the future. Some academics have predicted the rise of "cryptoviruses"—malware that invades your computer and encrypts all your files, making them unreadable. "The only way to get the data back will be to pay a ransom," says Stuart Schechter, a doctoral candidate in computer security at Harvard. (One night on a discussion board I stumbled across a few virus writers casually discussing this very concept.) Antivirus companies are writing research papers that worry about the rising threat of "metamorphic" worms—ones that can shift their shapes so radically that antivirus companies cannot recognize they're a piece of malware. Some experimental metamorphic code has been published by Z0mbie, a reclusive Russian member of the 29A virus-writing group. And mobile-phone viruses are probably also only a few years away. A phone virus could secretly place 3 a.m. calls to a toll number, sticking you with thousand-dollar charges that the virus's author would collect. Or it could drown 911 in phantom calls. As Marty Lindner, a cybersecurity expert at CERT/CC, a federally financed computer research center, puts it, "The sky's the limit."

The profusion of viruses has even become a national-security issue. Government officials worry that terrorists could easily launch viruses that cripple American telecommunications, sowing confusion in advance of a physical 9/11-style attack. Paula Scalingi, the former director of the Department of Energy's Office of Critical Infrastructure Protection, now works as a consultant running disaster-preparedness exercises. Last year she helped organize "Purple Crescent" in New Orleans, an exercise that modeled a terrorist strike against the city's annual Jazz and Heritage Festival. The simulation includes a physical attack but also uses a worm unleashed by the terrorists designed to cripple communications and sow confusion nationwide. The physical attack winds up flooding New Orleans; the cyberattack makes hospital care chaotic. "They have trouble communicating, they can't get staff in, it's hard for them to order supplies," she says. "The impact of worms and viruses can be prodigious."

THIS NEW AGE of criminal viruses puts traditional malware authors in a politically precarious spot. Police forces are under more pressure than ever to take any worm seriously, regardless of the motivations of the author.

A young Spaniard named Antonio discovered that last fall. He is a quiet 23-year-old computer professional who lives near Madrid. Last August, he read about the Blaster worm and how it exploited a Microsoft flaw. He became intrigued, and after poking around on a few virus sites, found some sample code that worked the same way. He downloaded it and began tinkering to see how it worked.

Then on Nov. 14, as he left to go to work, Spanish police met him at his door. They told him the anti-virus company Panda Software had discovered his worm had spread to 120,000 computers. When Panda analyzed the worm code, it quickly discovered that the program pointed to a site Antonio had developed. Panda forwarded the information to the police, who hunted Antonio down via his Internet service provider. The police stripped his house of every computer—including his roommate's—and threw Antonio in jail. After two days, they let him out, upon which Antonio's employer immediately fired him. "I have very little money," he said when I met him in December. "If I don't have a job in a little time, in a few months I can't pay the rent. I will have to go to my parents."

The Spanish court is currently considering what charges to press. Antonio's lawyer, Javier Maestre, argued that the worm had no dangerous payload and did no damage to any of the computers it infected. He suspects Antonio is being targeted by the police, who want to pretend they've made an important cyberbust, and by an antivirus company seeking publicity.

Artificial life can spin out of control—and when it does, it can take real life with it. Antonio says he did not actually intend to release his worm at all. The worm spreads by scanning computers for the Blaster vulnerability, then sending a copy of itself to any open target. Antonio maintains he thought he was playing it safe, because his computer was not directly connected to the Internet. His roommate's computer had the Internet connection, and a local network—a set of cables connecting their computers together—allowed Antonio to share the signal. But what Antonio didn't realize, he says, was that his worm would regard his friend's computer as a foreign target. It spawned a copy of itself in his friend's machine. From there it leapfrogged onto the Internet—and out into the wild. His creation had come to life and, like Frankenstein's monster, decided upon a path of its own.

Clive Thompson writes frequently about science and technology. His last article for the magazine was about mobile-phone culture.

The Fading Memory of the State

The National Archives struggles to ensure that endangered electronic records will be around for as long as the original Declaration of Independence.

David Talbot

THE OFFICIAL REPOSITORY of retired U.S. government records is a boxy white building tucked into the woods of suburban College Park, MD. The National Archives and Records Administration (NARA) is a subdued place, with researchers quietly thumbing through boxes of old census, diplomatic, or military records, and occasionally requesting a copy of one of the computer tapes that fill racks on the climate-controlled upper floors. Researchers generally don't come here to look for contemporary records, though. Those are increasingly digital, and still repose largely at the agencies that created them, or in temporary holding centers. It will take years, or decades, for them to reach NARA, which is charged with saving the retired records of the federal government (NARA preserves all White House records and around 2 percent of all other federal records; it also manages the libraries of 12 recent presidents). Unfortunately, NARA doesn't have decades to come up with ways to preserve this data. Electronic records rot much faster than paper ones, and NARA must either figure out how to save them permanently, or allow the nation to lose its grip on history.

One clear morning earlier this year, I walked into a fourth-floor office overlooking the woods. I was there to ask Allen Weinstein—sworn in as the new Archivist of the United States in February—how NARA will deal with what some have called the pending "tsunami" of digital records. Weinstein is a former professor of history at Smith College and Georgetown University and the author of *Perjury: The Hiss-Chambers Case* (1978) and coauthor of *The Story of America* (2002). He is 67, and freely admits to limited technical knowledge. But a personal experience he related illustrates quite well the challenges he faces. In 1972, Weinstein was a young historian suing for the release of old FBI files. FBI di-

rector J. Edgar Hoover—who oversaw a vast machine of domestic espionage—saw a *Washington Post* story about his efforts, wrote a memo to an aide, attached the *Post* article and penned into the newspaper's margin: "What do we know about Weinstein?" It was a telling note about the mind-set of the FBI director and of the federal bureaucracy of that era. And it was saved—Weinstein later found the clipping in his own FBI file.

But it's doubtful such a record would be preserved today, because it would likely be "born digital" and follow a convoluted electronic path. A modern-day J. Edgar Hoover might first use a Web browser to read an online version of the *Washington Post*. He'd follow a link to the Weinstein story. Then he'd send an e-mail containing the link to a subordinate, with a text note: "What do we know about Weinstein?" The subordinate might do a Google search and other electronic searches of Weinstein's life, then write and revise a memo in Microsoft Word 2003, and even create a multimedia PowerPoint presentation about his findings before sending both as attachments back to his boss.

What steps in this process can be easily documented and reliably preserved over decades with today's technology? The short answer: none. "They're all hard problems," says Robert Chadduck, a research director and computer engineer at NARA. And they are symbolic of the challenge facing any organization that needs to retain electronic records for historical or business purposes.

Imagine losing all your tax records, your high school and college yearbooks, and your child's baby pictures and videos. Now multiply such a loss across every federal agency storing terabytes of information, much of which must be preserved by law. That's the disaster NARA is racing to prevent. It is confronting thousands of incompatible data formats cooked up by the computer

Megabyte
1,024 kilobytes.
The length of a short novel or the storage available on an average floppy disk.

Gigabyte
1,024 megabytes.
Roughly 100 minutes of CD-quality stereo sound.

Terabyte
1,024 gigabytes.
Half of the content in an academic research library.

Petabyte
1,024 terabytes.
Half of the content in all U.S. academic research libraries.

Exabyte
1,024 petabytes.
Half of all the information generated in 1999.

SOURCE: UNIVERSITY OF CALIFORNIA, BERKELEY

Data Indigestion

NARA's crash data-preservation project is coming none too soon; today's history is born digital and dies young. Many observers have noted this, but perhaps none more eloquently than a U.S. Air Force historian named Eduard Mark. In a 2003 posting to a Michigan State University discussion group frequented by fellow historians, he wrote: "It will be impossible to write the history of recent diplomatic and military history as we have written about World War II and the early Cold War. Too many records are gone. Think of Villon's haunting refrain, 'Ou sont les neiges d'antan?' and weep.... History as we have known it is dying, and with it the public accountability of government and rational public administration." Take the 1989 U.S. invasion of Panama, in which U.S. forces removed Manuel Noriega and 23 troops lost their lives, along with at least 200 Panamanian fighters and 300 civilians. Mark wrote (and recently stood by his comments) that he could not secure many basic records of the invasion, because a number were electronic and had not been kept. "The federal system for maintaining records has in many agencies—indeed in every agency with which I am familiar—collapsed utterly," Mark wrote.

Of course, managing growing data collections is already a crisis for many institutions, from hospitals to banks to universities. Tom Hawk, general manager for enterprise storage at IBM, says that in the next three years, humanity will generate more data—from websites to digital photos and video—than it generated in the previous 1,000 years. "It's a whole new set of challenges to IT organizations that have not been dealing with that level of data and complexity," Hawk says. In 1996, companies spent 11 percent of their IT budgets on storage, but that figure will likely double to 22 percent in 2007, according to International Technology Group of Los Altos, CA.

Still, NARA's problem stands out because of the sheer volume of the records the U.S. government produces and receives, and the diversity of digital technologies they represent. "We operate on the premise that somewhere in the government they are using every software program that has ever been sold, and some that were never sold because they were developed for the government," says Ken Thibodeau, director of the Archives' electronic records program. The scope of the problem, he adds, is "unlimited, and it's open ended, because the formats keep changing."

The Archives faces more than a Babel of formats; the electronic records it will eventually inherit are piling up at an ever accelerating pace. A taste: the Pentagon generates tens of millions of images from personnel files each year; the Clinton White House generated 38 million e-mail messages (and the current Bush White House is expected to generate triple that number); and the 2000 census returns were converted into more than 600 million TIFF-format image files, some 40 terabytes of data. A single patent application can contain a million pages, plus complex files like 3-D models of proteins or CAD drawings of aircraft parts. All told, NARA expects to receive 347

industry over the past several decades, not to mention the limited lifespan of electronic storage media themselves. The most famous documents in NARA's possession—the Declaration of Independence, the Constitution, and the Bill of Rights—were written on durable calfskin parchment and can safely recline for decades behind glass in a bath of argon gas. It will take a technological miracle to make digital data last that long.

But NARA has hired two contractors—Harris Corporation and Lockheed Martin—to attempt that miracle. The companies are scheduled to submit competing preliminary designs next month for a permanent Electronic Records Archives (ERA). According to NARA's specifications, the system must ultimately be able to absorb any of the 16,000 other software formats believed to be in use throughout the federal bureaucracy—and, at the same time, cope with any future changes in file-reading software and storage hardware. It must ensure that stored records are authentic, available online, and impervious to hacker or terrorist attack. While Congress has authorized $100 million and President Bush's 2006 budget proposes another $36 million, the total price tag is unknown. NARA hopes to roll out the system in stages between 2007 and 2011. If all goes well, Weinstein says, the agency "will have achieved the start of a technological breakthrough equivalent in our field to major 'crash programs' of an earlier era—our Manhattan Project, if you will, or our moon shot."

petabytes (*see definitions on the previous page*) of electronic records by 2022 .

Currently, the Archives holds only a trivial number of electronic records. Stored on steel racks in NARA's 11-year-old facility in College Park, the digital collection adds up to just five terabytes. Most of it consists of magnetic tapes of varying ages, many of them holding a mere 200 megabytes apiece—about the size of 10 high-resolution digital photographs. (The electronic holdings include such historical gems as records of military psychological-operations squads in Vietnam from 1970 to 1973, and interviews, diaries, and testimony collected by the U.S. Department of Justice's Watergate Special Prosecution Force from 1973 to 1977.) From this modest collection, only a tiny number of visitors ever seek to copy data; little is available over the Internet.

Because the Archives has no good system for taking in more data, a tremendous backlog has built up. Census records, service records, Pentagon records of Iraq War decision-making, diplomatic messages—all sit in limbo at federal departments or in temporary record-holding centers around the country. A new avalanche of records from the Bush administration—the most electronic presidency yet—will descend in three and a half years, when the president leaves office. Leaving records sitting around at federal agencies for years, or decades, worked fine when everything was on paper, but data bits are nowhere near as reliable—and storing them means paying not just for the storage media, but for a sophisticated management system and extensive IT staff.

Data under the Desk

The good news is that at least some of the rocket science behind the Archives' "moon shot" is already being developed by industry, other U.S. government agencies, and foreign governments. For example, Hewlett-Packard, IBM, EMC, PolyServe, and other companies have developed "virtual storage" technologies that automatically spread terabytes of related data across many storage devices, often of different types. Virtualization frees up IT staff, balances loads when demand for the data spikes, and allows hardware upgrades to be carried out without downtime. Although the Archives will need technologies far beyond virtual storage, the commercial efforts form a practical foundation. The Archives may also benefit from the examples of digital archives set up in other nations, such as Australia, where archivists are using open-source software called XENA (for XML Electronic Normalizing of Archives) to convert records into a standardized format that will, theoretically, be readable by future technologies. NARA will also follow the lead of the U.S. Library of Congress, which in recent years has begun digitizing collections ranging from early American sheet music to immigration photographs and putting them online, as part of a $100 million digital preservation program.

But to extend the technology beyond such commercial and government efforts, NARA and the National Science Foundation are funding research at places like the San Diego Super-

computer Center. There, researchers are, among other things, learning how to extract data from old formats rapidly and make them useful in modern ones. For example, San Diego researchers took a collection of data on airdrops during the Vietnam War—everything from the defoliant Agent Orange to pamphlets—and reformatted it so it could be displayed using nonproprietary versions of digital-mapping programs known as geographic information systems, or GIS (*see "Do Maps Have Morals?" June 2005*). Similarly, they took lists of Vietnam War casualties and put them in a database that can show how they changed over the years, as names were added or removed. These are the kinds of problems NARA will face as it "ingests" digital collections, researchers say. "NARA's problem is they will be receiving massive amounts of digital information in the future, and they need technologies that will help them import that data into their ERA—hundreds of millions of items, hundreds of terabytes of data," says Reagan Moore, director of data-knowledge computing at the San Diego center.

Another hive of research activity on massive data repositories: MIT. Just as the government is losing its grip on administrative, military, and diplomatic history, institutions like MIT are losing their hold on research data—including the early studies and communications that led to the creation of the Internet itself. "MIT is a microcosm of the problems [NARA] has every day," says MacKenzie Smith, the associate director for technology at MIT Libraries. "The faculty members are keeping their research under their desks, on lots and lots of disks, and praying that nothing happens to it. We have a long way to go."

Now MIT is giving faculty another place to put that data. Researchers can log onto the Internet and upload information— whether text, audio, video, images, or experimental data sets— into DSpace, a storage system created in collaboration with Hewlett-Packard and launched in 2002 (*see "MIT's DSpace Explained," p. 50*). DSpace makes two identical copies of all data, catalogues relevant information about the data (what archivists call "metadata," such as the author and creation date), and gives each file a URL or Web address. This address won't change even if, say, the archivist later wants to put a given file into a newer format— exporting the contents of an old Word document into a PDF file, for instance. Indeed, an optional feature in DSpace will tell researchers which files are ready for such "migration."

Because the software behind DSpace is open source, it is available for other institutions to adapt to their own digital-archiving needs; scores have already done so. Researchers at MIT and elsewhere are working on improvements such as an auditing feature that would verify that a file hasn't been corrupted or tampered with, and a system that checks accuracy when a file migrates into a new format. Ann Wolpert, the director of MIT Libraries (and chair of *Technology Review*'s board of directors), says DSpace is just a small step toward tackling MIT's problems, never mind NARA's. "These changes have come to MIT and other institutions so rapidly that we didn't have the technology to deal with it," Wolpert says. "The technology solutions are still emerging." Robert Tansley, a Hewlett-Packard research scientist who worked on DSpace, says the system is a good start but cautions that "it is still quite new. It hasn't been tested or deployed at a massive scale, so there would need to be some work before it could support what the National Archives is looking at."

Digital Marginalia

But for all this promise, NARA faces many problems that researchers haven't even begun to think about. Consider Weinstein's discovery of the Hoover marginalia. How could such a tidbit be preserved today? And how can any organization that needs to track information—where it goes, who uses it, and how it's modified along the way—capture those bit streams and keep them as safe as older paper records? Saving the text of e-mail messages is technically easy; the challenge lies in managing a vast volume and saving only what's relevant. It's important, for example, to save the e-mails of major figures like cabinet members and White House personnel without also bequeathing to history trivial messages in which mid-level bureaucrats make lunch arrangements. The filtering problem gets harder as the e-mails pile up. "If you have 300 or 400 million of anything, the first thing you need is a rigorous technology that can deal with that volume and scale," says Chadduck. More and more e-mails come with attachments, so NARA will ultimately need a system that can handle any type of attached file.

Version tracking is another headache. In an earlier era, scribbled cross-outs and margin notes on draft speeches were a boon to understanding the thinking of presidents and other public officials. To see all the features of a given Microsoft Word document, such as tracked changes, it's best to open the document using the same version of Word that the document's creator used. This means that future researchers will need not only a new piece of metadata—what software version was used—but perhaps even the software itself, in order to re-create fonts and other formatting details faithfully. But saving the functionality of software—from desktop programs like Word to the software NASA used to test a virtual reality model of the Mars Global Surveyor, for example—is a key research problem. And not all software keeps track of how it was actually used. Why might this matter? Consider the 1999 U.S. bombing of the Chinese embassy in Belgrade. U.S. officials blamed the error on outdated maps used in targeting. But how would a future historian probe a comparable matter—to check the official story, for example—when decision-making occurred in a digital context? Today's planners would open a map generated by GIS software, zoom in on a particular region, pan across to another site, run a calculation about the topography or other features, and make a targeting decision.

If a historian wanted to review these steps, he or she would need information on how the GIS map was used. But "currently there are no computer science tools that would allow you to reconstruct how computers were used in high-confidence decision-making scenarios," says Peter Bajcsy, a computer scientist at the University of Illinois at Urbana-Champaign. "You might or might not have the same hardware, okay, or the same version of the software in 10 or 20 years. But you would still like to know what data sets were viewed and processed, the methods used for processing, and what the decision was based on." That

way, to stay with the Chinese embassy example, a future historian might be able to independently assess whether the database about the embassy was obsolete, or whether the fighter pilot who dropped the bomb had the right information before he took off. Producing such data is just a research proposal of Bajcsy's. NARA says that if such data is collected in the future, the agency will add it to the list of things needing preservation.

Data Curators

Even without tackling problems like this, NARA has its hands full. For three years, at NARA's request, a National Academy of Sciences panel has been advising the agency on its electronic records program. The panel's chairman, computer scientist Robert F. Sproull of Sun Microsystems Laboratories in Burlington, MA, says he has urged NARA officials to scale back their ambitions for the ERA, at least at the start. "They are going to the all-singing, all-dancing solution rather than an incremental approach," Sproull says. "There are a few dozen formats that would cover most of what [NARA] has to do. They should get on with it. Make choices, encourage people submitting records to choose formats, and get on with it. If you become obsessed with getting *the* technical solution, you will never build an archive." Sproull counsels pragmatism above all. He points to Google as an example of how to deploy a workable solution that satisfies most information-gathering needs for most of the millions of people who use it. "What Google says is, 'We'll take all comers, and use best efforts. It means we won't find everything, but it does mean we can cope with all the data,'" Sproull says. Google is not an archive, he notes, but in the Google spirit, NARA should attack the problem in a practical manner. That would mean starting with the few dozen formats that are most common, using whatever off-the-shelf archiving technologies will likely emerge over the next few years. But this kind of preservation-by-triage may not be an option, says NARA's Thibodeau. "NARA does not have discretion to refuse to preserve a format," he says. "It is inconceivable to me that a court would approve of a decision not to preserve e-mail attachments, which often contain the main substance of the communication, because it's not in a format NARA chose to preserve."

Meanwhile, the data keep rolling in. After the 9/11 Commission issued its report on the attacks on the World Trade Center and the Pentagon, for example, it shut down and consigned all its records to NARA. A good deal of paper, along with 1.2 terabytes of digital information on computer hard disks and servers, was wheeled into NARA's College Park facility, where it sits behind a door monitored by a video camera and secured with a black combination lock. Most of the data, which consist largely of word-processing files and e-mails and their attachments, are sealed by law until January 2, 2009. They will probably survive that long without heroic preservation efforts. But "there's every reason to say that in 25 years, you won't be able to read this stuff," warns Thibodeau. "Our present will never become anybody's past."

It doesn't have to be that way. Projects like DSpace are already dealing with the problem. Industry will provide a growing range of partial solutions, and researchers will continue to fill in the blanks. But clearly, in the decades to come, archives such as NARA will need to be staffed by a new kind of professional, an expert with the historian's eye of an Allen Weinstein but a computer scientist's understanding of storage technologies and a librarian's fluency with metadata. "We will have to create a new profession of 'data curator'—a combination of scientist (or other data specialist), statistician, and information expert," says MacKenzie Smith of the MIT Libraries.

The nation's founding documents are preserved for the ages in their bath of argon gas. But in another 230 years or so, what of today's electronic records will survive? With any luck, the warnings from air force historian Mark and NARA's Thibodeau will be heeded. And historians and citizens alike will be able to go online and find that NARA made it to the moon, after all.

David Talbot is Technology Review's *chief correspondent.*

False Reporting on the Internet and the Spread of Rumors: Three Case Studies

Paul Hitlin

Following the tragic events of September 11, 2001, a significant number of unsubstantiated rumors circulated around the Internet. One email pointed to the existence of prophecies by Nostradamus written hundreds of years earlier that predicted the attacks. Another accused Israel of masterminding the strikes and that thousands of Jews were told in advance to stay home from work that morning. The Internet allowed for a vast audience to spread these rumors along with the technology to facilitate their transmission, even though there was little evidence to support them and the rumors were later proven incorrect. Considering this spread of rumors, Stephen O'Leary (2002) writes:

> What may be hard for mainstream journalists to understand is that, in crisis situations, the social functions of rumor are virtually indistinguishable from the social functions of 'real news.' People spread rumors via the Net for the same reason that they read their papers or tune into CNN: they are trying to make sense of their world. (pg. 3)

O'Leary claims that these rumors fill a need for consumers of news that is very similar to the void that 'real news' fills. However, are the consequences the same? These Internet rumors help people to make sense of their world following a tragedy, although the lasting consequences are potentially much more harmful.

The Internet is certainly not responsible for errors in journalism. Every medium of news has a history of misreported stories. However, the nature of the Internet has created a new method for consumers to get their news and allowed for far greater numbers of people to become involved with the production and dissemination of news. As a consequence, cyberjournalism and the Internet have had real effects on both the process of reporting and subsequent public discourse.

How are errors in Internet journalism corrected online? What are the overarching consequences of errors that appear on Internet web sites? Jim Hall (2001) believes that one problem with instant news appearing on the Internet is that the way errors are handled does not adequately address the fact that an error was made. He writes, "The problem with instant news is that when it is wrong it tends to be buried, sedimenting into and reinforcing its context, rather than corrected" (p. 133). Errors of Internet reporting do not often get identified and corrected as they do in newspapers. Instead, even if the editors of the Web site where the error first appeared change their site to remove the error, often the same false information will have already spread throughout other Web sites and emails. These rumors can become part of a public folklore even if there are no facts to support the original reports.

This paper will first consider Hall's assertion that errors are buried rather than corrected, and will examine the reasons Internet reporting leads to false reports. Then, three case studies of significant false reports on the Internet will be compared to the theories behind cyberjournalism in order to understand why the errors occurred and the impacts of these stories. Investigating these three examples will help us to begin to understand how we can decrease the influence of false reports in the future.

The first case study is the plane crash of TWA flight 800 in 1996. Even before full investigations were conducted, the Internet was full of reports of missiles or other causes behind the crash, the impacts of which would reach as far as the White House. The second case study will examine Matt Drudge's report that former White House special assistant Sidney Blumenthal physically abused his wife. The third case study will take a look at the pervasive rumors that the death of former Bill Clinton aide Vince Foster was a murder, not a suicide, even though numerous investigations have concluded that these accusations are unsupported. This incident is a clear example of how partisan politics can play a role in the spread of false reports on the Internet.

There has been much discussion about what distinguishes a 'journalist' working for a mainstream news source from a self-titled 'reporter' who never leaves his/her computer and instead just links to reports on other sites. While these distinctions are important and worth discussing, it will not be within the realm of this study to draw out these distinctions. Instead, this paper will consider news reports that appear on the Internet regardless of whether or not the site displaying the report considers itself a news source. As we will see, public opinion can often be influenced as much from rumors on sites with little credibility as it can from more mainstream sources.

Reasons for Cyberjournalism Errors

Before considering the specific cases of false reporting, it is important to understand why the nature of the Internet may encourage reporting errors. Philip Seib (2001) points out that the Internet is not alone in containing factual errors. He writes, "the Web really is little different from other media in terms of its potential to abuse and be abused and its capability for self-governance" (pp. 129–130). The Internet itself, the actual technology, can not be held responsible for false reports since those reports have existed in all forms of media. However, there are qualities of the Internet and the manner in which news is reported on the Web that create differences in how frequently errors appear and what results as a consequence.

The causes of most cyberjournalism errors can be separated into four main categories. Let us now turn to each cause and examine it in turn.

1. The Need for Speed

The first and probably most significant reason for false reporting on the Internet is the 24-hour a day news cycle that the Internet promotes. With the development of newspapers, the news cycle was a daylong process that ended with having a story included in the next day's edition of the paper. This cycle changed with the expansion of cable television channels devoted entirely to news such as CNN and later MSNBC and Fox News. The cycle was expanded even further by the development of the Internet which is available to consumers 24-hours a day. Because of the constant need to keep both cable television and the Internet supplied with new information, expectations of news deadlines have shifted. As Seib notes, in the current information age, the deadline for reporters is always 'now' (p. 142).

Competitive pressures have also contributed to an emphasis being placed more on timeliness than accuracy. A number of Internet sites, such as Matt Drudge's *Drudge Report*, are one-person operations that issue reports on gossip and rumor without being constrained by traditional standards of reporting. These sites apply pressure to other news organizations to be the first to report a story or risk being scooped. Drudge himself believes that "absolute truth matters less than absolute speed" (Seib, 2001, p. 143). He also suggests that since we live in an information economy, complete accuracy is not possible or even necessary. Drudge focuses instead on immediacy and believes that the Web encourages this type of reporting (Hall, 2002, p. 148).

The pressure on reporters to be the first with a story has detracted from more traditional methods of journalism. Because the goal used to be to get a report into the next day's newspaper or that evening's nightly news television broadcast, reporters had more time for fact-checking. The 24-hour-a-day news cycle has decreased the time reporters have to assure accuracy and as a result, many errors found on the Internet can be attributed to the competitive pressure for journalists to be the first to break a specific news story.

2. The Desire to Attract 'Hits'

Competition among Web sites is also a cause for some false reports. Web sites have financial incentives to attract visitors to their sites, whether it is through advertising or a desire to widen the site's influence. Hall argues that journalism on the Web has promoted the idea that news is 'infotainment' and more at the mercy of the demands of the marketplace than to its audiences (Hall, 2001, p. 155). Web sites must fill the desires of consumers, or risk losing those consumers to other sites that either get the information first or are even more sensational in their reporting.

Furthermore, with the ability of Internet users to visit almost any news source in the world, as opposed to being confined to their local newspapers or television stations, the competition on the Web exacerbates the desire of sites to get the story first. Most news sites are updated several times a day, and competition forces those sites to get the story first or risk being thought of as irrelevant or out-of-date.

3. Political Gains

The specific source of many Internet rumors is often difficult to ascertain. However, certain rumors on the Internet are clearly promoted for partisan political gain and to advance a particular ideology.

Even after four investigations came to the same conclusions about Vince Foster's death, certain political groups were still spreading false reports in order to promote their own cause. For example, a fund-raising letter sent out by anti-Clinton groups asked for $1,000 donations in order to support the "Clinton Investigation Commission" which would investigate the claim that Foster was murdered (Piacente, 1997). Opponents of the Clinton administration perpetuated this false report to the exclusion of evidence in the case. These anti-Clinton groups were less concerned with accuracy than with forwarding a partisan agenda and the persistence of this specific rumor can be attributed to their political motives.

4. Attraction to Scandal

News, and specifically news on the Web, is often led by scandal and the concept of the spectacular rather than issues of depth (Hall, 2001, p. 137). For example, reports that TWA flight 800 was brought down by a missile were much more exciting than a report that a technical problem in the plane caused the crash. While some sites did wait for investigations into the cause of the crash to make conclusions about what actually brought the plane down, other sites used more dramatic rumors of missile fire to headline their reports. The competition between sites on the Web and the ability for consumers to move rapidly between those sites furthers the need for reporters to lead with scandal in order to catch consumers' attention. This desire for the spectacular, along with an emphasis on scandal, often leads to other false reports on the Internet.

Correction Policy, Social Cascades, and Online Credibility

Now that we have seen the four main reasons errors are found on the Internet, another key issue to understand is how those mistakes are corrected. There is still no singular method that Web sites use to correct errors, but as Seib (2001) writes:

> The easiest way to fix a mistake is simply to erase it and replace it with the correct information. That is a temptation unique to electronic publication, since there is no "original" version in the print or video archives ... This is fine for readers who come to the site after the correction has been made. But failure to post a formal notice of correction implies that there was never an error, and that is less than honest. (pp. 154–155)

The question of how to correct a mistake once it is discovered that causes Hall to suggest that the nature of Internet journalism reinforces the error's context rather than corrects the false information. While some retractions are clearly posted, as was the case with Matt Drudge following the accusations against Sidney Blumenthal, often the error has already spread to other sources. As a result, whether or not the original source is corrected no longer matters because the information will have already moved onto other places on the Web.

The result of this spread of Internet rumors is a phenomenon described by Cass Sunstein as one of 'social cascades.' Sunstein suggests that groups of people often move together in a direction of one set of beliefs or actions. He refers to this as a cascade effect (Sunstein, 2002, p. 80). Information can travel and become entrenched even if that information is incorrect. Sunstein argues that the Internet, with its wide reach and seemingly unending amount of Web sites and emails, greatly increases the likelihood of so-

cial cascades. Rumors can be passed to many users and spread quickly. The result is that the information appears believable solely due to the fact that the information has been repeated so many times. Richard Davis (1999) sums up the potential danger of this phenomenon:

> Anyone can put anything on the Internet and seemingly does. Often, one cannot be sure of the reliability of the information provided. Reliability diminishes exponentially as the information is passed from user to user and e-mail list to e-mail list until it acquires a degree of legitimacy by virtue of its widespread dissemination and constant repetition. (p. 44)

A number of other factors also contribute to the believability of information passed on the Internet. Richard Davis and Diana Owen (1998) discuss many of the reasons why 'new media,' consisting of the Internet, talk radio, and interactive television, often engage users in different ways than previous forms of news. They claim that much of new media relies on active participation by users rather than a more passive relationship between users and newspapers or earlier television programs. Davis and Owen describe the influence of this connection:

> The degree of involvement or interactivity with media is linked to the level of an audience member's media consumption and the strength of the effects of the communication. People who have a highly active relationship with a particular medium, such as callers to talk radio programs, may be more likely to establish a regular habit of attending to the medium and are more likely to be influenced by content than those whose acquaintance with the communication source is more casual. (p. 160)

Internet users who participate in online activities are not only more likely to be influenced by content they see online, but new media has a capacity to create strong psychological bonds between users and the media source. Davis and Owen add, "Individuals form personal relationships with their television sets and their computers. They treat computers as if they are people, talking to them, ascribing personalities to them and reacting to them emotionally when computers hand out praise or criticism during an interactive sessions" (p. 160). Users have greater influence over the content of media on the Web than in previous forms of media, whether it results from emailing articles of interest or responding to online polls and questionnaires. These interactions contribute to the perceived credibility that Internet users ascribe to information they receive over the Web. Stories that might be disregarded as false had they been disseminated through other forms of media often facilitate a social cascade effect if that information is spread online.

Having considered both why errors appear on the Internet and the difficulty in effectively correcting false information, let us now consider three cases of prominent false reports on the Internet and how those instances were handled.

Case Study One: The Crash of TWA Flight 800 in 1996

A clear example of how constant repetition of an erroneous report can result in widespread belief can be seen in the wake of the crash of TWA Flight 800. On July 17, 1996, the passenger flight left JFK International Airport in New York en route to Paris, but tragically crashed into the Long Island Sound. All 230 passengers and crew on board died.

Almost immediately, the National Transportation Safety Board (NTSB) began investigating the causes of the crash and rumors started to spread throughout the Internet as to what lead to the tragedy. Three main theories quickly surfaced as to what caused the crash: the crash was an act of terrorism conducted from onboard the flight; a mechanical malfunction was responsible for bringing down the plane; or the plane was shot down by a surface-to-air missile (Cobb & Primo, 2003, p. 104).

Some evidence initially indicated the crash could be a result of terrorism, either an onboard bomb or a projectile fired at the plane from the ground. The accident took place several days before the beginning of the 1996 Summer Olympics in Atlanta, which later become a target of a bombing attack. Some observers felt the timing of the plane crash indicated that it was somehow connected to international terrorism. In addition, numerous eyewitnesses reported having seen a streak of light approaching the plane before the explosion (Charles, 2001, p. 218). As the NTSB and the FBI began to investigate, numerous signals from the federal government indicated that all three potential theories were in play. As much as six months into a very public investigation, the NTSB was still declaring that all three theories remained as possibilities (Negroni, 2001). This did not change until March of 1997, when federal investigators began to dismiss theories of a missile bringing TWA Flight 800 down, claiming there was "no physical evidence" of such an attack (CNN.com, 1997).

As the investigation into the crash progressed and began to rule out terrorism, rumors persisted throughout the Internet that a government cover-up was concealing the real causes. At the forefront of those rumors was Pierre Salinger, a former press secretary to John F. Kennedy and correspondent for ABC News. Salinger insisted that he had a letter from French intelligence proving that a U.S. Navy missile ship shot down TWA Flight 800, and the FBI was covering up the act. Salinger's claims were reported in numerous news outlets. In addition, Salinger and several other journalists published a report in *Paris Match* stating that radar images existed that proved that a missile hit the plane (Harper, 1998, p. 85).

Salinger's credentials and his unwillingness to give up on his theory lent great credibility to the missile story. Many people on the Internet who believed the government was trying to hide something picked up on his writings. Interestingly enough, the letter that Salinger claimed had come from French intelligence was instead a memo that had been circulating on the Internet for several months written by a former United Air Lines pilot named Richard Russell.[1] As Mark Hunter writes in his Salon.com article, Salinger's insistence on promoting his conspiracy theory of both the missile and the FBI cover-up, even with scare evidence, actually harmed the real investigation by causing a significant distraction for investigators. It also caused further psychological stress on the family members of the victims of the crash who were forced to revisit the circumstances as a result of these repeated allegations.

By the time the NTSB issued its final report on the crash in August of 2000, much of the talk of conspiracy theories relating to the crash had disappeared. In 2001, the Federal Aviation Agency (FAA) acted in response to what was believed to be the actual cause of the crash and issued safety rules to minimize flammable vapors and decrease the risk of a tank igniting (Cobb & Primo, 2003, p. 117). However, the consequences of the crash rumors can be seen both in continuing public discourse and actions taken by upper levels of the federal government.

The immediate rumors following the crash about a possible bomb or missile attack led to direct government action. In the days that followed the accident, before much hard evidence was discovered, President Clinton issued a tightening of security at airports throughout the country in order to try to prevent any acts of terrorism (Cobb & Primo, 2003, p. 106). Clinton later created the White House Commission on Aviation Safety, led by Vice President Al Gore, which issued recommendations for improving airline safety (Cobb & Primo, 2003, pp. 110-111). Just the possibility of a terrorist or missile attack was enough for the federal government to react strongly and tighten security.

What role did the Internet play in promoting and maintaining the false rumors about the crash of TWA Flight 800? Internet sites were not alone in reporting the rumors about the crash. Many newspapers, including the *Washington Post* and *New York Times*, also reported the possibilities of a bomb or terror attack (Cobb & Primo, 2003, pp. 107-108). However, the Internet did allow for certain aspects of the story to persist even when the evidence against the rumors was mounting. For one thing, a letter written by Richard Russell that circulated by email throughout the Internet played a key role in Salinger's claims about a government cover-up. Whether or not Salinger knew the true source of the letter, the circulation of the note alone added some perceived credibility to the rumor. This Internet 'error' was not corrected and removed. Instead, as Hall suggested, the nature of the Internet embedded the rumor. The circulation continued even after the NTSB determined it was false: a clear example of a social cascade facilitated by the Internet, moving many to believe the government was hiding information and not telling the full story about the crash.

To further this notion about the impact of these rumors, one only has to look to the Internet today, more than seven years after the crash, to see how public discourse has been influenced. While the Internet is full of conspiracy theories and anti-government rhetoric, a simple search can still find many Web sites that maintain that the TWA crash was a government cover-up. A clear example is the Web site *whatreallyhappened.com*. One can still go to this site at any time and read about how the government is hiding secrets and promoting beliefs that the "witnesses who saw a missile hit the jumbo jet are all drunks" (whatreallyhappened.com, 2002). To any person deciding to conduct research into the causes of this plane crash today, the Internet is a rich resource consisting of both facts about the accident and significant rumor and innuendo.

Case Study Two: Sidney Blumenthal vs. Matt Drudge and Internet Libel

While some Internet rumors persist on numerous Web sites, others can be linked more closely with one specific site, as is the case with a report that appeared on Matt Drudge's Web site, *drudgereport.com*, in 1997. Matt Drudge's one-man newsroom is most well known for breaking the story about President Bill Clinton's Oval Office affair with a White House intern. Along with breaking that story, Drudge has had 'exclusives' with a number of other stories, some of which turned out not to be true at all. Included among these was the report that Bill Clinton had fathered an illegitimate black son, a report that was later proven to be false (Hall, 2001, p. 129).

On August 8, 1997, Drudge chose to report on his Web site allegations about White House special assistant Sidney Blumenthal. Writing about a Republican operative who was facing allegations of spousal abuse, Drudge issued the 'exclusive' on his Web site that included the following.

> The *Drudge Report* has learned that top GOP operatives who feel there is a double-standard of only reporting [sic] shame believe they are holding an ace card: New White House recruit Sidney Blumenthal has a spousal abuse past that has been effectively covered up.
>
> The accusations are explosive.
>
> "There are court records of Blumenthal's violence against his wife," one influential Republican [sic], who demanded anonymity, tells the *Drudge Report*. (Blumenthal, 2003, pp. 239-240)

Drudge goes on to write that one White House source claimed the allegations were entirely false and that Drudge had been unsuccessful in his attempts to contact Blumenthal regarding these charges.

Three problems existed for Drudge in relation to this story. First, no court records existed that claimed Blumenthal abused his wife. Second, Drudge had not in fact made any attempts to contact Blumenthal. And third, Sidney Blumenthal decided to sue Matt Drudge and the Internet carrier of his column, American Online (AOL), for libel after other conservative news sources such as the *New York Post* and talk radio programs picked up the story (Blumenthal, 2003, p. 241).

This false Internet report was unique in that the origin of the rumor on the Web was clear along with who was responsible for spreading the rumor. Because of this, Blumenthal did have an opportunity to confront his accuser, which he did the day after the report first appeared. Blumenthal and his lawyer sent a letter to Drudge demanding to know the sources of the report. If Drudge did not comply, Blumenthal threatened to take "appropriate action" (Blumenthal, 2003, p. 244). In direct response to the threat, Drudge printed a retraction on his Web site that read, "I am issuing a retraction of my information regarding Sidney Blumenthal that appeared in the Drudge Report on August 11, 1997" (Blumenthal, 2003, p. 247). Drudge never officially apologized for the specific claim, although he was quoted as saying, "I apologize if any harm has been done. The story was issued in good faith. It was based on two sources who clearly were operating from a political motivation" (Kurtz, 1997).

While the lawsuit proceeded against Drudge with the blessing of President Clinton and the White House, the final result was not nearly as dramatic as the initial report. In May of 2001, Drudge and Blumenthal settled the suit out of court, and Blumenthal agreed to pay $2,500 to Drudge to reimburse travel expenses (Kurtz, 2001). Blumenthal claimed that he settled the suit because Drudge had endless financial backing from conservative groups and the suit was doing little more than providing additional exposure for Drudge (Blumenthal, 2003, p. 784). One interesting side note to this case is that early in the process, a U.S. District judge had ruled that the Internet service provider, AOL, could not be a defendant in the libel case even though they had paid Drudge for his work. This decision was a significant victory for Internet service providers in protecting them from lawsuits concerning the content that appears on their own Web sites (Swartz, 1998).

Unlike the rumors about the TWA crash, this case study is much clearer in terms of who was responsible for placing the rumor online. Defamation of character is common in the Internet world, but Blumenthal viewed his lawsuit as an opportunity to make a larger point, "bringing the Internet under the same law that applied to the rest of the press" (Blumenthal, 2003, p. 471). Judging exactly how successful he was in doing so and whether future Internet sites will be as willing to publish unsubstantiated rumors is difficult. Drudge, for one, continues to publish numerous stories with seemingly little fear about being incorrect. However, this example does illustrate one occurrence where a retraction was issued on the same Internet site as the original error. Did the retraction correct the harm that resulted from a false story? Clearly Sidney Blumenthal did not feel so and continued his libel lawsuit even after the retraction was issued.

In addition, this news report was more a result of a partisan political agenda than it was an issue of Drudge trying to beat his competition by issuing an exclusive story not available on any other site. Drudge has been accused by many of having strong ties to conservative political groups who may have planted the Blumenthal story, but there seem to be no indications that other news sites were in competition with Drudge to be the first to issue this report. He would not thus have been facing a shortened time to check sources and facts. Drudge himself acknowledged that his sources for this story were acting on their own political agenda.

Case Study Three: The Suicide of White House Aide Vince Foster

Unlike the previous case study, the origins of the rumors involving the suicide of White House Aide Vince Foster are less clear. On July 20, 1993, the body of Vince Foster was discovered in a park in Washington, D.C. Foster had apparently committed suicide, and much of the initial evidence pointed to a self-inflicted gunshot wound as the cause of death. He had been showing tremendous signs of stress as he found himself the subject of political battles in Washington and a number of accusations against the Clinton administration. Foster had reportedly been very upset about the attention he was receiving in the "Travelgate" scandal and his role in questions about billing records involving Hillary Clinton and Whitewater investments (Tisdall, 1994). However, immediately after his body was found, rumors began circulating the Internet suggesting that Foster's death had not been a suicide. These reports claimed that the death was a murder that was covered-up by members of the Clinton administration who felt Foster knew too much about the Whitewater investigation being conducted by Independent Counsel Kenneth Starr.

Rumors of unresolved questions within the investigation of Foster's death began to spread throughout the Internet by members of conservative activist groups who made no secret of their hatred of President Clinton. Why was there no suicide note? Why were the keys on Foster's body not found at the scene, but only later, once the body was moved? What did the torn note say that was found near the body? Why were records missing from Vince Foster's office after the body was found? Those looking for sensational stories and rumors involving this story did not have to look hard on the Internet to find them.

The cascade effect of this story reached remarkable levels. Numerous Web sites published the rumor that Foster's death was a murder, including Matt Drudge's site (Scheer, 1999). Presidential candidate Pat Buchanan received criticism in 1996 by Jewish groups after an article published on his official campaign Web site claimed that Foster's death was ordered by Israel and that Hillary Clinton was secretly working as a Mossad agent (O'Dwyer, 1996). Rush Limbaugh, a conservative radio talk-show host, mentioned the accusations on his radio program and Representative John Linder, Republican of Georgia, even inserted the accusation into the record at Congressional hearings involving the Whitewater scandal (Atlanta Journal and Constitution, 1994). In fact, the rumors of murder were so persistent on the Internet and other mediums that a Time/CNN poll taken in 1995 during the Senate hearings of the aftermath of Foster's death showed that only 35 percent of respondents believed Foster's death was a suicide. Twenty percent believed he had been murdered (Weiner, 1995).

Rumors of a Clinton-led cover-up have continued to exist even after four separate investigations, conducted by the U.S. Park Police, the FBI, Special Counsel Robert Fiske, and Independent Counsel Ken Starr, all came to the same conclusion: Foster's death was a suicide. The persistent refusal to accept the conclusions of these investigations is demonstrated in a 1998 editorial in The Augusta Chronicle written five years after Foster's death. "Imagine [Ken Starr] ruling the Vince Foster killing a suicide when not one item of evidence would indicate suicide, but numerous items indicate obvious murder!" (The Augusta Chronicle, 1998).

Much of the persistent nature of these specific rumors can be traced to partisan political groups. Richard Scaife, a wealthy financier of many anti-Clinton groups, has been quoted as saying, "The death of Vincent Foster: I think that's the Rosetta Stone to the whole Clinton Administration" (Weiner, 1995). Scaife has supported groups, such as the Western Journalism Center, that have included work by Christopher Ruddy, a reporter who was dismissed by the New York Post for pursuing cover-up theories relating to the death. Ruddy, who refers to himself as part of the 'vast right-wing conspiracy' described by Hillary Clinton, has written and published numerous articles attacking both the Clinton administration and the Foster investigations. Even today, reports written by Ruddy questioning the investigations' findings can be found online (www.newsmax.com/ruddy/). In addition, fund-raising letters for conservative groups, including a 1997 letter from a group called "Clinton Investigation Committee," have been used to raise money to continue various investigations against Clinton, including the Foster case (Piacente, 1997). These organizations, Web sites, newspaper articles, and fund-raising letters, have all helped to perpetuate the rumors that Vince Foster's death was a murder, and somehow the Clinton administration was involved.

Because these rumors have persisted for years, their existence cannot be attributed to the timing pressure of the Internet news cycle. Instead, the theories involving Foster's death are a result of the desire for the sensational and partisan political efforts, in this instance from groups who opposed Bill Clinton. The possibility of a printed retraction seems impractical and would likely have no effect, since, unlike the Blumenthal case, there was no one specific site that started the rumors on the Internet, and because the rumors have extended far beyond the Internet into newspapers and even among members of Congress. The cascade effect of all of these rumors is that a certain contingent, in this case opponents of Bill Clinton, continues to believe that the Clintons were responsible for Vince Foster's death. The political consequences for such accusations, even after they have been disproved, can be far reaching because false information has to potential to unreasonably decrease the public's faith in public officials and the competency of their government.

Conclusion

The expansion of the Internet has great potential for promoting political discourse and allowing for far more citizens to be involved with the production and dissemination of news. Davis and Owen (1998) describe this positive potential:

> Increasingly, computer networks have become tools for political communication as well. Users gather political information, express their opinions, and mobilize other citizens and political leaders. The information superhighway is fast becoming an electronic town hall where anyone with a personal computer and a modem can learn about the latest bill introduced in Congress, join an interest group, donate money to a political candidate, or discuss politics with people they have never seen who may live half a world away. (pg. 110)

However, as these three case studies have shown, the potential for the Internet to be a conduit of false information or the spreading of rumors is also significant. The dilemma for those who are concerned about the role the Internet will play in the future of democracy will be to discover how to balance the positive democratizing aspects with the potentially harmful aspects that include the spread of false reports and misleading information.

The main goal of this investigation was to examine how errors of Internet reporting are handled online. These three case studies demonstrate that there is no single method as to how Internet errors are corrected. When one source for a rumor exists, as was the case with the Blumenthal story, a retraction is possible on that initial source which can somewhat lessen the impact of the false story. However, even that example was picked up by other mainstream newspaper and radio sources.

This study then supports Hall's assertion that the nature of the Internet reinforces the context of errors rather than corrects them. As seen with the Vince Foster case, significant numbers of people believed that his death was a murder even after several investigations had concluded otherwise. Public discourse was not shifted entirely even after the early reports were disproved or corrected. In fact, in all three of the cases presented here, the Internet rumors and false reports were picked up by other sources and continued to spread even after evidence pointed to contrary facts.

Another substantial conclusion that can be ascertained from this investigation is that Sunstein's assessment of social cascades is valid in regards to errors on the Internet.

For those people who are interested in finding evidence to support their views, even if the evidence itself is questionable, the Internet can be a tremendous facilitator. And the reach of the influence of these reports is not just to conspiracy theorists. Their impact can be seen even in actions taken by government officials, such as President Clinton after the crash of TWA flight 800. These social cascades can have important political consequences, whether on airline safety regulations or in the perceptions of political figures. A connection appears to exist between the capabilities of the Internet and the vastness of the social cascading that can occur as a result of rumor and innuendo.

How, then, should the potential for social cascading as a result of misleading information be balanced with the positive potential of the Internet? Not all scholars agree that the implications of an 'anything goes' attitude of Internet reporting is entirely negative. Davis and Owen (1998) make an argument relating to old media that an increase of tabloid journalism may not be entirely destructive because it "can foster a sense of intimacy with the public," and also attract viewers to news sources (pg. 209). This same line of reasoning can be applied to the Internet sites such as Matt Drudge's that spread rumor while using standards for verification that are less than those that are utilized by traditional media. Consequently, it is possible that the lowering of journalistic norms that is apparent online will not have entirely negative consequences if the result encourages more people to search for news and connect with other Internet users.

Even if it is true that the Internet's impact on journalism and the increase of false reports is not entirely negative, this investigation has demonstrated that harmful effects can result from the cascade effects of misinformation. The question that arises from this investigation is regarding how to control or combat the prevalence of errors on the Internet. Sidney Blumenthal acknowledged that one of the goals of his lawsuit against Drudge was to bring the Internet under the same type of libel laws that newspaper and television journalists must follow. However, Blumenthal's attempt at forcing the Internet "reporter" to face negative consequences as a result of his false report was unsuccessful, and further attempts by the government to regulate the content of the Internet seem likely to be impractical, costly, and ineffective overall. There is simply too much online content for the government to be able to enforce the same types of journalistic laws that other news mediums must follow, not to mention the potential for excessive government censorship.

At the same time, it is incredibly unlikely that the four reasons mentioned earlier in this discussion that cause errors in reporting, that is, the need for speed, the desire to attract hits, the goal of advancing a partisan agenda, and the attraction to scandal, will lessen and lower the competitive pressures on Internet journalists in the next few years. If anything, those pressures are likely to increase as more and more people turn to the Internet for their news. The only probable method for improving the accuracy of online reporting would be for news producers themselves to make better attempts at following voluntary guidelines that are closer to the standards used by old media sources. Offering guidelines for reporters to follow is not new. Sabato, Stencel, and Lichter (2000) describe a number of guidelines reporters should follow in reporting political scandals in their book entitled *Peepshow* and journalism schools have been teaching professional norms for decades. Other sets of standards that are usually applied to traditional news outlets could be applied to Internet sources as well. These standards, such as the need for multiple sources for issuing a report, do not guarantee complete accuracy in reporting, as can be seen with the recent scandals of newspaper reporters Jayson Blair of the *New York Times* and Jack Kelley of *USA Today*. However, attempts to follow these more traditional guidelines would lessen the frequency and impact of Internet reporting errors.

Seib agrees with the need for online reporters to voluntarily follow traditional ethics of reporting. In his predictions for the future of Internet journalism, he notes that it will be increasingly important for reporters to aim at fairness and accuracy. He writes, "The 'Drudge effect—shoot-from-the-hip sensationalism - will give online journalism a bad name if the public perceives it to be a dominant characteristic of this medium" (p. 162). The best way for journalists to deal with this perceived 'Drudge effect' and the potentially harmful impact of Internet rumors is to deliver a consistently fair and accurate news product. The marketplace will in time come to rely on the high-quality product more than the hastily put together news site that does not have a good track record of accuracy. Seib's faith in the public's desire for quality reporting is the most hopeful and promising view as to how to lessen the impact of social cascades based on misleading or false information.

Along with offering positive aspects of the Internet, Davis and Owen (1998) also write, "new technologies have enhanced opportunities for the mass dissemination of misinformation" (p. 200). As this study has shown, this rapidly expanding technology can have potentially harmful effects if false reports are spread without supporting evidence. In order for us to reap the positive effects of the Internet, which include added convenience and the possibility of increased political discourse, the dangers of false information must also be confronted. The most effective method to lessen the amount and impact of false Internet errors will be for news producers on the Web to follow traditional journalistic standards of fact-checking and sourcing. False reporting will not disappear, but, we must make ourselves aware of the various types of reporting that can be found on the Web and hope that market forces will encourage high-quality reporting as opposed to unsubstantiated rumors passing as news. Awareness of the potential for both types of reporting is

a central condition for encouraging effective and accurate online reporting.

References

The Atlanta Journal and Constitution (1994, July 29). "Hatemongers Who Cry Wolf . . ." Editorial, p. A14.

The Augusta Chronicle (Georgia) (1998, December 11). "Calls for Investigation, Not Cover-Up." Editorial, p. A4.

Blumenthal, Sidney (2003). *The Clinton Wars.* New York: Farrar, Straus and Giroux.

Charles, Michael T. (2001). "The Fall of TWA Flight 800." In Uriel Rosenthal, R. Arjen Boin, & Louise K. Comfort (Eds.), *Managing Crises: Threats, Dilemmas, Opportunities* (pp. 216–234). Springfield, IL.: Charles C. Thomas Publisher, Ltd.

CNN.com (1997, March 11). *NTSB: "No Physical Evidence" Missile Brought Down TWA 800.* Atlanta, GA: CNN.com. Retrieved October 18, 2003, from the CNN Interactive Web site: http://www.cnn.com/US/9703/11/twa.missile/

Cobb, Roger W., & Primo, David M. (2003). *The Plane Truth: Airline Crashes, the Media, and Transportation Policy.* Washington, D.C.: Brookings Institution Press.

Davis, Richard (1999). *The Web of Politics: The Internet's Impact on the American Political System.* New York: Oxford University Press.

Davis, Richard & Owen, Diana (1998). *New Media and American Politics.* New York: Oxford University Press.

Hall, Jim (2001). *Online Journalism: A Critical Primer.* London: Pluto Press.

Harper, Christopher (1998). *And That's the Way It Will Be: News and Information in a Digital World.* New York: New York University Press.

Hunter, Mark (1997). *The Buffoon Brigade: Pierre Salinger and His Conspiracy-Minded Colleagues are Stopping Investigators from Finding Out What Really Happened to TWA Flight 800.* San Francisco: Salon.com. Retrieved October 18, 2003, from the Salon.com Web site: http://www.salon.com/march97/news/news970326.html

Kurtz, Howard (1997, August 12). "Blumenthals Get Apology, Plan Lawsuit: Web Site Retracts Story of Clinton Aide." *The Washington Post,* p. A11.

Kurtz, Howard (2001, May 2). "Clinton Aide Settles Libel Suit Against Matt Drudge—At a Cost." *The Washington Post,* p. C1

Negroni, Christine (1997, January 17). *Six Months Later, Still No Answer to TWA Flight 800 Mystery.* Atlanta, GA: CNN.com. Retrieved October 18, 2003, from the CNN Interactive Web site: http://www.cnn.com/US/9701/17/twa/index.html

O'Dwyer, Thomas (1996, February 18). "Buchanan Web Site Blames Mossad for Clinton Aide's Death; Calls Hillary an Agent." *The Jerusalem Post,* p. 1.

O'Leary, Stephen (2002). *Rumors of Grace and Terror.* Los Angeles, CA: The Online Journalism Review. Retrieved September 29, 2003, from the Online Journalism Review Web site: http://www.ojr.org/ojr/ethics/1017782038.php

Piacente, Steve (1997, April 16). "Letter Claims Foster was Killed." *The Post and Courier (Charleston, SC),* p. A9.

Ruddy, Christopher (1999). "A Memo: The Unanswered Questions in the Foster Case." West Palm Beach, FL: The Christopher Ruddy Web site. Retrieved November 27, 2003, from Newsmax.com: http://www.newsmax.com/articles/?a=1999/2/8/155138

Sabato, Larry J., Stencel, Mark, & Lichter, S. Robert (2000). *Peepshow: Media and Politics in an Age of Scandal.* Lanham, MD: Rowman & Littlefield Publishers, Inc.

Scheer, Robert (1999, January 14). "More Sludge From Drudge: The Story that Clinton Fathered An Illegitimate Son Turns Out to be a Hoax." *Pittsburgh Post-Gazette,* p. A15.

Seib, Philip (2001). *Going Live: Getting the News Right in a Real-Time, Online World*. Lanham, MD: Rowman & Littlefield Publishers, Inc.

Sunstein, Cass (2002). *Republic.com*. Princeton: Princeton University Press.

Swartz, Jon (1998, June 23). "Free-Speech Victory For Internet; AOL Off the Hook in Landmark Libel Case." *The San Francisco Chronicle*, p. A1.

Tisdall, Simon (1994, February 7). "The Body in the Park." *The Guardian (London)*, p. 2.

Weiner, Tim (1995, August 13). "One Source, Many Ideas in Foster Case." *The New York Times*, pp. 1-19.

whatreallyhappened.com (2002, June 10). *Was TWA Flight 800 Shot Down by a Military Missile?* Retrieved October 18, 2003, from the whatreallyhappened.com Web site: `http://www.whatreallyhappened.com/RANCHO/CRASH/TWA/twa.html`

Note

1. For complete text of the Internet letter written by Russell, see (Harper, 1998, pp. 85-86)

The Level of Discourse Continues to Slide

By JOHN SCHWARTZ

Is there anything so deadening to the soul as a PowerPoint presentation?

Critics have complained about the computerized slide shows, produced with the ubiquitous software from Microsoft, since the technology was first introduced 10 years ago. Last week, The New Yorker magazine included a cartoon showing a job interview in hell: "I need someone well versed in the art of torture," the interviewer says. "Do you know PowerPoint?"

Once upon a time, a party host could send dread through the room by saying, "Let me show you the slides from our trip!" Now, that dread has spread to every corner of the culture, with schoolchildren using the program to write book reports, and corporate managers blinking mindlessly at PowerPoint charts and bullet lists projected onto giant screens as a disembodied voice reads

- every
- word
- on
- every
- slide.

When the bullets are flying, no one is safe.

But there is a new crescendo of criticism that goes beyond the objection to PowerPoint's tendency to turn any information into a dull recitation of lookalike factoids. Based on nearly a decade of experience with the software and its effects, detractors argue that PowerPoint-muffled messages have real consequences, perhaps even of life or death.

Before the fatal end of the shuttle Columbia's mission last January, with the craft still orbiting the earth, NASA engineers used a PowerPoint presentation to describe their investigation into whether a piece of foam that struck the shuttle's wing during launching had caused serious damage. Edward Tufte, a Yale University professor and influential expert on the presentation of visual information, published a critique of that presentation on the World Wide Web last March. A key slide, he said, was "a PowerPoint festival of bureaucratic hyper-rationalism."

Among other problems, Mr. Tufte said, a crucial piece of information—that the chunk of foam was hundreds of times larger than anything that had ever been tested—was relegated to the last point on the slide, squeezed into insignificance on a frame that suggested damage to the wing was minor.

The independent board that investigated the Columbia disaster devoted an entire page of its final report last month to Mr. Tufte's analysis. The board wrote that "it is easy to understand how a senior manager might read this PowerPoint slide and not realize that it addresses a life-threatening situation."

In fact, the board said: "During its investigation, the board was surprised to receive similar presentation slides from NASA officials in place of technical reports. The Board views the endemic use of PowerPoint briefing slides instead of technical papers as an illustration of the problematic methods of technical communication at NASA."

NASA's troubles lead to new critism of popular slide-show software.

The board echoed a message that Mr. Tufte and other critics have been trying to disseminate for years. "I would refer to it as a virus, rather than a narrative form," said Jamie McKenzie, an educational consultant. "It's done more damage to the culture."

These are strong words for a program that traces its pedagogical heritage to the blackboard or overhead projector. But the relentless and, some critics would say, lazy use of the program as a replacement for real discourse—as with the NASA case—continues to inspire attacks.

It has also become so much a part of our culture that, like Kleenex and Xerox, PowerPoint has become a generic term for any bullet-ridden presentation.

Speaking in PowerPoint

Critics say that Power-Point slide show software can confuse rather than edify. Edward Tufte, a professor at Yale University, has railed against the way NASA used the program in investigations of whether the space shuttle Columbia was in danger last January.

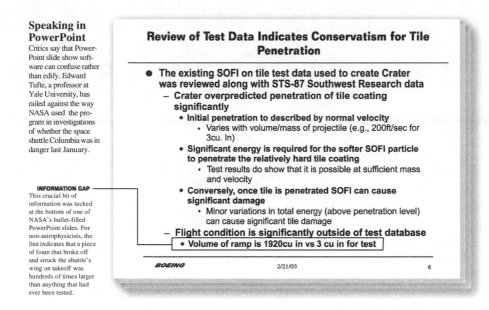

INFORMATION GAP

This crucial bit of information was tucked at the bottom of one of NASA's bullet-filled PowerPoint slides. For non-astrophysicists, the line indicates that a piece of foam that broke off and struck the shuttle's wing on takeoff was hundreds of times larger than anything that had ever been tested.

Dan Leach, Microsoft's chief product manager for the Office software, which includes PowerPoint, said that the package had 400 million users around the world, and that his customers loved PowerPoint. When early versions of Office for small business did not include PowerPoint, customers protested, he said, and new versions include it.

"We're proud of it," he said, pointing out that the product is simply a tool—"a blank for you to fill in" with ideas and information.

"I feel like the guy who makes canvas and the No. 2 green viridian paint," Mr. Leach said. "I'm being asked to comment on the art show."

His point is shared by plenty of people who say the criticism of PowerPoint is misdirected. "The tool doesn't tell you how to write," said Bill Atkinson, the creator of HyperCard, an earlier program considered by many to be the precursor to PowerPoint. "It just helps you express yourself," he said. "The more tools people have to choose from the better off we are."

It's likely, then, that PowerPoint is here to stay—everywhere. And not always for worse. At the wedding reception of Lina Tilman and Anders Corr last year in New Haven, Conn., guests showed two PowerPoint presentations. They were everything that slide shows usually are not: wry and heartfelt works that used the tired conventions of the form to poke fun at the world of presentations and celebrate the marriage.

NASA apparently still lacks a similar sense of irony. Earlier this month, the space agency held a three-day workshop in Houston to give reporters a first-hand view of its return-to-flight plans. Included in the handouts were dozens of PowerPoint slides.

UNIT 7

International Perspectives and Issues

Unit Selections

Key Points to Consider

• Use the Internet to examine the arguments for H1-B visas to the United States. What is your position on granting temporary visas to technical workers?

• It is often argued that information technologies have the potential to democratize politically oppressive regimes. Do you agree? Use "Dot Com for Dictators," and "Weaving the Authoritarian Web" in formulating your answer.

• Japanese youth seem to be forsaking networked computers for cell phones. Do you find a similar trend in the United States?

• Were you surprised to learn that employment in the American information technology sector was seventeen percent higher than in 1999? Do you think that the author of "The New Face of the Silicon Age," would be surprised? Why/why not?

Student Website

www.mhcls.com/online

Internet References

Further information regarding these websites may be found in this book's preface or online.

Information Revolution and World Politics Project
   http://www.ceip.org/files/projects/irwp/irwp_descrip.ASP

For the past several years, we have been hearing a great deal about a global economy, the exchange of goods and services and, though to a lesser degree, labor across national boundaries. Yet human beings have been trading across long distances for centuries. The discovery of Viking artifacts in Baghdad and sea shells in the Mississippi Valley are two of many, many examples. The beginnings of capitalism in the 15th century accelerated an existing process. But when most commentators speak of globalization, they refer increasingly to interdependent trade since the end of World War II[1] and, especially, the phenomena we have witnessed since the collapse of the former Soviet Union and the global availability of the Internet and satellite communications. Without the new information technologies, the global marketplace would not be possible. We can withdraw money from our bank accounts using ATM machines in Central Turkey, make cell phone calls from nearly anywhere on the planet, and check our email from a terminal located in an Internet café in Florence or Katmandu. They also make it possible for businesses to transfer funds around the world and, if you

happen to be a software developer, to employ talented—and inexpensive—software engineers in growing tech centers like Bangalore, India.

A piece of the global economy that is receiving belated attention is what becomes of those many millions of computers that are retired each year. Not long ago, one writer, dismayed at overblown predictions of growth in the computer industry, calculated that were the current claims accurate, discarded computers would cover all 3,679,192 square miles of the United States by the early years of the twentieth century.[2] Though the prediction was facetious, the problem of what to do with the detritus of the computer boom is real enough, as the excellent article from *The Progressive* shows ("China's Computer Wasteland").

Implicit in the bevy of books and articles on globalization is the worry that the 21st century may not be so American as the last. Not surprisingly, "of the Ph.D.'s in science and engineering awarded to foreign students in the United States from 1985 to 2000, more than half went to students from China, India, South Korea, and Taiwan." A piece on Indian programmers ("The New

Face of the Silicon Age") should be enough to keep chairs of American computer science departments awake at night. As a corrective, read David Patterson's short piece, "Restoring the Popularity of Computer Science." Though students seem to be voting with their feet about reports of smart, hard-working, and underpaid Indian software engineers, there is still plenty of work in the United States to go around. By May, 2004 the U.S. Bureau of Labor Statistics reported that employment in the American information technology sector was seventeen percent higher than in 1999.

Not all international consequences of computer technology are economic. One of the most exciting developments in theoretical computer science over the past two years is strong cryptography, the art of enciphering messages. For practical purposes, freely available cryptographic software can produce unbreakable codes. Governments, including our own, have worried about this for the past ten years. Whatever you might think about making wiretap-proof software available to criminals in the United States, it is being put to good use in countries with repressive governments. Authoritarian governments find themselves in a fix, according to "Dot Com for Dictators." Either they choose to shun the Internet with its ability to enable communication among dissidents and so languish economically, or jump on the information superhighway and look for ways to control it. Some regimes are using sophisticated censorship software to stay ahead of their wired opponents. Still others—Singapore is the best example—show that a country can have a tightly controlled political system and at the same time make effective use of information technology. While almost half of Singapore's citizens are Internet users, the ruling party still has a firm grasp on political power. In fact, there is some evidence that its tightly-controlled nature, as well as its size, has contributed to the government's effective use of e-government technology to allow for everything from marriage license applications to questions about genetic counseling to occur on-line.

In "Weaving the Authoritarian Web," Taylor Boas provides further evidence for this somewhat counterintuitive observation. "Far from trying to regulate the Internet by merely restricting diffusion," says Boas, "authoritarian countries such as China and Saudi Arabia are employing both technological and institutional means to control use of the Internet while also encouraging its growth."

We have included Sanjoy Majumder's piece, *Kabul's Cyber Café Culture*, because "for a country that has been brutally scarred by a war that has left little standing, the idea of an information revolution takes some getting used to." Afghans, it appears, are flocking to the Excelnet Café to pay $1 for an hour's broad band access. They are doing this in a country where the average income is less than $1 per day. And Internet entrepreneurs are making the same kinds of claims we have been hearing for information technology every since Marshall McCluhan announced the "global village" in the sixties. "It will empower the central government and unite our people, bringing us together," one of them says.

Meanwhile, the jaded Japanese, seem to have taken a step beyond the Internet. According to "Japan's Generation of Computer Refuseniks," Japanese teens have abandoned computers for Internet-enabled cell phones. Author Tim Clark introduces us to Tsukasa Amano, a fifteen year-old who "transmits as many as 200 e-mail messages" daily on her cell phone. Her brother, Chihiro, says his homework is almost entirely handwritten. Cultural norms, it appears, make Internet-enabled cell phones more attractive to Japanese teens than fully-featured computers.

The global interconnectedness that Marshall McCluhan observed forty years ago has only increased in complexity with developments in computer technology. Now instead of merely receiving one-way satellite feeds as in McCluhan's day, we can talk back through email, web sites, and blogs. It is not surprising that all of this communication is having unanticipated effects across the plant. Who, for instance, during the Tiananmen Square uprising of 1989 could have predicted that a newly market-centered China would also become a destination for America's computer trash? Or for that matter, who could have predicted, before the Soviet Union's collapse, that the U.S. one day would worry about a new kind of Russian attack—and that it could be thwarted by offering the perpetrators jobs in the computer industry. No one, which is why the study of computers in society, in international society, is so fascinating.

---

1. Merrett, Christopher D. "The Future of Rural Communities in a Global Economy." Retrieved 5/10/2004 from: http://www. uiowa.edu/ifdebook/features/perspectives/merrett.shtml

2. De Palma, Paul, "http://www.when_is_enough_enough?.com," *The American Scholar* 68, 1 (Winter, 1999).

China's Computer Wasteland

Benjamin Joffe-Walt

"Shhh. Shhhhhhhhhh!" the driver in Guangdong province whispers to us. He stares at the photographer out of the corner of his eye. When we stop, he won't even get out of the car. The photographer's every movement makes him jump a bit, and he receives the snap of her camera like the crack of a machine gun. "Careful!" he says. "They really will kill you."

We drive clandestinely, heads ducked, bodies curled up, eyes downward. "There, there it is!" the driver points. "They burn along the river." In front of us sprawl colossal piles of smoldering green computer circuit boards.

At first, Guiyu seems like any other rural Chinese town—flooded rice fields, streets swamped with produce vendors, migrant workers carrying bamboo on mopeds. But then you open the window. There is no smell more violent. The air is fierce, infected, as if the atmosphere itself had been viscously conquered by toxic paint, scorched bread, and burning plastic. An immediate noxious thickness enters your mouth, a toxic attack on all skin.

"I'm just trying to get some money," says Luo Yuan Chang, a newly arrived migrant from Hunan province who is burning old computers along the river. "Farming computers is more profitable than growing rice."

Computer waste from the West has made this poor mainland farming region an ecological disaster area. A large town along the Lianjiang River in southeastern China, Guiyu is the secret epicenter of illegal e-waste (electronic waste) processing in China. Workers there don't refurbish and sell the computers. They don't use them. Instead, they take hammers, chisels, and cutting torches to computers, keyboards, speakers, and other sorts of e-waste and smash them to bits for scrap metal, toner, gold, and reusable chips.

Chang stands shirtless atop scorched medical equipment, printing toner, and audio speakers. "I used to drive trucks, but I couldn't find a job so I had to come here and burn the rubbish," the forty-year-old says. "My family is here, and if I have no work we couldn't live, so I don't care how dangerous it is." When asked, though, he doesn't know much about the dangers involved.

It's plenty dangerous.

According to the Worldwatch Institute, workers breathe in all types of toxins: cadmium in chip resistors and semiconductors; beryllium on motherboards and connectors; brominated flame retardants in circuit boards and plastic casings; and lead, phosphor, barium, and hexavalent chromium in computer monitors.

The average CRT computer monitor contains four to eight pounds of lead, and the average LCD monitor contains four milligrams of mercury. Less than one-fourth of a teaspoon of mercury can contaminate more than 400 acres of a lake, making the fish unsafe to eat.

"There are many cases of lung problems, and the burning releases pollutants that cause diseases like silicosis, heart attacks, and pulmonary edema," says Dr. Chen at a local health clinic.

International watchdog groups estimate that the United States alone exported more than $1 billion worth of electronic waste to China last year while receiving virtually none from China. Though particularly pronounced in China, the e-waste of the Western world is being dumped all over Asia. *The Times of India* reports that "electronic waste is giving the country a big headache" and that India has become a "favorite dumping ground for countries like the U.S., Malaysia, Sweden, Canada, and Singapore."

Toxics Link, an Indian environmental group, claims that recycling a computer in India costs $2 on average, compared to $20 in the United States. Policymakers in the United States also understand the dynamics of dumping in Asia. After a pilot project to recycle computer monitors, the U.S. Environmental Protection Agency estimated that it is ten times cheaper to ship them to Asia than to recycle them in the United States.

China is not only a computer dumping ground. It also produces many of the 150 million computers that head out yearly on a peculiar round trip. For instance, IBM, Apple, Hewlett-Packard, Dell, and Sony all manufacture electronic goods in China. They then sell these products to Western countries. Finally, China gets them back as rubbish.

"Most of it is coming from recycling programs in countries that are trying to prevent pollution of their own territory," says Lai Yun, a Chinese environmentalist.

Today, more than 50 percent of U.S. households own a computer and have, on average, two to three old computers stored away in the basement or garage. Studies estimate that 315 million to 600 million computers in the United States will be obsolete by 2006.

"That's the same as a twenty-two-story pile of e-waste covering the entire 472 square miles of the City of Los Angeles," says the Computer TakeBack Campaign, an effort by a consortium of thirteen environmental organizations.

"Farming computers is more profitable than growing rice."

Two member groups, the Basel Action Network and the Silicon Valley Toxics Coalition, say in a report that 80 percent of e-waste collected in the United States is exported to Asia.

The United States is using "hidden escape valves to export the crisis to developing countries of Asia," the report states. "The poor of the world," it adds, are forced to "bear a disproportionate share of the e-waste environmental burden. This current reality is the dirty little secret of the electronics industry."

"The real crime," says Jim Puckett of the Basel Action Network, "is the unwillingness of countries like the United States and Japan to take responsibility for preventing the global dumping of their own toxic waste."

Guiyu is a cyber desert. Desolate mountains of electronic trash are everywhere, as hundreds of trucks drive over burnt circuit boards, the intricate crunch audible from almost a mile away. Dogs with diseased eyes are chained to e-waste "farmhouses" of moldy concrete walls. Circuit boards are used to hole up corrugated iron shacks housing migrants right next to heaps of junk along the river. The streams running through the migrants' riverside tenements are a blinding, shiny silver due to mercury and other toxins. Private traders import millions of gallons of water to the town and sell it at a premium to residents.

"Even if the work would kill me, I'd continue," says He Ti Guang, a wire cutter in an e-waste factory downtown. "I have no choice. My family is poor, so I came here to earn money." A thirty-five-year-old migrant from Sichuan province, Guang has warts, burns, and rashes up and down his arms.

"This waste is too hot, and it burns. My skin itches all the time," he says. "I think the wires are toxic, but I don't know."

His wife works in a plastics e-waste factory, melting old wires, computer monitors, TVs, and cellphones to be used for plastic chairs and thermoses.

"I've had many health problems," Li Sheng Cui says. "My body is weak and my stomach hurts when I laugh." She cringes and blinks erratically. "Your tongue tastes like sugar, and your skin is itchy," she says, holding her finger in her mouth. "It's impossible to wear a white shirt. You wash it and it turns yellow."

China's e-waste crisis is a byproduct of its unequal development. "China's opening to international markets and capital has greatly exacerbated the divide between urban middle class wealth and the rural poor," says Yun Xien, a local environmental activist. "E-waste is just one profitable coping mechanism for rural China."

E-waste sweatshops often sit in secluded areas off the street. Inside are migrant workers, usually women, stripping wires, banging circuits, and disassembling broken motors. Workers say the average salary for sweatshop work is $3 to $4 per day for men, and about half that for women.

"The law has no effect here, " says He Hai, who smuggled circuit boards to Guiyu as the e-waste boom took off. "Everyone here gets money from this kind of thing, so no one can afford to let it stop."

Hai says bribery is prevalent, as is intimidation. "Everything seems peaceful, but this place is very dangerous," he says. "The migrant workers fear the local people will beat them if they talk about it to anyone."

This is the underbelly of China's economic boom.

"The more developed areas won't do it," says Zhao Jun, who migrated to Guiyu twelve years ago as a teenager to work in e-waste. "This area was so poor, and it was hard to grow rice, so about a decade ago people began picking up rubbish to look for valuables. Gradually, they realized computer rubbish is better than other rubbish and started getting into e-waste. When I came, it was a one-story village with all dirt roads; now it's a city with big buildings and rich people."

Local residents got rich scouring the trash and brought in migrants to start scouring it for them. "The most dangerous and hardest jobs they give to the migrant workers," says Jun. "The locals who used to do the e-waste work are now wealthy e-waste bosses."

James Songqing is one such boss. His office is in a large building that makes up part of the new Juiyu skyline. He sits on his posh furniture next to a buddy holding a slingshot. Young women enter to pour them tea as Chinese soap operas play in the background.

Since my guide warned me that e-waste bosses want to keep all journalists out and would even kill me if they knew what I was doing, I pretend I'm interested in buying ten tons of bronze a month for a South African company.

"It is outside," Songqing says. On his front patio lie about two tons of untreated bronze in large white sacks.

It sells for $1.50 a kilo, he says. "It takes me two weeks to produce twenty tons of the stuff."

By my calculations, his street-side sweatshop is making upwards of $30,000 per month in profit.

Hai does not approve of this trade. "It's in the interests of our country to stop e-waste," he says. "We should stop e-waste altogether because it is foreign countries' rubbish."

Sound computer recycling programs are available. But, given the volume of e-waste produced each year, domestic reuse and recycling is wishful thinking for the time being.

Computers are not built to be recycled, environmentalists say, and their dismantling is extremely dangerous, labor-intensive, and costly.

The Computer TakeBack Campaign seeks to pressure "consumer electronics manufacturers and brand owners to take full responsibility for the lifecycle of their products." The groups in the campaign call on consumers to use their buying power to promote greater corporate responsibility, computer recycling, and a reduction in hazardous e-waste.

Outside the United States, there have been some successes. In May of 2001, the European Union adopted a directive that requires producers of electronics to take financial responsibility for the recovery and recycling of e-waste and to phase out the use of hazardous materials.

But reforms are lagging in the United States. "Brand owners and manufacturers in the U.S. have dodged their responsibility for management of products at the end of their useful life, while public policy has failed to promote producer take back, clean design, and clean production," says the Computer TakeBack Campaign.

We head back to the river to thank Chang. He is meandering on top of crumbled, smoking circuit boards, in a burning pile of e-waste. Chang must work late. He competes with eight other migrants, and he has a month-old baby.

We try to ask him more about his life, but his tune has changed. He is tight-lipped, redder in the face, unyielding. He gets frustrated immediately and says he has to go.

"I don't care for these questions of health and responsibility," he says. "Life is better here because I can get more money."

He turns away from us, coughs a bit, and bikes home along the banks of the Lianjiang River.

Benjamin Joffe-Walt is a freelance writer based in South Africa. Research for this article was supported by a grant from the Fund for Investigative Journalism, Inc.

The New Face of the Silicon Age

How India became the capital of the computing revolution.

Daniel H. Pink

Meet the pissed-off programmer. If you've picked up a newspaper in the last six months, watched CNN, or even glanced at Slashdot, you've already heard his anguished cry.

Now meet the cause of all this fear and loathing: Aparna Jairam of Mumbai. She's 33 years old. Her long black hair is clasped with a barrette. Her dark eyes are deep-set and unusually calm. She has the air of the smartest girl in class—not the one always raising her hand and shouting out answers, but the one who sits in back, taking it all in and responding only when called upon, yet delivering answers that make the whole class turn around and listen.

In 1992, Jairam graduated from India's University of Pune with a degree in engineering. She has since worked in a variety of jobs in the software industry and is now a project manager at Hexaware Technologies in Mumbai, the city formerly known as Bombay. Jairam specializes in embedded systems software for handheld devices. She leaves her two children with a babysitter each morning, commutes an hour to the office, and spends her days attending meetings, perfecting her team's code, and emailing her main client, a utility company in the western US. Jairam's annual salary is about $11,000—more than 22 times the per capita annual income in India.

Aparna Jairam isn't trying to steal your job. That's what she tells me, and I believe her. But if Jairam does end up taking it—and, let's face facts, she could do your $70,000-a-year job for the wages of a Taco Bell counter jockey—she won't lose any sleep over your plight. When I ask what her advice is for a beleaguered American programmer afraid of being pulled under by the global tide that she represents, Jairam takes the high road, neither dismissing the concern nor offering soothing happy talk. Instead, she recites a portion of the 2,000-year-old epic poem and Hindu holy book the Bhagavad Gita: "Do what you're sup-

posed to do. And don't worry about the fruits. They'll come on their own."

This is a story about the global economy. It's about two countries and one profession—and how weirdly upside down the future has begun to look from opposite sides of the globe. It's about code and the people who write it. But it's also about free markets, new politics, and ancient wisdom—which means it's ultimately about faith.

Our story begins beside the murky waters of the Arabian Sea. I've come to Mumbai to see what software programmers in India make of the anti-outsourcing hubbub in the US. Mumbai may not have as many coders per square foot as glossier tech havens like Bangalore and Hyderabad, but there's a lot more real life here. Mumbai is India's largest city—with an official population of 18 million and an actual population incalculably higher. It's a sweltering, magnificent, teeming megalopolis in which every human triumph and affliction shouts at the top of its lungs 24 hours a day.

Jairam's firm, Hexaware, is located in the exurbs of Mumbai in a district fittingly called Navi Mumbai, or New Mumbai. To get there, you fight traffic thicker and more chaotic than rush hour in hell as you pass a staggering stretch of shantytowns. But once inside the Millennium Business Park, which houses Hexaware and several other high tech companies, you've tumbled through a wormhole and landed in northern Virginia or Silicon Valley. The streets are immaculate. The buildings fairly gleam. The lawns are fit for putting. And in the center is an outdoor café bustling with twentysomethings so picture-perfect I look around to see if a film crew is shooting a commercial.

Hexaware's headquarters, the workplace of some 500 programmers (another 800 work at a development center in the southern city of Chennai, and 200 more are in Bangalore), is a silvery four-story glass building chock-full of blond-wood cubicles and black Dell computers. In one area, 30 new recruits sit through programming boot camp; down the hall, 25 even newer hires are filling out HR forms. Meanwhile, other young people—the average age here is 27—tap keyboards and skitter in and out of conference rooms outfitted with whiteboards and enclosed in frosted glass. If you pulled the shades and ignored the accents, you could be in Santa Clara. But it's the talent—coupled with the ridiculously low salaries, of course—that's luring big clients from Europe and North America. The coders here work for the likes of Citibank, Deutsche Leasing, Alliance Capital, Air Canada, HSBC, BP, Princeton University, and several other institutions that won't permit Hexaware to reveal their names.

Jairam works in a first-floor cubicle that's unadorned except for a company policy statement, a charcoal sketch, and a small statue of Ganesh, the elephant-headed Hindu god of knowledge and obstacle removal. Like most employees, Jairam rides to work aboard a private bus, one in a fleet the company dispatches throughout Mumbai to shuttle its workers to the office. Many days she eats lunch in the firm's colorful fourth-floor canteen.

While Hexaware's culinary offerings don't measure up to Google's celebrity chef and gourmet fare, the food's not bad—chana saag, aloo gobi, rice, chapatis—and the price is right. A meal costs 22 rupees, about 50 cents.

After lunch one Tuesday, I meet in a conference room with Jairam and five colleagues to hear their reactions to the complaints of the Pissed-Off Programmer. I cite the usual statistics: 1 in 10 US technology jobs will go overseas by the end of 2004, according to the research firm Gartner. In the next 15 years, more than 3 million US white-collar jobs, representing $136 billion in wages, will depart to places like India, with the IT industry leading the migration, according to Forrester Research. I relate stories of American programmers collecting unemployment, declaring bankruptcy, even contemplating suicide—because they can't compete with people willing to work for one-sixth of their wages.

Daniel H. Pink (*dp@danpink.com*) *is the author of* Free Agent Nation *and the forthcoming* A Whole New Mind.

Restoring the Popularity of Computer Science

Inaccurate impressions of the opportunities of 21st century CS are shrinking the next generation of IT professionals. You can help by dispelling incorrect beliefs about employment and by helping improve pre-college education.

David A. Patterson

Although universities were recently struggling to cope with an avalanche of computer science majors—some going so far as to erecting academic barriers to deflect the masses—they may soon need to reverse course and remove obstacles to the major, and even to recruiting to broaden participation in CS. Figure 1 tracks the change in popularity of the CS major among incoming freshmen over time in the U.S., which has been be a good predictor of graduates four to five years later [1].

Clearly, the CS major is now in a downward cycle in the U.S., especially for women. While the percentage of men intending to major in CS is no worse than the mid-1990s, the number of female CS majors is at a historic low. This drop is occurring while their academic numbers are increasing, as the majority of college students today are female. Colleagues outside North America suggest a similar decline in Europe. As an extreme example, a few CS departments were even closed in the U.K.

Everyone has an opinion as to why the CS numbers are down in this age group, so let me share mine: The expected negative impact of offshoring IT jobs in North America and Europe, and the current negative view of the CS profession by pre-college students, especially females. What can we do about these issues?

ACM's Job Migration Task Force has examined the impact of outsourcing extensively and is working to publish its findings, which we hope to complete this fall. I believe the truth will surely be better for our field than the worst fears of pre-college students and their parents. For example, Figure 2 shows the annual U.S. IT employment though May 2004. (The U.S. Bureau of Labor Statistics is about 15 months behind.)[1] Moreover, most of us believe things have gotten much better in the year since the survey was completed. Does anyone besides me know that U.S. IT employment was 17% higher than in 1999—5% higher than the bubble in 2000 and showing an 8% growth in the most recent year—and that the compound annual growth rate of IT wages has been about 4% since 1999 while inflation has been just 2% per year? Such growth rates swamp predictions of the

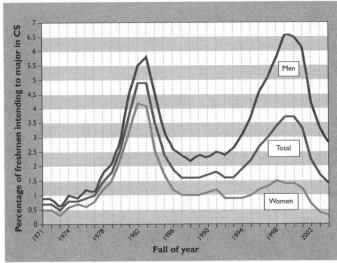

Source: HERI at UCLA

Figure 1. Computer science listed as probable major among incoming freshman.

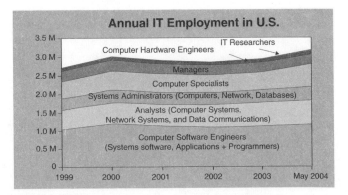

Figure 2. Annual IT employment in the U.S.

outsourcing job loss in the U.S., which most studies estimate to be 2% to 3% per year for the next decade.[2]

Regarding the negative CS impressions held by students not yet in college, we hope ACM's new Computer Science Teachers Association (CSTA) will help in this regard. CSTA is a membership organization that supports and promotes the teaching of CS and other computing disciplines. CSTA provides opportunities for pre-college teachers and students to better understand the computing disciplines and to more successfully prepare themselves to teach and learn. Remarkably, before ACM formed CSTA nine months ago, computer science was the only academic discipline within the U.S. high school curriculum without national professional representation.

To give you an idea what CSTA is trying to do to further the CS cause, here is the list of its existing committees: Curriculum, Equity, Finance, Funding Development, Governance, Membership, Policy and Advocacy, Professional Development, Publications and Communications, Research, and Standards and Certification (see csta.acm.org for details on all these groups and much more). I am particularly interested in the Equity committee, for I've long suspected that the drop in women CS majors was related to the initial unattractive impression of our field when high schools started teaching CS in the 1980s.

Although it only began in January, CSTA already has more than 2,000 members, and these members come from all over the world. CSTA members represent more than 60 countries and all 50 states in the U.S.

At the recent National Educational Computing Conference, panel speakers from Canada, Israel, Scotland, and South Africa described their current CS curriculum for students ages 12 to 18 and the issues that surround its implementation. They all emphasized the importance of supporting CS education as a means for ensuring the economic futures of their countries.

While all of the countries noted their efforts to implement a new national curriculum were initially hampered by issues such as lack of funding or insufficient time for teacher training, no point about the need for well-trained teachers was made more poignantly than by Michael Chiles from South Africa. He told the audience that the HIV/AIDS pandemic is taking the lives of so many teachers that it is becoming almost impossible to replace them. Not only are the teachers themselves dying, so many people in business are dying that industries looking for technically skilled workers are luring the healthy CS teachers away from the classroom.

This panel discussion led to a CSTA project to create a white paper that will provide an international perspective on successful models for CS curriculum development and implementation. Judith Gal-Ezer, the panel speaker representing Israel, serves as an international director to the CSTA Board.

What can you do to help? First, please try to counteract the widespread impression that the CS field is not a good one for the future. For example, you can help publicize real employment data and the results of ACM's upcoming outsourcing study.

Second, if you know pre-college teachers, please suggest they consider joining CSTA. Studies of teachers belonging to such organizations suggest they gain important knowledge and psychological support as well as establish networking relationships that provide opportunities to share curricula. The resulting reform is also more widespread and long lasting.

CSTA could also use specific help on some of their committees. The Research committee is looking for volunteers to assist on statistical analysis of surveys. The Standards and Certification committee needs volunteers to create a database of teacher certification requirements in different regions. It could also use more practicing teachers on its Curriculum committee. Finally, if you really care about the issue of pre-college education, join CSTA.

It's difficult to imagine a more important topic for our future than trying to change public opinion about career opportunities in CS and to improve pre-college education, so thanks in advance for your help.

Notes

1. Private communication, John Sargent, Office of Technology, Policy Technology Administration, U.S. Department of Commerce, July 2005. For clarity, Figure 2 combines the 12 official U.S. Department of Labor titles into seven related categories.
2. Private communication, William Asprey, Indiana University, July 2005.

Reference

1. Vegso, J. Interest in CS as a major drops among incoming freshmen. *Computing Research News 17*, 3 (May 2005); www.cra.org/CRN/articles/may05/vegso.

David A. Patterson (pattsn@eecs.berkeley.edu) is president of the ACM and the Pardee Professor of Computer Science at the University of California at Berkeley.

From *Communications of the ACM,* Vol. 48, No. 9, September 2005, pp. 25-26, 28. Copyright © 2005 by Association for Computing Machinery, Inc. Reprinted by permission.

Dot Com
for Dictators

Tales of cyberdissidents fighting government censors feed the conventional wisdom about the Internet's role as a powerful tool against tyranny. But if democracy advocates want to spur meaningful change, they must also recognize the Net's ability to change authoritarian regimes from within. As nations such as China embrace the Web to streamline government and boost economic growth, they also create opportunities for greater transparency, accountability, and freedom.

By Shanthi Kalathil

Call it Authoritarianism 2.0: Forced to choose between jumping on the information superhighway or languishing on the unwired byways of technology, many authoritarian regimes are choosing to go along for the Internet ride. In addition to helping autocratic rulers compete in the global economy, the Internet and other information and communication technologies (ICTs) can streamline authoritarian states and help them govern more effectively—attractive options for many leaders. In some of these countries, reform-minded officials are even using the Internet to increase transparency, reduce corruption, and make government more responsive to citizens.

But hardheaded autocrats aren't suddenly soliciting e-mail advice from dissenters. Controlling information has always been a cornerstone of authoritarian rule, and leaders are naturally suspicious of the Web. Public Internet access could expose large swaths of a population to forbidden information and images or galvanize grass-roots opposition, as has already happened in many countries where Internet users are growing in number and challenging oppressive governments. As a result, authoritarian regimes are deploying sophisticated censorship schemes to stay one step ahead of online dissidents.

Such instances of technological one-upmanship have created the appearance of an Internet arms race pitting would-be revolutionaries and democracy-hungry publics against states determined to block, censor, and monitor citizens. Indeed, anecdotes about empowered cyberdissidents, amplified by faith in the democratic nature of the

China

Leader: Hu Jintao

Total Population: 1.3 billion

Number of internet Users: 26.5 million

Freedom House Rating: Not free

The Official Line: The speed and scope of [information flows] have created a borderless information space around the world... the melding of the traditional economy and information technology will provide the engine for the development of the economy and society in the 21st century."—*Jiang Zemin, former chief of the Chinese Communist Party*

Reality Check: Despite leaders' glowing rhetoric, China blocks thousands of Web pages within its borders, encourages self-censorship among users, and blankets its domestic information technology industry with conflicting regulations. The country has also embarked on a comprehensive e-government program designed to maximize bureaucratic efficiency and discourage corruption.

technology, have helped spread the notion that the Internet ineluctably thwarts authoritarian regimes. Little surprise, then, that human rights advocates and press freedom organizations publicly condemn crackdowns on the Internet as violating technology's democratizing manifest destiny.

But technological censorship and its evasion, while relevant to any discussion of political freedom, represent only one part of a larger developmental puzzle. Even if the Internet does not necessarily contribute to the downfall of authoritarianism, the Web does help transform authoritarianism's modern expression. Although other programs censor and spread propaganda, e-government initiatives that reshape bureaucracy, dispense education and health information, and increase direct communication between officials and the public actually improve the quality of life for citizens and boost transparency. Understanding these distinct effects of technology is crucial for those interested in using the Internet effectively to increase political liberalization and improve governance in closed societies. Efforts by outside governments and activists to champion hackers and cyberheroes in authoritarian states may win headlines, but the more mundane task of supporting e-government programs is just as likely—if not more so—to foster lasting reform.

DIALING UP FOR DOLLARS

Historically, authoritarian states in developing countries provided economic benefits and stability in return for the right to rule. Authoritarian and semiauthoritarian regimes such as China, Malaysia, and Singapore have already thrown government weight behind domestic information technology industries that stimulate the local economy. Malaysia has long promoted its Multimedia Super Corridor as a haven for technology companies—complete with tax perks and hands-off censorship policies for investors. Vietnam, while struggling with economic reforms, nonetheless aims to develop a local "knowledge economy" based on a tech-savvy population of programmers. Even authoritarian regimes such as Myanmar (Burma) that are relatively wary of all forms of ICT often emphasize wiring those key industries that generate hard currency, such as tourism.

On the other hand, some authoritarian countries have significantly less incentive to promote Internet access within their borders. Isolated by an embargo and fearful of widespread Internet use, Cuba has chosen to restrict entrepreneurship and greater competition in its tiny Internet industry. Economic use of the Internet in Cuba has followed the country's general pattern of separating its external and domestic sectors, and thus the majority of Internet use occurs in the tourist and export-oriented industries. Also shunned by many foreign investors and governments for its shoddy human rights record, Myanmar has been slow to open to information technology development. A 1996 decree makes possession of even an unregistered telephone (much less a computer) illegal and punishable by imprisonment—a regulation the government has made good on over the years.

Yet, if cash-strapped authoritarian states wish to tap the global economy, they will face growing pressure to permit private investment and market-led development within Internet sectors. Prodded by the Association of Southeast Asian Nations (ASEAN), Myanmar is starting to liberalize its draconian ICT laws and invite technological investment from friendly neighbors. Institutions like the World Bank and the International Monetary Fund now encourage deregulating the telecommunications sector and opening it to investment, while entities like the World Trade Organization (WTO) require certain reforms in return for membership. China, for example, had to agree to foreign telecommunications investment to join the WTO. Such reforms can, in turn, reduce state influence in key economic sectors and promote local growth in domestic Internet industries.

Authoritarian states also use ICTs like the Internet to promote larger development goals. The state-supported All China Women's Federation (ACWF), for instance, helps rural women get accurate, up-to-date health information online through local organizations that have Internet access. Via its Web site, the ACWF also offers women anonymous counseling on issues such as rape and spousal abuse. In Cuba, where mass Web access remains restricted, authorities have been pursuing online health initiatives. The Ministry of Public Health's Infomed, one of Cuba's oldest networks, connects medical centers nationwide and uses e-mail lists to disseminate health alerts. Egypt, a semiauthoritarian country that has not attempted to censor the Internet, is developing technology-access community centers to promote rural education.

STREAMLINING THE STATE

In countries that embrace ICT development, authoritarianism is no longer solely the domain of creaky bureaucracies and aging dictators. By implementing e-government policies—such as wiring key industries and federal departments—states can guide Internet development to serve their own goals. As a result, authoritarian states are shedding years of inefficiency and waste, paring down unwieldy bureaucracies, and consolidating central authority through more efficient communication with remote provinces. Such advancements are seemingly antithetical to democratization, but expanding government Internet programs can also make regimes more transparent and allow citizens to directly express their concerns about government performance.

The semiauthoritarian country of Singapore, in particular, has led the world in revamping its bureaucracy and changing the way government interacts with citizens. Singapore's ICT sector is one of the world's most dynamic, and the city-state boasts sky-high Internet penetration rates, with an estimated 2.1 million citizens online out of a total population of 4.5 million. Singapore's crown Internet jewel is its eCitizen program, which smoothly integrates services from several government departments and packages them in a user-friendly way. Just about any action requiring interaction with the government can be performed online, and the list is constantly expanding.

Myanmar (Burma)

Leader: Than Shwe

Total Population: 42.2 million

Number of Internet Users: 500

Freedom House Rating: Not free

The Official Line: A 1996 decree promotes "the emergence of a modern developed state through computer science" but forbids the unanauthorized use of computers or computer networks.

Reality Check: Myanmar severely restricts freedom of speech and of the press, and Internet use in the country is minimal, limited primarily to elites. Harsh punishments deter the public from seeking clandestine access.

Under the eCitizen site's "Get Married" subheading, for instance, visitors can file notice for either a civil or Muslim marriage, scan a roster of justices of the peace, find out about pre- and post-marriage counseling programs, and even obtain a list of hospitals providing genetic counseling. By using the Internet to enhance government responsivenes s and quality of life, Singapore's ruling party has turned the Internet into an asset that increases citizens' satisfaction with their government.

Singapore, of course, is something of a special case—it has a tiny population of just 4.5 million and is hardly a full-blown authoritarian state. Opposition parties, for example, participate in regular elections that are held at constitutionally mandated intervals. But they face other obstacles.

As the U.S. State Department's 2001 human rights report delicately puts it, "Government leaders historically have utilized court proceedings, in particular defamation suits, against political opponents and critics.... Both this practice and consistent awards in favor of government plaintiffs have raised questions about the relationship between the Government and the judiciary and led to a perception that the judiciary reflects the views of the executive in politically sensitive cases." Moreover, as the report goes on to note, "The Constitution provides for freedom of speech and expression but permits official restrictions on these rights, and in practice the Government significantly restricts freedom of speech and of the press." Web sites, for instance, that the government considers political must be registered with the authorities. The established media, which is connected to the government and espouses uncritical views, has a strong Internet presence. Since most civil society groups tend to have some connection to the ruling People's Action Party (PAP), they too use the Internet in government-approved ways. When a handful of independent groups used the Internet to provide a platform for criticism of the PAP, the party responded with new regulations. Many of these independent sites quickly shuttered operations rather than risk

the continual regulatory ire of the PAP. The government's grip on power is generally aided by use of ICTs, which help modernize government operations and open communication channels between the government and the public. Civil society organizations' use of the Internet, on the other hand, has not yet proved a potent challenge to the PAP's mixture of official regulations and unspoken inducements to damp politically threatening speech.

Small and capable states such as Singapore can generally reap the benefits of e-government technology more quickly than large states with unwieldy bureaucracies. Nonetheless, across the board, many authoritarian regimes moved early and forcefully on e-government plans. In Egypt, the most politically significant Internet use takes place not among opposition groups but within the government itself. During the last two decades, Egypt computerized regional governments and then connected them through a national network. The country now has a central government Web site, and about 500 other government entities are online. In April 2001, Egypt announced an e-government initiative to provide civil services and promote intragovernmental collaboration using a technological infrastructure provided by Microsoft.

Egypt

Leader: Hosni Mubarak

Total Population: 70.7 million

Number of Internet Users: 560,000

Freedom House Rating: Not free

The Official Line: "The technology that portrays itself to be global, needs to be truly so not only in terms of reach, but more importantly in terms of equal access and mutual benefit.... These new technologies need to be geared towards the advancement of the developing world."—*President Hosni Mubarak*

Reality Check: Egypt is one of the few countries in the Middle East to forgo a coordinated Internet censorship scheme, while heavily promoting the use of Internet technology for development. However, recent arrests of Internet users indicate the government remains sensitive to dissenting opinion online.

China, which uses the term "informatization" to describe the incorporation of ICTs into all spheres of life—political, economic, and social—is developing a particularly ambitious e-government plan. In addition to implementing a comprehensive project called Government Online to make services and information available to the public, individual Chinese ministries are partnering with private companies to eliminate corruption. By using online procurement auctions, ministries can eliminate layers of middlemen, along with traditional opportunities for graft. In major cities, municipal Web sites not only provide helpful local information but also solicit feedback on projects, such as large-scale construction work. These initiatives have yet to reach poverty-stricken interior provinces, but even government officials there are beginning to think creatively about Internet kiosks and basic Internet training.

E-government provides the citizens of authoritarian regimes with important benefits. True, such programs can also help strengthen authoritarian states, particularly if they augment central authority. Some governments may also be interested only in the facade of improved governance. Yet cynical power calculations are not the sole reason officials in these countries pursue e-government initiatives. Internal reformers may attempt to use such measures as a basis for political liberalization, if not outright democratization. In China, for instance, midlevel officials have expressed the desire to use the Internet to increase government transparency and bolster accountability.

LESS CONTROL IS MORE

For all their power in creating the architecture for national Internet development, many authoritarian regimes have realized that adapting to the information age means relinquishing a measure of control. Savvy leaders understand they simply cannot dominate every facet of the Internet and rarely erect foolproof fire walls. Indeed, countries such as Malaysia and China allow a freer information environment online than they do in traditional print and broadcast media. Many employ measures of "soft control" to shape the boundaries of Internet use.

Cuba

Leader: Fidel Castro

Total Population: 11.2 million

Number of Internet Users: 60,000

Freedom House Rating: Not free

The Official Line: The Ministry of Computing and Communications' mission is "to prompt, facilitate and organize the massive use of information, communication, electronics and automation technology services and products to satisfy the expectations of all spheres of society."

Reality Check: The Cuban government restricts popular use of the Internet to individuals and organizations that are supportive of the regime. In the future, the general public is likely to gain access only to preapproved Internet sites.

Regimes often promote self-censorship—a task easily accomplished in an authoritarian atmosphere—rather than official censorship, access restrictions, and other forms of overt control. Such governments also encourage private Internet companies to filter content or police users. Moreover, years of ideological conditioning and the threat of punitive action keep citizens from crossing the boundaries of politically acceptable Internet use, making it easy for authorities to sustain an environment where comprehensive censorship is unnecessary.

Iran

Leader: Mohammad Khatami

Total Population: 66.6 million

Number of internet Users: 250,000

Freedom House Rating: Not free

The Official Line: Iranian state radio has announced that "steps have been taken so that the entire population can use Internet services around the country."

Reality Check: Internet service providers have multiplied recently, but so have regulations. A commission dominated by religious hard-liners (and some intelligence officials) has recently been set up to monitor news Web sites deemed illegal.

Authoritarian countries seeking to encourage domestic Internet industries can also present a wide array of politically unthreatening, domestically generated content that satisfies the demands of most Internet users, whose basic online needs often mirror those of residents in advanced industrialized democracies. Want to e-mail a friend, get news on a favorite sports team, or check local weather? It's easy to do in China without ever having to use proxy servers to access government-blocked Web pages. China's own private and state-owned Internet companies have generated a staggering body of information—all in Mandarin Chinese, using the People's Republic's own simplified characters—that falls largely within the boundaries of the country's harsh content restrictions. Whether via rules stipulating that all online news must flow from official sources or by making examples of those who transgress regulations, China's government has created a domestic Internet for domestic consumption.

The concept that subtler forms of ideological influence might prove effective has extended to many propaganda departments as well. In authoritarian countries where the government has taken an active interest in the Internet, the official newspaper is generally one of the first government organs to establish an online presence, which may be substantially more engaging and inviting than stodgy print counterparts. In Vietnam, the Communist Party's official *Nhan Dan* newspaper was among the first government bodies to go online in 1999. China's *People's Daily* Web edition provides not only the official take on news but a snazzy English site with links to, among other things, Chinese government white papers. The Chinese-language version features a popular chat room, called the Strong Country Forum, where users can and do debate issues related to national security, international relations,

179

and China's global role. Unsurprisingly, such discussions feature a distinctively nationalistic tinge. These forums can provide the government with a subtler means of ideological control than the blunt instrument of official rhetoric.

REWIRING REGIMES

These rarefied forms of ideological control did not evolve overnight. Many governments have shaped Internet policy by imitating each others' policies and techniques. In China, where both domestic and foreign observers are examining the Internet's impact, officials have long sought to emulate Singapore's success in neutralizing the Web as a medium for political opposition. Authoritarian countries in the Middle East, such as the United Arab Emirates, also look to Singapore's successful e-government and e-commerce programs. For its part, China is formally advising Cuba on ICT policies and has sent Chinese Information Industry Minister Wu Jichuan to Cuba to explore joint projects. Even in Myanmar, where Internet access is tightly controlled, the government is borrowing technology strategies (or at least tech-friendly lingo) from authoritarian neighbors in ASEAN.

The Internet may be empowering autocrats, but it is also forcing them to reassess, adapt, and, in some cases, make critical changes. True, e-government programs can streamline the state, extend the central government's reach, and increase citizen support, but they also represent a hidden opportunity for political liberalization. It is a mistake to discount them simply because they come from within authoritarian governments themselves. Yet many Western policymakers and activists tend to regard autocratic moves toward e-government as mere window dressing, focusing instead on using technology to strengthen popular opposition movements. The latter approach deals with means—such as anticensorship techniques—instead of the presumably desirable ends of increased openness.

Heightened political reform and more responsive governance require not only combating censorship but also promoting Internet use that tangibly benefits citizens of authoritarian regimes while increasing government transparency. Approaches currently under consideration by the U.S. Congress, such as unblocking Web sites or offering anonymizing software to citizens in authoritarian nations, will commit large sums of money to fixing only one small piece of the greater liberalization puzzle. Rather than treating the Internet as an innately liberating tool that, if unleashed in closed societies, will release a tide of opposition sentiment, policymakers should identify and support specific actions and Internet policies that are likely to promote openness in authoritarian countries. This approach should not preclude the opportunity to combat censorship. However, since countless nongovernmental organizations, private companies, and individuals are already working toward that goal, government-funded Western support should also help reformers within authoritarian regimes use technology to make government accountable and transparent—reformers who may not attract the media attention that dissidents and human rights campaigners command.

[Want to Know More?]

This article draws on research from Shanthi Kalathil and Taylor C. Boas's *Open Networks, Closed Regimes: The Impact of the Internet on Authoritarian Rule* (Washington: Carnegie Endowment for International Peace, 2003).

For an assessment of the Internet's ability to promote freedom globally, see Michael J. Mazarr's, ed., *Information Technology and World Politics* (New York: Palgrave, 2002). Another first-rate analysis of the Internet's democratizing impact in the developing world is *Launching Into Cyberspace: Internet Development and Politics in Five World Regions* (Boulder: Lynne Rienner, 2002) by Marcus Franda. For more on the challenges to the conventional wisdom surrounding the Web, read Andrew L. Shapiro's *"Think Again: The Internet"* (FOREIGN POLICY, Summer 1999).

Several sources provide excellent country- and region-specific case studies of the Internet's impact on authoritarian rule. For analysis on the Middle East, including Iraq and Syria, see Benjamin Goldstein's report **"The Internet in the Mideast and North Africa: Free Expression and Censorship"** (New York: Human Rights Watch, 1999), available on the Human Rights Watch Web site, and Jon Alterman's **"The Middle East's Information Revolution"** (*Current History*, Vol. 99, January 2000). Two of the best works on the much-studied intersection of globalization, commercialization, and the Internet in China are *After the Propaganda State: Media, Politics, and "Thought Work" in Reformed China* (Stanford: Stanford University Press, 1999) by Daniel C. Lynch and **"You've Got Dissent! Chinese Dissident Use of the Internet and Beijing's Counter-Strategies"** (Santa Monica: RAND, 2002) by Michael Chase and James Mulvenon. See also Kalathil's **"China's Dot-Communism"** (FOREIGN POLICY, January/February 2001). In **"The Weakest Links"** (FOREIGN POLICY, November/December 2002), Tobie Saad, Stanley D. Brunn, and Jeff House map the world based on nations' global Internet linkages.

Many human rights and press freedom organizations monitor Internet censorship in authoritarian countries. Some of the best studies include Reporters sans Frontieres' **"Enemies of the Internet,"** as well as the Committee to Protect Journalists' annual *Attacks on the Press* (New York: Committee to Protect Journalists, 2002). Both are available on those organizations' Web sites.

For links to relevant Web sites, access to the *FP* Archive, and a comprehensive index of related FOREIGN POLICY articles, go to www.foreignpolicy.com.

Aid organizations are beginning to get the message: The United States Agency for International Development (USAID), for example, has committed more than $39 million over five years to promote e-government, e-commerce, and ICT diffusion in Egypt. At present, however, there is little coordination or information sharing between various agencies and groups in the United States, much less internationally. Apart from USAID, other arms of the U.S. government are pursuing their own Internet-based initiatives, while recent anticensorship measures proposed in Congress by Republican Rep. Christopher Cox of California, among others, take no notice of these activities. If an Office of Global Internet Freedom (as suggested in proposed U.S. legislation) is to be established, it should have as its mandate not merely unjamming Web sites but also coordinating various government efforts to better achieve democratic reform.

Once strong-arm regimes open the door to technology, they may find it difficult to return to a culture of bureaucratic secrecy, unscrupulous abuse of power, and unaccountability. Using technology to illuminate murky government processes and craft better public services may not automatically lead to more politically liberal atmospheres, but these moves are helping to spur more government oversight—or at least create the expectation of it. authoritarian governments may not enter the information age with reform in mind, but it can be a welcome result.

Shanthi Kalathil is an associate at the Carnegie Endowment for International Peace. She is coauthor, with Taylor C. Boas, of Open Networks, Closed Regimes: The Impact of the Internet of Authoritarian Rule *(Washington: Carnegie Endowment for International Peace, 2003.)*

Weaving the Authoritarian Web

"Authoritarian countries such as China and Saudi Arabia are employing both technological and institutional means to control use of the Internet while also encouraging its growth. In doing so, they stand as counterevidence to much of the optimistic thinking about the Internet's effect on democratization...."

TAYLOR C. BOAS

In preparatory meetings leading up to the December 2003 World Summit on the Information Society in Geneva, the delegations of several authoritarian regimes reacted negatively to the hands-off approach to Internet regulation promoted by the United States and other advanced democracies. Saudi Arabia proposed that the development of the information society "shall be done without any prejudice whatsoever to the moral, social, and religious values of all societies"—values to which the Saudi government has appealed when justifying its censorship of the Internet. The Chinese delegation campaigned vigorously against a statement of support for the principles of free speech enshrined in the Universal Declaration of Human Rights. Ultimately, the summit's final declaration disregarded the objections that these and other authoritarian regimes had voiced during the negotiations, but their positions stand as a vivid reminder that not all countries accept a laissez-faire vision for the future of the Internet.

At first glance, the negotiating positions adopted by China and Saudi Arabia might seem to constitute evidence for the common belief that the Internet presents authoritarian leaders with a stark choice: either promote the development of an Internet that remains free from extensive government control, or exert control over the technology by restricting its diffusion within their borders. Whether because of inherent technological characteristics that complicate efforts to censor the Internet, or because countries are under pressure to align their policies with those preferred by the international community, many scholars have assumed that the only effective way to control the Internet is to limit its growth or even keep it out entirely.

They are wrong. Contrary to the assumption underlying many of the studies of Internet policies among autocratic regimes, governments can in fact establish effective control over the Internet while simultaneously promoting its development. Indeed, China and Saudi Arabia are two of the most prominent examples of this phenomenon. Far from trying to regulate the Internet by merely restricting its diffusion, authoritarian countries such as China and Saudi Arabia are employing both technological and institutional means to control use of the Internet while also encouraging its growth. In doing so, they stand as counterevidence to much of the optimistic thinking about the Internet's effect on democratization that pundits and politicians voiced during the net's early days and the technology boom of the late 1990s.

CONTROLLING THE INTERNET

The Internet was initially designed as a technology that would not lend itself to centralized control. The original engineering decisions that gave rise to this characteristic were a product of the specific economic, political, and social environment in which the Internet was created. In part, the technological characteristics of the early Internet derived from the norms of its designers and initial user community—a small group of engineers and academics who were wary of bureaucracy, trusted each other, and worked well through consensus rather than a centralized hierarchy. In light of this culture, they made specific choices about the design of the technology that rendered the network resistant to efforts at centralized control. An even more important influence on the technological configuration of the early Internet were the military imperatives for its development. The US Department of Defense was the sponsor and progenitor of the Internet's precursor network, the ARPANET, and the packet-switching technology on which it was based was designed to frustrate attempts at centralized control so that communications capacity could not be disabled by an enemy attack on a key portion of the network. The particular characteristics of the Internet that served to frustrate attempts at centralized control involve what is called the "end-to-end arguments" in network design. As guidelines for the design of computer networks, the end-to-end arguments state that complexity and control should be implemented at the ends of the network (the multiple computers and individual users that are interconnected); the core of the network performs simple data transfer functions that do not require knowledge of how the ends are operating. Because the Internet was built around an end-to-end design, one cannot control the entire network through control of a small number of centralized nodes. Control can be exerted at the ends of the network, but as these ends multiply, controlling the entire network by controlling the ends becomes less and less feasible.

While a control-frustrating technological architecture suited the needs and preferences of the Internet's designers and initial user community, the technology has since spread into a number of environments in which centralized control of information is a more desirable feature. One of the most important of these major shifts involves the global diffusion of the Internet. With Internet use in the developing world growing rapidly, the Internet is moving into a number of authoritarian countries where standards of information control are quite different from those in the United States. The leaders of these countries generally recognize the tangible benefits that the Internet has to offer, such as the promotion of economic development and the provision of online government services. Yet they worry that Internet use might pose political threats, challenge state control of economic resources, or offend local cultural sensitivities. To reap the benefits of the technology while avoiding what they see as negative ramifications, some leaders would prefer to exert greater centralized control over Internet use.

The idea of an inherently control-frustrating Internet rests on the assumption that the network's architecture is incapable of fundamental change. But many of the same characteristics that made the Internet hard to control make it a flexible technology as well. Unlike the telephone network, which was designed specifically for voice traffic, the core of the Internet was not optimized for any particular service. At the time of its creation, there was little sense of what services the Internet would need to support in the future, so the network's core was built as a set of simple, flexible tools. Any service that conforms to the published protocols for addressing and transmitting information can be implemented at the ends of the network without altering the center. The Internet's central mechanisms simply move information indiscriminately; the core of the network does not need to know if it is transmitting packets from an e-mail, a website, streaming audio, or some as-of-yet uninvented service. Thus, the characteristics of the Internet as a whole can be altered by adding new protocols that will help the technology meet the needs of operating in new environments.

CENSORS AT THE GATEWAYS

The Internet is much less a single network of individual users than a network connecting separate computer networks. Networks are interconnected through a gateway; behind the gateway, each individual network can be configured in any number of ways. Conceptually, therefore, it may well make more sense to think of the Internet's component networks as its ends than to view individual users as the outer edge of a single, seamlessly interconnected Internet.

Controlling the *entire* Internet by controlling each of its component networks would remain a nearly impossible task. But no governing authority realistically seeks to control the whole Internet in this fashion. Rather, authorities attempt to control a relevant subset of Internet users. The administrators of corporate computer networks, for instance, often monitor employees' usage and block certain types of non–work-related traffic. Users who have a choice of networks will always be able to switch to a more liberal environment. For those with no realistic choice, however, the distinction between control of the entire Internet and control of a network attached to the Internet is largely irrelevant. For them, the choice is between access to a restricted Internet and access to nothing at all.

Such is the situation in many countries where the authoritarian regimes are developing national computer networks with connections to the Internet. While in most democracies a number of individual Internet service providers (ISPs) maintain separate links to the global Internet, under authoritarian regimes all Internet users may effectively be members of a single national network. Even where there are multiple ISPs within a country, international connections to the global Internet are often channeled through a single government-controlled gateway. Indeed, the image of the Internet's global diffusion, in which a single transnational network makes inroads into countries around the world, is something of an inaccurate picture. What has occurred historically is the development of national computer networks (typically under the guidance of the state) that are then connected to the Internet.

Given the political, economic, and social conditions prevailing in many authoritarian-ruled countries, it is not surprising that their governments have sought to establish technological measures of control over the portions of the Internet within their borders. Authoritarian regimes are typically central players in the growth of their countries' information infrastructures, and the conditions under which this technological development takes place are far removed from those that prevailed in the early days of the Internet in the United States. Rather than an environment in which military imperatives and engineering culture demand a control-frustrating network, authoritarian countries are places in which political elites typically seek a fair degree of control over information flow. Given the flexibility of Internet technology at the macro-level, one would expect authoritarian regimes to build architectures of control into their "ends" of the Internet.

THE SAUDI CASE

Saudi Arabia's approach to the Internet has been strongly influenced by the pressures of a conservative society, with significant public concern over pornography and material offensive to Islam, and considerable societal support for censorship of this type of content on the Internet. In addition, Saudi Arabia is a monarchy in which the royal family is quite sensitive to criticism and dissent; it is particularly cognizant of the threat posed by overseas opposition groups. Because of these conditions, Saudi Arabia has moved very slowly in its approach to the Internet. The country's first connection was established in 1994, but public access was delayed until 1999 while authorities perfected their technological mechanism for Internet control. Saudi Arabia has chosen to permit multiple, privately owned ISPs, but all international connections to the global Internet pass through a gateway maintained by the Internet Services Unit (ISU) of the King Abdulaziz City for Science and Technology, the Internet's governing authority in the country. Effectively, all Internet use within Saudi Arabia can be thought of as taking place within a single national network.

In Saudi Arabia, the government has found support for its censorship regime among conservative Islamist groups that are primarily concerned about pornography.

This concentrated network structure has facilitated the technological control of Internet content, a goal about which Saudi authorities have been quite open. Since the debut of public access in Saudi Arabia, all traffic to the global Internet has been filtered through a set of proxy servers managed by the ISU, aiming to block information that authorities consider socially or politically inappropriate. Market conditions have facilitated this imposition of censorship, with Saudi Arabia outsourcing the provision of censorship software to foreign firms that specialize in this area. Saudi authorities rely on a pre-set list of sexually explicit sites contained in a computer program that has been customized with the addition of impermissible political and religious sites. In addition, the ISU's website includes forms with which the public can request that sites be blocked or unblocked; officials report an average of 500 block requests and 100 unblock requests per day.

CHINA'S INTERNETS

China in its approach to the Internet has sought a strategy that will allow it to promote widespread market-based diffusion of the technology while still retaining government control. In contrast to Saudi Arabia, in which all blocking takes place at a single international gateway, Internet control in China is more diffuse. It is difficult to ascertain the specific technological details of this case because China has been much less open about the configuration and extent of its censorship regime. All evidence suggests, however, that China employs multiple, overlapping layers of Internet control that have been effective at limiting the access of the majority of users. Blocking specific web pages on the basis of IP address has been the most common; a similar procedure can block e-mails sent to or received from a host computer. Beginning in September 2002, authorities implemented a more sophisticated system capable of blocking pages dynamically, based on either keywords in the web address (URL)—prohibiting Google searches on specific terms, for instance—or keywords in the actual web page requested. These methods of blocking are a step beyond previous strategies and mechanisms employed elsewhere, since they do not rely on a preexisting blacklist of prohibited websites.

At the level of the international gateway, the cornerstone of China's Internet control has been its system of interconnecting networks. While promoting rapid proliferation of the ISPs that offer Internet access to end-users, actual connectivity to the global Internet has long been channeled through a small number of interconnecting networks with ties to government ministries or important state companies. Four interconnecting networks were initially established in 1996; the number has since grown to nine. As the Ministry of Information Industries has licensed additional networks, it has made certain they are under effective state control. Moreover, the structure of this market is more concentrated than the number of interconnecting networks implies; the top two networks, ChinaNET and China Netcom, jointly control 81 percent of international bandwidth. Most national-level Internet filtering is implemented by the International Connection Bureau, based on a set of computers belonging to China-NET owner China Telecom. And the major networks routinely exchange information about specific websites that they seek to block.

IN THE CAFÉS AND CHAT ROOMS

In addition to blocking mechanisms implemented at the level of the interconnecting network, China has extended its management of Internet architecture by establishing control at the level of ISPs, Internet cafés, and chat rooms. These points of access to the Internet number into the thousands, and most are thoroughly private entities without the same ties to the regime as the interconnecting networks, so direct government imposition of technological control is less of an option here. At this more diffuse level, authorities implement an architecture of control indirectly, through their legal influence over these intermediaries and their creation of a market environment in which cooperation with authorities is good business practice. Technological measures of censorship at a centralized level are thus augmented by additional filtering at a level much closer to the individual user.

China's Internet regulations make ISPs, Internet cafés, and chat rooms responsible for online content, and the threat of sanctions (and occasional largescale crackdowns) has encouraged these entities to implement their own technological measures of control. It is likely that at least some filtering methods are implemented by ISPs instead of (or in addition to) the interconnecting networks. For their part, many Internet cafés have chosen to install blocking software to limit what their patrons can view, and chat rooms use a technology that scans for potentially sensitive postings and sends them to a webmaster for review. In addition to these filtering measures, ISPs and Internet cafés have been required to implement technological architectures that facilitate government surveillance. Regulations introduced in October 2000 require ISPs to keep logs of Internet traffic for 60 days and deliver the information to authorities on request. Many Internet cafés have installed software that allows public security bureaus to track user records and monitor Internet traffic remotely.

Evidence from the cases of Saudi Arabia and China confirms the view that the architecture of the Internet is not inherently control-frustrating, even if this characteristic was a feature of the early Internet in the United States. Rather, the logic of end-to-end network design allows authoritarian governments to construct national computer networks attached to the Internet in ways that facilitate technological control. In Saudi Arabia, a single gateway to the global Internet effectively creates a single national network within the country. Even in the case of China, where infrastructure is more developed and international connections to the Internet are more diffuse, influence over intermediaries through legal or market channels allows for the creation of control-facilitating technological architectures.

PERFECT VS. EFFECTIVE CONTROL

Those skeptical of arguments about Internet control routinely point to the myriad ways in which determined users can circumvent technological measures of control. Indeed, evidence from Saudi Arabia, China, and many other authoritarian countries confirms that some individuals are finding ways to elude government censors. Saudi authorities have acknowledged that many users are finding ways to access forbidden websites, often through the use of overseas proxy servers. Wealthy Internet users who find this avenue blocked can always dial into unrestricted accounts in neighboring Bahrain—a common

practice in the days before public access was permitted in Saudi Arabia. Chinese Internet users can attempt to circumvent controls in a variety of ways, from the use of peer-to-peer file-sharing systems to entering the URLs of blocked pages in ways that may fool censorship mechanisms. In the Chinese case, ongoing arrests of online dissidents confirm that people are successfully engaging in types of Internet use that the government seeks to block. And in each of these countries, it is more difficult to exert technological control over the use of e-mail than it is to filter access to international websites.

> *China employs multiple, overlapping layers of Internet control that have been effective at limiting the access of the majority of users.*

In addressing the implications of these inevitable cracks in national firewall systems, it is important to distinguish between perfect control and effective control of the Internet. Ultimately, libertarian perspectives on Internet control are concerned with the individual: will the government be able to prevent me from doing what I want to do online? For the most determined and technology-savvy users, only perfect architectural constraints will be able to control their online activity. But the perspective of authoritarian governments, or of any authority seeking to exert control over the Internet, is different. For them, the goal is almost never perfect control, attempting to thwart the evasive maneuvers of every enterprising individual. Rather, authoritarian leaders seek to exert control with an external criterion of success—control that is in effect "good enough" to serve any number of objectives, including regime stability and protection of local culture. Effective control of this sort may not be capable of changing the behavior of the last tenth of a percent of Internet users, but this small number is rarely enough to seriously challenge the goals that most authoritarian regimes are trying to pursue.

THE COST OF CIRCUMVENTION

It is in establishing and enforcing effective rather than perfect control over the Internet that institutional constraints on Internet use come most clearly into play. In contrast to the architectural characteristics that render certain types of Internet use easier, more difficult, or impossible, institutional constraints consist of the legal regulations, market conditions, and social norms that exert an influence on what individual users do with the technology. To understand the interplay of these two categories of constraints, an economic interpretation is useful, with unrestricted Internet access thought of as a good demanded by different numbers of users depending on the price.

In this economic model, most consumers are quite happy using the Internet for entertainment, online games, communication with friends, and access to officially sanctioned news sources; they place a low value on circumventing controls, especially with regard to political information. Similarly, some percentage of users will always demand unrestricted access to the Internet even at extremely high prices; they will spend money for technology to circumvent censorship, engage in illegal political communication at the risk of punishment, and ignore disapproval from members of society who frown on lawless activity. As these costs are raised, however, demand for unrestricted Internet access shrinks. The government's goal is not to set the cost so high that demand is completely eliminated; rather, authorities seek to reduce this demand to the point of political insignificance.

Law, social norms, and market forces that raise the cost of unrestricted Internet use allow for a much more effective implementation of control than architectural constraints alone. Arguably, the establishment of perfect technological control is impossible short of cutting off access to the global Internet. For this reason, countries such as Cuba and Burma have chosen control of access rather than extensive content censorship as their strategy for Internet regulation. For countries that promote widespread access to the Internet, however, filtering alone is insufficient. In the absence of perfect architectures of control, technological constraints are most effective when they interact with alternative, institutional constraints. If firewalls can be circumvented with sophisticated technology or international phone calls, the high price of these activities helps to render this architectural constraint effective. If tech-savvy patrons of Internet cafés can configure their browsers to access pornographic or dissident websites, they will be stopped only by the ingrained knowledge that such behavior is socially unacceptable, or that café managers may be observing their Internet use and could report their transgressions to authorities.

"BIG MAMA" IS WATCHING

The cases of Saudi Arabia and China illustrate how governments can leverage institutional constraints in combination with technological filters to establish effective control over Internet use. In Saudi Arabia, the government has found support for its censorship regime among conservative Islamist groups that are primarily concerned about pornography. Social norms against viewing material deemed offensive to Islam encourage self-censorship among users, as do legal prohibitions on accessing forbidden content and the possibility that surveillance mechanisms can identify violators. Attempts to view blocked sites are greeted with a message that all access attempts are logged; ISPs are required to keep records on the identity of users and provide such information to authorities if requested. In addition to these legal and normative sanctions, market conditions (such as the high price of dialing into an ISP outside of the country) have also discouraged those who would seek to obtain unrestricted Internet access in Saudi Arabia.

In China, the use of institutional constraints on Internet access has been even more extensive, probably a result of the greater challenge of exerting purely technological control over a broader and more diffuse Internet. One major way that China promotes self-censorship involves regulation of users. Authorities have engaged in high-profile crackdowns on various dissidents and individuals who run afoul of the regulations by engaging in politically sensitive communication. Examples include Huang Qi, who operated a website with news about the Tiananmen massacre, and members of the Falun Gong, who disseminate their materials online. Sentences of several years in prison are common for such offenses, undoubtedly deterring others who might have the inclination to engage in similar activity.

Periodic crackdowns on the Internet cafés and chat rooms that allow patrons to engage in prohibited activities have encouraged these intermediaries to police their own users. In addition to implementing the technological measures of censorship and surveillance, China's Internet cafés have added elements of human control to comply with regulations. Managers tend to observe closely their users' surfing habits, especially after a series of crackdowns and closures of Internet cafés in 2001. Similarly, most chat rooms employ censors known as "big mamas" who screen postings and delete those that touch on prohibited topics. The operators of major Internet portals, who are forbidden to post information that "undermines social stability," have steered clear of anything potentially sensitive, offering primarily entertainment, sports information, and news from official sources.

Even where regulations do not specifically require it, market conditions have encouraged the private sector to comply with the state's broad goals for the Internet. Doing business in China means maintaining good relations with the government; for Internet-related businesses, this means complying with the state's overall designs for the technology, both written and unwritten. In early 2000, for example, more than 100 of China's major Internet entrepreneurs signed a pledge to promote self-discipline and encourage the "elimination of deleterious information [on] the Internet."

JUST A TOOL

Ultimately, the Internet is a tool, a medium of communication much like any other. It has no inherent political logic. As a tool, its political impacts will depend largely on who controls the medium and in what manner they seek to use it. In countries such as Mexico and Indonesia, where authorities have taken a more hands-off approach to Internet regulation, protesters and civil society groups were able to use the Internet for organization and pressure politics in ways that may have contributed to regime change. There are few such opportunities in Saudi Arabia and China with their extensive government control of the Internet by both technological and institutional means.

In speculating about the longer-term prospects for the Internet under authoritarian regimes, one should recall that accurately predicting the impact of a flexible technology is an inherently difficult enterprise. However, given the flexible nature of Internet technology, its specific design will reflect the social, political, and economic environment in which it is developed. Where these conditions do not favor a liberal technology, it is unlikely that one will emerge.

Of course, the institutional constraints that influence Internet use—law, the market, and social norms—are similarly capable of change over time even when they exhibit a certain degree of stickiness. To say that China's laws and market environment or the social norms prevailing in Saudi Arabia currently support government control of Internet use does not mean that they will continue to do so 50 years hence. While it is not an automatically control-frustrating technology, a more liberal future for the Internet is certainly possible. But that future will depend largely on the institutional variables shaping the evolution of Internet technology and the manner in which it is used—not on any inherent characteristic of the Internet itself.

TAYLOR C. BOAS is a *doctoral candidate in political science at the University of California, Berkeley, and coauthor, with Shanthi Kalathil, of* Open Networks, Closed Regimes: The Impact of the Internet on Authoritarian Rule *(Carnegie Endowment for International Peace, 2003).*

Kabul's cyber cafe culture

By Sanjoy Majumder

When Kabul-based businessman Sabir Latifi opened his internet cafe in the Afghan capital last December, he had little idea what to expect.

After all, he had only logged on to the internet for the first time ever just a few weeks earlier.

He had heard about the world wide web from friends but did not even know what e-mail was.

"People talked about this being the internet era. I wondered how an era could be named after the internet," Mr. Latifi told BBC News Online.

Six months later he has learned a lot more and has grown proportionately more ambitious, hoping to become the country's first privately-owned internet service provider (ISP).

For a country that has been brutally scarred by a war that has left little standing, the idea of an information revolution takes some getting used to.

Only two years ago, the Taleban banned the use of the internet by anyone but the government.

But like people in many other developing countries around the world, Afghans are realising that their best chance of catching up is by taking a technological leap of faith.

High-end technology

One person who needs little convincing is Bennet James Bayer, the American managing director of the Afghan Wireless Communication Company (AWCC).

Started by an Afghan living in New York, Ehsan Bayat, AWCC is the country's only GSM mobile phone network and launched the country's first cyber cafe last year at the Kabul Intercontinental.

Fittingly, for a country where the modern straddles the traditional, it was tested during the loya jirga—a grand assembly of tribal chieftains and clan leaders which chose Hamid Karzai as the country's president.

Mr. Bayer points out that to make up for lost ground, Afghanistan was using high-end technology which is still a premium service in the West.

Afghans access the net through a wireless broadband system which actually means high-capacity lines and faster connections.

"Quite a few Afghan children are starting to use the mobile wireless environment and we are looking at that as a very rapidly growing business environment," says Mr. Bayer.

"It's a bit similar to Japan where they use PDAs, different kinds of phones and computers to access the internet through Bluetooth [a technology that uses radio to communicate rather than cables]."

Keeping in touch

It is hard to relate this world view with the dusty streets of Kabul, with its kebab stalls, vegetable carts, curio stores and chaotic traffic.

But at the Excelnet Cafe, the enthusiasm is hard to miss.

The eight terminals are all occupied and 10 Afghans wait patiently for their turn, squeezed on to a wooden bench.

One reason for its popularity is that it is the cheapest one in town, charging $1 for an hour's access.

That is lower than the $3 charged by most of the others, but still quite expensive in a country where the average income is less than $1 a day.

Zabiullah, an English language instructor, is not put off, however, and has bought himself a $50 card allowing him use of the internet for two hours every day.

He spent some time in India and Pakistan which is where he became familiar with the internet and now uses it to catch up on news, friends and even to prepare for an exam.

"When I came back to Afghanistan, there were no internet facilities," he says, his face breaking into a shy smile.

"It's so good to be able to use it to hear from my friends and find out about what's happening around the world."

Like Zabiullah, law student Aurush Siddiqui learned how the internet worked while living in the Pakistani capital, Islamabad.

He, too, uses it to keep in touch with the friends he made there and to learn more about legal practices around the world.

Crucial role

Sabir Latifi is banking on people like Zabiullah and Aurush and believes they hold the key to his future.

"We want to broaden the use of the internet for the younger generation," he says.

"I hope to then bring the cost of access to below $1, and even open a centre at Kabul University, making it free for college students."

Most of those who use Kabul's four internet cafes are young, men and women, using it mainly to stay in touch, chat and to find out about opportunities abroad or to study.

"But increasingly people are using it to pursue their own interests, such as growing crops," adds Mr. Bayer.

Its use in business transactions is not lost on Mr. Latifi, who says he is encouraging business owners to use e-mail, open their own website and get in touch with their customers directly.

"At the moment, to send a message from Kabul to Jalalabad [140 kilometres] you have to actually travel there by road since the phone lines don't work."

"If you have an internet facility, it'll take five minutes."

Both AWCC and Mr. Latifi are spreading their internet facilities to the provinces.

In a country where ethnic divisions have pitted provincial warlords against each other, Sabir Latifi believes it could play a critical role.

"It will empower the central government and unite our people, bringing us together," he says.

"The Taleban banned the use of the internet because they did not want Afghans to be part of the world and see the freedom that people elsewhere were enjoying."

"It's our chance, we have to grasp it."

Japan's Generation of Computer Refuseniks

Most teens and young adults in Japan rarely use computers to surf the World Wide Web. Instead they use cell phones to access a scaled-down wireless Web. The result: A growing computer literacy problem among Japan's youth.

Tim Clark

Yasushi Takashita smiled sheepishly when his slender girlfriend Rika, clinging to the train stanchion next to him, suggested he use the Internet to search for some college-related information he needs.

"I don't know how to use a PC," he admitted as the yellow Chuo Line train car bumped out of Yoyogi, an area in central Tokyo with a high concentration of private prep schools.

Takashita, a 19-year-old cram school student hoping to enter a four-year college this spring, is not alone. A surprising number of Japan's high school students graduate without learning how to use a personal computer, let alone the Internet.

How can this be in gizmo-crazed Japan? The answer lies in a combination of educational policy, peer pressure, and most importantly, the dramatic increase in the use of Internet-enabled cell phones in Japan over the last four years.

"Five years ago, before cell phone e-mail came into such widespread use, all college students felt the need to own their own PCs," says Hiroshi Hanamoto of the online marketing firm Promotions. "Today, students with cell phone mail can easily get by without buying their own computers. Besides, they don't have the money."

Peer pressure is a critical factor pushing students to own cell phones rather than computers. Almost every teenager in Japan has a mobile telephone with an e-mail address, and the fastest, easiest, and least expensive way to join the crowd is to subscribe to a mobile phone service.

Indeed, the primary motivation for a Japanese student to go online these days is not to use the Internet, but to get an e-mail address—far cheaper and easier to do with a cell phone than a computer.

For less than $100 and a few minutes of paperwork, a student can take home a phone and e-mail address from any number of retailers, which are often just a short walk from most train stations. Buying a personal computer means spending $500 or more, making room for the machine in limited space at home, and struggling to set up a dial-up, ADSL or cable Internet connection.

"Younger students in particular tend to feel that they don't need a PC if they have a cell phone. Some even say that if they had enough money to buy their own PC, they would rather upgrade to a better cell phone."

—Media strategist Minoru Sugiyama.

Mobile phones have replaced computers as the de facto e-mail terminal of choice for the majority of Japanese who are not in technology, finance, engineering or other computer-intensive occupations.

E-mail exchanges between high school and college students in Japan today take place almost exclusively via cell phones. High school clubs announce activities and meeting schedules via cell phone e-mail, and university class cancellation alerts are delivered primarily to handsets rather than computers. The reason is simple.

"Students have their handsets with them 24 hours a day, so they view messages immediately," says Hanamoto. "When they go to bed, it's on the nightstand next to them. Even if they have a computer at home, they may not bother checking mail on it."

Few universities allow students to check their school e-mail accounts off campus, so even students who use computers for e-mail tend to favor Web-based accounts like Hotmail.

A new government report claims that for the first time ever, more than half of the people in Japan are now using the Internet. But many are not using the Web at large—they're using cell phones to access a scaled-down, Japanese language mini-Web built for small screens, slower speeds and minimal keypunching.

Most of Japan's Internet users primarily frequent "official" sites provided by NTT DoCoMo and other wireless carriers.

The most common way to get to non-carrier Web pages is to send e-mail to an address advertised in magazines and on billboards, television or Web sites. Replies contain embedded URLs, enabling users to get to them by using the handset's 12-button keypad. Most users rarely enter a URL manually.

"News is all around us—there are televisions everywhere," says Nobuyuki Amano, 49. "I have no need to read the news on my cell phone."

"Typing an Internet address into a handset is a pain," says Chihiro Amano, an 18-year-old high school graduate who sends an average of 100 cell phone e-mail messages per day. "This past year I hardly used the PC at all. My homework problem sets were all handwritten."

Chihiro's younger sister, Tsukasa, 15, is even more engrossed in the cell phone lifestyle. Though she rarely talks on her mobile handset, on some days she transmits as many as 200 e-mail messages to her friends. Last month her telephone bill, consisting primarily of packet fees for e-mail messages, was about $213. During a five-minute interview in the Amano family's dining room, she received and responded to two e-mail messages.

Tsukasa and other young people here enter Japanese text into their handsets with amazing single-thumb speed, but are far less facile typing English and the ASCII-code periods, slashes, and colons that are the lingua franca of the Internet. But this hurdle—and the fact that most Web sites are not formatted for viewing on cell phones—only partially explains why few consumers venture onto the Internet from their handsets.

The main reason is that most simply do not feel the need to do so. The carriers' "walled gardens" are rich with preselected content. Consumers are bombarded with cell phone-specific offers, "specials" and other slick solicitations from magazines, television, billboards and direct-mail advertisements. Users get everything they need without having to search.

"There's almost no need for people to actively seek out information on their own," says Hanamoto. "Users are given information over cell phones—they don't proactively look for it. This passive acceptance of 'push' content reflects a fundamental problem with Japan's educational system."

The result is a surprisingly passive approach to information gathering and media use via cell phones. While news headline and summary services are available via the carriers' networks, they attract only a fraction of the number of subscribers to entertainment and "lifestyle" offerings, such as ringtone downloads, cartoon character screensavers, weather reports, map downloads and train timetables. Many news service subscribers are interested primarily in sports scores or other "flash" updates.

"News is all around us—there are televisions everywhere. I have no need to read the news on my cell phone," says Chihiro's father Nobuyuki Amano, 49.

None of the five cell-phone-carrying members of the Amano family use their handsets to read news stories, with one exception. During the World Cup soccer series held in Japan last year, Kazumi, Nobuyuki's wife, and Meguru, the couple's 12-year-old son, signed up for soccer match updates delivered by e-mail.

In the United States, the personal computer—which provides direct access to alternative news sources and multiple one-to-many channels for opinion expression—is the ultimate media literacy tool. In Japan, where few understand the term "media literacy," Internet-enabled cell phones play no such role.

"If asked whether mobile telephones are a positive factor in improving media literacy, I would have to say no. In fact, they are somewhat of a negative factor," says Minoru Sugiyama, 40, a Tokyo-based media strategist.

"Younger students in particular tend to feel that they don't need a PC if they have a cell phone," Sugiyama added. "Some even say that if they had enough money to buy their own PC, they would rather upgrade to a better cell phone and use more mobile services. But they tend to change their tune and get more PC-oriented as they approach graduation and job hunting."

Today, 17 percent of Japanese households—about 8.3 million—have broadband connections to the Internet. That number is expected to grow rapidly, but the cell phone seems for now to have displaced computer use to some extent, particularly among the young.

In part, this is due to the highly mobile lifestyle here, where it is not uncommon for children as young as 9 to commute 40 minutes or more by train to school every day. But in key ways, cell phones suit the Japanese mindset and communication style far better than computers.

"Cell phone mail in particular represents a very closed world, since people exchange mail almost exclusively with their existing circles of friends," says Promotions' Hanamoto. "It's not a gateway to a bright, broader view of reality. I can't equate online offerings available via cell phone with the Internet. Mobile is a great channel for intimate communications, but I wouldn't say it is especially useful in terms of broadening your horizons."

Tim Clark, author of the Japan Internet Report, serves as Senior Fellow at Tokyo-based venture incubator SunBridge and editor of the monthly Japan Entrepreneur Report. He is currently working on a book about service sector entrepreneurship with co-author Carl Kay.

UNIT 8

The Frontier of Computing

Unit Selections

Key Points to Consider

- 2003 marked the 30th anniversary of the publication of an essay entitled "Animals, Men and Morals" by Peter Singer in the New York Review of Books. This essay is often credited with beginning the animal rights movement. Singer argues that because animals have feelings they can suffer. Because they can suffer, they have interests. Because they have interests, it is, among other things, unethical to conduct experiments on them. Suppose scientists succeed in developing machines that feel pain and fear. What obligations will we have towards them? If this is difficult to imagine, watch the movie Blade Runner with Harrison Ford. What do you think now?

- The Overview to this unit says that the dollar value of the output of the meat and poultry industries exceeds the dollar value of the output of the computer industry. The Overview mentions one reason why we hear so much more about software than chickens. Can you think of others?

- Suppose you were provided with a digital assistant like those described in "Minding Your Own Business." One task of this assistant is to filter spam from your email. Now suppose you are provided with a real secretary to do the same task. Both of these assistants will make judgment calls. That is, based on what you have told them, each will make best guesses as to whether email is spam or not. How do you feel about your digital assistant making the occasional error? How do you feel about your secretary making a mistake?

Student Website
www.mhcls.com/online

Internet References
Further information regarding these websites may be found in this book's preface or online.

Introduction to Artificial Intelligence (AI)
http://www-formal.stanford.edu/jmc/aiintro/aiintro.html

Kasparov vs. Deep Blue: The Rematch
http://www.chess.ibm.com/home/html/b.html

PHP-Nuke Powered Site: International Society for Artificial Life
http://alife.org/

According to U.S. Census Bureau statistics not long ago, the output of the meat and poultry industry was worth more than the output of the computer and software industries. Though this is not exactly a fair comparison—computers are used to build still other products—it does get at something significant about computers: they figure more importantly in our imaginations than they do in the economy. Why is this? Part of the answer has to do with who forms opinions in developed nations. The computer is an indispensable tool for people who staff the magazine, newspaper, publishing and education sectors. If meat packers were the opinion makers, we might get a different sense of what is important. Recall "Five Things We Need to Know about Technological Change." Postman says that "Embedded in every technology there is a powerful idea....To a person with a computer, everything looks like data."

We can concede Postman's point but still insist that there is something special about computing. Before computers became a household appliance, it was common for programmers and users alike to attribute human-like properties to them. Joseph Weizenbaum, developer of Eliza in the 1970's, a program that simulated a Rogerian psychotherapist, became a severe critic of

certain kinds of computing research, in part, because he noticed that staff in his lab had begun to arrive early to ask advice from the program. In 1956 a group of mathematicians interested in computing gathered at Dartmouth College and coined the term "Artificial Intelligence." AI, whose goal is to build into machines something that we can recognize as intelligent behavior, has become perhaps the best-known and most criticized area of computer science. Since intelligent behavior, like the ability to read and form arguments, is often thought to be the defining characteristic of humankind (we call ourselves, after all, "homo sapiens"), machines that might exhibit intelligent behavior have occupied the dreams and nightmares of western culture for hundreds of years.

All of our ambiguous feelings about technology are congealed in robots. The term itself is surprisingly venerable, having been invented by the Czech playwright Karel Copek in 1921. They can be loveable like R2D2 from *Star Wars* or Robbie from *The Forbidden Planet* of a generation earlier. They can be forbidding but loyal, like Gort from "*The Day the Earth Stood Still.*" They can even be outfitted with logical safety mechanisms that render them harmless to humans. This last, an invention of

Isaac Asimov in *I, Robot*, is a good thing, too, since so many of our robotic imaginings look like *The Terminator*.

Still, it is wise to keep a cool head here. One way to think about advances in computing is to imagine what it is that computers actually do rather than what they might do. Not much, it turns out, but what they do, they do very quickly. A computer program is a precise set of instructions to carry out some pre-defined task. The more complex the task, the more complex the instructions, but the principle is the same. So it is not surprising that computers are at their best when asked to take over tasks—say keeping track of your progress toward graduation or what you owe the university—that are themselves routine. Computers have been less successful when asked to substitute their own "judgment," based on past behavior. Predicting future behavior based on the past is deeply human. "What's past is prologue," says Antonio in *The Tempest*. But some other wise person also said that "The devil is in the details." The infamous Microsoft paperclip homunculus springs immediately to mind. The problem here is that he was not so much helpful as annoying. In fact, were the past a perfect predictor of the future, and if computers could formalize the past, we might have effective spam filters, ones that would filter out ads for Viagra but not notification that we've been short-listed for a Pulitzer prize, a problem addressed in this unit. With this as background, we offer "Minding Your Business," a look at what is on the horizon in the world of digital assistants.

One area in which computers have changed and, then changed again, in just a few short years is the business of recorded music. Youthful readers of "Why Listening Will Never by the Same," may not find Teachout's predictions as unsettling as those of us who grew up on LP's: "One thing is already clear: hard though it may be to imagine life without records and record stores, it is only a matter of time, and not much time at that, before they disappear." But they will find the reason for this transformation fascinating: "Herein lay the true digital revolution," he says. "When recorded sound is converted to numbers, it exits the realm of objects and enters the realm of ideas." It also enters file-sharing networks, which record companies have tried so hard to control these past few years.

Futurists everywhere will recognize the name "Nahan Myhrvold." The former chief technology officer of Microsoft Research, became convinced, as he "flew around the world in his Gulfstream V jet attempting to get into the heads of inventors young and old … that a new global flowering of invention is possible." His new venture "has no mission other than to invent what … inventors believe should be—or can be—invented." When you read this interview ("Sparking the Fire of Invention") ask yourself if you trust technologists to understand that there is a world of difference between "should" and "can."

"Mind Control" considers how advanced software is being developed to alleviate chronic pain, enable quadriplegics to play video games and, perhaps one day, develop robot soldiers controlled by the thoughts of real soldiers far from the battle front. Though one should take these inventions and predictions with a grain of salt—futurists in the 60's thought we would all be commuting in levitated automobiles in short order—they give a sense of the excitement that surrounds computing.

Robots, the end of the record album, personal digital assistants, processors embedded in the brain, computing without bounds, the articles in this unit have ranged widely but with this common theme: none of the technologies described are fully-formed and, more to the point, their impact on society has, so far, not been large. Computing history is filled with bad predictions. Perhaps the most spectacularly wrong is widely attributed to Thomas Watson, head of IBM, who in 1943 is reputed to have said, "I think there is a world market for maybe five computers." But there have been many, many others. Will grid computing go the way of other good, but very complex, ideas? Will virtual reality analgesia not reduce reliance on opioids for the bulk of burn patients? Will captured electroencephalograms get stuck at the pong-playing stage? It is hard to know, of course. No one wants to be the next Thomas Watson.

MINDING YOUR BUSINESS

Humanizing gadgetry to tame the flood of information

PETER WEISS

A telephone call to Roel Vertegaal's lab may cause a pair of plastic-foam eyeballs to wiggle. Those peepers are attached to a desktop gadget that Vertegaal says could presage a generation of what you might call digital secretaries—particularly insightful ones at that. If Vertegaal looks at the shaking eyeballs, they'll suddenly stop and stare back at him and then patch the call through. If instead, Vertegaal doesn't establish eye contact with the little pop-eyed gizmo on his desk, an answering machine kicks into gear. That's because his digital secretary could tell in a glance that Vertegaal wasn't interested in taking the call.

Such interactions between Vertegaal, director of the human media lab at Queen's University in Kingston, Ontario, and the gadget, known as eyePROXY, are an experiment in a new style of human-machine interactions. Known as attentive-user interfaces, these combos of gadgetry and software are designed to make our growing staff of machines accommodate human behaviors. The goal is to render that entourage of technology more helpful and less annoying.

Cell phones, pagers, personal digital assistants (PDAs), laptops, and car navigation systems—the list of these devices lengthens as electronic intelligence and communications links infiltrate household and office items. There are now even prototype cooking spoons that tell you what temperature the batter is. As this corps of gizmos swells, a barrage of blinking lights, ring tones, beeps, vibrations, and other cues calls out for attention. "The volume of notifications … is becoming so large that people are having trouble dealing with it," Vertegaal says.

Consider the demands placed, for example, on nurses, with their many patients and even more health-care gadgets to mind. Add their family, community, and social obligations, and they're often at the edge of information overload, he says.

To alleviate this type of problem without having people limit their access to information, Vertegaal and other computer scientists are designing new software and hardware. "We are on a mission to change the way it feels to work with computers," says Eric Horvitz of Microsoft Research in Redmond, Wash. The fruit of all these efforts will be that digital devices "become a lot less like tools and a lot more like companions and collaborators who understand your intentions and goals," Horvitz predicts.

The scientists want to create the equivalent of the ideal personal human assistant, a flesh-and-blood helper who would recognize what input you need or want at any moment.

One way that researchers are pushing toward that goal is to develop attentive systems, such as eyePROXY, that monitor a person's eyes. Other systems scan a person for position, motion, gestures, and other body language. Yet others tune in to electronic sources, including schedules and sensors indicating where in the world the person is and what he or she is doing. With such information, the system then can ask itself questions about its user: Does he want to take an incoming phone call? Is she too wrapped up in a videoconference to bother?

EYE'LL BE WATCHING YOU Despite the current enthusiasm for multitasking and the proliferation of gadgets that demand a chunk of our attention, most people can effectively handle only a few inputs at a time. Psychologists find that an average person can hold only about seven unrelated chunks of information in his or her mind at any one moment.

Some computer scientists and engineers now see a chance to infuse psychological savvy into interactive devices. "We can take the results from psychology … and leverage them" by incorporating them into information tools that people use, Horvitz says.

New technologies, like eyePROXY, may provide machines with the power to observe, interpret, and communicate with their users on human terms. Some investigators say that there's no better place to start than with the face.

"A huge amount of information can be gleaned from watching someone's eyes," says Daniel Russell of IBM's Almaden Research Center in San Jose, Calif. For example, people often vie for one another's attention by means of a complex interplay of glances that make and break eye contact.

In the late 1990s, the IBM group that Russell now leads developed a compact video camera that determines where a person's eyes are pointing at any moment. The system exploits the red-eye effect that wrecks many a snapshot. In this context, light reflecting from the retina renders conspicuous the pupil's location, which a machine can then use to track the person's gaze.

Russell's lab has incorporated the camera into a prototype computer interface that he says could make the Web more effective as an educational tool. The system observes exactly what sentence or image on a Web page a person is focused on and how long he or she may be spending on a particular item—say, a division problem. With those data, the interface might then direct the student toward help with long division rather than with multiplication.

Such systems may enable computers to become better tutors for educational courses disseminated over the Web, Russell says. Anticipating only a small market for the camera, IBM made its design available for free to other researchers interested in eye-gaze tracking.

Vertegaal's group took up IBM's offer. The researchers have increased the camera's resolution and miniaturized its electronics so that the whole unit is now small enough to be mounted on a computer, a hat, or even a pair of eyeglasses.

The team has built the same technology into eyePROXY and communications devices, including cell phones, that recognize when a person is engaged in a face-to-face conversation. That way, even if his or her cell phone is on, it can take a message instead of permitting the phone to ring. This application might be considered a rudeness blocker.

Vertegaal's group has also incorporated the camera into gadgets that it calls "eyePLIANCEs." One of them, a floor lamp, turns on or off by voice command only when a person is looking at it. Another is a television that recognizes whether someone is watching it and, if not, pauses the action on its display. Such attentive devices can sum into an environment that can respond to or even anticipate a person's needs, Vertegaal's group proposes in the March *Communications of the ACM*.

A simpler sensor that can pick up information about eye behavior has been developed at the Massachusetts Institute of Technology (MIT). A small diode produces infrared light that's reflected off the eyeball and detected by a photodiode. The device was created by a team led by Ted Selker, director of MIT's Context-Aware Computing lab and former director of the IBM lab that created the eye-gaze tracker.

Named eye aRe units—a takeoff on the abbreviation for infrared—the devices can monitor such eye characteristics as the rate at which a person blinks. That can provide a window onto a person's mental and emotional state, Selker says. For instance, a rate near the high end of the typical range of 1 to 6 blinks per minute may indicate that the person is experiencing stress or fear.

Selker has several ideas about how such a sensing ability might be used. In one test, he and his colleagues programmed an eye-monitoring digital assistant to use blink-rate to infer whether someone preferred one type of music to another. In another experiment, they monitored people having conversations and found indications of which ones got along well.

MINDFUL MACHINES Besides eye-monitoring technologies, interface designers are also experimenting with methods for gauging other aspects of a person's state of being. Those include video systems that determine body position and head orientation and audio interfaces that listen to and interpret speech and other sounds in the environment.

For instance, for mobile individuals, Microsoft Research has made a prototype PDA souped-up with several sensors to automatically detect how the user intends to use it. These sensors include an accelerometer that tells the device whether it's upright, a touch sensor that indicates whether the device is being held, and a proximity sensor that reports whether there's a solid body—for example—a head, within arm's length of the device. With the accelerometer, this prototype can also determine whether its user is walking.

If wirelessly networked to the person's office gadgets, a PDA with even this limited bit of awareness about the person's activities could help redirect messages and other information to that guy or gal on the go.

Even if gadgets become better at discerning the information, computing, or communications needs of their users, they—like able assistants—still need to know when and how to get the user's attention.

For example, Selker and Ernesto Arroyo, also of MIT, compared whether brightening a light or heating up a mouse pad is the better way to grab a person's attention. They found that the light was good at quickly producing awareness. The heated pad, although it took longer to attract interest, was better at holding that attention, says Selker. Actually, he adds, the heat might be especially effective for getting a visually overloaded person's attention, say, when an emergency arises. The researchers reported these results in Miami last January at the International Conference on Intelligent User Interfaces.

Selker, Russell, and their respective teams have also been developing automotive versions of attentive interfaces. The systems are on the alert for signs of drowsiness, for example, and may blare the car radio, make the steering wheel quiver, or provide other feedback to jar the driver back into a more alert or safety-conscious state.

ALL IN THE FAMILY Some skeptics, such as artificial intelligence pioneer John McCarthy, emeritus professor at Stanford University, ask whether making devices more attentive could make them more annoying. "I feel that [an attentive interface] would end up training me" to accommodate it rather than providing a worthwhile service, McCarthy says.

Rather than adding people-reading senses to machines, Microsoft Research's Horvitz and his colleagues favor developing sophisticated software tools to analyze the continuous stream of personal information that's already flowing through the computers and other digital equipment that people routinely use. This software sifts out signs of what the user is doing or might want to do in the near future.

The Microsoft researchers, for example, are developing ways to analyze and disseminate data to create systems that hold back low-priority distractions, such as an e-mail notice for discount Viagra, while—in a sensitive, courteous manner—pushing through urgent messages, such as the arrival of a crucial document in the mail room.

The team recognizes that examples abound of smart gadgets or software functions that aren't smart enough. An overzealous digital assistant, such as the infamous animated paperclip that pops up in the word-processing program Microsoft Word, can annoy and get in the way.

Horvitz and his team recently developed a system, represented to computer users by a cartoon genie, that scans incoming e-mail, recognizes whether the message might require scheduling of an appointment, and offers to set one up. By slightly increasing the time delay before the genie sprang forward to volunteer its services, the interface transformed from something "terrible" to a seemingly "smart, intuitive person," Horvitz recalls.

These researchers are also developing software systems that mine such information troves as e-mails, calendar appointments, logs of network use, and organizational charts identifying someone's bosses and underlings. If unobtrusive information from passive observations by cameras and microphones is available, that's included, as well.

The forte of the Microsoft Research group is developing mathematical models that can incorporate such information and—even without full knowledge about a person's present location and activities—calculate probabilities of what he or she will want to do or might want to know. To do this, the researchers are trying to make the model assess the information in the less-than-precise way that people do.

More specifically, these models work by assigning the equivalent of dollar values to pieces of information to be delivered to someone and to the cost of interrupting that person to present the information. By these calculations, the software may opt to interrupt a person if he is gazing out the window but not if he is briefing the CEO.

"The magic of the kind of work we do here is that we do not change the way people work," Horvitz says. "We don't say, Hold your eyes in a certain way, but we pick up on all the things going on in your life."

Even if attentive devices work seamlessly, all these possibilities for scrutiny may smack of Big Brother to some people. "That can be a potentially sensitive issue," acknowledges Horvitz.

Why Listening Will Never Be the Same

by Terry Teachout

LAST YEAR, for the first time, blank compact discs outsold pre-recorded ones. This statistic has been widely reported in the news media, usually in connection with the fact that sales of pre-recorded CD's in the U.S. dropped by 10 percent in 2001. To most observers of the music business, all this was further proof that the recording industry is in a state of acute crisis. But nowhere was it suggested that the CD-R (to use the trade name by which blank, recordable CD's are known) might be anything more than a superior replacement for the now-obsolete audio cassette—much less that its burgeoning popularity is the latest sign of a radical and irreversible change in the way we experience music.

Just as significant, and even less well known, is the fact that 31 million Americans to date have used their personal computers to share music files—that is, to send recordings to one another over the Internet. It is no secret that record companies see file-sharing as a threat to their existence, for which reason they are futilely attempting to impede its use, mostly through aggressive litigation and the introduction of new software that would make it harder to copy a CD. Again, however, the wider implications of this development have gone mostly unexplored. Anyone reading a typical newspaper story about file-sharing would be likely to conclude that the process, for all its unprecedented technical sophistication, does not differ in any essential way from making a cassette copy of a favorite album and giving it to a friend.

Of course, when it comes to the effects of technology on culture, skeptics are in good company. The prophets of the 20th century, utopian and dystopian alike, were in no doubt that middle-class Americans would by now be routinely conversing on picture phones and traveling to work in personal aircraft, *à la* George and Jane Jetson. And even as they were wrong about that, none of them foresaw the rise of the Internet, or the speed with which a relatively simple application like e-mail would become part of the everyday routine of tens of millions of people around the world.

I do not claim the gift of prophecy, but I have been using computers in my daily work for 25 years, longer than most Americans, and in that time I have acquired a healthy respect for their culture-shaping power. At the same time, I have become aware of a paradox: just as it is very difficult to grasp the potential of a new technology if one does not actually use it, using it can make it seem so routine as to be unremarkable. Since comparatively few people over the age of thirty have downloaded music files from the web and "burned" them onto CD-R's, they may find it hard to imagine how these technologies work, or to understand the dramatic impact they are having. By contrast, people *under* thirty, having spent their whole lives with personal computers, tend to take CD-burning and file-sharing for granted, and are less prone to speculate about their implications.

Let me, then, offer some thoughts on what it feels like to use the new computer-based listening technologies, and on how they are changing our larger musical culture and its existing institutional structures.

FIRST, A little history. For three-quarters of a century, records were made by a process now known as analog recording. In its earliest form, a musician would sing or play into the large end of a megaphone-like horn, which funneled the resulting sound waves to a recording needle. The waves made the needle vibrate, and the vibrating needle incised a correspondingly wavy groove into a rotating wax plate or cylinder. When the process was reversed, by the consumer, a needle placed in a groove would move in such a way as to generate new vibrations that resembled the original sound waves and could be used to reproduce them.

This process was replaced by today's digital recording, invented in 1976. In creating such a recording, a computer is used to convert sound waves not into an analogous physical object—a wavy groove in a wax plate, or an electronically recorded array of magnetized particles on a strip of plastic tape—but into a sequence of descriptive binary digits. When *this* process is reversed, the digits are first decoded and only then used to generate a fluctuating electrical signal analogous to the original sound waves. This signal is sent to a loudspeaker, which converts it into new waves closely resembling the original ones.

The initial advantage of digital recording was that it offered a more accurate way to reproduce sound. With the introduction in 1983 of the laser-scanned compact disc, in which sounds are stored in actual digital form rather than (as was the case with the first digital recordings to be commercially marketed) etched into the needle-cut grooves of a vinyl disc, it was widely thought that the digital revolution was complete. The larger significance of the break with analog recording was yet to penetrate. It was simply this: instead of manufacturing physical objects from which sounds could be reconstituted, engineers were now converting those same sounds into strings of numbers. As a result, it was no longer necessary to own the physical object in order to reproduce the music. All one needed was the numbers.

Herein lay the true digital revolution. When recorded sound is converted to numbers, it exits the realm of objects and enters the realm of ideas. To put it another way, it becomes pure information, transmissible from person to person by an infinite variety of means. In theory, I could call you up on the phone and read aloud a string of numbers representing a recorded performance of Beethoven's Fifth Symphony, and you in turn could write those numbers down, type them into a computer, and eventually translate them back into sound. The only catch is that such a "conversation" would last for weeks, or however long it would take to read out the millions of binary numbers comprising a digitized version of a piece of music. Hence the importance of the Internet, which allows computer users around the world to transmit digitized data over commercial telephone lines.

AT FIRST, admittedly, it was impractical to do this. So great was the sheer volume of information packed into a single CD that it required hours to transmit even a fairly short piece of music. But two recent developments have changed this situation dramatically. The first is the rapidly spreading availability of broadband cable modems that give high-speed Internet access to ordinary computer users. The second is the invention of MP3, the popular "data-reduction" software that compresses sound recordings into data files small enough to be stored on the hard drive of a personal computer, sent via e-mail, or downloaded from websites.

Such files can also be downloaded from "peer-to-peer" file-sharing sites, the best known of which is the now-defunct Napster. These sites are web-based clearing houses that allow their users to make MP3 files available for free to all other users. In addition, many record labels have launched or are launching on-line delivery systems from which their recordings can be downloaded for a fee.

How easy is it to do these things? I own an iBook, a laptop computer made by Apple. Bundled into its software is a program called iTunes. Whether I am downloading music directly from the web or uploading from CD's I already own, the process is the same.

I have already uploaded about 190 hours of music onto my iTunes player, ranging from sonatas and symphonies to bluegrass and rock-and-roll. The exercise is so simple that I was able to start using the player without bothering to look at an instruction manual. I insert one of my recorded compact discs into the computer and click a few keys. The computer then takes the contents of the disc—all of it or any combination of tracks, just as I choose—and converts them into MP3 files that are stored on my hard drive. It takes about 30 seconds to "rip" a three-minute song from a CD. Downloading works the same way, and just as fast: it recently took me all of thirteen seconds to download an MP3 file of a three-minute song by Ella Fitzgerald from amazon.com.

To play any of the 2,300 selections that are now on my iTunes player, I go to the "library" screen, find the title, and click on it twice. The music begins playing instantly. I like to listen through headphones, but if I wanted, I could also connect a set of external speakers to my computer, or use it as a component in my stereo system, just like a CD player. Since MP3 files are compressed, the resulting sound is not of the highest possible quality, but my forty-six-year-old ears are rarely capable of telling the difference between an MP3 file and the original CD from which it has been ripped.

My iTunes player also burns CD-R's. In a matter of seconds, I can instruct it to record up to 75 minutes' worth of MP3 files from my computerized library, arranged in any order I want. Within a few minutes, I have a custom-made compact disc that I can play on my stereo, give to a friend, or drop in a mailbox and send to my mother. Should I find that process laborious, I can e-mail the same files to anyone equipped to receive them.

If, after reading this, you still doubt the power of the new computer-based technologies, consider: what I have done is to pack the equivalent of seven shelves' worth of CD's into a plastic box not much larger than a stack of eight issues of COMMENTARY. This box also contains the personal computer on which I do my writing and from which I send my e-mail. I can use it whenever and wherever I want—at my desk, in a hotel room, on a plane. Were I to find the box insufficiently portable, I could also purchase an iPod, Apple's version of a Walkman, into which the contents of my iTunes player can be dumped in about twenty minutes. An iPod is roughly the size of a cellular phone, and at present costs about $300.

None of these devices is a science-fiction fantasy. They are on sale now, and I use them every day.

AS PEOPLE start using personal computers in the way I have just described, their relationship to the experience of listening to recorded music will change accordingly.

The nature of this experience has yet to be adequately described by theorists of art, most of whom make flawed assumptions about the nature of what the Marxist critic Walter Benjamin, in his 1935 essay of the same name, called "the work of art in the age of mechanical reproduction." Benjamin, for example, feared the loss of authenticity that he thought would be an inevitable consequence of the mass production of replicas of art works, a process that (in his words) substitutes "a plurality of copies for a unique existence." Conversely, André Malraux, writing in *Le Musée imaginaire* (1947), praised the prospect of a democratic "museum without walls" made possible by the widespread availability of just such replicas and reproductions.

In fact, however, traditional museums, rather than falling into desuetude, now attract larger audiences than ever, precisely because they offer viewers the opportunity to see handmade art objects whose existence *is* unique. Even the most unsophisticated museum-goer quickly comes to realize that no reproduction of a painting by Rembrandt or Cézanne can possibly convey more than the smallest part of the impact of the original.

But music is very different. Unlike a painting, the score of a Schubert song is not an art object in and of itself. It is a set of instructions that, if followed faithfully, will cause the object to be made manifest—once. But if music exists only through the act of performance, a recording of a Schubert song, being also a performance, does not bear the same relationship to a live performance that a reproduction of a painting does to the original. It is *not* a mere "replica," but an independent and fully valid way of experiencing the song.

Indeed, a record album can be, and usually is, an art object in its own right. I own several thousand CD's, each of which comprises a series of musical selections arranged in a specific order and (normally) intended to be listened to in that order. Some were recorded in concert, but most were created in a studio, often with the help of studio-specific techniques like tape splicing and overdubbing. Such famous albums as Glenn Gould's 1955 recording of the Bach "Goldberg" Variations, Frank Sinatra's *Only the Lonely*, Miles Davis's *Kind of Blue*, or the Beatles' *Sgt. Pepper's Lonely Hearts Club Band* are not attempts to simulate live performances. They are, rather, unique experiences existing *only* on record, and the record itself, not the music or the performance, is the art object.

Since 1950 or so, objects like these have been the most significant forms of musical experience in the West—far more significant than live performances, and arguably even more so than specific musical compositions. Nor have they been rendered irrelevant by digital technology, any more than *Citizen Kane*

made *War and Peace* irrelevant. But now something else is happening: when I load any one of these "objects" onto my iTunes player, I am opening myself up to the possibility of experiencing it in a completely new way.

All at once, the concrete object—the original album, with its cover art, liner notes, and carefully arranged sequence of tracks—ceases to exist. In its place is a string of abstract digits that I can manipulate at will. If I want, I can listen to the twelve songs that make up *Only the Lonely* in the order that they appear on the album. But I can also listen to them separately, in a different order, as part of a Frank Sinatra "greatest hits" sequence of my own devising, or in any other way that suits my fancy. Instead of permitting an artist or a record company to tell me how to listen, I am making my own choices.

This enhanced capacity for choice is central to the appeal of computer-based listening systems. Should I care for only one track on a CD, I can buy that CD, load it onto iTunes, and throw away the original disc. Or I can go to a website and download only that one song—which is just what young, computer-literate music lovers are increasingly doing. Instead of buying pop albums containing two or three good songs, they acquire the songs they like and listen to them in contexts of their own choosing. If record companies will not give them the power to make those choices themselves, they will take the power into their own hands by swapping MP3 files with friends, or downloading them from file-sharing sites.

THE SPREAD of computer-based listening has already started to alter the way records are made and marketed. A young jazz pianist who recently signed with a major label told me in conversation that to get people to buy his CD's, he now has to give them "something they can't get by going to hear me at a club, or downloading a couple of tracks off the web." Instead, he has to make albums that are strong from start to finish—a unified experience, not just "a studio jam session or a bunch of unrelated selections." And, he added, "it's not just the music either. The packaging has to contribute to the total ef-

fect, too. Interesting liner notes, interesting art—all that really matters now."

Indeed it does, more so than ever. But such efforts, however ambitious and thoughtfully conceived, are still doomed to failure. In the not-so-long run, the introduction of online delivery systems and the spread of file-sharing will certainly undermine and very likely destroy the fundamental economic basis for the recording industry, at least as we know it today. Nor can there be much doubt that within a few years, the record album will lose its once-privileged place at the heart of Western musical culture.

And what will replace it? I, for one, think it highly likely that more and more artists will start to make their own recordings and market them directly to the public via the web.* Undoubtedly, new managerial institutions will emerge to assist those artists who prefer not to engage in the time-consuming task of self-marketing, but these institutions will be true middlemen, purveyors of a service, as opposed to record labels, which use artists to serve *their* interests. And while most artists will also employ technical assistants of various kinds, such as freelance recording engineers, the ultimate responsibility for their work will belong—for the first time ever—to the artists themselves.

What form that work will take is another question entirely. Prior to the invention in 1948 of the LP, popular musicians usually recorded not albums but specific songs or pieces of music that were released on single 78's and meant to be experienced individually. Perhaps, then, there will never be another *Only the Lonely* or *Kind of Blue*, but, once again, only individual selections like "One for My Baby" or "All Blues." Or possibly new modes of presentation will evolve, in the same way that Internet "magazines" are developing web-specific features like "The Corner," a chatty group-discussion page that has become the most widely read department of *National Review Online*.

To be sure, this prospect is understandably disturbing to many older musicians and music lovers, given the fact that the record album has played so pivotal a role in the culture of postwar music. Nor do I claim that life without records will necessarily be better—or worse. It will, however, be *different*, just as the lives of actors were irrevocably changed by the invention of the motion-picture camera in ways that no one could possibly have foreseen in 1900.

One thing is already clear: hard though it may be to imagine life without records and record stores, it is only a matter of time, and not much time at that, before they disappear. Unlike museums and opera houses, they serve a purpose that technology has rendered obsolete. The triumph of the digit—along with the demise of the record album as culture-shaping art object—is at hand.

---

* The London and San Francisco Symphony Orchestras, as well as a growing number of individual classical musicians, have already responded to the decline of the major classical record labels by starting to make and distribute their own CD's, though they are not yet generally available for direct downloading. For a discussion of the effects of file-sharing on classical music, see my essay, "What Killed Classical Recording?" (COMMENTARY, May 2001).

TERRY TEACHOUT, COMMENTARY's *music critic, is the author of* The Skeptic: A Life of H. L. Mencken, *forthcoming in November from HarperCollins.*

From *Commentary*, September 2002, pp. 57–60. Copyright © 2002 by American Jewish Committee. Reprinted by permission of the publisher and author.

THE INTELLIGENT INTERNET

THE PROMISE OF SMART COMPUTERS AND E-COMMERCE

Information and communication technologies are
rapidly converging to create machines that understand us,
do what we tell them to, and even anticipate our needs.

William E. Halal

We tend to think of intelligent systems as a distant possibility, but two relentless supertrends are moving this scenario toward near-term reality. Scientific advances are making it possible for people to talk to smart computers, while more enterprises are exploiting the commercial potential of the Internet.

This synthesis of computer intelligence and the Internet is rapidly creating a powerful new global communication system that is convenient, productive, and transformative—the Intelligent Internet. Here are three simple examples of what should become common soon.

- The UCLA Cultural Virtual Reality Laboratory has developed a Web site that recreates ancient Rome. Visitors are able to virtually walk around 3-D images of reconstructed temples, monuments, and plazas as though they were living in Rome 2,000 years ago. The head of UCLA's lab calls it "a kind of time machine."

- Amtrak has installed speech recognition software to replace the button-pressing menus that drive many people mad. Now you can talk to a virtual salesperson named Julie to get train schedules, make reservations, pay for tickets, and discuss problems. Customers are happier, and Amtrak is saving money.

- The Waldorf-Astoria Hotel in New York City leases out a five-by-seven-foot videoconferencing system that allows guests to hold virtual meetings with other people at remote locations. Business people find it so useful that the system is always busy.

It may seem foolhardy to claim that the Internet will soon thrive again when economies around the globe struggle out of recession. After all, it was the unrealistic type of endless growth we heard during the dot-com boom that caused today's economic pain. But forecasts conducted under the TechCast Project at George Washington University indicate use should reach 30% "takeoff" adoption levels during the second half of this decade to rejuvenate the economy. Meanwhile, the project's technology scanning finds that advances in speech recognition, artificial intelligence, powerful computers, virtual environments, and flat wall monitors are producing a "conversational" human-machine interface.

> "WE ARE POISED AT THE CUSP OF ANOTHER MAJOR TECHNOLOGY TRANSITION, MUCH AS THE 1980S BROUGHT THE PC AND THE 1990S BROUGHT THE INTERNET."

These powerful trends will drive the next generation of information technology into the mainstream by about 2010. Rather than forcing us to hunch over a keyboard, this Intelligent Internet should allow people everywhere to converse naturally and comfortably with life-sized, virtual people while shopping, working, learning, and conducting most social relationships.

E-COMMERCE TECHNOLOGY TIMELINE

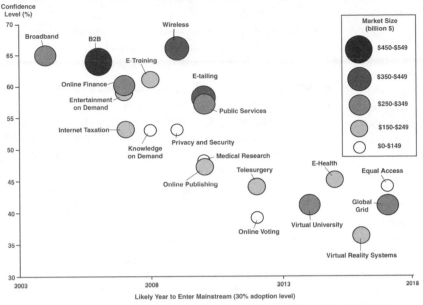

Confidence Level (%)

NOTES: "Likely Year" is the most likely year that each e-commerce is expected to reach its stated adoption level in industrialized nations. Adoption levels are defined as a percent of the total that is possible. For instance, broadband is defined as the percent of households, while e-tailing is the percent of retail sales. "Confidence Level" is the confidence experts place in their forecast of "Likely Year." "Market Size" is a relative measure of the econimic market resulting from each e-commerce service, on a scale from a low of less than $150 billion to a high of about $550 billion. See www.TechCast.org, "Emerging Technoligies," THE FUTURIST (November-December 1997); and "The Top Ten Emerging Technologies," THE FUTURIST (July-August 2000).

ORIGINAL GRAPH CONSTRUCTION BY PAUL WILLIAMS, GWU GRADUATE ASSISTANT.

Broadband High-speed channels (DSL, cable, Ethernet, and satellite) are used in 30% of homes: 2004.
B2B 30% of commercial transactions are conducted online: 2006.
E-Health Online systems are used 30% of the time to prescribe drugs, order lab tests, monitor patients, etc.: 2015.
Entertainment on Demand 30% of music, movies, games, and other entertainment is sold online: 2007.
Equal Access Most (90%) of underprivileged people have Internet access: 2017.
E-tailing 30% of goods and services are sold online: 2010.
E-Training Distance learning (Internet, video, e-mail) is the main method used in 30% of training programs: 2008.
Global Grid Half of the world population has access to PCs, Internet, etc.: 2017.
Internet Taxation Internet sales are taxed by major nations: 2007.
Knowledge on Demand Focused educational programs are used online to serve 30% of specific needs: 2008.
Medical Research 30% of clinical research is conducted using computerized systems: 2010.
Online Finance 30% of banking, investments, and other financial services are performed online: 2007.
Online Publishing 30% of newspapers, magazines, journals, and books are sold online: 2010.
Online Voting ATM-type machines or PCs on the Internet are used in 30% of elections: 2012.
Privacy and Security A majority of the public feels safe about the privacy and security of their information: 2009.
Public Services 30% of government services (auto registration, licenses, fees, etc.) are conducted online: 2010.
Telesurgery Surgical procedures are performed at remote locations: 2012.
Virtual Reality Systems are used by 30% of the public to experience exotic environments (Mars), entertainment (games, virtual sex), education, testing designs, etc.: 2016.
Virtual University Distance learning (Internet, video, e-mail) is the main method used in 30% of courses: 2014.
Wireless Web phones, handheld devices, etc., are used by 30% of the population for Internet, video, etc.: 2009.

ECONOMIC MATURING OF THE INTERNET

The TechCast system, formerly called The GW Forecast, is a database-driven Web site in which panels of experts provide online estimates to carefully researched questions. The estimates are pooled automatically to produce the best possible forecast of when each technology is likely to take off, the associated confidence level, and size of the potential market—in real time.

ABOUT THE GW FORECAST AND TECHCAST

The George Washington University Forecast of Emerging Technologies (GW Forecast) is a research project initiated by William Halal, management professor, that has been in operation for a decade. In order to provide a source of funding to support this work, TechCast was formed two years ago as a limited liability corporation (LLC), with the goal of commercializing the results. TechCast is jointly owned by Halal and the other officers of the project, by George Washington University, and by partner George Mason University. TechCast intends to offer individuals and organizations access to the information on its new Web site, www.TechCast.org, on a subscription basis.

Results are presented in the E-Commerce Technology Timeline for 20 applications of e-commerce. The expert panel convened for this study comprises 38 authorities from a variety of backgrounds, including CEOs of high-tech firms, technology officers, scientists and engineers, consultants, academics, and futurists. Not all experts respond to every question, so the typical number of respondents averages 22. Delphi forecasts of this type are generally considered sound if they use a dozen or more experts, which makes these results fairly reliable.

These results portray a striking scenario in which the dominant forms of e-commerce—broadband, business-to-business (B2B), online finance, entertainment-on-demand, wireless, e-training, knowledge-on-demand, electronic public services, online publishing, e-tailing—grow from their present 5%–20% adoption levels to 30% between 2004 and 2010. TechCast considers the 30% penetration level significant because this roughly marks the "take-off point" when technologies move from their early-adopter phase into the mainstream, where they permeate economic and social life. Andrew Grove, former CEO of Intel, told *Business Week* (May 5, 2003), "Everything we ever said about the Internet is happening now."

Many think the Internet is mainstream now, but that's only true for nonpaying use, such as surfing for free information. As of 2003, commercial operations involving monetary exchange were limited to about 23% for broadband, 10% for e-tailing, 12% for B2B, 10% for distance learning, and 5% for music. And these are the most popular Internet applications. Others hardly register in adoption levels at all.

TechCast's other results suggest that more-complex applications—online voting, e-health, the virtual university, virtual reality, and the global grid—are likely to follow later. These forms of e-commerce lag because they involve more exotic and costly technology, difficult institutional changes, and new forms of consumer behavior. Making the virtual university a reality, for instance, requires professors to switch from traditional lectures to communication technologies that are poorly developed, college administrators to justify the economic feasibility of more expensive systems, and students to feel comfortable and trusting in a virtual setting. E-health demands a similar transformation among physicians, hospitals, and patients.

The remaining developments in our forecast—taxation, privacy and security, computerized research, telesurgery, and equal access—should appear at varying times throughout the next two decades. These applications differ because they do not serve major new social needs but involve modifications of existing systems.

Interwoven through these advances in e-commerce are other trends leading to a new generation of intelligent systems expected to emerge during the same time period. The TechCast project calls it TeleLiving—a conversational human-machine interface that allows a more comfortable and convenient way to shop, work, educate, entertain, and conduct most other social relationships [see THE FUTURIST, January-February 2003]. The following are a few of the advances in speech recognition, artificial intelligence, powerful chips, virtual environments, and flat-screen wall monitors that are likely to produce this intelligent interface.

■ Reliable speech recognition should be common by 2010.

- IBM has a Super Human Speech Recognition Program to greatly improve accuracy, and in the next decade Microsoft's program is expected to reduce the error rate of speech recognition, matching human capabilities.

- MIT is planning to demonstrate their Project Oxygen, which features a voice-machine interface. Project director Rodney Brooks says, "I wanted to bring the machine into our world, a machine that will look you in the eye, let you ask questions in casual English, and answer them the same way."

- Amtrak, Wells Fargo, Land's End, and many other organizations are replacing keypad-menu call centers with speech-recognition systems because they improve customer service and recover investment in a year or two. Analysts think most companies will make the conversion soon.

- Internet search engines such as Google and Yahoo operate voice-recognition systems that help users find what they seek.

- General Motors OnStar driver assistance system relies primarily on voice commands, with live staff for backup;

the number of subscribers has grown from 200,000 to 2 million and is expected to increase by 1 million per year. The Lexus DVD Navigation System responds to over 100 commands and guides the driver with voice and visual directions.

- Even more pervasive yet simpler, Sprint offers voice dialing on most cell phones and networks.

■ Smart computers will be learning and adapting within a decade.

- The Defense Advanced Research Projects Agency is developing a hypersmart computer that can maintain itself, assess its performance, make adaptive changes, and respond to different situations.

- The Department of Energy is creating an intelligent computer that can infer intent, remember prior experiences, analyze problems, and make decisions.

- IBM's "autonomic computing" program will allow servers and networks to solve problems and reconfigure themselves to accomplish a goal, just as organisms rely on an autonomic nervous system to regulate heartbeat and body temperature.

- Norton provides PC software that can eliminate virus infections, optimize computer performance, fix registry mistakes, and perform other tasks without user intervention.

- AI is being used to intelligently guide human action figures in computer games, such as *Sims, Metal Gear Solid, Unreal Tournament*, and *Halo*.

- Pattern matching and text parsing are used to improve searches by Google and AltaVista.

- BCC Corporation estimates total AI sales to grow from $12 billion in 2002 to $21 billion in 2007.

■ A new generation of computer power is here.

Intel and AMD are introducing 64-bit processors to replace the 32-bit chips that brought us the Windows operating system a decade ago. The 64-bit chips mark a new generation of computer power that features cinematic displays rivaling the most sophisticated science-fiction movies, accurate speech recognition, and artificial intelligence.

■ Virtual robots/environments will populate the Web by 2010.

- Virtual robots, or avatars, are becoming common, such as Ananova, a female robot who presents weather reports. In Japan, Yuki Terai is a virtual rock star who has become a national idol.

- "There" is a multimedia Web site featuring 3-D computer-generated environments populated with avatars that interact with users and other avatars.

- According to the CEO of Native Minds, a virtual robot maker, "The Internet will be filled with robots by 2010."

■ **Flat wall monitors should become common in a few years.**

- Sales of liquid crystal display (LCD) monitors now surpass cathode ray tube (CRT) sales, introducing an era of flat monitors that use one-third the power of CRTs. "Ultimately, the flat panel is less expensive," according to a Dell manager.

- Leading TV makers are all bringing out 60-inch wall-mounted digital TV monitors.

- Albeit expensive now, as the switch from CRTs to LCDs gathers momentum, costs and prices should fall dramatically, making $1,000 wall monitors the size of a movie screen fairly common. A fully functional three-by-five-foot wall monitor should sell for less than $500.

These are formidable undertakings, to be sure, and some may not succeed as planned. But such remarkable developments promise to transform the human-computer interface. Powerful new scientific capabilities are being applied now for simple uses, and if current trends hold, a modest version of the talking computer made famous in *2001: A Space Odyssey* should be available about 2010. Rather than use a keyboard or mouse, the PC will disappear into a corner while we talk to life-sized virtual persons on large wall monitors.

A few years ago, Microsoft chairman Bill Gates claimed, "The future lies with computers that talk, see, listen, and learn." This view is now supported by computer industry leaders. Robert McClure of IDC stated recently, "What the graphical user interface was in the 1990s, the natural user interface will be in this decade." Sony President Kunitake Ando expects the PC of 2005 to be a more personalized, intelligent system, acting as a "teacher, agent, and guide." Ian Pearson at British Telecom sees a resumption of Internet growth in 2005 and 2006, driven by "better interface technology ... and artificial intelligence." And computer scientist Ray Kurzweil forecasts, "It will be routine to meet in full-immersion virtual reality for business meetings and casual conversations in five to seven years."

THE NEXT INFORMATION TECHNOLOGY [IT] GENERATION

The enormous gap between today's depressed IT industry and the vibrant trends noted above signifies that we are poised at the cusp of another major technology transition, much as the 1980s brought the PC and the 1990s brought the Internet.

The economic recession left in the wake of the dot-com bust may linger awhile, but all technological revolutions go through a similar boom-and-bust cycle. The introduction of railroads, telephones, and radios invited wild speculation similar to the dot-com bubble. But a few years after the inevitable crash, renewed economic growth and more prudent business practices caused these fledgling industries to boom again.

A similar resumption of growth is likely for dot-coms. Economically sound e-practices are common now and

should continue to expand. As the economic recession runs its course, venture capital is also appearing to support new startups. And broadband is reaching the critical 30% take-off level, which will soon create huge markets for exciting new applications that need lots of bandwidth. The Tech-Cast Project participants therefore see no serious obstacles to the first wave of relatively straightforward e-commerce services noted in the forecast, which is likely to reach the 30% adoption level during this take-off period running roughly from 2005 to 2010.

This time, however, the intelligent interface holds the key to putting today's underutilized IT to work. Many more examples like those noted above are being developed by Web entrepreneurs, and competition could mount as customers demand these attractive new benefits. The first "wired generation" of college students is entering work, expecting the unlimited bandwidth and sophisticated Internet features they grew accustomed to on campus. The nagging problem of selling entertainment online—the digital rights management conundrum—is also likely to be resolved soon, which could unleash a huge market for music, videos, movies, and other intellectual property.

These emerging markets are perfect for the lifelike, conversational multimedia of TeleLiving, encouraging a new generation of IT that should be extremely appealing and relieves today's exploding complexity. Ninety percent of Americans say today's computers are too complex and time-consuming. The huge advantages of this next-generation IT could fuel demand for the Intelligent Internet to blossom sometime around 2010, as the trends above suggest. *Business Week's* special issue, "The E-Biz Surprise" (May 5, 2003), noted, "The Web is the same age color TV was when it turned profitable."

Almost any social transaction—teleworking with colleagues, buying and selling online, education, consulting with your physician, entertainment, or just a casual talk with a distant friend—could soon be conducted in a conversational mode, speaking with life-sized images as comfortably as we now use the telephone and television. It should feel as though virtual people are right there in the same room with you.

This scenario is not without uncertainties. Cynicism persists over unrealized promises of AI, and the Intelligent Internet will present its own problems. If you think today's dumb computers are frustrating, wait until you find yourself shouting at a virtual robot that repeatedly fails to grasp what you badly want it to do. And this forecast for a glorious IT future may seem extravagant amidst the dismal mood of IT today.

The main obstacle is a lack of vision among industry leaders, customers, and the public as scars of the dot-com bust block creative thought. Yes, the dot-com boom was unrealistic to a large extent, but it was driven by a powerful image that inspired huge gains in many areas. Bold innovations always require equally bold imagination, and so unleashing pent-up demand for online social transactions will require an imaginative understanding of how IT can improve life in the difficult years ahead. The evidence suggest the future lies in developing an Intelligent Internet, and that the world could benefit enormously by focusing on this concept with clarity and determination.

About the Author

William E. Halal, director of the TechCast Project (formerly The GW Forecast), is a professor of management in the Department of Management Science, Monroe Hall, George Washington University, Washington, D.C. 20052. Telephone 1-202-994-5975; Web site www.TechCast.org or www.gwforecast.gwu.edu; e-mail halal@gwu.edu.

Originally published in the March/April 2004 issue of *The Futurist,* pp. 27-32. Copyright © 2004 by World Future Society, 7910 Woodmont Avenue, Suite 450, Bethesda, MD 20814. Telephone: 301/656-8274; Fax: 301/951-0394; [&url]http://www.wfs.org[&stop]. Used with permission from the World Future Society.

SPARKING THE
FIRE
OF INVENTION

ONE OF THE MOST **RADICAL** BUSINESS IDEAS OF THE 21ST CENTURY
MAY BE THE CREATION OF A **NEW METHOD OF INVENTION—**
INDIVIDUALISTIC, GLOBAL, AND NOT BOUND TO **CORPORATE MISSIONS**.

NATHAN P. MYHRVOLD HAS **NO INTEREST** IN COMPETING WITH MICROSOFT—BUT HE
DOES MEAN TO **CHALLENGE THE VERY METHOD** OF INNOVATION PRAC-
TICED AT THE COMPANY HE LEFT **FOUR YEARS** AGO.

EVAN I. SCHWARTZ

The 44-year-old founder of Microsoft Research and former chief technology officer of the Seattle giant argues that virtually all big corporations, even wealthy ones, lack motivation to pump money into projects outside their existing product lines. In other words, they tend to discourage *invention*, the often subversive effort to isolate new problems and generate unexpected solutions. "Invention is a side effect [at corporate labs], not the focus," Myhrvold says. "Most large organizations have a mission, and invention often takes you in another direction. When it comes to mission versus invention at most companies, mission wins." Even small companies such as Silicon Valley startups, he notes, are often loath to support invention outside their core markets.

Yet this very reluctance has opened a world of opportunity, Myhrvold believes. "You can't outdevelop Microsoft," he says. "But you can out*invent* Microsoft."

And that's exactly what Myhrvold and former Microsoft chief software architect Edward Jung have set out to do at Bellevue, WA-based Invention Science, a hothouse of ideas where staff have free rein to cross-pollinate insights from information technology, biotechnology, and nanotechnology—three domains that Myhrvold feels are converging to make powerful new technologies possible. In recent months, the organization has quietly hired some two dozen inventors, along with the patent attorneys and licensing experts needed to support them and get their ideas to market. It's the culmination of more than two years of travel, study, and planning by Myhrvold and Jung, who first set up an independent Bellevue research shop called Intellectual Ventures in 2000 (*see "The Invention Factory," TR May 2002*). The company serves as the parent for Invention Science.

The new venture, Myhrvold says, has no mission other than to invent what the inventors believe should be—or can be—invented. "Invention is the secret sauce," Myhrvold says. "It has the highest concentration of value compared with any task in a company. But because it's so risky, it also has the lowest amount of focused effort." Showing what can happen when that effort is intensified is Myhrvold's main reason for creating the laboratory, which he is funding in part from his own Microsoft-made fortune.

Myhrvold isn't the only one to see new value in cross-disciplinary collaborations where invention itself is the primary goal. In fact, more and more ventures dedicated

MILESTONES

1940

The U.S. Census Bureau eliminates "inventor" as a separate job category

solely to invention have been popping up in recent years—including Walker Digital, a business systems developer in Stamford, CT, and Invent Resources, a smart Lexington, MA, consultancy whose slogan is "Invention on Demand" (*see "Independent Inventors Incorporated,"*). And the mindset is spreading to the corporate world as well: at research-driven companies like brainstorming firm Generics Group of Cambridge, England, engineers are actually paid to spend a subset of their time on personal projects, stuff that typically has little or nothing to do with what their clients are doing—yet. Even young firms like Google, in Mountain View, CA, are getting into the act: the search engine leader encourages employees to devote 20 percent of their time to developing their own far-out ideas. The belief at such companies is that creative people are fueled by freedom to find problems that interest them. "Our employees are coming up with ideas anyway," says Google cofounder Sergey Brin. "We just provide them with time to test whether those ideas work."

This freedom to pursue invention for its own sake is the main hallmark of today's climate. It's been argued that moments of invention are little different from the rest of the research and development process—they are simply a matter of applying "normal problem solving to the right problem space," says David N. Perkins, a principal investigator at Harvard University's Project Zero, a 35-year effort to understand human creativity. But a close look at the process of invention reveals that some problems are so hard that they're "unreasonable" to even consider during the normal R&D process—or worse, they're completely hidden. Dedicated inventors "can recognize latent opportunities, problems that people don't even know they have," Perkins says.

No one personifies this mindset more than Myhrvold. As the affable, bearded physicist, photographer, and paleontologist flew around the world in his Gulfstream V jet attempting to get into the heads of inventors young and old, he became convinced that a new global flowering of invention is possible. For one thing, he says, the Web and other powerful information technologies make sharing knowledge easier than ever, enabling people with great ideas to attract capital and marketing firepower more readily. Meanwhile, the very pace of technological progress is picking up. Myhrvold foresees what he calls a new age of exponential growth, in which converging technologies will bring unpredictable but important changes—at a pace comparable to that of microchip miniaturization, famously described by Moore's Law. But what inventors require to generate this kind of growth, he

concluded, is focused, long-term support, like the access to patent and licensing experts he and Jung are providing to their staff.

Ultimately, Myhrvold and others funding pure invention are out to debunk the perception that research labs make sense only when they are part of an existing corporate structure—one that includes development, manufacturing, distribution, and marketing. Until the 1980s, Myhrvold points out, businesses had a similar attitude toward software, believing that it was only valuable when bundled along with hardware. Bill Gates and others thoroughly disproved that theory. In the same way, "We think invention can be valuable in and of itself," says Myhrvold.

"Invention is the new software"

MORE POWER TO THE LITTLE GUYS

The new climate for invention, say Myhrvold and others, is the result of four major trends. The first is the reemergence of invention outside big corporations. For nearly a century, the innovations of large corporate research centers such as Bell Labs or General Electric overshadowed those of inventors working alone or in small groups. But now a constellation of forces is bringing the individual inventor and small technology companies—and sometimes small teams within large firms—back to the fore.

The change marks a comeback for those iconoclastic souls who still call themselves inventors—the people considered the driving force of the economy in the days of Thomas Edison, Alexander Graham Bell, and the Wright brothers. From the 1920s and '30s onward, with the rise of giant technology-based companies like GE, AT&T, and DuPont, invention became co-opted by corporate labs that had to answer to management hierarchies. Within corporate labs, inventors were reclassified as "researchers." In 1932, the year after Edison died, more U.S. patents were granted to corporations than to individuals for the first time, and in 1940, the U.S. Census Bureau eliminated "inventor" as a job category.

At big companies, the emphasis gradually moved from invention to what legendary economist Joseph A. Schumpeter called the second and third stages of technological change: *innovation*, in which ideas are transformed into marketable products and services, and *diffusion*, which sees those products and services distributed across markets. Companies adopted the view that invention by itself was only a tiny part of business success; for every $1 spent on basic research, the conventional wisdom went, $100 would be spent on development and $1,000 on commercialization. Since great ideas often fail, and the best or most original product doesn't necessarily win in the marketplace, the inventor came to be perceived as a relatively minor player in the equation. The dot-com boom of the late 1990s skewed this model to new extremes, as billions of dollars were staked on the conviction that the Web was changing everything about commerce, without much in the way of marketable inventions.

REINVENTING BIOLOGY, VIRTUALLY

Elite researchers team up across institutes to create a powerful biotech tool

Sometimes, thinking big means thinking small. For an audacious collaboration known as the **Nanosystems Biology Alliance**, the goal is nothing less than to invent a "nanolab," a chip one centimeter square that can sense 10,000 different proteins and other molecules in a single blood cell, looking for signs of impending disease and helping to identify malfunctioning molecular pathways that could be regulated with drugs.

Reaching that goal will require a combination of advances in nanotechnology, microfluidics, and "systems biology," which views cells as if they consisted of vast chemical circuits. So the alliance is thinking big as well: it includes researchers in eight labs at three West Coast scientific institutions.

To cofounder **Leroy Hood**, the alliance represents how it's possible to push the boundaries of invention by bringing top inventors together—even if they're separated by geography. "If you want to solve a problem, why not get the best people together to work on it?" says Hood, who is also president of Seattle's Institute for Systems Biology.

The alliance's elite eight include people like James Heath, a Caltech chemist and nanotechnology pioneer; Michael Phelps, a University of California, Los Angeles, scientist who coinvented positron emission tomography (PET); and Hood himself, the coinventor of the automated DNA sequencer. Hood's hope is to combine the group's mental firepower to build a handheld device that could detect everything from the early signs of cancer to the molecular changes associated with heart disease.

Financing their work from existing academic grants, the alliance members have spent most of the last year learning about each other's fields, trading postdocs, and exchanging lots—*lots*—of e-mail. But the alliance "is not completely virtual, or it would not work," says Heath. He and the members of his Caltech group visit Hood's lab frequently and swap equipment and materials. Also helping to keep the whole extended collaboration together: "We have a strong and shared vision of where we want to go," Heath says. "That drives everything." *Wade Roush*

Now, with big corporate research laboratories focusing more and more on shorter-term product cycles, many see a growing opportunity for small companies, academic researchers, and individual inventors to generate breakthroughs that have longer-term impact. Anthony Breitzman, vice president of CHI Research, a Haddon Heights, NJ, patent analysis firm, reports that big corporations still have a wide lead in patent filings, especially in areas such as aerospace, motor vehicles, oil and gas, computing, and plastics, where research is expensive and small companies don't have the resources to compete. But Breitzman notes that "there *are* areas where small companies are really competing." In biotechnology, pharmaceuticals, and medical electronics—fields where every company is drawing on the same base of knowledge about the human body and the genome—about 25 percent of patents are being issued to small companies and individuals (*see "Reinventing Biology, Virtually," this page*). A disproportionate number of those are "high-impact patents," Breitzman says, inventions that actually do become significant products in the marketplace.

The second trend: burned by the often vague schemes that passed for breakthrough thinking in the late 1990s, venture capitalists, in particular, have become far more selective, often insisting that the companies they back have significant, patented inventions that will shield their investments from competition. Attention to invention is becoming more rigorous across all areas of technology, says MIT engineering professor David Staelin. Staelin cofounded an MIT venture mentoring program that currently advises about 70 student- and faculty-led startups; he says 85 percent of the companies were formed around patentable inventions, from a smart golf club that tells users how to improve their swings to exoskeletons that help people in rehab.

The new emphasis on invention pays off. CHI Research combs patent databases for "highly cited" patents, ones that are frequently referenced in papers and later patents. According to CHI, the stocks of companies with a high proportion of these highly cited patents have greatly outperformed both the S&P 500 index and the stocks of companies with low numbers of highly cited patents (*see "Investing in Invention Pays Off," this page*). "Highly cited patents correlate to [stock market] success," says Breitzman.

·MILESTONES

1981

In *Diamond v. Diehr*, the U.S. Supreme Court rules that software can be patented.

INVENTING LOCALLY, MARKETING GLOBALLY

Thirdly, the Internet and other ubiquitous communications tools are enabling new global connections. Inventors everywhere are able to not only access patent databases, troves of online technical specifications, and genomic repositories but also take advantage of e-mail and collaborative software tools to brainstorm across borders and tap international markets. A record 49.9 percent of U.S. patents awarded in 2003 listed at least one non-U.S. citizen as a coinventor. Foreign entities will

INDEPENDENT INVENTORS INCORPORATED

A sampling of companies and organizations that exist chiefly to incubate new inventions—often for hire

ORGANIZATION	ORIGINS	DESCRIPTION	SAMPLE INVENTIONS
Invention Science Bellevue, WA	Started by former Microsoft executives Nathan Myhrvold and Edward Jung	In-house inventors explore convergence of information technology, nanotechnology, biotechnology; 25 employees	New types of lasers
Walker Digital Stamford, CT	Launched in 1999 by Jay Walker, creator of priceline.com	Develops and licenses business-related technologies; 40 employees	USHomeGuard, a system of surveillance webcams and civilian spotters
Invent Resources Lexington, MA	Formed in 1992 by former MIT physicist Richard Pavelle and electronics engineer Sol Aisenberg	Consults with clients to test ideas and develop prototypes; four employees	Electronic time stamp; advanced microwave ovens
Generics Group Cambridge, England	Established in 1986 by electrical engineer Gordon Edge	Brainstorms new products and consults with clients on development; more than 200 employees	Advanced fuel cells; strong cardboard can for carbonated drinks
Sarcos Research Salt Lake City, UT	Created in 1983 by roboticist Stephen Jacobsen	Develops products for government and commercial clients; 50 employees	Robotic arms and hands for industrial and prosthetic uses
Deka Research and Development Manchester, NH	Launched in 1982 by independent inventor Dean Kamen	Develops products to improve patient quality of life and increase mobility; 200 employees	Home dialysis machine; stair-climbing wheelchair; Segway human transporter

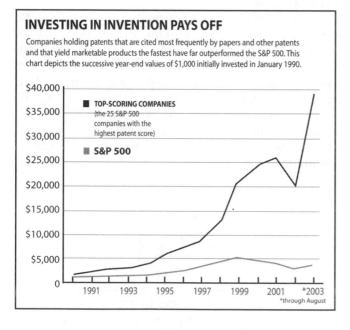

INVESTING IN INVENTION PAYS OFF

Companies holding patents that are cited most frequently by papers and other patents and that yield marketable products the fastest have far outperformed the S&P 500. This chart depicts the successive year-end values of $1,000 initially invested in January 1990.

likely account for the majority of U.S. patent filings from 2004 onward, predicts CHI's Breitzman. Some two dozen countries now produce significant levels of U.S. patents per capita, a figure that is highly correlated with higher GDP and standards of living (*see the Global Invention Map, p. 76*).

For high-cost nations like the U.S. and Britain, this worldwide competition—which is intensifying as other countries beef up their educational systems and intellectual-property protections, and firms outsource high-tech jobs to lower-wage regions—means that professionals must prove their worth by moving up the intellectual-property value ladder. Instead of just completing assignments that are handed to them, employees need to be more inventive and more original in their thinking—often by finding new problems to tackle in the first place. Former U.S. labor secretary Robert Reich, now a professor at Brandeis University, identifies two growing categories of work in today's economy. The first he calls "symbolic analysis"; it involves the application of in-depth knowledge and includes jobs in R&D, design, and engineering. The second is "personal services" such as those provided by retail clerks, security guards, and hospital attendants. "Only the first [category] is commanding better pay and benefits," Reich notes. "This category includes identifying and solving new problems." In a nutshell, that's exactly what inventors do.

The leveling of the international playing field enhances the long-standing premium on original thinking, and smart companies are becoming more and more open to licensing inventions from smaller competitors, wherever they may be. "We're scanning the horizon for new ideas outside the company," says Simon Beesley, professional-audio marketing manager for Sony Professional Services Europe, a 1,200-employee division of Sony. "We're not as closed as we were ten years ago." He cites as an example the company's rollout of Hypersonic Sound, a directional-audio system developed by U.S. inventor Elwood "Woody" Norris (*see "The Sound War," p. 50*). Sony is bundling the invention as part of plasma screen audiovisual systems. But Beesley says it is also selling the technology to dozens of retailers, banks, and museums across Europe

MYHRVOLD AND THE INVENTION FACTORY

Q&A with the former Microsoft mogul

TECHNOLOGY REVIEW: What kinds of inventors have you hired?

NATHAN MYHRVOLD: We have a staff of 20 to 25 people, plus 10 or 15 outside affiliated inventors. Lots of fantastic people. One reason they're successful is that they have a giant experience base. A large fraction of our inventors are women. At one brainstorming session, we looked around and noticed that men were in the minority, and that white men were in the minority among the men.

TR: How many inventions are you currently working on?

MYHRVOLD: We have many hundreds of ideas under investigation. We invent in solid-state physics, in electronics, in software, nanotech, biotech, biomedical. We're about following our inspirations, as opposed to working on any preordained problems.

TR: Are there any good models for invention Science?

MYHRVOLD: The model for what we are doing now was set in the 19th century. Edison and Bell and Tesla and lots and lots of others had invention-oriented businesses back then. Invention was a big thing. The world is due for this to come back.

TR: Do you foresee competition?

MYHRVOLD: We'd welcome competition. We hope our inventions spawn other inventions. I hope there are people who get fantastically wealthy building on our ideas. There is a real opportunity for small groups of people to make incredible contributions. Silicon Valley and Wall Street will rise to the challenge if great new ideas are created.

TR: What didn't you know when you started your invention lab?

MYHRVOLD: What has surprised me most is how well we have been able to get inventors to play off one another and collaborate in brainstorming. We have a couple very exciting inventions involving new kinds of lasers. If you asked me if we could have done that, I would have said no two years ago. I would have even said no before going into the sessions where we invented these things. I had the key idea on both. But one person can provide only 25 percent of the bridge across the Grand Canyon. That's only enough to get you to fall to the bottom. You need lots of help. If you can get a rapport going among inventors with different backgrounds, you can accomplish amazing things. *Evan I Schwartz*

that are "clamoring" to build products, machines, and exhibits that can beam audio narration or marketing pitches to one customer at a time. "Every time I show this to someone," Beesley says, "they come up with a new idea for using it."

PEERING INSIDE INVENTION

That fits with the final trend—toward a new appreciation of how the cognitive process of invention actually works. Invention is so steeped in the myth of accidental discovery that one might conclude it's like playing the lottery. For example, there is the tale of Percy Spencer, the researcher at Waltham, MA-based Raytheon who reportedly noticed that a radar tube in his lab melted the candy bar in his pocket—resulting in the microwave oven. Chance can indeed be a key element of invention. But from their studies, Myhrvold and others have come to realize that truly "accidental" inventions are rare and are usually exaggerated in hindsight—sometimes to justify why researchers deviated from what they were supposed to be doing. Most of these stories leave out the fact that these researchers were keenly observant and were deliberately trying to invent new things all the time.

In fact, invention is now being recognized as a more focused, deliberate process, enacted by people who are especially good at finding new problems and who often work and think differently from typical researchers and technicians. Sarcos Research of Salt Lake City is a case in point. The 50-employee invention shop, which CEO Stephen Jacobsen calls a "skunk works for hire," develops prototypes and licenses them to firms such as Merck, Pfizer, Disney, Sony, Lucent, and the Palo Alto Research Center.

MILESTONES

2004

U.S. patent filings from foreign entities are expected to surpass those from U.S. entities for the first time.

By mixing ideas from biology and engineering, Sarcos's researchers have built everything from high-precision catheters for maneuvering inside the bloodstream to robot dinosaurs for Hollywood. But Jacobsen himself—the inventor of the Utah Arm, the world's most advanced robotic arm replacement for humans—may be the company's most unconventional thinker. Visual representations preoccupy Jacobsen to such an extent that he says he has virtually no recollection of nonvisual data, such as dates. He visualizes the progression of the hundreds of inventions he has worked on in terms of how their intricate shapes were formed and assembled over time. After enlarging a device such as a microchip or a nanosensor in his mind and setting it spinning and twisting, he can go about constructing it and writing the software for it. "What I remember is the geometry," he says.

Few people may think as visually as Jacobsen, but everyone can be more inventive, the experts say. "We've got a prefrontal cortex that works as an experience simulator," says Harvard psychologist Daniel Gilbert. "We can have experiences in our heads before we try them out." With practice, just about anyone can learn visualization and other high-level thinking skills that help to create new concepts and translate them into practical technologies, Gilbert says. Inventor Jay Walker—the founder of Walker Digital, the creator of priceline.com, and the holder of more than 200 business process patents in industries ranging from retail to gaming to health care—agrees. "Can anyone learn to do improv, or to become a pianist or a chef or a wine taster?" he asks. "Sure. Anyone with above-average intelligence can do those things. But it takes years and years to train your brain to do it well. Invention is the same way."

So in addition to leaping across disciplines and challenging assumptions, inventors visualize results and embrace uncertainty—which is another reason a bigger proportion of invention may be taking place outside the traditional corporation. "All the conventional wisdom works against invention," says Walker. "The field of management is about reducing the risk of bad outcomes involving people; the field of engineering is about reducing the risk of bad outcomes involving technology. But invention is about taking risks that will almost certainly fail in order to find the unlikely breakthrough."

By that logic, brainstorming laboratories like Myhrvold's Invention Science are almost certain to produce lots of failures—but also, perhaps, the occasional big idea that changes the world … and later gets called an accident.

Evan I. Schwartz is a Technology Review *contributing writer and the author of* Juice: The Creative Fuel Driving Today's World-Class Inventors, *forthcoming in September.*

Mind Control

Matt Nagle is paralyzed. He's also a pioneer in the new science of brain implants.

Richard Martin

Matthew Nagle is beating me at Pong. "OK, baby," he mutters. The creases in his forehead deepen as he moves the onscreen paddle to block the ball. "C'mon—here you go," he says, sending a wicked angle shot ricocheting down the screen and past my defense. "Yes!" he says in triumph, his voice hoarse from the ventilator that helps him breathe. "Let's go again, dude."

The remarkable thing about Nagle is not that he plays skillfully; it's that he can play at all. Nagle is a C4 quadriplegic, paralyzed from the neck down in a stabbing three years ago. He pilots a motorized wheelchair by blowing into a sip-and-puff tube, his pale hands strapped to the armrests. He's playing Pong with his thoughts alone.

A bundle of wires as thick as a coaxial cable runs from a connector in Nagle's scalp to a refrigerator-sized cart of electronic gear. Inside his brain, a tiny array of microelectrodes picks up the cacophony of his neural activity; processors recognize the patterns associated with arm motions and translate them into signals that control the Pong paddle, draw with a cursor, operate a TV, and open email.

Nagle, 25, is the first patient in a controversial clinical trial that seeks to prove brain-computer interfaces can return function to people paralyzed by injury or disease. His BCI is the most sophisticated ever tested on a human being, the culmination of two decades of research in neural recording and decoding. A Foxborough, Massachusetts-based company called Cyberkinetics built the system, named BrainGate.

After we play Pong for a while, I ask Nagle to try something I'd seen him do in a video: draw a circle. This is more fundamental and difficult than playing Pong. Drawing a circle freehand is a classic test of motor function, a species marker. Legend has it that Leonardo da Vinci was among the few humans who could sketch a perfect one.

Today, Nagle barely gets to imperfect. The line keeps shooting off the screen or crossing itself. Maybe it's my presence or fatigue or some subtle shift in Nagle's brain chemistry due to who knows what. Abe Caplan, the Cyberkinetics technician overseeing the computer gear that dominates a corner of Nagle's room at New England Sinai Hospital, urges him on softly.

The room fills with static—the sound of another human being's thoughts.

"I'm tryin', dude," Nagle says, cursing softly. "C'mon, you bitch."

Caplan taps on one of his keyboards to adjust a setting, averaging the system's motion prediction over a longer time to smooth out the line. Finally, Nagle manages to produce a collapsed half circle. He's exhilarated but clearly exhausted. As they finish the session, Caplan nods his head toward the computers and says, "Want to hear it?"

He flicks a switch, and a loud burst of static fills the room—the music of Nagle's cranial sphere. This is raw analog signal, Nagle's neurons chattering. We are listening to a human being's thoughts.

Roughly the size of a deflated volleyball, your brain weighs about 3 pounds. Its 100 billion neurons communicate via minute electrochemical impulses, shifting patterns sparking like fireflies on a summer evening, that produce movement, expression, words. From this ceaseless hubbub arose *Ode to Joy*, thermonuclear weapons, and *Dumb and Dumber*.

Nobody really knows how all that electricity and meat make a mind. Since Freud, scientists have wrangled over "the consciousness problem" to little effect. In fact, it's only in the past 20 years that researchers have learned how to listen in on—or alter—brain waves. Neuroscientists can record and roughly translate the neural patterns of monkeys, and thousands of humans with Parkinson's disease and epilepsy have cerebral pacemakers, which control tremors and seizures with electrical impulses.

John Donoghue, head of neuroscience at Brown University and the founder of Cyberkinetics, eventually wants to hook BrainGate up to stimulators that can activate muscle tissue, bypassing a damaged nervous system entirely. In theory, once you can control a computer cursor, you can do anything from drawing circles to piloting a battleship. With enough computational power, "everything else is just engineering," says Gerhard Friehs, the neurosurgeon from Brown who implanted Nagle's device.

For now, that engineering remains a challenge. Cyberkinetics is just one of a dozen labs working on brain-computer interfaces, many of them funded by more than $25 million in grants from the US Department of Defense, which frankly envisions a future of soldier-controlled killer robots. Before that can happen, BCIs must become safe enough to be implanted in a human, durable enough to function reliably for years, and sensitive enough to pick up distinctive neural patterns. Many physicians doubt useful information can ever be extracted from neural activity, and some who believe in the promise of BCIs worry that putting one into Nagle's head was premature, even reckless, considering less invasive technological options still on the table—electrode-studded skullcaps or devices that rest on the brain's surface. They worry that a failure could set the entire field back a decade.

"The technology required is very complex," Donoghue admits. "There are still many issues to be resolved. But it's here. It's going to happen. Just look at Matt."

On July 3, 2001, Matthew Nagle and several friends went to a fireworks display at Wessagussett Beach, 20 miles south of Boston. The 6' 2", 180-pound Nagle had been a football standout at Weymouth High and was a devoted Patriots and Red Sox fan. That summer he was driving a van delivering kitchenware and had just passed the postal service exam. As Nagle and his buddies were leaving the beach, one of them got into a scuffle. Nagle jumped out of the car to help his friend. "The last thing I remember is sitting in the car," Nagle says. "My friend told me I went over to this guy and he pulled a knife."

The 8-inch blade entered the left side of Nagle's neck just under his ear, severing his spinal cord. Nagle spent four months in rehabilitation before moving back to his parents' house. He can't breathe without a respirator, and though he has at times managed to wiggle a finger, doctors give him no chance of regaining the use of his limbs. Nagle's mother ran across the BrainGate experiments while researching spinal-cord injuries online, and she brought him an article about Cyberkinetics from *The Boston Globe*. Nagle, who had been trying unsuccessfully to wean himself from the ventilator, begged his doctors for the chance to be the first subject. "My mother was scared of what might happen, but what else can they do to me?" Nagle rasps, jutting his chin at his wheelchair. "I was in a corner, and I had to come out fighting."

Nagle's doctor contacted the people running the trial. "A week later I got a call," Nagle says. "I told them, 'You can treat me like a lab rat, do whatever. I want this done as soon as possible.'"

Nagle turned out to be an ideal subject—young, strong-willed, and convinced that he will walk again. The only problem: Because Nagle's brain had been cut off from his spinal cord, no one knew if he could still produce the coherent neural signals necessary for movement. It wouldn't matter how well the BrainGate could read patterns if Nagle's brain was broadcasting noise. Donoghue's experiments had used healthy, fully functioning monkeys.

"That was the great unknown," says Donoghue. "When he thinks 'move left,' were we going to get one neuron firing one time, 20 the next time? Or maybe not anything? Could he still imagine motion enough to make those cells modulate, to change those spikes?"

There was only one way to find out: implant the chip.

On the morning of June 22, 2004, Friehs—an expert in gamma knife surgery, which uses focused radiation to treat brain diseases like Parkinson's—opened Nagle's skull using a high-speed drill called a craniotome. With a number 15 scalpel, he carefully sliced through the protective membranes that surround the brain.

The living brain is a gory sponge, a mass of blood vessels shot through with a delicate mesh of fiber. Magnetic resonance imaging allowed Friehs to plot in advance the region on Nagle's motor cortex most likely to provide readable arm-movement signals to the BrainGate. One revelation of BCI research has been that brain functions are highly distributed: Any spot within a given region can provide neural signals to operate a prosthetic. Get the BrainGate to the right place, and it would pick up signals not just from the neurons it touches, but from important neural clusters nearby as well. Using a small pneumatic inserter, Friehs tapped in the tiny array—100 electrodes, each just 1 millimeter long and 90 microns across at its base. Friehs closed Nagle's skull with titanium screws, leaving a tiny hole. Through that he threaded gold wires from the array to an external pedestal connector attached to Nagle's skull. Matthew Nagle was now part biological, and part silicon, platinum, and titanium.

It took Nagle three weeks to sufficiently recover from surgery to start learning to use the BrainGate. The first session would answer Donoghue's foremost question: Could Nagle's brain still produce usable signals?

As Donoghue looked on, Caplan asked Nagle to think left, right, then relax. "When we watched the system monitor, we could plainly see that neurons were briskly modulating," Donoghue recalls. "My reaction was 'This is it!'"

Nagle had even more confidence. "I learned to use it in two or three days—it's supposed to take 11 months," he says. "I totally knew this was going to work."

Four months after the operation, I watched Caplan take Nagle through a typical training session. He tracked Nagle's mental activity on two large monitors, one of which displayed a graph of red and green spiking lines. Each spike represented the firing of clusters of neurons. As Nagle performed specific actions in his mind's eye—move arm left, move arm up—the electrodes picked up the patterns of nearby neuron groups. Then BrainGate amplified and recorded the corresponding electrical activity. Over dozens of trials the computer built a filter that associated specific neural patterns with certain movements. Later, when Nagle again mentally pictured the motions, the computer translated the signals to guide a cursor.

Then they moved on to some more complicated neural gymnastics, with Nagle willing a large green cursor onto a picture of a money bag that popped up in different spots onscreen. Sometimes the cursor moved shakily, or shot off course; sometimes it landed almost immediately where Nagle wanted to place it. It was like watching a 3-year-old learn to use a mouse. Slowly, the cursor grew more controlled. The machine was memorizing Nagle's characteristic neural firing patterns.

"Let's see what you can do with this thing, Matt," Caplan said.

Nagle turned the TV on and off and switched channels (trapped in his hospital room, he's become a daytime-TV addict). Then he opened and read the messages in his dummy email program. "Now I'm at the point where I can bring the cursor just about anywhere," he said. "I can make it hover off to the side, not doing anything. When I first realized I could control it I said, 'Holy shit! I like this.'"

What are you thinking about when you move the cursor? I asked.

"For a while I was thinking about moving the mouse with my hand," Nagle replied. "Now, I just imagine moving the cursor from place to place." In other words, Nagle's brain has assimilated the system. The cursor is as much a part of his self as his arms and legs were.

Fresh out of Boston University undergrad, John Donoghue went to work at the Fernald School, a facility for mentally handicapped children in Waltham, Massachusetts. His boss, Harvard neuroanatomist Paul Yakovlev, had studied in Russia under Ivan Pavlov, who turned his conditioned-reflex work with dogs and bells into the first map of the human motor cortex—left foot controlled here, right foot over there, and so on. At Fernald, Yakovlev and assistants like Donoghue spent hours a day slicing human brains, mostly damaged or defective ones, into 1/1,000-inch sections for study.

Whenever he looked up from his microscope, Donoghue could see the results of those defects roaming the halls of Fernald. Looking for ways to help people recover from cerebral injury, he became interested in plasticity, the brain's ability to adapt and form neural pathways. "By understanding how the plasticity of the brain can be captured and controlled," Donoghue says, "I believed we could promote the recovery of function in severely impaired patients." He set out to learn the grammar and syntax of interneuron communication.

Ten years later, with a PhD in neuroscience from Brown, Donoghue was using microelectrodes to record neural activity in rats, one neuron at a time. It wasn't enough. "Listening to just one neuron is like hearing only the second violinist," says Donoghue. "With multiple neurons, it's like hearing the whole orchestra." The problem was, nobody knew how to record multiple neurons reliably.

In 1992, he went to the Society for Neuroscience meeting in search of a solution. "I went to every poster session that had innovative multielectrode recording methods," Donoghue says, "and finally I found Dick Normann."

Normann is the kind of person who shows up often in the history of scientific revolutions: more tinkerer than basic researcher, more inventor than visionary. In the early 1990s he created the Utah electrode array, a thin substrate of silicon that rests on the surface of the cortex, embedding platinum-tipped electrodes into the gray matter. Normann designed it to send signals into the brain, as part of a visual prosthetic. Donoghue realized it could also be an uplink.

A few weeks after the conference, he visited Normann's lab in Utah. "We placed the implant in a cat, went to lunch, and let the animal recover," Donoghue says. "When we came back we had good signals. It worked!"

Other researchers were chasing the same goal. In 2002, Miguel Nicolelis, a neurobiologist at Duke, provided the best evidence yet of the brain's plasticity. He and his team plugged 86 microwires into the brain of a monkey and taught the animal to use a joystick to move an onscreen cursor (the reward: a sip of juice). After the computer had learned to interpret the animal's brain activity, Nicolelis disconnected the joystick. For a while, the monkey kept working it. But he eventually figured it out. The monkey dropped the joystick and stopped moving his arm; the cursor still moved to the target. As the monkey calmly downed another swallow of juice, Nicolelis' lab fell silent in awe. The mammalian brain could assimilate a device—a machine.

Now the cursor is as much a part of him as his arms and legs ever were.

Still, the Utah array had a few advantages over other designs. It "floats" with the movement of respiration and blood pumping, remaining stable in relation to the surrounding neurons. Years of refinement stripped much of the metal away, making it more biocompatible and less likely to cause scarring. By 2003, Donoghue and Normann had tested the device, now called BrainGate, in 22 monkeys. That got them the FDA approval they'd been looking for: a small trial with five human subjects. Their first was Matthew Nagle.

At a conference in 2002, Anthony Tether, the director of Darpa, envisioned the military outcome of BCI research. "Imagine 25 years from now where old guys like me put on a pair of glasses or a helmet and open our eyes," Tether said. "Somewhere there will be a robot that will open its eyes, and we will be able to see what the robot sees. We will be able to remotely look down on a cave and think to ourselves, 'Let's go down there and kick some butt.' And the robots will respond, controlled by our thoughts. Imagine a warrior with the intellect of a human and the immortality of a machine."

Some scientists have further suggested that implants designed to restore cognitive abilities to Alzheimer's and stroke victims could enhance the brainpower of healthy people. There's talk of using BCIs to stifle antisocial tendencies and "program" acceptable behavior.

Of course, as spooky as these scenarios may be, they first require that BCIs actually work. A few months into the trial, Donoghue's device looks safe enough, and it clearly reads useful (albeit rudimentary) signals from Nagle's brain. No one knows if it will still work a year from now, much less five or ten. If Nagle's brain rejects the implant, other researchers might shy away from implants altogether. "The key is what functions you want to restore," says Duke's Nicolelis. "If you only want to play a videogame or turn on your TV, you don't need to get into the brain. It's really a question of cost-benefit and risk. That's why I'm concerned about things moving too fast; we need to know more about the risks of leaving these things in people's heads for long periods. We don't know much yet."

That's why some BCI researchers are looking for less invasive methods. A team of Austrian researchers taught a quadriplegic patient to open and close a prosthetic hand using an electrode-studded skullcap that picked up electroencephalograms, waves of electricity generated by the entire brain. It was impressive, but the patient required five months of training to pull it off. And this past Decem-

ber, researchers at the Wadsworth Center in Albany, New York, reported that a patient was able to move a cursor around on a monitor using externally detected signals— no implant. Another group has tried an electrode array that rests on the surface of the brain without penetrating the cortex. "I don't think anybody really knows which method is going to be the safest and still give detailed pictures of brain activity," says Wadsworth's Gerwin Schalk.

Donoghue remains convinced that the only way to give people with immobile bodies full interaction with their environment is through embedded electrodes. "No other method gives you the power and clarity you need to transform this noisy signal into something that a patient can use," he says. "The people who question whether this will really work, I don't think they realize how much has already been done. We've got a 1,098-day monkey, who had a working BCI for almost three years. The question is, how long do you want to keep doing this in monkeys?"

Nagle has the fervor of the saved. He's convinced that BrainGate will restore him to movement. "It's just around the corner," he says. "I know I'm going to beat this." Already he can control a prosthetic hand—it's an eerie sight, rubberized, disembodied fingers grasping and relaxing on a tabletop a few feet from the motionless Nagle. "Thirty-nine months I've been paralyzed," he says. "I can stick with it another two years, till they get this thing perfected."

But controlling a robotic hand is a long way from walking. Near the end of our interview, I ask Donoghue if he thinks he's giving Nagle false hope for a cure.

"I don't know that it's false," he replies. "It's hope."

From *Wired,* Issue 13.03, March 2005, pp. 113-116, 119. Copyright © 2005 by Richard Martin. Reprinted by permission of the author.

Index

Index

Test Your Knowledge Form

We encourage you to photocopy and use this page as a tool to assess how the articles in *Annual Editions* expand on the information in your textbook. By reflecting on the articles you will gain enhanced text information. You can also access this useful form on a product's book support Web site at *http://www.mhcls.com/online/*.

NAME: DATE:

_____

TITLE AND NUMBER OF ARTICLE:

_____

BRIEFLY STATE THE MAIN IDEA OF THIS ARTICLE:

_____

LIST THREE IMPORTANT FACTS THAT THE AUTHOR USES TO SUPPORT THE MAIN IDEA:

_____

WHAT INFORMATION OR IDEAS DISCUSSED IN THIS ARTICLE ARE ALSO DISCUSSED IN YOUR TEXTBOOK OR OTHER READINGS THAT YOU HAVE DONE? LIST THE TEXTBOOK CHAPTERS AND PAGE NUMBERS:

_____

LIST ANY EXAMPLES OF BIAS OR FAULTY REASONING THAT YOU FOUND IN THE ARTICLE:

_____

LIST ANY NEW TERMS/CONCEPTS THAT WERE DISCUSSED IN THE ARTICLE, AND WRITE A SHORT DEFINITION:

We Want Your Advice

ANNUAL EDITIONS revisions depend on two major opinion sources: one is our Advisory Board, listed in the front of this volume, which works with us in scanning the thousands of articles published in the public press each year; the other is you—the person actually using the book. Please help us and the users of the next edition by completing the prepaid article rating form on this page and returning it to us. Thank you for your help!

ANNUAL EDITIONS: Computers in Society 06/07

ARTICLE RATING FORM

Here is an opportunity for you to have direct input into the next revision of this volume.
We would like you to rate each of the articles listed below, using the following scale:

1. **Excellent: should definitely be retained**
2. **Above average: should probably be retained**
3. **Below average: should probably be deleted**
4. **Poor: should definitely be deleted**

Your ratings will play a vital part in the next revision.
Please mail this prepaid form to us as soon as possible.
Thanks for your help!

RATING	ARTICLE	RATING	ARTICLE
	1. Five Things We Need to Know About Technological Change		34. The Level of Discourse Continues to Slide
	2. Whom to Protect and How?		35. China's Computer Wasteland
	3. On the Nature of Computing		36. The New Face of the Silicon Age
	4. The Productivity Paradox		37. Restoring the Popularity of Computer Science
	5. The Big Band Era		38. Dot Com for Dictators
	6. The New Gatekeepers		39. Weaving the Authoritarian Web
	7. The Software Wars		40. Kabul's Cyber Cafe Culture
	8. Brain Circulation: How High-Skill Immigration Makes Everyone Better Off		41. Japan's Generation of Computer Refuseniks
	9. Software		42. Minding Your Business
	10. Letter from Silicon Valley		43. Why Listening Will Never Be the Same
	11. When Long Hours at a Video Game Stop Being Fun		44. The Intelligent Internet
	12. The Computer Evolution		45. Sparking the Fire of Invention
	13. Making Yourself Understood		46. Mind Control
	14. Back-to-School Blogging		
	15. Structure and Evolution of Blogspace		
	16. New Technologies and Our Feelings: Romance on the Internet		
	17. From Virtual Communities to Smart Mobs		
	18. Making Meaning: As Google Goes, So Goes the Nation		
	19. Conquered by Google: A Legendary Literature Quiz		
	20. The Copyright Paradox		
	21. You Bought It. Who Controls It?		
	22. Electronic Voting Systems: the Good, the Bad, and the Stupid		
	23. Small Vote Manipulations Can Swing Elections		
	24. To Size Up Colleges, Students Now Shop Online		
	25. Facing Down the E-Maelstrom		
	26. Point, Click…Fire		
	27. The Doctrine of Digital War		
	28. Why Spyware Poses Multiple Threats to Security		
	29. Terror's Server		
	30. Homeland Insecurity		
	31. The Virus Underground		
	32. The Fading Memory of the State		
	33. False Reporting on the Internet and the Spread of Rumors: Three Case Studies		

(Continued on next page)

BUSINESS REPLY MAIL
FIRST CLASS MAIL PERMIT NO. 551 DUBUQUE IA

POSTAGE WILL BE PAID BY ADDRESEE

McGraw-Hill Contemporary Learning Series
2460 KERPER BLVD
DUBUQUE, IA 52001-9902

NO POSTAGE
NECESSARY
IF MAILED
IN THE
UNITED STATES

ABOUT YOU

Name

Date

Are you a teacher? ☐   A student? ☐
Your school's name

Department

Address   City   State   Zip

School telephone #

YOUR COMMENTS ARE IMPORTANT TO US!

Please fill in the following information:
For which course did you use this book?

Did you use a text with this ANNUAL EDITION?   ☐ yes ☐ no
What was the title of the text?

What are your general reactions to the *Annual Editions* concept?

Have you read any pertinent articles recently that you think should be included in the next edition? Explain.

Are there any articles that you feel should be replaced in the next edition? Why?

Are there any World Wide Web sites that you feel should be included in the next edition? Please annotate.

May we contact you for editorial input?   ☐ yes ☐ no
May we quote your comments? ☐ yes ☐ no